SHAKESPEARE STUDIES

EDITORIAL BOARD

Harry Berger Jr.
The University of California, Santa Cruz

David M. Bevington
The University of Chicago

Catherine Belsey
University of Wales College of Cardiff

Michael Bristol
McGill University

S. P. Cerasano
Colgate University

Barry Gaines
The University of New Mexico

Jean E. Howard
Columbia University

Lena Cowen Orlin
University of Maryland, Baltimore County

John Pitcher
St. John's College, Oxford

Maureen Quilligan
Duke University

Alan Sinfield
The University of Sussex

Peter Stallybrass
The University of Pennsylvania

SHAKESPEARE STUDIES VOLUME XXVIII

EDITED BY
LEEDS BARROLL

BOOK REVIEW EDITOR
Susan Zimmerman

Madison • Teaneck
Fairleigh Dickinson University Press
London: Associated University Presses

© 2000 by Associated University Presses, Inc.

All rights reserved. Authorization to photocopy items for internal or personal use, or the internal or personal use of specific clients, is granted by the copyright owner, provided that a base fee of $10.00, plus eight cents per page, per copy is paid directly to the Copyright Clearance Center, 222 Rosewood Drive, Danvers, Massachusetts 01923 [0-8386-3871-6/00 $10.00 + 8¢ pp, pc.]

Associated University Presses
440 Forsgate Drive
Cranbury, NJ 08512

Associated University Presses
16 Barter Street
London WC1A 2AH, England

Associated University Presses
P.O. Box 338, Port Credit
Mississauga, Ontario
Canada L5G 4L8

The paper used in this publication meets the requirements of the American National Standard for Permanence of Paper for Printed Library Materials Z39.48-1984.

International Standard Book Number 0-8386-3871-6 (vol. xxviii)
International Standard Serial Number 0582-9399

All editorial correspondence concerning *Shakespeare Studies* should be addressed to the Editorial Office, *Shakespeare Studies,* Fine Arts 447, University of Maryland (Baltimore County), Baltimore, Maryland 21250. Manuscripts submitted without appropriate postage will not be returned. Orders and subscriptions should be directed to Associated University Presses, 440 Forsgate Drive, Cranbury, New Jersey 08512.

Shakespeare Studies disclaims responsibility for statements, either of fact or opinion, made by contributors.

Contents

Foreword	11
Contributors	13

Articles

Punctuating Shakespeare JONATHAN CREWE	23
Mary Frith, Alias Moll Cutpurse, in Life and Literature GUSTAV UNGERER	42
Rethinking the Discourse of Colonialism in Economic Terms: Shakespeare's *The Tempest,* Captain John Smith's Virginia Narratives, and the English Response to Vagrancy PAUL A. CEFALU	85

Symposium: Material Culture

Material Culture: Introduction PETER STALLYBRASS	123

Material Texts

Whitewash and the Scene of Writing JULIET FLEMING	133
Erasable Tablets as Tools for Musical Composition JESSIE ANN OWENS	139
Used Books WILLIAM H. SHERMAN	145
Size Matters DAVID SCOTT KASTAN	149
Vox Piscis: Dead Men Shall Ryse Agayne KATHLEEN LYNCH	154

Ben Jonson's Head
    JEFFREY MASTEN   160

Murder in Guyana
    PATRICIA PARKER   169

The Art of the Lacuna
    STEPHEN ORGEL   175

The Triumph of King James and his August Descendants
    ANA MARY ARMYGRAM   184

Clothes, Properties, Textiles

"The 'Signification' of William Reynolds's Clothes"
    KATHERINE DUNCAN-JONES, ed.   191

"His Apparel Was Done Upon Him": Rites of Personage in
Foxe's *Book of Martyrs*
    LAURIE SHANNON   193

Handkerchiefs and Early Modern Ideologies of Gender
    WILL FISHER   199

Elizabeth's Embroidery
    MAUREEN QUILLIGAN   208

Cheerful Givers: Henslowe, Alleyn, and the 1612 Loan Book
to the Crown
    S. P. CERASANO   215

The Secret History of Richard Bellasis
    LENA COWEN ORLIN   220

Creating a Silk Industry in Seventeenth-Century England
    LINDA LEVY PECK   225

Languages of Materiality

Words as Things
    MARGRETA DE GRAZIA   231

The Matter of Sounds
    GARY TOMLINSON   236

The Language of Framing
    RAYNA KALAS   240

Shakespeare Writing Matter Again: Objects and Their
Detachments
   JONATHAN GOLDBERG   248

When We Were Capital, or Lessons in Language: Finding
Caliban's Roots
   IAN SMITH   252

Trinket, Idol, Fetish: Some Notes on Iconoclasm and the
Language of Materiality in Reformation England
   JAMES J. KEARNEY   257

Review Article

Playing Companies and the Drama of the 1580s: A New
Direction for Elizabethan Theatre History?
   PAUL WHITFIELD WHITE   265

Reviews

John H. Astington, *English Court Theatre 1558–1642*
   HERBERT BERRY   287

Peter Beal, *In Praise of Scribes: Manuscripts and their
Makers in Seventeenth-Century England*
   LAETITIA YEANDLE   291

David Bevington and Peter Holbrook, eds., *The Politics of
the Stuart Court Masque*
   R. MALCOLM SMUTS   295

Cyndia Susan Clegg, *Press Censorship in Elizabethan
England*
   CECILE M. JAGODZINSKI   302

Viviana Comensoli and Paul Stevens, eds., *Discontinuities:
New Essays on Renaissance Literature and Criticism*
   JEAN E. HOWARD   305

Jonathan Dollimore, *Death, Desire and Loss in Western
Culture*
   MARIO DIGANGI   308

Marshall Grossman, ed., *Aemilia Lanyer: Gender, Genre,
and the Canon*
   KAREN ROBERTSON   310

Marshall Grossman, *The Story of All Things: Writing the Self in English Renaissance Narrative Poetry*
    JUDITH H. ANDERSON   317

Elizabeth Hanson, *Discovering the Subject in Renaissance England*
    MIHOKO SUZUKI   321

Jonathan Gil Harris, *Foreign Bodies and the Body Politic: Discourses of Social Pathology in Early Modern England*
    BRUCE R. SMITH   323

Skiles Howard, *The Politics of Courtly Dancing in Early Modern England*
    PETER HOLBROOK   327

Constance Jordan, *Shakespeare's Monarchies: Ruler and Subject in the Romances*
    KATHERINE EGGERT   333

Theodore B. Leinwand, *Theatre, Finance and Society in Early Modern England*
    DOUGLAS S. BRUSTER   337

Ania Loomba and Martin Orkin, eds., *Post-Colonial Shakespeares*
    PETER ERICKSON   339

Ned Lukacher, *Time-Fetishes: The Secret History of Eternal Recurrence*
    MARGUERITE R. WALLER   342

Megan Matchinske, *Writing, Gender, and State in Early Modern England: Identity Formation and the Female Subject*
    KATHLEEN LYNCH   345

Peter E. McCullough, *Sermons at Court: Politics and Religion in Elizabethan and Jacobean Preaching*
    JOHN H. ASTINGTON   351

Anne Lake Prescott, *Imagining Rabelais in Renaissance England*
    PHILIPPA BERRY   353

Bruce R. Smith, *The Acoustic World of Early Modern England: Attending to the O-Factor*
    JOAN PONG LINTON   356

Alan Stewart, *Close Readers: Humanism and Sodomy in Early Modern England*
    JEFFREY MASTEN   361

Margaret Tudeau-Clayton, *Jonson, Shakespeare, and Early Modern Virgil*
    REBECCA BUSHNELL   366

Index   369

Foreword

Shakespeare Studies is very pleased to offer in Volume XXVIII its first symposium, *Material Culture,* conceived and organized by Peter Stallybrass. In addition to examining the conceptual divorce between "material" and "culture" that began in the early modern period, the symposium addresses the materiality of Renaissance textual culture and the production and circulation of material goods. It provides brief commentaries from twenty-two scholars, representing a variety of disciplines, under three rubrics: "Material Texts," "Clothes, Properties, Textiles," and "Languages of Materiality." In his introduction to the symposium, Stallybrass elucidates the individual and collective significance of the commentaries.

Volume XXVIII also continues a recent innovation, that is, a review article that comments at length on important historical and theoretical issues in early modern studies. In this edition, Paul Whitfield White examines approaches and assumptions in recent studies of the development of the English theater between 1580 and 1630. There are three additional essays as well, contributed by Jonathan Crewe, Gustav Ungerer, and Paul A. Cefalu. Crewe's essay serves as a prolegomenon that would resituate the issue of punctuating Shakespeare's texts; Ungerer provides a documentary record of historical evidence concerning Moll Frith and comments on contradictions between this record and her fictional personae; and Cefalu examines Captain John Smith's Virginia narratives and *The Tempest* as early modern "colonialist" texts that are primarily concerned with economic relationships among the European colonists themselves. Volume XXVIII also contains twenty-one reviews of important new scholarly studies.

Plans for Volume XXIX include an essay on court politics during the first fourteen months of James I's reign, and another on issues of early modern costume and clothing, together with a forum that will be directed by Bruce Smith and entitled "Body Work."

LEEDS BARROLL

Contributors

JUDITH H. ANDERSON is Chancellors' Professor of English at Indiana University. She is currently working on metaphor, an extension of *Words That Matter,* her recent book on cultural linguistics.

JOHN H. ASTINGTON is Professor in the Department of English, University of Toronto, and author of *English Court Theatre 1558–1642* (1999).

HERBERT BERRY is an Emeritus Professor of English in the University of Saskatchewan.

PHILIPPA BERRY is Fellow and Director of Studies in English at King's College, the University of Cambridge. She has just published *Shakespeare's Feminine Endings: disfiguring death in the tragedies* (1999).

REBECCA BUSHNELL is Associate Dean for Arts and Letters and Professor of English at the University of Pennsylvania. She has written books on Sophocles, Renaissance tyrant tragedy, and English humanism.

PAUL A. CEFALU is Assistant Professor of English at Lafayette College. He is currently completing a book on the relationship between habit and moral identity in early modern English texts.

S. P. CERASANO, Professor of English at Colgate University, is writing a biography of the actor-entrepreneur Edward Alleyn.

JONATHAN CREWE teaches English and comparative literature, and directs the Dartmouth Humanities Center. He is currently editing several plays and the narrative poems for the new Pelican Shakespeare.

MARGRETA DE GRAZIA is Clara M. Clendenen Term Professor in English at the University of Pennyslvania. She has edited with Stanley Wells the *New Cambridge Companion to Shakespeare* (forthcoming) and is currently completing *"Hamlet" and Epochal Change*.

MARIO DiGANGI is Assistant Professor of English at Lehman College, CUNY. He is the author of *The Homoerotics of Early Modern Drama* (1997) and of essays on sexuality and gender in Renaissance culture.

KATHERINE DUNCAN-JONES prepared a New Arden edition of *Shakespeare's Sonnets* published in 1997. She is currently writing a biography of Shakespeare.

KATHERINE EGGERT is Associate Professor of English at the University of Colorado, Boulder. She is the author of *Showing Like a Queen: Female Authority and Literary Experiment in Spenser, Shakespeare, and Milton* (2000).

PETER ERICKSON is author of *Patriarchal Structures in Shakespeare's Drama* and *Rewriting Shakespeare, Rewriting Ourselves*. He is coeditor of *Shakespeare's "Rough Magic": Renaissance Essays in Honor of C. L. Barber*, and of *Early Modern Visual Culture: Representation, Race, Empire in Renaissance England*.

WILL FISHER is Assistant Professor of English at Lehman College, City University of New York. He is currently completing a book about the construction of gender through detachable parts such as beards, hair, codpieces, and handkerchiefs in early modern England.

JULIET FLEMING is a Lecturer in the Faculty of English at Cambridge University. She is completing a book on early modern writing practices.

JONATHAN GOLDBERG is Sir William Osler Professor at Johns Hopkins University. His most recent book is *Desiring Women Writing: English Renaissance Examples*.

PETER HOLBROOK is Lecturer in English at the University of Queensland, Australia, and coeditor with David Bevington of *The Politics of the Stuart Court Masque* (1998).

Contributors

JEAN E. HOWARD is Professor of English at Columbia University. Her recent books include *The Stage and Social Struggle in Early Modern England* (1994) and, with Phyllis Rackin, *Engendering a Nation: A Feminist Account of Shakespeare's English Histories* (1997). She is at work on *Theater of a City: Social Change and Generic Innovation on the Early Modern Stage.*

CECILE M. JAGODZINSKI is Coordinator of Collection Management at Milner Library, Illinois State University. She is the author of *Privacy and Print: Reading and Writing in Seventeenth-Century England.*

RAYNA KALAS is a doctoral candidate at the University of Pennsylvania. She is currently completing a thesis entitled "Frames, Glass, and the Technology of Poetic Invention."

DAVID SCOTT KASTAN is Professor of English and Comparative Literature at Columbia University. He has written widely on English Renaissance literature and culture, his most recent book being *Shakespeare after Theory* (1999). He also serves as a general editor of the Arden Shakespeare, and he is editing *1 Henry IV* for that series.

JAMES J. KEARNEY is a Ph.D. candidate in English literature at the University of Pennsylvania. He is currently completing a dissertation on the materiality of the book in Reformation England.

JOAN PONG LINTON is Associate Professor of English at Indiana University. She is currently working on the cultural interplay between the stake and the stage in the performance of agency.

JEFFREY MASTEN is Associate Professor of English at Northwestern University. He is currently completing a book called *Spelling Shakespeare, and Other Essays in Queer Philology;* with Wendy Wall, he edits *Renaissance Drama.*

ANA MARY ARMYGRAM is the Distinguished Randall McLeod Marmoreal Professor of Textual Bibliography at the University of Trona.

Contributors

STEPHEN ORGEL is the Jackson Eli Reynolds Professor of Humanities at Stanford. His most recent book is *Impersonations: The Performance of Gender in Shakespeare's England* (1996). A volume of his essays, *Authorities and Fictions,* is forthcoming.

LENA COWEN ORLIN is Research Professor of English at the University of Maryland Baltimore County and Executive Director of the Shakespeare Association of America. She is author of *Private Matters and Public Culture in Post-Reformation England* (1994) and editor of *Material London, ca. 1600* (2000).

JESSIE ANN OWENS is Professor of Music at Brandeis University. Her 1997 book, *Composers at Work: The Craft of Musical Composition 1450–1600,* received the 1998 ASCAP Deems Taylor Prize. Professor Owens is President-elect of the American Musicological Society.

LINDA LEVY PECK is Professor of History at George Washington University. The author of *Northampton: Patronage and Policy at the Court of James I* (1981), *Court Patronage and Corruption in Early Stuart England* (1990), and editor of *The Mental World of the Jacobean Court* (1991), she is currently completing a book entitled *Consuming Splendor: Britain in the Age of the Baroque.*

KAREN ROBERTSON is Adjunct Associate Professor of English and Women's Studies at Vassar College. She recently coedited (with Susan Frye) *Maids and Mistresses, Cousins and Queens: Women's Alliances in Early Modern England,* and is completing a book on Pocahontas among the Jacobeans.

LAURIE SHANNON is Assistant Professor of English at Duke University. She is currently completing a book entitled *Sovereign Amity: Figures of Friendship in Shakespearean Contexts.*

WILLIAM H. SHERMAN is Associate Professor of English at the University of Maryland. He is the author of *John Dee: The Politics of Reading and Writing in the English Renaissance* and the coeditor (with Peter Hulme) of *"The Tempest" and Its Travels.*

BRUCE R. SMITH, Professor of English at Georgetown University, is the author of *Homosexual Desire in Shakespeare's England, The Acoustic World of Early Modern England,* and *Shakespeare and*

Masculinity. His most recent work is concerned with the phenomenology of bodily experience in early modern England.

IAN SMITH is Assistant Professor of English at Lafayette College. He is currently completing a book on race, rhetoric, and national identity in early modern England.

R. MALCOLM SMUTS is Professor of History at the University of Massachusetts at Boston and President of the North American Society for Court Studies. His publications include *Court Culture and the Origins of a Royalist Tradition in Early Stuart England* (1987) and *Culture and Power in England, 1585–1685* (1999).

PETER STALLYBRASS is Professor of English at the University of Pennsylvania. He has just completed a book with Ann Rosalind Jones entitled *Renaissance Clothing and the Materials of Memory.*

MIHOKO SUZUKI is Associate Professor of English at the University of Miami. She is the author of *Metamorphoses of Helen: Authority, Difference, and the Epic,* and has recently completed a book entitled *Subordinate Subjects: Gender, the National Popular, and Literary Form in England, 1588–1688.*

GARY TOMLINSON is Annenberg Professor in the Humanities and Chair of the Department of Music at the University of Pennsylvania. His most recent book is *Metaphysical Song: An Essay on Opera.*

GUSTAV UNGERER, Professor of English Literature at the University of Berne, retired, is currently completing papers on London prostitution in the 1590s, on Mary and George Newborough, and on the sexual transgressions of the four Brookes. He is also doing research into the Mediterranean background of *The Merchant of Venice,* as well as the first black and Moorish servants in English households and in soap factories in Seville (1520).

MARGUERITE R. WALLER is Professor of English and Women's Studies at the University of California, Riverside. She is the author of *Petrarch's Poetics and Literary History,* and articles on gender construction in early modern texts.

LAETITIA YEANDLE is Curator of Manuscripts at the Folger Shakespeare Library in Washington, D.C.

SHAKESPEARE STUDIES

ARTICLES

Punctuating Shakespeare

Jonathan Crewe

> In restoring the authour's works to their integrity, I have considered the punctuation as wholly in my power; for what could be their care of colons and commas, who corrupted words and sentences? Whatever could be done by adjusting points is therefore silently performed, in some plays with much diligence, in others with less; it is hard to keep a busy eye steadily fixed upon evanescent atoms, or a discursive mind on evanescent truth.
> —Samuel Johnson, *Preface to Shakespeare*

JOHNSON'S ATTITUDE TOWARD editorial punctuation can't be called the standard eighteenth-century one since Theobald felt bound to justify many specific decisions about punctuation in his edition of Shakespeare.[1] Before and after Johnson, however, many (probably most) editors have considered punctuation "wholly within [their] power," and have repunctuated Shakespeare's text no less silently than Johnson did, according to the conventions of the moment. They have done so without necessarily sharing Johnson's justifying beliefs, namely that Shakespeare's texts are extensively corrupted, that Shakespeare's printers cared nothing for punctuation, and that punctuation marks are in any case only fugitive atoms in an otherwise stable print cosmos. To this day, repunctuation, often silent, remains a prerogative assumed by those editing Shakespeare's texts for the mass market and even for fairly restricted academic circulation. Quotation of modernized texts is still more the rule than the exception in Shakespeare criticism, scholarship, and teaching.

Attempts to resist or come explicitly to terms with modernization (a practice that encompasses spelling, orthography, typography, and format no less than it does punctuation) are not new. Nor have they been wholly absent in recent criticism and editorial practice. After briefly discussing some peculiarities of punctuation in different Shakespearean texts as well as consistencies in the scrivener Ralph Crane's punctuation, the editors of the new Oxford

Shakespeare observe that they have tried to repunctuate the early texts as sparingly as possible.[2] Readers interested in the punctuation of the original texts are then referred to the same editors' old spelling edition. This queasiness about modernizing punctuation attests to the larger fact that scholarly rigor, historical interpretation, and postmodern theory have increasingly converged in anti-interventionist or restorative editorial practices.[3] "Unediting" Shakespeare, as Leah Marcus has called it, calls for textual recovery or restoration rather than alteration. Historicizing and postmodern impulses clearly converge in the current editorial preference, highlighted by the Oxford Shakespeare, for multiple, contextually situated, nonhierarchized texts of any Shakespeare play where more than one text exists.[4]

Insofar as specifically modernizing editorial practices still seem embedded in twentieth century modernist aesthetics, or seem alternatively to be relics of a nineteenth century dream of universal progress toward ever greater rationality, efficiency, clarity, and order, they are subject to both historical and postmodern strictures.[5] Stephen Orgel has effectively challenged the editorial assumption that what seems obscure to us in Shakespeare was necessarily plain to Shakespeare's contemporaries. Editors who attempt to clarify are thus by no means necessarily restoring a clarity the play once possessed as text or performance; on the contrary, they may well be replacing systematic obscurity with their own anachronistic form of clarity.[6] Yet despite all recent editorial revisionism, the question of punctuation has remained somewhat neglected.[7] Although the approximate basis on which Shakespearean texts were punctuated is not particularly mysterious, discussions of the topic continue to be surprisingly uncertain, contradictory, and imprecise. That situation is partly due to the different historical and intellectual frames in which discussion has taken place, and the different purposes it has served; yet, cumulatively, the unsettled questions (as distinct from conscious avowals of uncertainty) aren't trivial. Such, at least, is the view I take in this paper, against the possible Johnsonian counterview that neither punctuation nor anyone's beliefs about it ever rise to the level of significance. Thus it is not clear to me, on the one hand, what modernizers believe they are doing (or neglecting) when they modernize, and it is almost equally unclear to me what antimodernizers believe can be accomplished (or made interpretively accessible) by conserving the punctuation in the early texts of Shakespeare. Borrowing a now-discarded phrase from Milton criticism, I will go even further. I will suggest that punctuation remains something of an "untransmuted lump" for both queasy modernizers and antimodernizing historicists.[8] In this paper, I hope to begin the process of transmutation, proceeding in the spirit of Random Cloud's manifesto for textual studies: "simply to establish critical rapport between our on-going speculations and documentary evidence."[9] I shall, however, conclude with one modest practical proposal, and one observation about the specific limits to editorial modernization of the punctuation in Shakespearean texts.[10]

Before continuing, I should admit that my topic might seem thankless for at least two reasons. Arguments *for* modernization seem practically redundant. The almost ubiquitous practice continues to justify itself as a market necessity, and for most purposes of teaching, performance, and literary reading. That general situation is unlikely to change soon, although the heuristics of antimodernization *have* entered public consciousness through the Oxford Shakespeare and controversies surrounding it. Arguments against modernizing are, on the other hand, difficult to pursue as productively with regard to punctuation as they have been with regard, for example, to emendation and textual conflation. Critiques of those practices continue to produce a high editorial and critical yield; in contrast, critiques of modernization in spelling and punctuation promise little more than repetitious generalities and uncertain, local gains.[11] Yet the fact remains that modernization constitutes the most ubiquitous and least heralded form of editorial intervention in the Shakespearean text, one that not even the Oxford editors can avoid. That fact calls for commensurate critical engagement.

My point of departure will be Stephen Booth's influential edition of the sonnets. Booth cites Sonnet 16, 9–12:

> So should the lines of life that life repaire
> Which this (Times pensel or my pupill pen)
> Neither in inward worth nor outward faire
> Can make you live your selfe in eies of men.

According to Booth, the reader of a modernized text only may forfeit meanings present in the quarto "because of his habit of expecting punctuation and spelling to control logical relationships methodically."[12] Booth supplements this remark by observing that (a) "spelling and punctuation probably result from a printer's whims, errors, or idiosyncrasies," and (b) that "logic and the narrowed potential" of modern language force modern readers to choose between alternatives that remain suspended in the 1609 Quarto. Perhaps Booth's comment about idiosyncracy can be read as summarizing conclusions arrived at in modern textual editing from McKerrow through Greg and Bowers, namely that punctuation in the first printed Shakespearean texts does not represent the author's intentions but rather the choices of individual compositors.[13] Even if that is what Booth means, however, he doesn't say it, and the readers to whom his edition is addressed will not necessarily know enough to fill in. Nor, in fact, is it clear to me that that is what he means; his unqualified statement stands. Furthermore, nothing indicates whether he is consciously rejecting beliefs about punctuation in the early texts of Shakespeare (whether authorial or compositorial) that have been in circulation at least since Percy Simpson's *Shakespearean Punctuation* (1911).[14]

Roughly speaking, the position taken by Simpson and some of his successors is that Shakespeare and/or his compositors proceeded intelligibly under rules of punctuation outlined by, among others, Richard Mulcaster in his *Elementarie* (1582) and George Puttenham in his *Arte of English Poesie* (1589). It does not have to be assumed that Shakespeare or the compositors referred to these texts as handbooks, but, failing proof to the contrary, we can accept that the rules represented a reasonably secure working consensus (see our own elementary composition texts and electronic grammar programs). Let us first hear Mulcaster, in chapter 21 of the *Elementarie*, under the heading "Of Distinction" (the standard neoclassical rhetorical term for breaking up continuous vocalization into discursive units):[15]

> This title of *distinction* reacheth verie far, bycause it containeth all those characts and their vses, which I called before signifying, but not sounding, which help verie much, nay all in all to the right and tunable vttering of our words and sentences, by help of those characts, which we set down and se in writing. The number of them be thirtene, and their names be *Comma, Colon, Period, Parenthesis, Interrogation, long time, shorte time, sharp accent, flat accent, streight accent, the seuerer, the vniter, the breaker.*[16]

"Long time" and "short time" refer to "the long or short pronouncing of syllabs, and ar not alwaie to marked ouer that syllab" (149). The "seuerer," "vniter," and "breaker" refer to diaresis, hyphen as a linking device (for example, in *for-think*), and double hyphen (=), already on the way out of the printer's repertoire, as a device for separating syllables, as in *ma=gi=strate*. Mulcaster treats parentheses as directions to pronounce the phrase they embed "with a lower and quicker voice," as in *"Bycause we ar not able to withstand the assalt of tentation (such is the frailtie of our natur) therefore we praise God"* (148). Standard punctuation marks are thus "elementary," as is a standard rhetorical way of conceiving their functions. (Mulcaster's treatment attests as well to the numerical reduction and standardization of punctuation marks in print culture as distinct from manuscript culture; here I shall narrow the field even further by focusing on sentence punctuation marks rather than, for example, apostrophe, hyphen, and accents that Mulcaster treats under "Distinction.")[17] Let us momentarily note that Mulcaster says nothing about semicolons, then coming into use, as Ben Jonson does several decades later in his *English Grammar,* first printed in the 1640 Folio.[18] Let us note as well, for future reference, that Mulcaster personifies linking and separating marks ("the seuerer, the vniter, the breaker") as Puttenham does with rhetorical figures, thereby investing them with agency.

Puttenham largely concurs with Mulcaster, although he factors in both lineation and caesura as specifically poetic forms of punctuation. He argues that these are really of more concern to poets than the basic forms of punctuation poets share with prose writers. Modern editors have tacitly concurred, since, apart from limited attempts to correct apparent compositorial errors, Shakespearean poetic language and lineation have remained untouchable. Covering the same bases as Mulcaster, Puttenham writes:

> The aunctent reformers of language inuented three maner of pauses, one of lesse leasure then another, and such seuerall intermissions of sound to serue (besides easement to the breath) for a treble distinction of sentences or parts of speech, as they happened to be more or less perfect in sence. The shortest pause of intermission they called *comma,* as who would say a peece of speach cut of. The second they called *colon,* not a peece, but as it were a member for his larger length, because it occupied twise as much time as a *comma.* The third they called *periodus,* for a complement or full pause, and as a resting place and perfection of so much former speach as had bene vttered, and from which they needed not to passe any further, vnles it were to renew more matter to enlarge the table.[19]

It is against Mulcaster's and Puttenham's elementary norms that deviations, eccentricities, and possibly "dramatic" effects in early modern English punctuation—and compositorial practice—need to be read in the first instance. Apparent deviations or eccentricities may importantly include exceptionally heavy or light punctuation (or the absence of punctuation in some passages), significant variations in this respect being evident across the corpus of Shakespearean texts. A marked preference for light punctuation has been ascribed, admittedly on slender evidence, to Shakespeare as author.[20]

On what, then, does Booth base his claim that printers' whims, errors, or idiosyncrasies alone "probably" determine compositorial punctuation? Improbable on the face of it, the claim is unsupported, and Booth makes no explicit response to well-entrenched views to the contrary. Perhaps we can further test Booth's claim with an imaginary example. Below, I have quoted a speech from *Measure for Measure* (a play I happen to have been editing recently) in its folio version, and then in an imaginary version that should be conceivable under whim-error-idiosyncrasy hypothesis:

(1) 'Tis one thing to be tempted (*Escalus*)
 Another thing to fall: I not deny
 The Iury passing on the Prisoner's life
 May in the sworne-twelve have a theefe, or two
 Guiltier then him they try; what's open made to Iustice,
 That Justice ceizes. What knows the Lawes
 That theeues do passe on theeues?

(2.1.17–23)

(2) 'Tis one thing to be tempted *Escalus*)
 Another thing. To fall; I not deny.
 The Iury passing on the Prisoner's life
 May in the sworne-twelve have? A thiefe or two!
 Guiltier then him they try what's open made to Iustice.
 That Iustice, ceizes. What! knowes, the Lawes:
 That, theeues do-passe on theeues.

(2.1.17–23)

If we have never come across a passage like this anywhere in Shakespeare, aside from Peter Quince's prologue to the mechanicals' play in *A Midsummer Night's Dream,* that is because, however wide the range of variation, Shakespearean punctuation is governed by intelligible, explicit, regular norms—and, in fact, by more than those explicit norms, as we shall see.[21] Even now, departure from those norms induces something akin to vertigo. The point about Peter Quince, as Lysander observes, is that "he knows not the stop." Evidently Shakespeare's compositors did know the stop: The onus is on Booth to prove otherwise.[22]

Perhaps the least contentious of Booth's claims is the one that modern punctuation, unlike its early modern counterpart, is methodical and logically directive. That statement does virtually recapitulate one made by Percy Simpson in *Shakespearean Punctuation* (1911): "we base our punctuation now on structure and grammatical form; the old system was largely guided by the meaning." The editors of the current Oxford Shakespeare reiterate: "the imposition on Shakespeare's syntax of a precisely grammatical system of punctuation reduces ambiguity and imposes definition on indefinition" (xxxvii). These propositions readily and quite convincingly support the belief that "rhetorical" punctuation mainly comprised directives for public speaking, reading aloud, stage performance, or (at a minimum) the subvocalization of texts in the process of reading. Implicitly, the early modern printed text is a voiced text, the modern one a read text.[23]

If this assumption is correct, it should follow that modernizing punctuation in Shakespeare's texts will indeed have "material" or "substantive" effects, and will do so on a massive scale. When editors modernize Shakespearean punctuation they will, in effect, be subjecting rhetorically composed and presented texts to logical analysis after the fact, and then silently incorporating the results into those texts. One set of directives will be erased and replaced by another in what might count—unlike a good deal of intuitive, sporadic emendation—as a major instance of cultural translation.[24] Booth corrects for this alteration by printing the 1609 texts of the sonnets alongside the modernized ones and by explicitly drawing attention to some possible negative consequences of modernization. Other editors insert prefatory disclaimers or, like the Oxford ones, direct readers to an old-spelling edition. It appears to me that two assumptions now underlie much of this criticism and editorial practice: first, that different, antithetical systems, one "rhetorical" and the other "logical," distinguish early modern from modern punctuation; and, second, that the respective systematicity of the two systems differs importantly in degree, the logical, system being (logically, one must suppose) more systematic.

As I have stated them, these assumptions seem ready-made for deconstruction, yet deconstruction is not what I mainly wish to attempt here. Instead, I wish to introduce some qualifications and caveats. First, when scholars begin from the strong premise that current punctuation *is* systematic and logically directive, they may too readily draw questionable or overpolarized reverse-inferences about "rhetorical" punctuation. It will then too easily follow that "rhetorical" (a.k.a. "dramatic" or "elocutionary") punctuation, practically devoid of logic or system, necessarily tolerates ambiguity, free association, and suspension of meaning in language. But does it, at least in the minds of its early modern proponents and users?[25] Moreover, is the historical difference between rhetorical and logical punctuation so fully polarized that editorial modernization really amounts to full-scale systemic (or epistemic) conversion? What, in fact, is the magnitude of the change wrought by modernization, and along what axis should it be aligned?

To take up these crucial questions, I shall turn to a recent, systematic, and wide-ranging survey of Western punctuation by M. B. Parkes titled *Pause and Effect*. As regards modernization, Parkes still makes a point similar to Booth's, and one consistent with the conclusions since 1911 that I have previously cited. Parkes too endorses a broad distinction between premodern punctuation as rhetorically directive and modern punctuation as logically directive. He takes a passage from Thomas Nashe's *Pierce Pennilesse* as his Elizabethan example:

> Having spent many yeeres in studying how to live, and liv'de a long time without mony: having tired my mouth with follie, and surfetted my minde with vanitie, I began at length to looke backe to repentaunce, & addresse my endevors to prosperitie: But all in vaine, I sate up late, and rose eraely [*sic*], contended with the colde, and conversed with scarcitie: for all my labours turned to losse, my vulgar Muse was despised & neglected, my paines not regarded or slightly rewarded, and I my selfe (in prime of my best wit) laid open to povertie. (88)

Parkes argues that "colon marks draw attention to the rhyming words ... which appear at the end of each *colon*. The period contains four *cola* (the average number according to Cicero) and the antithesis between the first two and the last two has been emphasized by introducing the third *colon* with a capital letter. The carefully balanced *commata* have been separated by commas" (88–89). Parkes then observes that when McKerrow repunctuated the text in his magisterial 1910 edition he "[divided] the single period into three sentences and [applied] semicolons—which neither Nashe nor his printer had employed, although they were widely used at the time—[thus indicating] his preference for a logical analysis of the text" (89). Breaking up longer discursive units into short, separate sentences remains a hallmark of editorial modernization even in our time, the assumed gain in logicality presumably offsetting rhetorical losses.

What emerges from Parkes's analysis is still the single apparent certainty that modernization means system and logicality in punctuation. It follows either implicitly or explicitly that those traits were absent or highly attenuated in "rhetorical" punctuation. A broad shift from orality to print culture, and from vocalization to silent reading, can readily be aligned with this implied trajectory from the rhetorical to the logical, even if commensurate cultural explanations seem lacking or often tendentious.[26] Yet complications emerge in connection with Parkes's example no less strikingly than they do in connection with Booth's. Parkes notes without further elaboration that the specifying function of punctuation marks depends at any time on the "immediate context" (88). The functioning of punctuation marks in any particular case cannot therefore be decided by referring to a general system (or a general *lack* of system). That proposition holds, no matter what regularities may observed among the texts of any particular period, and no matter what systematizations may have been attempted by rhetoricians and grammarians.

The introduction of context lets in more than Parkes seems to bargain for. It threatens his own generalizations as well as all the others cited so far, including the one between clear-cut logical and rhetorical alternatives. "Context" will supervene everywhere. Parkes's evident attempt to restrict the scope of context by confining it to the "immediate" will be unavailing. Since Parkes doesn't specify the immediate context of *Pierce Pennilesse,* one might think first of Richard Jones's printing house, where Nashe's text was set in type, but how immediate can that context be, given the wide range of factors determining the practice of any Elizabethan printer? Moreover, Parkes ascribes a high degree of rhetorical directiveness to the punctuation in his example. To whom should that be credited, author or printer? Or is something like coauthorship being posited? Parkes's additional stipulation of "literary" context implicitly shifts directive agency from compositor to author, thereby further straining at the bounds of the immediate.[27] Finally, given Nashe's performative aspirations, the example Parkes chooses is arguably at the extreme "rhetorical" end of the prose range, not an average specimen. Indeed, Parkes shortly goes on to contrast the Nashe passage with one by Bacon, whose aim to transmit knowledge calls, we are told, for logical-rhetorical "balance" (89), authorial intention again getting the credit. Parkes adds that this balance still doesn't satisfy Bacon's nineteenth-century editor, who unequivocally "prefers logical analysis" (89) and therefore splits up Bacon's extended discursive units into shorter sentences.

My point isn't that Parkes errs by introducing context, but that in doing so he effects an untheorized and methodologically troublesome shift from system to context. His own procedure graphically illustrates the risks of uncontrollable multiplicity and analytical circularity that arise with the introduction of context. The performative Nashe and the didactic Bacon are hardly average specimens but preconceived polar opposites; not too surprisingly, the performative Nashe's punctuation turns out to be highly rhetorical, while the didactic Bacon's punctuation turns out to be relatively logical. In other words, Parkes evidently finds what he expects to find in both these strongly marked cases; at the same time, more is being claimed for authorial intention than is being convincingly attributed to any immediate context. In short, the casual introduction of context does too much and too little for our understanding of punctuation; it leaves us where we were, but now with a mandate, the implementation of which will prove extraordinarily difficult and perhaps unrewarding, to consider particular circumstances in every case.

That is not all. Parkes's discussion of both Nashe and Bacon has its own context in *Pause and Effect*. That discussion appears in a section titled "The Impact of Printing: A Precarious Balance Between Logical and Rhetorical Analyses" (87). If Parkes correctly reads the history of print, it follows that "logical" preference and analysis must always have been formally available in print culture. Indeed, Parkes identifies Isidore of Seville (ca. 560–636) as an important precursor of all those who, in manuscript and subsequent print culture, have tried to subject "pointing" to a highly rationalized, logical discipline: "Writing was no longer merely the record of the spoken word but could also signal directly to the mind through the eye. For this reason, Isidore preferred silent reading to ensure better comprehension of the text: 'for understanding is instructed more fully when the voice of the reader is silent'" (21). Isidore thus separates the cognitive/ideographic potential of writing from both its "voiced" potential and from longstanding, systematic punctuation aligned with the classical rhetoricians' "parts of discourse" (21) (*cola, commata, distinctio, periodus*, etc.).[28] Some early modern humanists, among them the printer Aldus Manutius and his grandson, influentially endorsed grammatical rather than rhetorical punctuation.[29]

Two interim conclusions may be drawn. First, the history of print does not move along a simple trajectory from orality to literacy, or from rhetoric to logic, and no study of Shakespearean punctuation can be organized simply on that basis. Contingent assumptions about the richness or regulative latitude of rhetorical culture need at least to be treated with caution.[30] Second, for no phase in the history of script does the thesis of randomness or mere whim in punctuation appear to hold up.

Now, let me add that the term Parkes more crucially inserts into the history of punctuation than "context" is "analysis." What this unheralded insertion brings into view is the fact that the segmentation of written or printed discourse always *entails* linguistic analysis, whether we call that analysis rhetorical, logical, grammatical, or some combination of these (in fact, these categories inevitably overlap and circulate in the production and analysis of discourse).[31] How the segments are conceived, named, or thought to function in relation to one another has indeed differed historically, yet the both the immanence and the overlapping of systems of linguistic analysis in the composition and reproduction of texts seems like a basic datum for any kind of interpretation.[32] Both that fact and attempts either to obscure or highlight it are evident in all the early modern texts I have so far mentioned. It is to those texts and their implications for current editors and critics we must therefore return.

Mulcaster, Puttenham, and Jonson broadly concur in deriving punctuation from natural respiration. The segmentation of discourse is dictated, in this view, by the rhythm of human breathing, and punctuation marks indicate breathing spaces of varying duration.[33] This view, both commonsensical and "rhetorical," at least temporarily suspends questions about the relation between punctuation and the grammatical articulation of discourse *(sententiae, clausulae),* thus supplying further evidence for the widely held view that English Renaissance culture is overwhelmingly a rhetorical culture. Part of the explanation for this almost exclusively rhetorical focus may, however, be that grammar was taught primarily in relation to the classical languages and silently transposed—and presupposed—in discussions of vernacular writing. There was certainly no shortage of grammatical primers, Lily's being the best known one of the period. At least as important for critical purposes as the respiratory rationale Mulcaster, Puttenham, and Jonson share, however, is their widely differing contextualization of that rationale. It is with these differences as much as the shared rationale that modern editors and critics need to contend.

Let us accept that the writers I have named situate punctuation in a phonocentric frame, and that their doing so enables them to naturalize punctuating conventions that, if not wholly arbitrary, are always products of linguistic analysis. It takes no more than a moment's reflection to recognize that the natural (or comfortable) span of a breath has been very differently construed at different times in the history of print. The fact that we often feel earlier texts to be overpunctuated, or alternatively feel that sentences in earlier texts are too long (just try running a paragraph of *Areopagitica* through a contemporary electronic grammar program) does not mean that the physiology of breathing has changed over time.[34] The truth, rather, is that different writers (and epochs) have differed both in their commitment to linguistic naturalism and in their construal of it.[35]

The most aggressively and exclusively naturalist view taken by any of the authors I am considering is the one propounded by Jonson in his *English Grammar*. Having begun his book by asserting that "Grammar is the art of true, and well speaking a Language: the writing is but an accident," Jonson goes on to say: "For, whereas our breath is by nature so short, that we cannot continue without a stay to speake long together; it was thought necessarie as well for the speakers ease as for the plainer deliverance of the things spoken, to invent this means, whereby men pausing a pretty while, the whole speech might never the worse be understood."[36] Like much of Jonson's criticism, the fragmentary *Grammar* consists almost entirely of unacknowledged but identifiable borrowings, including shamelessly extensive ones from Mulcaster.[37] Yet Jonson is unusually reductive: here the "invention" of punctuation simply follows "nature" as understanding follows speaking. This somewhat imperious naturalism is ironically belied by Jonson's own folio punctuation, if we accept A. C. Partridge's reading, based in turn on Herford and Simpson. Drawing a sharp line *between* Shakespeare and Jonson, Partridge claims that Jonson's punctuation is "academic, critical, and logical" (130). Indeed, says Partridge, "between 1600, when Jonson began to take punctuation seriously, and 1616, when he piloted his First Folio through the press, his ideas advanced to the 'elaborate and overloaded system' that Simpson describes as 'ultra logical.'"[38] Yet it is in the same period that Jonson asserts that, in matters of punctuation, invention simply follows nature. The almost comical failure of Jonsonian linguistic naturalism, as distinct, perhaps, from the success of Shakespearean (or Mulcasterian) naturalism, now almost goes without saying, both naturalisms, however, being conventional. On Partridge's showing, one would be inclined to regard Jonson's punctuation less as a product of nature than of Jonson's obsessive pursuit of sole, dictatorial control, a phenomenon about which modern critics have had much to say.

Mulcaster's naturalism is less intransigent though possibly more insidious than Jonson's. If history (or literary history) has effectively denaturalized Jonson's punctuation, the same cannot confidently be said about Mulcaster's. Let us recall, for example, that when Mulcaster discusses the function of the period, he writes that it is "a small round point, which in writing followesth a perfit sentence, and in reading warneth us to rest there, and to help our breath at full, as *The feare of God is the beginning of wisdom*" (148). Rhetorically understood, a perfect sentence is a complete and self-sufficient unit of voiced utterance, its closure dictated only by the need for our breath to be "helped." The "perfit sentence" Mulcaster quotes is, however, short enough to render the rhetorical rationale dubious: it could certainly be spoken without exhausting the breath, or be incorporated into a significantly longer sentence that could still be spoken without running out of breath. The "perfit" quality of the particular sentence may therefore be inferred to include its grammatical completeness, its tacit logic, and its authoritative finality. Perhaps that would be "understood" by Mulcaster and his readers, but it would no less likely be "forgotten." What is being naturalized here is a rhetorical analysis of punctuation, but evidently a great deal is bound up with that naturalizing act: little less than a projected cultural or ideological totality. Thus, within the limits to which punctuation can be pedagogically dictated—against the resistance of error, whim, and eccentricity—Mulcaster's rules dictate more than the simple mechanics of written discourse. We must assume that our "logical" rules, composition courses, and electronic grammar programs do so as well, though that investigation lies beyond the scope of my paper.

What applies to Mulcaster largely applies to Puttenham, though in Puttenham's case "sense" begins to emerge alongside vocal delivery as a criterion, as does the necessary concurrence between rhetorical, grammatical, and logical protocols if language is to *make* sense. (Puttenham explicitly invokes "logic" in a later passage than the one I will cite.)[39] Moreover, punctuation begins to be denaturalized and linked, as is typical of the entire *Arte of English Poesie*, to cultural imperatives and hierarchies. Without "distinction," says Puttenham, language is barbarous:

> There is no greater difference betwixt a ciuill and a brutish vtterance then cleare distinction of voices; and the most laudable languages are alwaies most plaine and distinct, and the barbarous most confuse and indistinct: it is therefore requisit that leasure be taken in pronuntiation,

> such as may make our wordes plaine & most audible and agreable to the eare; also the breath asketh now and then to be releeued with some pause or stay more or lesse; besides that the very nature of speach (because it goeth by clauses of seuerall construction & sence) requireth some space betwixt them with intermission of sound, to th'end they may not huddle one vpon another so rudely & so fast that th'eare may not perceiue their difference (77).

Here, the continuum between nature and culture, sound and sense, breath and invention has clearly been interrupted, with civil determinants bidding for precedence over natural ones. No longer definitively aligned with bodily necessity or comfort, punctuation is on the way to becoming the endlessly reiterated signifier of culture rather than of nature, of civilization as opposed to barbarism. (Perhaps we should recall again here that not "knowing the stop" also becomes a decisive marker of class distinction between gentry and mechanicals in *A Midsummer Night's Dream*.) In Puttenham's work, and perhaps after it, punctuation signifies with a vengeance; a high degree of regularity becomes the implicit condition on which it does so. At the same time, grammar ("clauses of seuerall construction and sence") gets implicitly aligned with rhetoric as a codeterminant, while the segmentation (spacing) of discourse becomes the abstract condition of its articulation *as* discourse, not merely a bodily necessity. Here, as elsewhere in the *Arte,* Puttenham comes far closer to enunciating a general linguistic theory linked to cultural construction than do either Mulcaster or Jonson. In short, Puttenham is resituating neoclassical punctuation theory in his comprehensive and still undercontextualized early modern cultural anthropology.

How we are to "read" English punctuation after Puttenham—that is, roughly the same English punctuation as Mulcaster's, but with its import drastically redetermined—is far from clear. What little we know about the book's dissemination and critical reception (including Sir John Harington's famous snub in favor of Sidney's *Apology*) does not allow us to pronounce definitively on the *Arte*'s direct influence or lack of influence.[40] Nor is it easy to determine whether the book should be read as representative or eccentric in its time. What can be said is that the *Arte* invests punctuation as such with *possible* contemporary significances that call for notice by both critics and editors; it also calls attention to the increasing plurality of significations attached to punctuation in Shakespeare's time. How cultural theory and printing-house practice impinged on one another during the decades in which Shakespeare's plays were being printed may remain unfathomable, but we cannot assume that they were simply discontinuous, or that variations imply only individual whim or eccentricity.

If we must say, then, that the punctuation of Shakespeare's texts still brings us back in the final analysis to compositorial or printing-house practice—in that sense, to the "material" text—as the principal object of investigation, it is certainly not enough to pursue the investigation as if the "material" were sealed off from the realm of signification and active cultural construction. Our tendency to segregate the material site of printing from the larger culture is fostered by our belief in the mindless, wayward, "humble" scrivener or compositor, evidently the rude mechanicals of modern editorial criticism.[41] It appears that early modern punctuation is a site of conflicting as well as overlapping signification, and of active cultural construction. It is also overdetermined in theory and practice to a degree that makes it difficult to determine the precise magnitude and nature of the changes wrought by modernization. The overdeterminations are both specifiable and subject to further discovery, however, and the mere difficulty of factoring them in is not reason enough for the silence largely maintained on the subject by modernizing editors, even of upscale, scholarly editions, and by antimodernizing historicists. Even if only more elaborate disclaimers are called for, those disclaimers need to be pro forma or merely repetitious. They, together with whatever punctuation studies may still be in the works, could contribute to the rapport sought by Random Cloud between criticism and documentary evidence.

Let me briefly conclude now by returning to the beginning of this paper, where I referred to the specific limits of editorial modernization. These limits are generally not ones established in principle. The fact is that no amount of repunctuation can convert Shakespeare's logic and syntax into ours, as innumerable efforts to clarify attest, and that not only because the passion and irrationality of dramatic speakers may be mimed in many instances. Furthermore, modernizing punctuation, which often involves removing or redistributing commas, semicolons, and colons, and breaking up long discursive sequences into short sentences, always represents a messy compromise between the early texts and our own conventions. Whatever they may signify, the "distinctions" and discursive units *(cola, commata)* of early modern composition continue to assert themselves against all modernizing efforts. In many editions of Shakespeare, as well as in our reading of the plays, they still frequently override our strict rules about the function of commas, semicolons, and colons, and about the formation of "perfit" sentences.

Notes

1. For a good summary of eighteenth-century Shakepeare editing, see Marcus Walsh, *Shakespeare, Milton, and Eighteenth Century Editing: The Beginnings of Interpretive Scholarship* (Cambridge: Cambridge University Press, 1997), 111–99.

2. William Shakespeare, *The Complete Works,* ed. Stanley Wells and Gary Taylor (Oxford: Clarendon Press, 1986), xxxvii. On Crane's possible responsibility for punctuation in the Shakespeare Folio, see A. C. Partridge, *Orthography in Shakespeare and Elizabethan Drama* (Lincoln: University of Nebraska Press, 1964), 172–74.

3. I see no need to quibble here about distinctions between (old) historical and (new) historicist practices since the difference is immaterial for my purposes.

4. See Leah Marcus, *Unediting Shakespeare* (New York: Routledge, 1996). In our revisionist moment, Random Cloud's "FIAT *f* FLUX" might well serve as the rallying cry for postmodern critics of textual stabilization by modern editors. See Random Cloud, "FIAT *f* LUX," *Crisis in Editing: Texts of the English Renaissance,* ed. Randall McLeod (New York: AMS Press, 1994), 61–172, and also David Greetham, "Editorial and Critical Theory: From Modernism to Postmodernism," *Palimpsest: Editorial Theory in the Humanities* (Ann Arbor: University of Michigan Press, 1993), 9–28.

5. On the ideological frames of Shakespeare editing since the nineteenth century, see Marcus, *Unediting Shakespeare,* 17–25.

6. Stephen Orgel, "Introduction" to Shakespeare's *The Winter's Tale* (Oxford: Clarendon Press, 1996), 6–11.

7. For example, the word "punctuation" does not appear in the index to Marcus's *Unediting Shakespeare,* nor does she discuss the issue. Like many, she focuses primarily on textual variants.

8. Stanley Fish recalls a phase in which Books 11 and 12 of *Paradise Lost* were dismissed as "an untransmuted lump of futurity." See Stanley Fish, "Transmuting the Lump: *Paradise Lost,* 1942–1979," *Doing What Comes Naturally* (Durham, N.C.: Duke University Press, 1989): 247. As one of the current editors of the new Pelican Shakespeare, I include myself among the queasy modernizers, here attempting to come to terms with my own practice.

9. Random Cloud, "Introduction," *Crisis in Editing,* x.

10. A. C. Partridge, *Orthography,* lists various modern approaches and conclusions to punctuation research, including A. W. Pollard's, from 1911 to 1964. Because I believe that punctuation studies have languished in recent times, partly for methodological reasons and partly, perhaps, on account of the empirical difficulties and limits revealed by earlier studies, I have not tried to form a coherent overview of the post-1964 field.

11. Retaining Shakespearean spelling and punctuation may effect a salutary, general estrangement of the text in the service either of denaturalization or of historical objectification. Neither of these rationales is strongly urged, however, in current criticism nor editing. Nor, for that matter, is "antiquing" of the text for aesthetic or culturally nostalgic reasons.

12. Stephen Booth, ed., *Shakespeare's Sonnets* (New Haven: Yale University Press, 1977), xv.

13. It is on this basis more than any other that modern editors have felt punctuation of Shakespearean texts to be "wholly within [their] power."

14. Cited in Partridge, *Orthography*, 131.

15. A practice not always followed in manuscript culture from late antiquity onward, so-called *scripta continua* producing a wholly unpunctuated and uncapitalized text for the reader to punctuate. These texts could generally not be sight-read.

16. Richard Mulcaster, *The First Part of the Elementarie Which Entreateth Chefelie of the Right Writing of our English Tung* (London: Thomas Vautrollier, 1582).

17. See, among others, M. B. Parkes, *Pause and Effect: An Introduction to the History of Punctuation in the West* (Berkeley and Los Angeles: University of California Press, 1993).

18. Ben Jonson, *The English Grammar, The Works of Ben Jonson*, ed. C. H. Herford and Percy and Evelyn Simpson, 10 vols. (Oxford: Clarendon Press, 1957), 8:453–554. Some have regarded the introduction of the semicolon as the momentous beginning of a broad historical shift from "rhetorical" to "logical" punctuation. See Partridge, *Orthography*, 136.

19. George Puttenham, *The Arte of English Poesie*, in Gregory Smith, ed., *Elizabethan Critical Essays*, 2 vols. (Oxford: Clarendon Press, 1904), 2:77–78.

20. Partridge, *Orthography*, 130–40. If the evidence were firmer, something important might be inferred about Shakespeare's specific resistance to any systemization, a resistance that would, however, have been negated to varying degrees by his own compositors.

21. This point has already been well made by Stephen Orgel, "What Is an Editor?" *Shakespeare Studies* 24 (1996): 23–29. Orgel writes: "The idea that spelling and punctuation have no rules in the period, and are a function of the whim of the compositor, the whole concept of *accidentals*, has come under heavy scrutiny" (24).

22. I would suggest, more affectionately, I hope, than censoriously, that Booth's punctuation theory betrays a hippie-era wistfulness for a state of plentitude to be accessed simply by the undoing of modern regulation. Booth's virtually unpunctuated quatrain makes his preference clear.

23. To the extent that this generalization holds up, the "voiced" nature of Shakespearean texts has recently been subsumed by Bruce Smith in what he calls the early modern soundscape, an audio-historical reconstruction predicated on a general "phenomenology of audition." In Smith's account, the Globe functions as an acoustic resonator; early modern audition does not have to be wholly imaginary since some of Smith's contentions can be put to the test in the new Globe Theatre. See Bruce Smith, *The Acoustic World of Early Modern England: Attending to the O Factor* (Chicago: University of Chicago Press, 1999).

24. The practice of modernization can indeed be defended *as* cultural translation, subject to whatever criteria of evaluation might apply. Walter Benjamin supplies the theoretical frame in which all cultural transmission inevitably consists in cultural translation. For Benjamin, the historical gaze, in contrast to the anthropological one, discloses only the melancholy vista of accumulating ruin. See Walter Benjamin, "The Task of the Translator," and "Theses on the Philosophy of History," *Illuminations*, trans. Harry Zohn (New York: Schocken Books, 1968): 69–85, 253–64.

25. For what it's worth, Marlowe's *Edward II* turns on the fatal potentiality—

and manipulability—of ambiguity unresolved by punctuation. The "unpointed" sentence capable of being taken as a command to kill the king reads *Edwardum occidere nolite timere bonum est.* The king dies if the comma is placed after "timere," but lives if it is placed after "nolite." Unpointed, the sentence leaves it up to reader to decide, but also allows "deniability" (innocent intent and/or innocent misunderstanding) if the king is put to death.

26. The entire issue thus falls into the vexed debate regarding the priorities of orality and literacy. Silent reading is attested at least since the famous anecdote, recalled by Parkes, in which, before his conversion, St. Augustine was startled to see St. Jerome reading silently. In that anecdote, silent reading is evidently connected to inwardness, spirituality, and perhaps theological rigor as distinct from public, affective, power-seeking, rhetorical performance. Parkes additionally notes that St. Augustine's apostrophizing invocation of the dead requires that this texts be voiced.

27. This slippage back to authorial intention recurs frequently in discussions of early modern punctuation. The literary context might be taken to comprise, inter alia, the decade in which *Pierce Pennilesse* was written; the patronage system in which it solicited attention; the milieu of the disaffected university wits; the competitive, agonistic performance in which Nashe and others continued to engage after the Marprelate controversy; the anti-Ciceronianism of Nashe's "extemporal style," conspicuously marked in the passage cited; the Elizabethan emergence of literary prose and the literary personality; the problematic reinscription of cultural masculinity during the Elizabethan period. And so on. In short, literary context provides only a weak and doubtful basis for reading early modern punctuation.

28. We can by no means say that the ideographic potential of language—or its writtenness and mechanical reproducibility for that matter—play no part in the calculations of Shakespeare or his compositors. The sonnets alone, or especially, prove otherwise, as, does Shakespeare's marked attention to both voiced and inaudible letters.

29. For a summary, see A. C. Partridge, *Orthography,* Appendix 8 "Aldus Manutius on the Use of Symbols," 191–92.

30. Bruce Smith's argument in *The Acoustic World* for the primacy of audition represents a powerful, theoretically astute response to the textualizing propensities of post-structuralism rather than being an unconditioned return to phonocentrism. It is worth remarking that historical and phenomenological approaches to early Shakespearean texts cannot wholly coincide.

31. A. C. Partridge, *Orthography,* asserts that "Ben Jonson, like Aldus Manutius, favored the logical theory of pointing; Richard Mulcaster and Shakespeare preferred a *partly* rhythmical system. He adds, however, that "these were not regarded as rival systems, for the reason that each permitted much latitude in individual practice" (130).

32. Innumerable theoretical disclaimers notwithstanding, historical editors and interpreters still tend to treat "recovered" early texts of Shakespeare as ones restored to historical immediacy and unconditional legibility. Likewise, while admitting that context is always constructed, those historicists frequently take the historical contexts they invoke as given or self-evident.

33. By the middle of the seventeenth century, it had become a rule of thumb that the time interval (or breathing space) signified by different punctuation marks observed the proportion 1, 2, 3, 4. In other words, the comma designated a pause for one beat, a semicolon for two, a colon for three, and a period for four. Mulcaster

doesn't include the semicolon, although it was already coming into use by printers.

34. Or that respiration varies cross-culturally, since Americans often find British texts overpunctuated.

35. This linguistic naturalism continues to be transmitted through Shakespeare's works unless they are more drastically modernized than they usually are, our preference for "logicality" notwithstanding.

36. Jonson, *The English Grammar,* vol. 8, 551.

37. On Jonson's other sources, from Quintilian and Martianus Capella to Scaliger and Ramus, see Jonson, *Works,* vol. 9, 165–210.

38. Partridge, *Orthography,* 137.

39. Thomas Wilson discusses punctuation in his *Art of Logic* (1553) rather than his *Art of Rhetoric,* using a epistolary example that has sometimes been identified as the source for Peter Quince's Prologue.

40. Sir John Harington, *A Brief Apology for Poetry,* in Gregory Smith, *Elizabethan Critical Essays,* (Oxford: Clarendon Press, 1904), vol. 2, 196. It seems unlikely that Shakespeare's compositors were directly influenced by the *Arte,* but they were not foreigners to the culture in which it was produced.

41. In a forthcoming work, Jeff Masten anatomizes some specifically Cold War editorial fictions regarding compositors.

Mary Frith, Alias Moll Cutpurse, in Life and Literature

Gustav Ungerer

I

MARY FRITH'S SEXUAL AND GENDER identities remain elusive for various reasons. For one thing, the source material that has come down to us is fragmentary, male-oriented, and prejudiced; for another, any argument based on the published biography is bound to be fallacious considering that the biographers were committed to adjusting their subject in conformance to the stereotyped criminal of fictional biography. In point of fact, their attempt to explain Mary Frith's seemingly enigmatic sexuality simply amounted to labeling her as a sexual aberration, a prodigy, a monster. Once dehumanized, she was slotted into different sexual categories regardless of the fact that some of them were contradictory. Thus, she is represented as a transvestite usurping male power, as a hermaphrodite transcending the borders of human sexuality, as a virago, as a tomboy, as a prostitute, as a bawd, and even as a chaste woman who remained a spinster.

Moreover, the ongoing debate about the sexual and gender identity of Mary Frith has mainly drawn on her fictional representations as Moll Cutpurse in the criminal biography and as the Roaring Girl in Middleton and Dekker's play.

Thus a crucial problem that the steadily growing Moll Cutpurse studies have failed to address is whether Moll Cutpurse was a historical or a fictional figure. Can the anonymously published biography, *The Life and Death of Mrs. Mary Frith. Commonly Called Mal Cutpurse. Exactly Collected and now Published for the Delight and Recreation of all Merry disposed Persons* (London: for W. Gilbertson, 1662; Wing L 2005), be acknowledged as the authentic and authoritative biography of Mary Frith or must it be categorized as one of those early factual fictions that appropriated historical figures of

HE ROARING GIRLE:

OR,

MOLL CUT-PURSE.

As it hath lately beene Acted on the Fortune-stage by the Prince his Players.

Written by T. Middleton and T. Dekkar.

My case is alter'd, I must worke for my living.

Printed at London for Thomas Archer, and are to be sold at his Shop in Popes head-pallace, neere the Royall Exchange, 1611.

Original woodcut of Mary Frith on the title page of the first edition of Middleton and Dekker's play, *The Roaring Girl* (1611). Courtesy of the National Portrait Gallery, London.

the underworld in order to put them through a mythologizing process from which they emerged as mythic figures shorn of their personal histories? Elizabeth Spearing, the modern editor of *The Life*, although aware of the problem, leaves it unsolved. On the one hand, she owns that the figure of Moll Cutpurse assumed various forms in the course of the seventeenth and eighteenth centuries, but, on the other, she is inclined to believe that the text she has edited "is certainly the only one that gives anything like an account of the actual woman rather than a mythical figure, or that could derive from information given by the original 'Moll,' Mary Frith herself."[1]

The editor, I am sure, would have adopted a different stance on the nature of the biography if she had consulted the chapbook version printed in 1662 on behalf of the publisher George Horton: *The Womans Champion; or The Strange Wonder Being a true Relation of the mad Pranks, merry Conceits, Politick Figaries, and most unheard of Stratagems of Mrs. Mary Frith, commonly called Mall Cutpurse, living near Fleet-Conduit; even from her Cradle to her Winding-Sheet. Containing several remarkable passages touching the Constable, Counters, and Prisoners, and her last Will and Testament to Squire Dun, as a Legacy for his later days. With her divining Prophesie, concerning wicked Plots, and Hell-bred Conspiracies. Extracted from the Original; Published according to Order* (London, printed for G. Horton, living in Fig-Tree Court in Barbican, 1662, Wing W 3323B). In 1651 and 1652, Horton had been instrumental in fashioning the myth of the highwayman James Hind. He was responsible for the publication of at least five Hind biographies, besides a collection of crude dramatic sketches, all of them being part of a concerted scheme to lay hands on Hind in order to pass him off as a defender of royalism.[2] In like manner, the hacks working for George Horton in Barbican and William Gilbertson lay hands on Mary Frith, transmuting her into a royalist and, what is more, into a female highway robber who masterminded the feats and pranks of both the mythic James Hind and Richard Hannam. The author(s), as will be discussed below, consciously transgressed the generic principles of male criminal biography and the order of gender hierarchy.

The text of the fictional memoirs of Moll Cutpurse was made accessible to later generations by the epitome published in captain Alexander Smith's *A Complete History of the Lives and Robberies of the Most Notorious Highwaymen, Shoplifts, and Cheats of Both Sexes* (London, 1719, ii, 137–52). It is Captain Smith, an uninhibited plagiarist and manipulator, who is mainly responsible for misleading modern critics into taking a piece of fiction for the actual record of Mary Frith's career.[3] Smith did not content himself with lifting the abstract from the 1662 *Life,* but seized the opportunity to tamper with the text, vamping up some further episodes of a sensational character such as Moll's robbery of general Fairfax on Hounslow Heath, which will be commented on in part II. To rely on Smith as purveying historical evidence on metropolitan criminality and on the organization of the female underworld amounts to distorting the known facts.[4]

The purpose of this article is thus an effort to recover at least some of the historical documentation for Moll Frith's life that has been displaced or distorted by her biographer(s). Accordingly, I have appended an addendum, a "Documentary Life," and syntheses of the extant texts (including the contribution made by the visual arts to the mythmaking process). This addendum serves as the documentary basis for the essay that I shall be offering here and that I have organized as follows.

Part II, which follows immediately, addresses the mythmaking process of transmuting the historical figure of Mary Frith into the mythic Moll Cutpurse. It will be shown that the main strategy the author(s) pursued was to integrate scanty historical records into the preexisting parameters of criminal biography as they had been evolved for male criminals and, if need be, to transcend or invert the pattern.[5] As a result of this transmutation, Mary Frith suffered the same fate at the hands of her anonymous pseudobiographers as did Hind and his like. Moll Cutpurse, as she has come down to us in the text published in 1662, is a mythic construct made up of invented facts and conditioned by absences and displacements; or to put it in other terms, the historical figure, who already in her lifetime had gone through a mythologizing process, was reduced to a depersonalized entity. Part III is conceived as a contribution to the ongoing academic debate about the sexual ambiguity of the mythic Moll Cutpurse. It breaks new ground in examining the sexual and gender identities of the historical Mary Frith in the light of her marriage to Lewknor Markham and in analyzing her career as a pickpocket, as a Tarltonesque entertainer and licensed broker. Contemporary studies have invariably focused on the representation of Moll Cutpurse's sexuality and gender and have thereby turned a blind eye to the fact that the real-life Mary Frith was creating, for gain, her own public persona as a cross-dressing performer. Cross-dressing was her professional signature. I am arguing that she was a liminal figure striving to carve a niche for herself, however marginal, in the entertainment business of Southwark and the City of London.

II

It is doubtful that the author(s) charged to produce the criminal biography of Mary Frith had access to the inside information that archival research has brought to light. In any case, the amount and reliability of biographical data at his/their disposal is quite irrelevent if we bear in mind that whatever material he/they drew on was invariably trimmed to conform to the formula of criminal biography. Thus, *The Life and Death of Mrs. Mary Frith* deconstructs itself as factual fiction by transmuting the historical Mary Frith into the conventional figure of the sinner turned penitent who commits her crimes to paper as a warning to future generations; into the criminal who has espoused the royalist cause; into the highway robber who besides performing her own deeds is glorified as the plotter of Hind's and Hannam's raids on Cromwell's money convoys; and into the popular outcast defending the poor and the oppressed against rapacious lawyers. Worst of all, she is simultaneously represented as a sexual monster.

Before focusing our attention on the reductive process, it is advisable to settle the question of authorship. Elizabeth Spearing has applied to the soi-disant memoirs and confessions of the seventeenth-century lawbreaker a computer test program that has been developed to fathom out the veracity of the confessions of twentieth-century lawbreakers. The result would seem to support the likelihood that three different writers may have been working on the criminal biography. Her findings lend some weight to my view that the publishers William Gilbertson and George Horton engaged a team of male writers to piece together a biography and a chapbook in order to capitalize on the sensational career of a woman who, despite her illiteracy, worked up her way from cutpurse to cross-dressed entertainer and to licensed broker, thus breaking into the male-dominated business world of the entertainment industry and early capitalism.

This theory is somewhat strengthened by the fact that the biography falls into three incoherent, uncoordinated, and at times contradictory parts. The first part, the address to the reader (3–5), initiates the process of pruning away the individual features of Mary Frith.

Written in the style of mock learning, it stresses the matchlessness of the heroine in presenting her as *"the Oracle of Felony,"* the *"*Prodigy of *those* Times *she lived in,"* and *"Epicoene Wonder,"* a "Virago," and a "Bona Roba," that is, a prostitute. The last slur is one of the major contradictions between the three parts. The writer, somehow aware of the biographical reduction and of the incoherence of the three parts, thought fit to add an apology to the Reader, asking him to *"Excuse the Abruptnesse and Discontinuance of the Matter, and the severall independencies thereof."* He presumed to palm off the responsibility for the lack of narrative coherence to the character of Mary Frith, observing *"that it was impossible to make one piece of so various a Subject, as she was both to her self and others, being forced to take her as we found her though at disadvantage"* (5). The "we" may be as pluralis majestatis or the slip of a slipshod writer giving away the multiple authorship.

The second part (7–17) is a standarized fictional biography, tracing Mary Frith's family background, her childhood, education, and dislike of domestic chores up to the point when the *"Colossus of Female* subtlety in the wily Arts and *ruses* of that Sex" stood "upon her own leggs" (17). The writer assumes the voice of a third-person narrator whose analysis of the heroine's gradual development into a sexual and social outsider betrays a remarkable sense of psychological insight. This writer may well have had some "personal knowledge of the subject," as Elizabeth Spearing argues (xii); but as we will see, he nonetheless committed some "factual blunders" in making up for the lack of authentic biographical material.

The third part (17–73), inscribed as a first-person narrative, pursues the editorial policy of making the reader believe that "Mal Cutpurse's *Diary"* is an autobiographical confession, a "Defence and Apology," committed to paper by the heroine, in a state of grace, for the edification of the reader.[6] This part falls into two sections, the first running from page 17 to page 49, the second from page 49 to page 73. There is an unmistakable break on page 49, a "Discontinuance of the Matter," to put it in terms of the first writer. It marks the moment when the third biographer, run short of jests and pranks, begins to drift away from his subject and to foreground contemporary history. From now on the autobiography reads like a diatribe against Cromwell, his Protectorate, and "the sanctified Delusions" of the Puritans.

The insousiance with which three putative writers approached their task as well as their indifference to the basic facts of Mary Frith's life is borne out by the inaccurate dates of birth and death.

Mary Frith (see addendum) died on 26 July 1659. The second writer, not sure about the date, has brought himself to admit that he failed to "ascertain the Week" and "Moneth of her Nativity" (8), and the writer of her memoirs has her record: "I bid . . . Adieu this Threescore and Fourteenth year of my Age" (72). Her age, however, does not square with the date of birth given by the writer of the standardized biography. If she died at the age of seventy-four in 1659, she must have been born in 1585. The text suprisingly reads that she "was Born *Anno Domini,* 1589, in *Barbican,* at the upper end of *Aldersgate* street" (8). The chapbook version makes the same mistake, adding that Mary Frith was born "in the Parish of St. *Giles's* Cripplegate, near *Barbican*" (sig. A2r). The place of birth may have been prompted by George Horton's address in Barbican.

Mary Frith's will, dated 6 June 1659, was not accessible to the biographers. But as the formula of criminal biography required a will, the third biographer had no scruples in allowing free rein to his creative imagination. On the one hand, he kept in line with the literary tradition in passing off Mary Frith as a generous patroness throughout her life; on the other, he had the sangfroid to make her say that "I did make no *Will* at all, because I had had it for so long before to no better purpose" (73). Thus the fictionalized Mary Frith reports at the end of a criminal life that she spent £1,400 "in good Gold . . . out of my *kind heartedness*" on "my old Friends, the distressed Cavaliers, to help them in their compositions" (72). She would have "very well liked" to emulate the example set by Edward Alleyn, the actor, in endowing a charitable foundation, a school and "*Almes Houses,*" but she regrets that she has less than £100 left "to command." She has, however, given £30 to her "Maids" (73). The rest of her "Estate in Money Movables and Household *Goods*" she leaves to her "Kinsman *Frith,* a Master of a Ship, dwelling at *Redriffe* [Radcliff], . . . as next of Kin" (73). This is a complete departure from what actually happened. The historical Mary Frith left the "remainder" of a "meane estate" to her married niece and executrix Frances Edmonds, £20 to ther kinsman Abraham Robinson and 12d. to Abraham's father James Robinson (see addendum).

The three biographers and most modern critics in their wake have ignored the fact that on 23 March 1614 Mary Frith was married to Lewknor Markham, esquire, at St. Mary Overies, Southwark (see Addendum). The second collaborator sacrifices historical evidence to the fictional policy of creating the portrait of a hermaphrodite who chose to remain single. Thus he explains that Mary Frith had sought the company of a shoemaker, but when "she found the fellow made an absolute prey of her Friendship," squandering the money "she with difficulty enough provided," she left him. This negative experience and other swindles "not only took her off from the consideration or thought of Wedlock, but reduced her to some advisement which way she might maintain her self single" (15).

The fictional drive to cook up biographical data and manipulate historical events is most apparent in the third writer's adaptation of Mary Frith's career to the pattern set up by George Fidge, in his 1651/52 campaign, whose aim was to fashion the myth of James Hind as a royalist highwayman. Fidge, a royalist sympathizer, had politicized Hind, appropriating him as an ideological instrument with which to denounce the hated rule of the protectorate;[7] and the anonymous biographer, in accordance with the standardized royalist criminal, encoded Mary Frith as a staunch defender of royalism, tracing the origin of her nickname Mary Thrift to King Charles's entrance into the city of London in 1639. Thus, he has his fictional Mary Frith report that she threw a party in honor of the king's return to London "After that unnatural and detestable Rebellion of the Scots in 1638" (43), which the pacification of Berwick, in 1639, put an end to, to the disadvantage of the king's cause. As she knew that it was "usual with the *Roman* and modernly with the *Italian* Courtezans to be very splendid in publique Works, as erecting of Bridges or Aqueducts, Cause-wayes, making of Moles, or cutting Passages," she "resolved to show" her "Loyal and Dutiful Respects to the *King*" (43) in undertaking "to supply *Fleet-street* Conduit adjacent to" her "House with Wine, to run continually for that triumphal Day" (44). "And as the *King* passed by," she grasped his hand, "saying, *Welcome Home,* CHARLES." This "celebrated Action . . . being the Town talk, made people look upon" her "at another rate then formerly. 'Twas no more *Mal Cutpurse* but Mrs. *Mary Thrift*," her "neighbours using" her thereafter "with new respect and civility" (44). The celebration of the king's entrance, as narrated by the mythic Mary Frith, is cast in the episodic style of the traditional jest-biography. The nickname Mary Thrift (see Addendum) originates from her activity as a dynamic broker and was coined between 1614 and 1620. It has nothing whatever to do with the historical events of 1639.

The royalist code and the anecdotal form of the jest-biographies enabled the writer of the memoirs to embed his mythic Moll Cutpurse into the contemporary historical background. She is represented as a partaker of the civil war and as a witness committed to defending the royalist cause. Thus, she did not only hobnob with King Charles in 1639, but she branded Cromwell as an "ambitious Usurper" (69). She also took John Pym and the parliamentarians to task for their "desperate Fatal conspiracy against the renowned States-man, the Earl of *Strafford,* Lord Deputy of Ireland" (50). To revenge his execution, which took place on 12 May 1641, she published the pamphlet of "a solemne *Bull baiting*" in the Bear Garden, in which she called the "Bull that threw off all the Dogs . . . *Strafford*" and her own "Dogs that played at him" John Pym and Oliver St. John (50). She also defied Robert Devereux, third Earl of Essex, who in June 1641 had been appointed Lord General and Supreme Commander of the Parliament's forces on land. She changed the headgear of her fighting dogs to orange, the Earl's colors, "and with the usual stile given that Earle by the Cavaliers," she "called the *Bull*" at the Bear Garden "its Oxcellency" (59).[8]

In weaving the historical Mary Frith into the fictional texture of a criminal biography, the writer of the memoirs displayed some originality. He applied, as mentioned above, the generic formula of the royalist criminal to Mary Frith and in doing so he went to the length of transgressing the formula. George Fidge had elevated the highwayman James Hind to the heights of a royalist hero in 1652 and now, in 1662, the anonymous biographer(s), in like manner, lionized Mary Frith, transmuting her into a female highway robber. This was a daring regendering of the generic principle. Highway robbery, the male crime par excellence, was now hailed as the female crime par excellence.[9] This implied the reversal of the gendered criminal code with the mythic Mary Frith masterminding the mythic exploits of James Hind and Richard Hannam.

It is, of course, extremely improbable that Mary Frith as a metropolitan pickpocket should ever in real life have rubbed shoulders with Hide and Hannam, let alone have hatched and supervised their robberies. Her boast that she set "most of the chief of" Hind's feats as "the Wyer that moved that Engine in all his great prizes" (65–66) is pure fiction. This consideration also applies to the only joint venture in the battlefield: the raid on a money convoy that was on its way "to pay their Souldiers at *Oxford* and *Gloucester*" (65). Moll and Hide justified their assault arguing that it was "the Commonwealths Money which those great Thieves at *Westminster* had Fleeced out of the Publique to pay the[i]r *Janizaries,* who maintained them in their Tyranny and Usurpation: while the Loyal and the Honest Subject was Ruined and Undone by their Taxes, Plunderies, twentieth part, and Sequestrations of their Estates" (65).

Alexander Smith in his *History of the Lives and Robberies of the Most Notorious Highwaymen* (1719) stretched the heroic formula to preposterous lengths. Prompted by one of the pranks about "*Walker* a notable *Pick-pocket,*" who, disguised as "a Commander in the Army," stole "a rich Gold Watch set with Diamonds from my Lady Fairfax, the Generals Wife," while she was attending a presbyterian service in St. Martin's Church, Ludgate Hill (62–63), Smith capped the theft with the report of Mary Frith's heroic assault on General Thomas, third Baron Fairfax. He would have the reader believe that Fairfax, the founder of the New Model Army, was held up by Mary Frith on Hounslow Heath, shot through the arm, relieved of two hundred jacobuses, and left with two horses killed on the Heath. For this offense she was committed to Newgate Prison, from where she procured her release by paying Fairfax £2,000.[10]

Smith had no second thoughts about casting an urban female criminal, who used London as her haunt, in the role of a highway robber prowling on the fringes of the city and keeping a lookout for the general. As he was catering for a vast readership, Smith had learned how to pander to the tastes and instincts of readers who preferred tales about a single highwayman cavaliering on a heath in the outskirts of a town to tales about crimes committed in towns by well-organized gangs.[11] Smith, making no bones about his antirepublican sentiments, pounced upon any opportunity to discredit the Fairfaxes. Thus, he also concocted the report that Zachary Howard raped Anne Vere, Lady Fairfax, and her daughter Elizabeth.[12]

Another stereotyped feature of the criminal biography was the portrayal of the biographee in the role of criminal-as-sinner. Mary Frith's biographers adhered to this code. Thus, she introduces her memoirs in the guise of the penitent sinner, entreating her readers "with all Fairness and Candor, and the pity of a *Sessions House Jury,* to hear me in this my Defence and Apology" (17).[13] But contrary to her initial protestation, the memoirs turn out to be a glorification of her pranks and crimes rather than a condemnation of them. Her abrupt repentance when facing death and her confession that she "never lived happy minute" in this world till she "was leaving of it" (72) do not ring true. The ambivalence of her moral attitude derives from the native tradition of the coney-catching pamphlets.[14]

The moral ambivalence also manifests itself in the criminal's stereotyped role as protector of the poor against injustice and social discrimination. Moll Cutpurse shares with other criminal biographees a sharp political awareness and a keen sense of justice. In the fashion of James Hind, who indulges in lecturing on the corrupting power of money,[15] she poses as the defender of the oppressed, the underprivileged, the exploited, laying bare the corruption of the moral guardians of the state, the rapacity of the lawyers and clergymen, and the abuses committed by petty constables and selfish politicians. Thus, she "sympathized" with a coiner who was hanged at the beginning of the civil war for counterfeiting and clipping half-crowns out of sheer "Necessity," as she puts it; and following a well-established journalistic device, she records his very last words allegedly spoken under the gallows: *"That he was adjudged to die but for Counterfeiting of a Half Crown, but those that Vsurped the whole Crown and stole away its Revenue, and had Counterfeited its Seal, were above justice and escaped unpunish'd"* (25).[16] She enjoys recounting how she took her revenge on a vainglorious constable who had committed her to the Counter for a "Rat," that is for beng drunk. Her hilarious account reads like one of those free-floating pranks that came to be written down in the vein of the popular jest-biographies (25–30).[17] On Sundays she used to observe the custom "to be charitable . . . to the Prisoners of *Ludgate* and *Newgate* (45) and she spontaneously offered £50 to secure the release of the "famous Wrastler" Cheney (64), a friend of her and of Hind's, who is remembered in Hind's epitaph.

III

Because of the inevitable mythologizing generated by the scarcity of biographical data about Mary Firth, what then is to be claimed or suggested concerning her gender and sexual orientation, questions that have dominated recent study? One approach to this problem is, I think, her marriage to Lewknor Markham, esquire, of Nottingham, possibly an elder son of the author Gervase Markham. The marriage bond was signed on 23 March 1614 in St. Saviour's, Southwark, a stone's throw from the Hope and Globe theatres, the Bear Garden, and the stews. Shakespeare's youngest brother, Edmund, a professional actor, had been buried there on 31 December 1607 to the sound of the great bell.[18]

The heterosexual marriage imparted an air of cultural normalcy to Mary Frith's status as a notorious member of the underworld and to her threatening anomaly as an autonomous woman. Obviously, she was not unmarriageable; she was neither a monster as given out by her biographers, nor did she correspond to Middleton and Dekker's hermaphroditic ideal, as represented in *The Roaring Girl*, who refuses to marry. The registers of biological and social normalcy do not imply that she must have shared the gender orientation of those Jacobean women who conformed to the role enforced on them by the patriarchal system. She turned out to be a self-fashioning individual who had taken to transvestism as an alternative strategy for economic survival. A close examination of the few extant documents yields the impression that she was a scheming and calculating woman with an ingrained instinct for upward social mobility and determined to exploit to the full the ambiguous legal position of women under common law.

Mary Frith took advantage of her rise in status as a married woman in claiming to be, as the case required, either a *feme sole,* a single woman, or a *feme covert,* a married woman under coverture whose legal identity was covered by her husband. As *feme sole,* she could pose both as a spinster, as Mary Frith, and as a married woman, as Mary Markham, who with respect to property and business was as independent of her husband as if she were unmarried. As *feme covert,* however, she could not contract and was liable to lose her right for independent action with regard to property and real estate as well as her right to sue and be sued on her own behalf. Thus, in 1624 when Richard Pooke, hatmaker, sued "Mary Frith alias Markham of London, Spinster," for some unpaid beaver hats, the attorney warned Pooke not to sue her as *feme sole* under the name of Mary Frith, for she had already defeated other complainants by claiming that she was *feme covert,* married "to one Markham." She did, indeed, resort to this legal double game in defending herself against Pooke's complaint, arguing "that she is Maryed to the same Markham and soe being a *feme Covert,* she cannot be ympleaded as *feme Sole*" (see addendum).[19]

Even without knowing the terms of Mary Frith's marriage settlement, we can define her status as that of a *feme sole* merchant. She obviously entered her marriage on condition that she had the right to run a business on her own account. Her union with Lewknor Markham should presumably be seen as a marriage of convenience contracted with a view to avoiding the discrimination and disabilities resulting from coverture and to exploiting the loopholes in the definition of gender boundaries. What arouses suspicion is her deposition made in the 1624 trial. It emerges from there that she did not quite remember how many years she had been married to Lewknor Markham (see addendum). The suspicion is strengthened by Pooke's attorney who stated that Markham had "not lived with her this tenne yeares or thereabouts." This could mean either that the two had never lived physically together as husband and wife or, in legal parlance, that they had not lived together as *baron and feme,* that is, as one legal person under the law of coverture. Whatever this may mean, Mary Frith was operating a lost property office as *feme sole.* On the one hand, the former cross-dressed pickpocket had gained the status of a married woman—she had become, as it were, a conformist; on the other, she was still a nonconformist in running a business of her own. This alternative view on marriage does not correspond to the view of Moll Cutpurse expressed in Middleton and Dekker's play.[20]

There is no denying that Mary Frith as *feme sole* or, to put it in terms of Defoe's *Roxana,* as "a Masculine in Politick Capacity," had seized an occupation in the dynamic market of stolen goods, a market that was mainly dominated by men. The reputation of her brokery is attested by Henry Killigrew, gentleman, who on being robbed in February 1621 relied on the services of her office. He had "heard howe" by her "meanes many that had had their pursses cutt or goods stolen," had recovered their goods owing to her experience and connections. In the present case, the local authorities collaborated with the broker. The constable of the parish of St. Bride's arrested the alleged pickpocket and took her to Mary Frith's office to be cross-examined there. Richard Dell, the husband of the alleged pickpocket, was so shocked at the news that his wife was being detained in Mary Frith's office that he demanded her immediate release from that company. For him Mary Frith, in 1621, was "a notorious infamous person . . . well knowne & acquainted with all theeves & cutpurses." What he did not realize is that she had a commission to examine alleged pickpockets and the right to monitor criminal behavior.

The row over the moral qualifications and professional competence of Mary Frith is quite comprehensible. Both wranglers were right; Richard Dell in denouncing Mary Frith as being a broker who owed her unchallenged position to her ties with the underworld; and Mary Frith in asserting that she was empowered by a royal or rather local license to interrogate petty lawbreakers. As a female broker, she was straddling the elusive border between the legal and illegal world obviously in connivance with the civic authorities, which had a vested interest in collaborating with a woman who was "acquainted with all theeves & cutpurses" in London. Given the fact that there was neither an effective statute against receiving stolen goods nor a professional police force, the local authorities, in the interest of crime control, welcomed women as paralegal intermediaries in the return and custody of stolen goods. Mary Frith was by no means the only female broker, but she was the most dynamic and best organized, whose dual role as collaborator with the underworld and the authorities guaranteed a steady supply of stolen goods for the brokerage.[21]

For a lifetime Mary Frith was scheming to outwit the guardians of law and order. When they first laid hands on her in 1600 and 1602, she was heading for a long period of trials and tribulations as a pickpocket (see addendum). The tenor of the prosecution leaves no doubt about the criminal offenses she had committed: in 1600 she was prosecuted on suspicion of having stolen the purse of an unknown man and in 1602 the purse of Richard Ingles. It is important to note that the indictments of 1600 and 1602 do not mention that she was prosecuted for having committed a gender transgression as a woman dressed up in male attire.

Mary Frith's deviant behavior as a transvestite dates from about 1608. Her cross-dressing coincides with her intrusion into the male dominated organization of the Bankside entertainment industry. Bearing in mind her later intrusion into the dubious trade of brokerage, it does not seem hazardous to speculate that her transvestism was a commercially and professionally motivated ploy to increase her income. It would definitely be dangerous to diagnose the case of Mary Frith as that of a lower-class woman in quest of her sexuality; hers is far more likely to be the case of a pickpocket turned transvestite for gain. The strategy she hatched up by 1608 was well thought out. To put it in terms of John Chamberlain, she "used to go in mans apparell," conspicuously flaunting her cross-dressing, and thereby "challenged the feild of" the town fops. It stands to reason that the "gallants" displaying their sartorial excesses would gather to watch her pageantry and cheer or jeer her only to be fleeced by a pack of pickpockets working hand in glove with the showwoman. Her unconventional lifestyle required a good store of apparel to keep it up and a heavy purse.

The examination conducted by the Bishop of London in January 1612 bears out that her new career as a public figure dressed up in male attire was designed as a commercial joint venture between herself and a gang of footpads. Thus, she "confessed" to having "vsually associated her selfe with Ruffinly swaggering & lewd company as namely with cut purses, blasphemous drunkards & others of bad note & of most dissolute behauiour." The examination also confirms that while mounting her street and floor shows she was deftly practising her light-fingered art: she "confesseth" to the Consistory of London that "she is commonly termed Ma[ll] Cutpurse of her cutting of purses."²²

Mary Frith's cross-dressing expertise confirms that there was a relationship between transvestism and crime. Most women who cross-dressed publicly in London, as Marjorie Garber has noted, were simply aping a fashion that affected all classes well into the 1620s, but the transvestite movement was also misused as a stratagem to commit theft. Women on the Continent fared no better. The European paradigm of the criminal female transvestite that emerges from Rudolf M. Dekker and Lotte C. van de Pol's study of over one hundred female cross-dressers, who, between 1550 and 1839, were active in the Netherlands also applies to Mary Frith: to wit, a young unmarried woman of the lower classes living on the edge of poverty resorts to male disguise and associates herself with accomplices.²³

Within two or three years Mary Frith became a Bankside personality whose showmanship caught the attention of four playwrights: John Day (1610), Thomas Middleton, Thomas Dekker (1611), and Nathan Field (1611). Day's jest-biography, "A Booke called the Madde Prancks of Merry Moll of Bankside, with her walks in Man's Apparel and to what Purpose" has been lost, but its title and Moll's alleged ride or progress through the City of London on Banks's famous "dancing horse" Morocco may give us an inkling of what her street performances must have been like (see *The Life,* 36–37). If the title of Day's jest-biography advertises Mary Frith as an outdoor prankster performing her feats and tricks on the thoroughfares of Bankside and London, it emerges from the examination conducted by the Bishop of London that she must also have been a shrewd indoor entertainer. It is on record that she "voluntarily confessed that she had long frequented all or most of the disorderly & licentious places in this Cittie as namely she hath vsually in the habite of a man resorted to alehowses, Tavernes, Tobacco shops and also play howses there to see plaies & pryses." Needless to say that these haunts, the theaters included, were an ideal hunting ground for a criminally minded pack of thieves waiting for Mary Frith's beck and call. What better "pryses," that is, presses, crowds, to relieve of their purses than guests in taverns, befuddled by drink and dazzled by Moll playing on her lute and singing a bawdy song and most likely performing a jig, or guests in a tobacco shop mesmerized by Moll smoking a pipe. As Robert Greene alleged, pickpockets thrived under the screen cast by the music of popular entertainers (see Addendum).

Mary Frith, Alias Moll Cutpurse, in Life and Literature

The climax of Mary Frith's career as an entertainer was her stage appearance at the Fortune Theatre in an afterpiece to a performance of Middleton and Dekker's play *The Roaring Girl* sometime in April 1611. Her appearance was orchestrated as a highlight and duly announced by the dramatists in the epilogue:

> The Roaring Girl herself, some few days hence,
> Shall on this stage give larger recompense.

Mary Frith's performance proved both a highlight and a turning point, for the subsequent measures taken by the authorities against her were so stern that within two years she abandoned her career as a cross-dressed entertainer to begin a new one as a broker. She was apprehended and detained in Bridewell where like all the inmates she was put through the grueling ordeal of corporal chastisement. In compliance with the rules of the governors, she had to account to them, in their weekly routine sessions, for her misbehavior and immorality. The examinations were thorough and extensive. In other cases of unruly women (I am thinking of Mary Newborough, Lucy Morgan, Katherine Arden, Mary Digby) their examinations are still untapped.[24] Unfortunately, in the present case the Bridewell Court Books for 1611 have been destroyed. However, we do know what happened at the Fortune Theatre because Mary Frith, relapsing into her old style of life, was again committed to Bridewell in December 1611 and eventually indicted in the palace of the Bishop of London in January 1612. There before John King, Bishop of London, Dr. Thomas Edwardes and Robert Christian, notary public, she confessed that she was "at a play about 3 quarters of a yeare since at the FFortune in mans apparell & in her bootes & with a sworde by her syde. . . . And also sat there vppon the stage in the publique viewe of all the people there presente in mans apparell."

Mary Frith was fully aware of the crucial importance of her solo performance in one of the leading commercial theaters. Endowed with an inborn talent for playing up to street and tavern audiences, she performed with great aplomb. She seized the opportunity to bring home to the audience that her self-fashioned cultural identity as a public persona, that is, as a female entertainer in male disguise, was not identical with her private self. Thus, she let it be known in unmistakable words that she was not a transvestite, nor a hermaphrodite, nor a sexually ambiguous character of any kind. She addressed the audience of the Fortune Theatre, some 2,340 spectators, telling them unashamedly and disarmingly "that she thought that many of them were of opinion that she was a man, but if any of them would come to her lodging, they should finde that she is a woman." This declaration was classified by the ecclesiastical judges as "immodest & lascivious speaches" that she "also vsed at that time." There was, however, nothing lascivious about the reaffirmation of her womanhood. Her disclosure may also have been meant as a rejection of Middleton and Dekker's fictional representation of her as a hermaphroditic ideal.[25]

Mary Frith's message, then, was that the crossing of gender boundaries was not transgressive and disruptive, nor immoral and reprehensible, and hence was not punishable. The guardians of public morality disagreed. They looked upon a cross-dressed woman as a deliquent arrogating the sexually active role of man and consequently stigmatized her as a whore.[26] The Bishop of London, therefore, suspected Mary Frith of being a prostitute. He "pressed" her "to declare whether she had not byn dishonest of her body & hath not drawne also other women to lewdnes by her perswasions & by carrying her selfe lyke a bawde." Whereupon Mary Frith "absolutly denied that she was chargeable with eyther of these imputacions." Almost all modern critics, misled by the criminal biography, have sided with the Bishop of London in identifying Mary Frith as a prostitute and bawd. It is true, as has been recently argued, that cross-dressing and prostitution were alternative social strategies that women pursued for social, economic, and security reasons.[27] Yet there is no evidence available to prove that Mary Frith was a cross-dressed prostitute.

Mary Frith's interactive address to a live audience was quite in line with the popular traditions as observed by the comedians. The spectators flocked to the theater in expectation of being entertained by one of those afterpieces that the Fortune was famous for and that were to cause the Middlesex magistrates in October 1612 to issue an order banning the performance of all afterpieces in England. The order ruled that all "Jigges, Rymes and Daunces after their playes" must be abolished because "by reason of certayne lewde Jigges, songes, and daunces vsed and accustomed at the play-house called the Fortune in Goulding-lane divers cutt-purses and other lewde and ill-disposed persons in greate multitudes doe resorte thither at th' end of euerye playe, many tymes causing tumultes and outrages, wherebye His Majesties peace is often broke and much mischiefe like to ensue thereby."[28]

There is good reason to believe that it was not so much the fact

Mary Frith, Alias Moll Cutpurse, in Life and Literature 59

that a woman in male dress entertained an audience in a public theater—after all the authorities had been tolerating her dress violations, outdoor pranks, and unlicensed entertainments in Southwark and the city of London for some years without intervening—as the uncontrollable concourse of the additional spectators wanting to see the afterpiece and the throng of cutpurses in league with Mary Frith that alarmed the authorities and led them to arrest her in April 1611 in order to prevent a repetition of her solo performance. It was apparently less for her deviancy and breach of the sumptuary laws than for her threat to peace that the authorities clamped down on Mary Frith, committing her to a house of correction where she could be broken in and reformed. She offered some resistance in 1611, but by 1614 she gave in, turning over a new leaf as a broker. Thus a potential actress was disciplined and what looked like an initial step toward a professional career with Prince Henry's company of actors was thwarted, nipped in the bud by the authorities. Ironically, she retaliated as a broker by keeping in touch with the underworld. Whether her husband played a decisive role in her transition remains unknown.[29]

Mary Frith's single (or perhaps repeated) appearance at the Fortune was hardly an extempore performance. It was, no doubt, a cooperative theatrical enterprise undertaken for the profit of all the parties involved. It can be inferred from the epilogue to *The Roaring Girl* that Mary Frith mounted the boards of the Fortune Theatre with the consent of the two authors and that, after the scripted play was over, the company of players conceded to her the freedom of the stage for her nonscripted performance. It would also seem logical for her to take the advice and assistance of John Shank, the company's leading comedian, who was renowned for his jigs.[30] She remained silent on all the preparations that must have gone into her performance, but she confessed to the Bishop of London that "there vppon the stage in publique viewe of all the people there presente in mans apparrell," she "playd vppon her lute & sange a songe" and made "some other immodest & lascivious speaches," for let us say about half an hour, the average length of an afterpiece.

Mary Frith's stage performance as a lutenist and singer in the afterpiece of *The Roaring Girl* must also be placed in the performing tradition set by Richard Tarlton. There are some astonishing parallels between the two entertainers. Both were upstarts with lower-class backgrounds and links with the underworld. They developed their skills as solo entertainers in the subculture of the London taverns. Tarlton, a tavern owner, obviously sharpened his performance skills as a tableside jester before becoming a professional comedian, a national celebrity renowned for his indecorous jigs.[31] In like manner, Mary Frith practiced her art both in the streets, as we know from the title of Day's jest-biography, and in haunting the taverns and tobacco shops, as she confessed to the Consistory Court. She "had long frequented all or most of the disorderly & licentious places" in London, resorting "to alehowses, Tavernes, Tobacco shops." The taverns and alehouses were ideal places of low-life community gathering where she could learn how to establish a relation of interactive fellowship with the public and how to capture the communal spirit of indoor entertainment. There she conceivably had opportunity to develop her skill as a cross-dressed instrumentalist and singer of bawdy and burlesque songs.[32] Presumably she was less adept than Tarlton at extemporizing, at exploring the subversive and irreverent oral culture of the alehouses, "the new-founde phrases of the taverne," but she was his equal in acquiring a reputation as a heavy drinker.[33] Finally, what marks her out as a Tarltonesque entertainer, who after Tarlton's example took over the stage at the end, is the fact that, despite the low art form she was practising as an unlicensed amateur performer, she appealed to the lower classes, the groundlings of the Fortune Theatre, and also drew the middle-class audiences, the gallants she used to challenge in their own field.

Mary Frith, a seasoned entertainer in her twenties, must have been at the peak of her creative ability when she boarded the stage of the Curtain. She had made a name for herself as a street and tavern performer, as a light-fingered instrumentalist and dancer of jigs, who apparently sensed that the time was ripe to confide to her audiences that her cross-dressing had nothing to do with her sexual identity and should be taken for what it was: a simple trick of the trade consisting in a costume change. In her promotion of this view, her male dress or playing apparel had become, as it were, her signature as a popular entertainer.[34] A graphic demonstration of the costume change is afforded by the unauthorized woodcut of the original edition of *The Roaring Girl*. It shows the image of a woman dressed up in male clothes, brandishing a sword, smoking a pipe, but not playing the lute. The caption, printed lengthwise on the left-hand margin, reads: "My case is alter'd, I must worke for my liuing." The wording sealed the demystification of Mary Frith's sexual and gender ambiguity, signaling her desire to legitimate her profession and to earn her livelihood as a cross-dressed entertainer. The subversive woodcut was censored and replaced by an alternative one (see Portraits, below).

Besides the tavern and the street, the tobacco shop was the third of Mary Frith's venues, where she built up her image as a female smoker. Her stage portrait on the 1611 title page of *The Roaring Girl* shows her smoking a pipe, and the fictional biography dishes up an absurdly crude anecdote about an "unlucky knave, at a Grocers shop," who gave her a "Pipe full of *Gunpowder,* covered at Top with Tobacco" (23). The tobacco shops offered her not only the possibility of indulging in the latest fashion of smoking, but also in practising her self-taught art as a music entertainer and, what must be taken into account, in pursuing her profession as a pickpocket. Support for this interpretation comes from the contemporary dramatists who established a correlation between tobacco, music, and lecherousness. Thus, it became a stage convention about 1599 to poke fun at the gallants who affected smoking tobacco and playing the bass viol da gamba to ensnare women. The foppish Fastidius Brisk in Ben Jonson's *Every Man Out of His Humour* (1599) plays on the viol while smoking and courting Saviolina.[35] Gregory Gudgeon, the city lecher in Thomas Middleton's *The Family of Love* (1602), keeps "a viol da gambo and good tobacco."[36]

Mary Frith was not the first female devotee of tobacco in England, but presumably the first to resort to the tobacco shops, which were the exclusive haunts of men.[37] We have it on Thomas Hariot's authority that by 1589 "men & women of great calling as else, and some learned Phisitians also" were indulging in the new custom of smoking or "drinking" earthern or silver pipes. Paul Hentzner and Thomas Platter attest in their travel accounts that smoking in England became a national recreation in the late 1590s, and Edmund Howes in his sequel of John Stowe's *The Annales or Generall Chronicle of England* confirms that by 1615 smoking was "commonly used by most men & many women."[38]

The civic and ecclesiastical authorities obviously found fault with the example set by Mary Frith as a smoker. In the first place, a woman frequenting the tobacco shops, which were reserved for men, meant to them an infringement of gender boundaries and, second, an arrogation of class privileges. The authorities considered smoking as becoming the upper classes but as unbecoming to the lower orders. King James in his proclamation issued on 17 October 1604 levied a heavy custom on the weed and distinguished between "the better sort" of people who "have and will use the same with Moderation to preserve their Health," and "a number of riotous and disordered Persons of mean and base Condition, who, contrary to the use which Persons of good Calling and Quality make thereof, do spend most of their time in that idle vanity."[39] Mary Frith inevitably fell under the category of "disordered Persons" and of prostitutes, such as Joan Woodshore, who in 1611 was also charged with selling tobacco.[40] She was, therefore, bound to be reprehended by the Bishop of London for addicting herself to the wanton pleasure of smoking and of making music in public, both thought to be inventions of the devil made to inflame the passions of the addicts and of the listeners and to entice them to fall into debauchery.

Addendum

Knowledge of Mary Frith's life remains fragmentary. There is much work that remains to social historians specializing in criminal history to save the record of Mary Frith's life from oblivion. I have, however, attempted to make up for the present lack of interest in Mary Frith as a historical figure, for without some reliable biographical data there is no way of assessing her public persona, nor of finding out to what extent the printed biography of 1662 departs from historical records in accommodating the protagonist to the formula of criminal biography. The following biographical survey is indebted to the researches of other critics, in particular to Mark Eccles, who has unearthed biographical records that have passed unnoticed in Moll Cutpurse studies, but it also contains hitherto unpublished documents.

Documentary Life

[Ca. 1584–85] The date of birth given in the biography is 1589 (see Spearing, *Counterfeit Ladies,* 8). The reasons why it does not make sense have been given above.

1600 Mary Frith began her career as a purse snatcher about 1600. She, Jane Hill, and Jane Styles, were all three spinsters dwelling in the City of London, indicted by the Justices of Middlesex for having snatched, on 26 August 1600, "bursam cordi ad valorem ijs et vndecem soldi in pecuniis numeratis . . . de bonis Cattalis et denariis," that is, a purse kept in a breast pocket and containing 2s and 11d in cash, from an unknown man at Clerkenwell. The endorsement of the record reads "Billa vera," true bill, "Mary Ffrythe confesseth at Examinacion of Jane Styles & Jane Hill." See Greater London Record Office, Middlesex Sessions Rolls, MJ/SR/384/41. Mark Eccles in "Mary Frith, the Roaring Girl," *Notes and Queries* 32

(1985): 65–66, gives a very short abstract without mentioning the two accomplices and surprisingly adding that the trial jury found her not guilty.

The indictment contradicts Moll Cutpurse's statement made in the fictional autobiography that she "never Actually or Instrumentally cut any Mans Purse, though I have often restored it" (quotations are taken from Spearing's edition, 71). It also disproves Spearing's opinion that Mary in her teens was not so much drifting "into a criminal life-style" (xx). The origin of Mary Frith's nickname, Moll Cutpurse, has to be sought in her early status as a lower-class woman groomed as a cutpurse.

The petty crime that led to the arrest of the fifteen-year-old Mary Frith reveals that in her formative years as a delinquent she was plying her craft with two female partners. She was obviously working in a small female gang to reduce the risk of detection. Partnership with two women is likely to have been less combative than a partnership with men as regards dividing the loot into equal shares. Their efficiency, however, must have been rather poor when compared to the nimbleness of hand of their colleagues who at the Oxford commencement celebrations of October 1602 relieved Sir Thomas Bodley of his cloak and Sir Richard Lea of two jewels to the value of 200 marks. See letter of John Chamberlain to (Sir) Dudley Carleton in Paris dated 2 October 1602, *Calendar of State Papers, Domestic, Elizabeth, 1601–1603, with Addenda, 1547–1605*, ed. Mary Anne Everett Green (London 1870). For the types of gangs operating in England see A. L. Beier, *Masterless Men: The Vagrancy Problem in England 1560–1640* (London: Methuen, 1985), 128–31.

Potential pickpockets used to drift into delinquency at an early age. Thus all the members of a gang of nineteen "cutpurses" whom Simon Forman, in 1598, "had in Examination abought" the theft of his "purse" were between fifteen and twenty years old. The youngest, Jeames Harborte (James Herbert?), was fifteen, that is, Mary's age, Roger Goth was sixteen, and the oldest, Jhon Tucke and Robarte Frenche, were twenty years old. See Bodleian Library, MS Ashmole 195, fol. 196v. There were academies specializing in introducing boys into the art of stealing. Such a "schole howse" for pickpockets was denounced to Lord Burghley in 1585. It had been "sett upp" by one Wotton, gentleman and former merchant at Smart's Quay near Billingsgate, "to learne younge boyes to cutt purses." See J. A. Sharpe, *Crime in Early Modern England 1550–1750* (London: Longman, 1984), 114.

Contrary to what these instances and to what the rogue and coneycatching pamphlets make us believe, London was not in the grips of a highly structured fraternity of pickpockets. Ian W. Archer in his groundbreaking study *The Pursuit of Stability: Social Relations in Elizabethan London* (Cambridge: Cambridge University Press, 1991), chap. 6, makes clear that as far as thieving is concerned, there is little to suggest the professionalism and network described in Greene's pamphlets.

1602   On 18 March 1602, the cordwainer Thomas Dobson and the silktwister William Simons, both dwelling in the parish of St. Giles outside

Cripplegate, gave bonds to Nicholas Collyn, justice of Middlesex, that "Marya FFrithe" should appear at the next session of gaol delivery on suspicion of having taken "a purse with XXVs of Richard Ingles." See Greater London Record Office, Middlesex Sessions Rolls, MJ/SR/400/121. A brief abstract is given by Eccles in *Notes and Queries*.

As early as 1602 Mary Frith was apparently doing business in the neighborhood of the Fortune theatre where in the spring of 1611 she was to give her public stage debut. As no associates were implicated, Mary may have been operating on her own. In any case alignments among pickpockets, as Archer has shown, were impermanent and rapidly shifting (209–10).

1608   On 13 May 1608, "Maria Feith de Southworke," spinster, and John Clementes, servant to Edward Carrell, of Hastings, Sussex, both men being soldiers, gave bond to justice Nicholas Collyn to prosecute and give evidence against Edward Welles and Gilbert Dadson on suspicion of felony. See Greater London Record Office, Middlesex Sessions Rolls, MJ/SR/462/60. A brief abstract omitting information on Mary Frith's partners is given by Eccles, *Notes and Queries*.

This record is valuable for more than one of reason. First, it proves that by 1608 Mary Frith had made up her mind to settle in Southwark, the entertainment district notorious for its theaters, brothels, and the Bear Garden. Second, it suggests that her lifelong myth of mannishness may be traced back to her early acquaintance with soldiers. This partnership with soldiers, possibly disbanded soldiers, is bound to have cast a shadow on her reputation.

1609   On 8 September 1609, "Maria ffrythe," living in the parish of St Olave, Southwark, "Spinster," burgled ["intrauit"] the house of Alice Bayly in St Olave by night ["tempore nocturno"] and stole £7 7s in money ["septem libris et septem solides . . . in pecunijs"], "twoe angells of gold," "one twentie shillinge peece of gold," "twoe half crownes of gold," a gold ring ["annulum aureum"] rated at 6s, and "twoe cristall stones sett in seluer" valued at 20d. Public Record Office, ASSI 35/52/6/m. 18. There is an abstract in Jane Baston, "Rehabilitating Moll's Subversion in *The Roaring Girl*," *Studies in English Literature 1500–1900,* 37 (1997): 317–35, taken from J.S. Cockburn, ed., *Calendar of Assize Records: Surrey Indictments, James I* (London, 1982).

At the bottom of the record, an addition in a different hand reads that Mary Frith, in March 1610, was found not guilty. I think this does not necessarily mean that she did not break into the house. She may have arranged with Alice Bayly, who was present at the hearing, to return part of the stolen goods. Deals with victims were popular, as J.G. Bellamy has shown in *The Criminal Trial in Later Medieval England* (Toronto, 1998), because the stolen goods, in the event of a conviction, would be confiscated by the crown. The formula "tempore nocturno," as noted by Bellamy, does not imply that an offense was committed in the darkness (84–85).

Mary Frith, Alias Moll Cutpurse, in Life and Literature   65

1610   On 7 August 1610, John Day, playwright and collaborator with Thomas Dekker in a number of plays, entered in the Stationers' Register a jest-biography, "A Booke called the Madde Prancks of Merry Moll of the Bankside, with her walks in Man's Apparel and to what Purpose." No copy has been preserved. It is certainly not a play as suggested in the *Dictionary of National Biography* under Day. For Paul A. Mulholland, the editor of Thomas Middleton and Thomas Dekker's *The Roaring Girl. The Revels Plays* (Manchester, Eng.: Manchester University Press, 1987), the entry in the Stationers' Register was likely "the earliest dependable reference to the real Moll" (13). All the above quotations of *The Roaring Girl* are taken from the Mulholland edition.

The title confirms that Mary Frith was plying her trade in Southwark, where by 1608 she had obviously emerged as a roaring girl. Endowed as she was with a theatrical talent, she had chosen the neighborhood of the Bankside theatres in the parish of St. Saviour's to mount her street performances and indoor floorshows in male dress. She can claim the status of a marginal entertainer who evaded the licensing system. She was, however, no innovator. She simply joined the transvestite movement, which after its eruption in the 1570s and 1580s had subsided in the 1590s to flare up again about 1605 and that was to reach its peak in the 1620s. See chapter 6 in Linda Woodbridge, *Woman and the English Renaissance: Literature and the Nature of Womanhood, 1540–1620* (Urbana: Illinois University Press, 1984).

Mary Frith was also a lutenist. Her unlicensed playing in taverns and streets went against the 1606 regulations issued by the company of musicians in the interest of public order. Offenders were fined 3s. 4d. for each infringement to the regulations. See Walter L. Woodfill, *Musicians in English Society from Elizabeth to Charles I* (Princeton, 1953; rpt New York: Da Capo Press, 1969), 14. For music performances, which according to Robert Greene in 1592, were misused as cloaks for larceny, see A. L. Beier, 97–98.

1611   On 27 January 1612, Mary Frith was summoned by the bishop's court of London to answer charges of public immorality. The text of the interrogation, preserved in the Consistory of London Correction Book, has been published by Mulholland in his edition of *The Roaring Girl,* Appendix E; and by Spearing, *Counterfeit Ladies,* xiv–xv. I am, however, quoting the text of the examination from Mulholland's paper "The Date of *The Roaring Girl,*" *Review of English Studies* 28 (1977): 18–31, for being the most reliable (see note 22). I have modernized the punctuation of the quotations.

The personal voice of Mary Frith has left an indelible impression in the court proceedings. Her confessions reveal what John Day meant by "her walks in Mans Apparel" across London's entertainment district. They also disclose that she extended her operations to the underworld of the city of London. She must have embarked upon her new career as a cross-dressed roaring girl some time after 1602. She was an experienced theatergoer when, in about April 1611, she made her stage debut at the Fortune playhouse "in mans apparell & in her bootes & with a sword by her syde." E. K. Chambers is right in observing that her stage appearance had been carefully orchestrated by the playwrights and Prince Henry's company of actors. See his *Elizabethan Stage* (Oxford: Clarendon Press, 1923), iii, 297, and my discussion in part III.

Mary Frith also confessed to being still "associated . . . with cut purses" and to frequenting the "lewd company" of "blasphemous drunkardes & others of bad note & most dissolute behaviour." Her confession casts new light on her relations with the organized underworld of thieves. Although she had entered a new phase in her career after 1602, she had not severed her ties with her old companions. Her connections with them, as a matter of fact, remained a lifelong commitment and stood her in good stead as an entertainer, theatergoer, and broker.

Mary Frith's defense before the bishop's court makes evident that she had already been punished for her "misdemeanors," particularly for her sensational transgression perpetrated at the Fortune playhouse. She had been committed to Bridewell, where, like all the inmates, she must have undergone the regular punitive regime of reform consisting of corporal punishment and hard work, a process that used to last two or three months for nonrecalcitrant inmates. There she shared her lot with many other cross-dressed women, among them Joanna Goodman, who in 1569 was whipped for dressing as a male servant, and Mary Wakeley, who in 1601 was detained for her misconduct as a transvestite. See Jean E. Howard, "Cross-dressing, The Theatre and Gender Struggle in Early Modern England," *Shakespeare Quarterly* 39 (1988): 418–40.

Katherine Cuffe suffered the same fate, in February 1599, for cross-dressing as a boy and "for her wicked lyfe and great offence" committed within the boundaries of the Inner Temple. She confessed to the court which met in Bridewell on 13 February 1599 that Ambrose Jasper, the cook of the Inner Temple, had asked her "to come in boyes apparrell" to his room "for that he would not haue her come in her owne apparell least that she should be espyed." In compliance with her lover's cunning strategem, she turned up in male disguise, flouting the rules of an all-male academic institution. She "laye" with Jasper "allnight" and he "had th'vse and carnall knowledge of her bodye a little before Christmas last." Thomas Webster, the porter, "dwelling at the Temple gate," was also examined and confirmed the defendant's account. So was Thomas Lucey, Jasper's servant, who gave witness that Katherine Cuffe "came once in boyes apparrell hauing a doblett and hose and a cloke and a hatt." As Jasper refused to appear, a warrant was issued for his arrest; and the court meeting on 5 November 1599 ruled that he was to be arraigned (Bridewell Court Books, IV, f. 61–62v, 67r, 105r, 120v; there are further entries on this case).

The routine correction of the inmates dressed in blue garments was beating hemp and flax; and to believe Thomas Dekker, a close observer of Mary Frith's career, she was indeed subjected to beating hemp. In the last scene of his play *If It Be Not Good, the Devil Is in It* (1611/12), the devils report to Pluto that Moll Cutpurse has not yet come to the underworld, for "Shee has bin too late a sore-tormented soule" and "was beating hemp in bridewell to choke theeues." See *The Dramatic Works of Thomas Dekker*, ed. Fredson Bowers (Cambridge: Cambridge University Press, 1966), 3:5.4.105–12.

In Mary Frith's case the reformatory policy failed. After her release she was caught again trespassing against public morality "vpon Christmas day" 1611 "at night." She was arrested "in Powles Church," obviously St. Paul's Walk, "with her peticoate tucked vp about her in the fashion of a man with a mans cloake on her to the great scandall of diuers persons who vnderstood the same & to the disgrace of all womanhood." The constable who apprehended her sent her back to Bridewell, where she spent the Christmas season in confinement, waiting to be summoned by the Consistory of London on 27 January 1612.

The bishop of London, it seems, could not make up his mind to withdraw all the charges brought against Mary Frith. When he "pressed" her "to declare whether she had not byn" sexually incontinent as a prostitute and "bawde," she "absolutely denied that she was chargeable with eyther of these imputacions." The bishop, nonetheless, "thought fit to remand her to Bridewell . . . vntill he might further examine the truth of the misdemeanors inforced against her without laying as yet any further censure vppon her." There are bound to have been many more interrogations conducted by the governors of Bridewell. Unfortunately, the volume of the Bridewell Court Books covering the years 1611 to 1616 was destroyed by fire.

1612   John Chamberlain, the learned observer of town and court life, helps to bridge the gap in the Bridewell Court Books. In a letter, addressed to Sir Dudley Carleton and dated 12 February 1612, he reported that "last Sonday Mall Cut-purse a notorious bagage (that used to go in mans apparell and challenged the feild of divers gallants)," was taken back to St. Paul's Cross to do penance in public. The bitter tears she shed in penance, I think, can be interpreted as a well-rehearsed act of histrionics performed to entertain the public; for Mary Frith, as Chamberlain noted, was later suspected of having been "maudelin druncke." In any case, her dramatic talents saved her from a prolonged detention in Bridewell. For Chamberlain's letter see Norman Egbert McClure, ed., *The Letters of John Chamberlain* (Philadelphia, 1939), 1:332–35; and Spearing, *Counterfeit Ladies*, xvi.

Mary Frith's efforts at self-definition as a cross-dressed entertainer were played out as much in outdoor as in indoor venues. As Chamberlain put it, she used "to go in mans apparell," walking the streets of London and Southwark disguised as a man. It was during these urban perigrinations that she pursued her sartorial rivalry with the gallants of London and Southwark and that she must have hatched out her policy to take advantage of her male disguise as her signature of a cross-dressed entertainer. Parading as a gallant, as an object of wonder, simply involved a change of costume; in public she performed the part of a man in order to eke out a living. Thus her own signature style contributed to the perpetuation of her myth as a mannish woman.

1614   On 23 March 1614, Lewknor Markham and Mary Frith were married at St. Saviour's (St. Mary Overbury), Southwark. They paid 4d. for the wedding ceremony and 4d. for the license granted by the bishop of Winchester. Only three out of thirteen couples that were married at St. Saviour's in March 1614 had a marriage license. See Greater London Record Office, Registers of Marriages, Parish Registers of St. Saviour's, P 92/SAV/376. The microfilm of the Parish Registers, X 097/284, does not record the fee paid. The Registers have been published by John V. L. Pruyn, "Weddings at St. Saviour's, Southwark, from A.D. 1606 to 1625," *The Genealogist*, n.s. (1890), 6:145 ff; the Markham/Frith marriage is listed in vol. 7 (1891), 96, without the fee. Mark Eccles for his note consulted *The Genealogist*. The marriage license has not been preserved in the Greater London Record Office nor in the Hampshire Record Office.

Marriage and ownership conveyed status and respectability. Mary Frith's marriage to an esquire of Nottingham (see 1624 entry) provides a key to approaching the mystery of her sexual and gender identity as well as to explaining her new career as a broker. Her scheme to open up a fencing business is likely to have matured while she was frequenting the London alehouses; for brokerage was originally a sideline of the innkeepers. For the innkeepers' double role see George Daniel Ramsay, *The City of London in International Politics at the Accession of Elizabeth Tudor* (Manchester, Eng.: Manchester University Press, 1975); and Salgado, 131.

The identity of Lewknor Markham has remained elusive despite my searches in printed sources and the extensive searches made by a record agent in several archives. Lewknor was in some way connected to Gervase Markham, the writer, possibly one of his elder sons. He must have been christened Lewknor after a godparent (X. Lewknor) or a close relative.

1621   It appears from a Star Chamber bill, edited by Margaret Dowling in "A Note on Moll Cutpurse—'The Roaring Girl,'" *Review of English Studies* 10 (1934): 67–71, that by 1621 Mary Markham, alias Mary Frith, alias Mary Thrift, alias Mal/Moll Cutpurse, was running a licensed fencing business or lost property office in the city of London, which she had been building up after 1612 with the help of her close ties with the underworld. She had made her way from pickpocket to street entertainer, walking the streets in conspicuous male disguise and thereby issuing, as John Chamberlain put it, a sartorial challenge to "divers gallants" or fops. She had now achieved notoriety as the receiver of stolen goods, that is as the entrepreneur of a metropolitan-based brokerage. By the time the transvestite controversy reached its height, she had given up the status of a criminal and had succeeded in arrogating the position of a paralegal intermediary to herself, which enabled her to mediate between the victims and the pickpockets, between authorities and the underworld. The events mentioned in the bill are here given in chronological order; the punctuation of the bill has been modernized.

The victim was Henry Killigrew, gentleman, son of Sir Henry Killigrew and nephew of Sir William Killigrew.[41] He was robbed one Saturday night in February 1621 and on Sunday repaired to the office of Mary Frith to seek help. The circumstances of the robbery, as told by Mary Frith in her defense made before the Court on 4 June 1621, do not appear to be framed. She testified that when Killigrew was walking down Blackhorse Alley, he was accosted by a nightwalker asking for some wine. He offered her instead "some kindnesse," which she understood as a signal to take him to a "place" of assignation rather than to a tavern. It then happened, as Mary Frith put it in a euphemism for carnal knowledge, that "whilst he was in priuate familarity with" that prostitute, she "priuilie tooke forth of his pockett certen peeces of gold and some seales and other thinges." The moment Killigrew "was trussinge" the "pointes," that is the buttons of his trousers, "she was gone."

The following day, as Mary Frith certified, Killigrew came to see her "and desired her to doe her endeauour to try if she could by any meanes fynd out the pickpockett or helpe him to his monie," for he had "heard howe" by her "meanes many that had had theire pursses cutt or goodes stollen, had beene helped to theire goodes againe and diuers of the offenders taken or discouered." She did prove helpful. The nightwalker had made the mistake to point out to Killigrew the window of her husband's flat, and thus it happened that when Killigrew took Mary Frith to have a look at the house, she identified Richard Dell, gentleman, and Margaret Dell, his wife, as the tenants of the flat. The constable of the parish of St. Bride's in Fleet Street then arrested Margaret Dell on suspicion of being the pickpocket and took her to Mary Frith's house for Killigrew to verify if she was the woman who had relieved him of eight pieces of gold and seven silver seals. When he saw her face to face, he "confidently affirmed," according to Mary Frith, "that he thought her to be the woman." On this evidence, Margaret Dell, on 23 February 1621, was taken before Sir Thomas Bennett, who committed her to the Counter prison.

On 2 May 1621, Richard Dell and his wife, Margaret, lodged a complaint about wrongful imprisonment in the Court of Star Chamber against Giles Allen, goldsmith, the constable of the parish of St. Bride's, Francis Goddard, haberdasher, Henry Killigrew, gentleman, Edward Thacker, Edward Florie,[42] and Mary Markham, alias Mary Frith, alias Mary Thrift, alias Mal Cutpurse. It emerges from their bill that Richard Dell, outraged that his wife was being questioned in Mary Markham's house, demanded that his wife be removed from her company, for, as he said, Mary Markham was "a notorious infamous person, and such a one as was well knowne & acquainted with all theeves & cutpurses." She refused Dell's accusation, asserting that she had a royal commission to examine all such persons. She therefore advised Dell to leave her house before he would be beaten by Killigrew and Florie. In her defense of 4 June, she threatened that if the Dells "gaue" her "any ill wordes or language, she . . . might and did giue them some reply in some tart or angry manner agayne."

Mary Frith's reputation as a dubious broker lasted unabated until her death. Some hitherto unknown allusions in ephemeral publications, which spawned from the printing presses of the Commonwealth, attest her unbroken notoriety. *Merlinus Anonymus . . . for the year 1653,* a mock almanac by the royalist Samuel Sheppard, has the following calendar entry for 11 March: "Mrs. Frith tax'd for conivance and acquitted by a Jury of pick pockets, 1645."[43] Quite pregnant is the twenty-third query in *Endlesse Queries: or An End to Queries, Laid down in 36 Merry Mad Queries for the People's Information* (1659), a copy of which was acquired by the publisher George Thomason on 13 June 1659, a week after Mary Frith had signed her will. The query reads: "Whether Mrs. *Mary Frith* commonly called by some *Mall Cut-purse,* having formerly done so good service at the *Bear Garden,* and many other things for the good of the Nation, being now aged and having no children of her own body lawfully begotten, as ever I heard of, might not do a pious Act to appoint one to succeed her to help the people to their purses again when she is gone?" A satirical coupling of the contested faculties of William Lilly, the astrologer of the Parliament, and of Mary Frith, the retriever of stolen goods, occurs in Sir John Berkenhead's *Paul's Churchyard. Libri Theologici, Politici, Historici, Nundinis Paulinis (una cum Templo) prostant venales . . . Done into English for the Assembly of Divines* (1651/52, Wing B 2970). A copy of this catalogue of vendible books, written by the supervisor of the royalist propaganda machine, was acquired by George Thomason on 6 July 1659, the very day Mary Frith died. Berkenhead listed a joint book venture of Lilly and Frith as item twelve under the title "*Pancirolla Medela.* A way to find out things lost and Stoln; by the said *William Lilly.* With a *Clavis* to his book, or the Art of his Art. By Mistris Mary Frith." Berkenhead poked fun at the dubiosity of their divining professions, clinching his mordant satire with a bawdy double entendre on the book's key and on the impotence of Mary Frith to beget children though dressed as a man.

1624   In 1624, Richard Pooke, hatmaker, sued "Marye Frith alias Markham of London, Spinster," in the Court of Requests for the unpaid bill for some beaver hats that she had bought about 1616. She had made a down payment of £3 when the Sheriff's court ordered her arrest, but now in 1624 he asked for the rest of the bill to be paid. Pooke was warned by his attorney not to sue the defendant under the name of Mary Frith, for she had already "overthrowne two or three severall" complainants "in their accions brought against her there by reason she was Maryed to one Markham who hath not lived with her this tenne yeares or thereabouts." She was now putting forward, Pooke complained, the same argument in her defense, saying "that she is Maryed to the same Markham and soe being a *feme Covert,* she cannot be ympleaded as a *feme Sole.*" In fact, she stated on 24 November 1624 that she had paid for the hats and confessed that "shee was marryed unto one Lewknor Markham in the County of Nottingham, Esquire, about some Seaven yeares sithence at the parish Church of Saint Mary Overies in Southwarke." See Eccles, *Notes and Queries.*

Mary Markham, a woman of the lower class, committed a double breach of the sumptuary laws in flaunting beaver hats and wearing male dress; it was a violation of both class and gender boundaries. Beaver hats were notoriously expensive. They were priced at up to 40s. in 1583 as Philip Stubbes records in *The Anatomie of Abuses.* Her sartorial extravagance can be traced back to the days when she used to challenge the beaver gallants who indulged in lavish apparel. For beaver hats see Marjorie Garber, "The Logic of the Transvestite. *The Roaring Girl* (1608)," in *Staging the Renaissance: Reinterpretations of Elizabethan and Jacobean Drama,* ed. David Scott Kastan and Peter Stallybrass (New York: Routledge, 1991), 221–34.

1644   It is on record in the Bridewell Court Books that the governors who sat on Friday, 21 June 1644, "thought fitt & ordered . . . that Gilbert Stopford, Katherine Killingham alias Killigrew, Anne Parrett, Mary Frith, Margery Houghton, Robert Crockett and Mary Thornton shal bee delivered & discharged out of the Hospital of Bethlem, London, being recouered of their former sences & may bee kept & provided for in any other place as well as in the hospitall of Bethlem. And that they bee every of them respectively sent to the severall Parishes from whence they came." See Bridewell Court Books, vol. 9/129.

I have found no further references to Mary Frith in volume 9, which covers entries from 14 October 1642 to 7 July 1658, but there are some more to the other inmates mentioned above in the Court Books. Katherine Killigrew was detained more than once. She had been discharged before by the court which sat on 24 March 1642 and sent back to the parish of St. Botolph outside Bishopsgate to be looked after by the church wardens and overseers of the poor. Anne Parrett was again detained in 1644. The court meeting of 23 November 1644 ruled that she should be released and sent back to her parish of St. James Garlickhithe (Bridewell Court Books, 9/161).

Why Mary Frith was declared insane and hospitalized in Bethlehem Hospital, which is described as a filthy rundown place, remains a matter of speculation. The inhuman maintenance of the inmates was subsidized by the parishes. The administration, the running of the asylum, and the atrocious therapy, which consisted in beating and punishing the inmates, rested with the governors of Bridewell. Considering that Mary Frith had a natural gift for impersonating, she may have been shamming madness in order to avoid the political turmoils of the first civil war (1642–45) and the pressure that was put on all the citizens of London, women of all classes and children included, to do statute labor for the fortification of the city in 1642–43.

Her detention in Bethlehem Hospital did not prove harmful to her public image as a woman of masculine spirit. She may have sided with the four hundred distressed women, "Tradesmens wives and Widdowes" who in January–February 1642 delivered a petition to Parliament and who on 8 August 1643 mounted a demonstration and a blockade of Parliament's entrances. Such an incident obviously inspired Henry Neville, the author of the satirical pamphlet *The Parliament of Ladies, or Divers remarkable passages of Ladies in Spring-Garden, in Parliament assembled* (1647), a copy of which was acquired by George Thomason in May 1647, to discredit Mary Frith. The "Forces of the City," the pamphleteer facetiously noted, "under the command of *Mall Cutpurse,* and *Mall Sebran,* two very able members, were appointed to guard the House" on Friday, 8 April 1647. The two female soldiers, veritable spitfires, "being there placed with pipes in both their mouths, with fire and smoake in a very short time, had almost choaked both the passage and the Passangers" (13, 14). On 16 August 1647, the House of Commons ordered its guards "to observantly keep all the passages, and with all to clear them from those clamorous women, which were wont to hang in clusters on the staires, and before the doores of the Parliament."

James Allen was harping on the very same string. He was one of the many university wits contributing commendatory prose and verse in several languages to James Strong's satirical poem *Joanereidos: or, Feminine Valour: Eminently discovered in Westerne Women* (1645), a copy of which George Thomason bought on 9 June 1645. In terms lifted from the beginning of Virgil's *Aeneid,* he facetiously commiserated with Moll Cutpurse and the female petitioners of the London mob who used to be dismissed disparagingly as fishwives from Billingsgate (as prostitutes) in antiroyalist tracts:

> Armes and the man I sing, whose lines rehearse
> The Westerne wenches doughty deeds in verse
> More high then (earst) the acts of *Guy* of *Warwicke,*
> Southamptons *Beavoys* or the *Knight* of *Barwicke,*
> Assist *Mol Cut-purse* and the warlike bands
> That march towards Bellings gate with eager hands.
> (sig.A2v; punctuation modernized)

For Bethlehem Hospital see G. Salgado, chap. 10; for female labor in 1642/43 see Norman G. Brett James, *The Growth of Stuart London* (London: Allen and Unwin, 1935), 268–77; for the female petitioners see Patricia Higgins, "The Reaction of Women, with Special Reference to Women Petitioners," in *Politics, Religion and the English Civil War,* ed. Brian Manning (London: Arnold, 1973), 177–222; for female demonstrations see Ann Marie McEntee, " 'The [Un]Civill-Sisterhood of Oranges and Lemons': Female Petitioners and Demonstrators, 1642–53," *Prose Studies* 14 (1991): 92–111.

1659 An early transcript of Mary Markham's will and testament, dated 6 June 1659 and proved on 24 July 1660, is kept in the Prerogative Court of Canterbury Wills and Administration (Public Record Office, The Family Records Centre, PROB 11/299/106–107). Here follows the text I have transcribed from the seventeenth-century transcript:

In the name of God Amen.
I Mary Markham, alias, FFrith, of the parish of St Bride, alias Bridgett, in FFleetstreete, London, Widdow, being aged and sicke and weake in body, but of good mind and memorie and vnderstanding, for all which I doe most humbly thanke my most gracious and mercifull Creator ffor the quieting of my mind and the settling of the small part and remainder of that meane estate which it hath pleased God of his greate mercie and goodnesse to lend[?] to mee in this world of Sorrowes, doe make this my last Will and Testament in manner and fforme ffollowing. (That is to say,) FFirst, I doe giue and bequeath my soule into the handes of my most gracious Creator, who by his onely power breathes the breath of life into mee, hopeing and confidently beleiuing that all my manifould and grevious sinnes are and shalbe freely pardoned and washed away in, by and through the sheding and powering and of the most precious bloud and the bitter Sufferinges and passion of my most blessed Redeemer and Saviour Jesus Christ and that after this transitorie and mortall life is ended, my soule and body shalbe reunited and enioy everlasting blisse and felicity with him in his heavenly Kingdome for ever and ever, Amen; my body I leaue vnto the Earth, whence it came, to bee decently buried in Christian buriall within the parish Church or Church yarde of St Brides aforesaid in such sort and manner as my Executrix hereafter named in her discretion shall thinke most fitting.

Item I giue vnto my Kinsman Abraham Robinson twenty poundes of Lawfull mony of England. And I giue vnto James Robinson, father of the said Abraham, twelue pence. All the rest and remainder of all my personall estate whatsoever, my iust debts by mee oweing and my legacies in this my will giuen and bequeathed, being first paid and discharged, I fully and wholly giue and bequeath the same vnto my neece and kinswoman Frances Edmonds, wife of George Edmondes, with my will and desires that they shalbee and remaine vnto her owne sole vse, benefitt and behoofe soe longe as she liveth. And I doe make the said FFrances Edmondes sole Executrix of this my last Will & Testament.

In witnesse whereof I the said Mary Markham, alias FFrith, haue herevnto sett my hand and Seale the sixth day of June in the yeare of our Lord God one thousand six hundred ffifty Nine. The marke of Mary Markham, alias FFrith, Subscribed, sealed and published by her the said Mary Markham, alias FFrith, as and ffor her last Will and Testament in the presence of vs Richard Hulet, Ralph Warfeild, Abraham Robinson.

This will was proued att London before the Right Worshipfull William Metcalf[?], Doctor of Laws, Master Keeper or Comissary of the Prerogatiue Court of Canterbury lawfully constituted the foure and twentieth day of July in the yeare of our Lord God according to the computacion of the Church of England one thousand six hundred and sixty. By the oath of Frances Edmondes, the sole Executrix named in the said Will, to whome Admon. of all and singular the goods, chattells and debts of the said deceased was graunted and committed, she being ffirst sworne truely to administer the same[?] according to the tenor and effect of the said Will.

The original will kept at the PRO in Kew, PROB 10/930, as Suranganee Perera has been so kind as to inform me, has either been misfiled or, more likely, has not survived. This is the case of about 20 percent of original wills. There is, therefore, no way of finding out what the testator's "marke" may have been like. One can only speculate that the "marke" may have been a cross or that, if Mary Frith, like many of her female contemporaries, was semiliterate with reading but with no writing skills, she may have set down her initials as did Mary Arden, Shakespeare's mother, in 1579. What Mary Arden's "marke" and seal looked like, see Park Honan, *Shakespeare: A Life* (Oxford: Oxford University Press, 1998), pl. 7 and pp. 14–15. Critics, however, have allowed their imagination free rein. Thus, Arthur Freeman's *Elizabeth's Misfits. Brief Lives of English Eccentrics, Exploiters, Rogues, and Failures, 1580–1660* (New York: Garland, 1978), contains a chapter on "The Roaring Girl" that mainly draws on the stereotyped biography. Freeman seems to have known the transcript of the will, taking it for the original and inventing the story that it was signed with a "spidery" X, "which extreme illness may account for" (214–14). The "spidery" cross has become a "shaky" one in Spearing's Introduction to *Counterfeit Ladies* (xiii). Freeman, moreover, misquotes his brief extracts taken from the will. He says that Mary Frith bequeathed her body "to the cart, whenever it come." The will, however, sticks to the formula that she left her body "vnto the Earth, whence it came." He also states that Abraham Robinson received £12; in fact he got 12p.

The formulaic phrasing of the will follows the standard pattern. The will was obviously written down by a clerk of the prerogative court. Originally, it must have been made up of three probate documents: the will, the inventory, and the account of the "personall estate" or movable goods, which used to provide a reliable insight into the value of the testator's property. Unfortunately, only a fair copy of the will has survived; the other two documents must have been destroyed owing to the chaotic state of probate administration during the Commonwealth. For probate documents and wills see Amy Louise Erickson, *Women and Property in Early Modern England* (London: Routledge, 1993), 15, 34, 35.

The will proves that Mary Markham, née Mary Frith, died a wealthy woman. She left a legacy of £20 to her kinsman Abraham Robinson and enough money for the sole executrix, her niece Frances Edmonds, to pay an extra fee for the funeral and burial rites. Frances Edmonds complied with her aunt's request to be "decently buried in Christian buriall within the parish Church" of St. Bridget's in Fleet Street, a privilege confined to those of greater wealth and higher standing. For death and burial practices see Clare Gittings, *Death, Burial and the Individual in Early Modern England* (London: Routledge, 1984).

The will seems to corroborate that Mary Frith's marriage to Lewknor Markham must have been a marriage of convenience. On the one hand,

Mary Markham acknowledges her status of widowhood and the assumption of her husband's name; on the other, she expresses no desire to be buried next to her husband who had the titled status of an esquire. It is likewise surprising that a woman who was renowned for her mannishness should have appointed her niece as sole executrix and not her kinsman Abraham Robinson. She thus conformed to the practice observed by widows in appointing female relatives as executrices or life had taught her to confide more in women than in men.

Mary Frith died on 26 July 1659 and was buried in the church of St. Bridget's in Fleet Street on 10 August. Frances Edmonds saw to it that her aunt was not buried in the churchyard. For the date see Sir John Ellis, ed., "The Obituary of Richard Smyth . . . being a Catalogue of all such persons as he knew in their life," *Camden Society Publications* 44 (1949): 51; see also A. H. Bullen's entry in the *Dictionary of National Biography*.

Portraits

All the portraits of Moll Cutpurse that have come down to us conform to pictorial stereotypes that bear no resemblance to the likeness of the real-life Mary Frith.[44] The three-quarter length portrait that had been bound into the British Library copy of the criminal biography (shelfmark C. 127.a.25) takes up the defamation of Mary Frith as a pickpocket and sexual aberrant. It represents Moll Cutpurse as president of the metropolitan thieves the moment she is delivering an academy lecture on the art of stealing. She wears male garments fashionable in the 1640s; the lower end of her doublet is provocatively unbuttoned; the hilt of her sword, obviously a phallic symbol, is just visible on her left side; her sleeves are slashed and her right arm akimbo; her hair is cut in male fashion; her broad-brimmed hat, perched atop her head, is cocked backwards over her head, which protrudes from her neck at an unnatural angle. With her left arm raised in the posture of a lecturer, she is addressing an audience of docile disciples. The caption, some couplets printed below the portrait, identify her as a female monster:

> *See here the* Presidesse *o'th pilfring* Trade,
> Mercuryes *second,* Venus's *onely* Mayd.
> *Doublet and breeches in a* Un'form *dresse,*
> *The female* Humurrist, *a Kickshaw messe.*
> *Heres no* attraction *that your fancy greets,*
> *But if her* FEATURES *please not, read her* FEATS.[45]

The only visible listeners are an eagle on a perch protruding from the left at the level of the speaker's face, a lion reclining on a desk in the left front row and an ape squatting on another desk in the right front row. The lion and ape are poorly done. The king of animals is reduced to the size of a decrepit midget or dog and the ape is scratching its anus. The emblematic meaning of the animal iconography may be decoded as follows. The eagle, a symbol of royal authority, signals the message that Moll Cutpurse is the uncrowned queen of pickpockets endowed with an exceptionally sharp eye for her victims. The lion, emaciated and exhausted, a mere shadow and inversion of its reputed majesty, seems to remind the beholder that Moll, despite her male dress, cannot assume man's part in generation. The figure of the ape may have been inspired by a passage in the fictional biography, according to which the aged Moll "played with . . . several sorts of Creatures of pleasure and imitation; such as . . . Baboons, Apes, Squirrels, and Parrots" (61). But the unknown engraver seems rather to have been prompted by Christian iconography and to have used the ape either as a symbol of female vanity, wantonness, frivolity, and ruse or as a *figura diaboli*. If so, the ape's obscene gesture invokes the evil picture of Moll as a monster in human shape.[46] The emblematic animals and the portrait, as Judith Petterson Clark argues, place the engraving in the tradition popularized by the Jan Berra engravings of the "Five Senses."[47]

A seventeenth-century woodcut of a similar image has been identified as the prototype of all other versions. This shows a support to the eagle's perch, which makes that part of the composition somewhat more convincing.[48] There is, therefore, some justifiable doubt as to whether the print was really published with the criminal biography. It looks as if it was added to the printed biography some decades after its publication in 1662. Four copies of this print and two different versions are known to me.[49] A print was bound into the British Library copy, but it was removed some years ago when the book was rebound presumably because it was taken for a later addition. A clipped print is pasted onto the flyleaf of Alexander Dyce's copy of *The Roaring Girl,* which is in the Victoria and Albert Museum, London. The print reproduced by A. H. Bullen as frontispiece in the fourth volume of *The Works of Thomas Middleton* (Boston, 1885) differs from the print bound into the Folger Shakespeare Library copy of Nathan Field's *Amends for Ladies* (1639). The Folger print was published by W. Richardson, an eighteenth-century publisher and print seller and is of better quality than the print reproduced by Bullen. There are also textual variants. The Folger print adds the caption "Moll Cut-Purse" and the last but one line reads *"Here no* attraction *that your fancy greets"* whereas the Bullen copy has *"Heres no* attraction *that your fancy greets."*[50]

The plain woodcut in the Bodleian Library copy of the chapbook version *The Womans Champion* (1662) displays the stylized side view of Moll Cutpurse as a highway robber galoping across a bleak countryside on a black horse. She blows a trumpet and holds a message in her right hand. This print obviously underscores the myth propagated by the biography and chapbook that Mary Frith was a highway robber.

A quite different print shows the half-length portrait of a young woman smartly clad in Caroline fashion, sitting on a stool and checking her dressing-up clothes. She wears a long flowing robe, a conical ruff, a broad-brimmed hat, and her hair is cut short in male fashion. In her right hand she holds a mirror and in her left a spy glass. An eagle is perched on her left shoulder. The caption reads:

> Visu pervincit summi iovis aies acuto.
> Not soe quick sighted is the Eagle for her pray
> As I new fashions spie to make me gay.

The copy of the print in the National Portrait Gallery lacks the Latin line. It is pasted onto an illustrated edition of James Granger's *A Biographical History of England* (1769), which formerly belonged to the first director of the National Portrait Gallery, George Scharf. It has some lines of verse inscribed on the back in what appears to be a seventeenth-century hand:

> Fain would I tell thy merry pranks
> And all thy varyous Arts rehearse
> But MALL thy deedes throughout all
> . . . .
> Shine bryghter than in prose or verse.[51]

There are some doubts as to the portrait's likeness. A. M. Hind has identified the print as representing "Seeing," one of a series of engravings of the "Five Senses" that is attributed to the Dutch engraver Jan Barra who settled in London about 1623.[52] What speaks against identifying the portrait as Mary Frith's is the sitter's representation as a fashion-conscious courtesan in her early twenties on the lookout for upper-class clientele. When Barra came to England,

Mary Frith was in her late thirties or early forties. W. A. Thorpe is mistaken in identifying this print as the model for a series of frescoes at Park Farm, Huntingdonshire, which he takes to be portraits of Moll Cutpurse.[53]

The woodcut printed by Nicholas Okes on the title page of Middleton and Dekker's *The Roaring Girl* is the best known portrait of Moll Cutpurse.[54] At first sight, the full-length portrait does look like an authentic visual representation of Mary Frith's advertised stage appearance at the Fortune "in mans apparell & in her bootes & with a sword at her syde," and it has the backing of Andrew Gurr's authority that it is an accurate rendering of her solo performance.[55] On careful examination, however, it becomes evident that the woodcut portrays the boy actor who performed the stage Moll. He/she wears a hat, adorned with a brooch in the shape of a flower, and ruffled shoes; a doublet and full-knee breeches, their sides tied below the knees; a cloak slung over his/her left shoulder. He/she provocatively wields a sword in his/her left hand and holds a lit pipe in his/her right hand. The woodcut cannot claim to be an authentic rendering of Mary Frith's stage appearance because he/she is portrayed without a lute but with a pipe. Mary Frith, as she confessed to the Bishop of London, "playd vppon her lute & sange a songe" on the stage of the Fortune. She did not mention that she smoked a pipe on the stage. The woodcut is rather a stereotyped version of how the man/woman, the *Hic Mulier,* was defined in the contemporary pamphlets.[56]

A strikingly different variant of this title-page woodcut is kept in the National Portrait Gallery and the British Library. In this alternative woodcut, Moll Cutpurse wears her hat askew; her head is turned to the left; her collar is open; she holds an unsheathed sword in her right hand and her pipe in her left; her cloak is evenly spread over her shoulders; her shoes are not ruffled. Her face and body shape are unmistakably a woman's. It stands to reason that what has come to be considered a variant or alternative must be the original woodcut advertising the sensational appearance of Mary Frith at the Fortune Theatre. This is borne out by the following irregularities. The first edition of *The Roaring Girl* came out in 1611 without a license of the Stationers. The first entry in the Stationers' Register is dated about 18 February 1612 and is matched by a fine of 7d. to be paid by its publisher Thomas Archer. The subversive portrait of a potential female actress on the title page of the authorized edition was unthinkable. It fell a victim to censorship. Nicholas Okes, therefore, was constrained in 1611 to issue the title page with a new woodcut. If the original woodcut was meant to convey the likeness of the real-life protagonist, then Mary Frith was not a mannish woman.[57] The caption of the woodcut reads: "My case is alter'd, I must worke for my liuing." It is obviously borrowed from Ben Jonson's comedy *The Case Is Altered* (acted 1597/98, printed 1609) and alludes to the various revelations of identity in its final scene.

The portrait of Moll Cutpurse allegedly painted by Sir Peter Lely is a literary hoax dished up by Daniel Defoe to peddle the Moll Cutpurse mania. Mrs. Bridges, one of the garrulous Old Maids in Defoe's "Satire of Censorious old Maids," which appeared in John *Applebees Original Weekly Journal,* 6 April 1723, gives free rein to her wagging tongue in qualifying a young girl as "a very Indifferent Creature, she'll be as far from Beauty, as *Moll Cut-Purse* was from Handsome." Nelly, the youngest of the old maids, provoked by Mrs. Bridges, retorts that "you wrong *Moll Cut-Purse,* I assure you I have seen her Picture, an Original of Sir Peter Lely's, and I can Vouch she was a very comely Jade." There are good grounds for disbelieving Nelly's statement. As Defoe's contribution to the Journal was conceived as a satire, the argument between the two censorious maids must be read as a joke made at the expense of loquacious women.[58] The same argument about Moll Cutpurse's physical attraction is put forward in Defoe's *Moll Flanders* (1722).

Notes

1. Janet Todd and Elizabeth Spearing, eds., *Counterfeit Ladies: The Life and Death of Mal Cutpurse, The Case of Mary Carleton* (London: William Pickering, 1994), x. I have not been able to consult Randall S. Nakayama's edition of *The Life and Death of Mrs. Mary Frith Called Moll Cutpurse* (New York: Garland, 1993). Spearing has edited the text of the British Library copy, shelfmark C. 127.a.25; a second copy from the library of Robert George Windsor-Clive, first Earl of Plymouth, was sold at Christie's on 30 May 1986. See Judith Petterson Clark's unpublished dissertation, *The Life and Death of Mrs. Mary Frith, Commonly Called Mal Cutpurse (1662): An Annotated Facsimile Reprint* (Miami University, Oxford, Ohio, 1989). The present owner of the Plymouth copy is known to Clark. Her scholarship outdoes Spearing's.
2. Lincoln B. Faller, *Turned to Account: The Forms and Functions of Criminal Biography in Late Seventeenth- and Early Eighteenth-Century England* (Cambridge: Cambridge University Press, 1987), 8–13.
3. Alexander Smith has been exposed as a manipulator of criminal records in John J. Richetti's *Popular Fiction Before Richardson: Narrative Patterns 1700–1739* (Oxford: Oxford University Press, 1969), 45–48; and in Faller's *Turned to Account,* 167–73.
4. On this ground, objection must be raised against the Moll Cutpurse material

in, for instance, Gamini Salgado's *The Elizabethan Underworld* (London: Dent and Sons, Ltd., 1977), 42–44; John L. McMullan's *The Canting Crew. London's Criminal Underworld 1550–1700* (New Brunswick, N.J.: Rutgers University Press, 1984), chaps. 6 and 8. McMullan's study, despite its reliance on fictional material, is one of the best studies of London crime up to 1700. A. H. Bullen's entry in the Dictionary of National Biography is an amalgam of the factual and the fictional. The same considerations apply to J. L. Rayner and G. T. Crook, *The Complete Newgate Calendar* (London, 1926), i, 169–79; Pearl Hogrefe, *Tudor Women: Commoners and Queens* (Ames: Iowa State University Press, 1975), 89–90; Antonia Fraser, *The Weaker Vessel: Woman's Lot in Seventeenth-Century England* (London: Methuen, 1985), 171–72.

5. For the typology of criminal biography see Faller, *Turned to Account,* part 1.

6. Sara Heller Mendelson points out that no example has survived of a female diary written by a woman of the lower class. See her paper "Stuart Women's Diaries and Occasional Memoirs" in *Women in English Society 1500–1800,* ed. Mary Prior (London: Methuen, 1985), 183.

7. For genre, such as the criminal biography, as a political code see Lois Potter, *Secret Rites and Secret Writing: Royalist Literature, 1641–1660* (Cambridge: Cambridge University Press, 1989), chap. 3; for the royalism of the mythic Hind, see Faller, *Turned to Account,* chap. 1.

8. Moll Cutpurse has been associated with bull baiting in *The Witch of Edmonton* (1621), written by Thomas Dekker in collaboration with William Rowley and John Ford. Cuddy Banks, the clown, proposes teasingly to Dog, the metamorphosed devil about to quit the service of Elizabeth Sawyer, the witch, that if he has "a mind to the Game, either at Bull or Bear, I think I could prefer you to Mal-Cutpurse." What the clown actually means is that he would prefer the devil to Moll Cutpurse in the shape of a dog in order to bait the bulls or the bears. See *The Dramatic Works of Thomas Dekker,* ed. Fredson Bowers, (Cambridge: Cambridge University Press, 1966), 3:5.1.160–61.

9. For the highwayman's special status in the hierarchy of criminals, see Faller, *Turned to Account,* chap. 8; and Jennifer Kermode and Garthine Walker, eds., introduction to *Women, Crime, and the Courts in Early Modern England* (London: University College London Press, 1994), 5–6.

10. John Wilson, *Fairfax. A Life of Thomas, Lord Fairfax, Captain-General of All the Parliament's Forces in the English War, Creator and Commander of the New Model Army* (London: J. Murray, 1985), dismisses the incident as gossip (122, 202). Clements Robert Markham and Mildred A. Gibb, in their biographies of Fairfax, the former published in 1870, the latter in 1938, did not even think the spurious incident worth mentioning. Cyrus Hoy in his "Introductions, Notes, and Commentaries to Texts" in *The Dramatic Works of Thomas Dekker,* ed. Fredson Bowers (Cambridge: Cambridge University Press, 1980), 3:13–14, takes the alleged exploits Mary Frith accomplished on Hounslow Heath at face value.

11. See Faller, *Turned to Account,* 178–81.

12. Faller notes that the Fairfaxes had no daughter called Elizabeth, 171, 270 n. 68.

13. For the penitent criminal in rogue biography see Faller, *Turned to Account,* chaps. 5 and 6.

14. For the ambivalence of the moral frame of the rogue biography see Paul Salzman, *English Prose Fiction 1558–1700: A Critical History* (Oxford: Clarendon Press, 1985), 206, 217–18.

15. For Hind see Faller, *Turned to Account,* 187.

16. Tampering with the coinage out of economic self-interest was a capital

crime, which for men was punishable by hanging and quartering. See Alan Macfarlane, *The Justice and the Mare's Ale* (Oxford: Blackwell, 1981), chap. 3.

17. "Rat" is one of the numerous antedatings in this biography, most of them taken from thieves' cant. "Rat" in the sense of "a drunken man or woman arrested by the watch and taken by the constable of the Counter" was already current in 1635. See Eric Patridge, *A Dictionary of the Underworld* (London: Routledge and Kegan Paul, 1968). The first entry in the *OED* dates from 1700.

18. S. Schoenbaum, *William Shakespeare. A Compact Documentary Life* (Oxford: Oxford University Press, 1978), 29. I wish to record my thanks to the Nottinghamshire Archives and Nottinghamshire County Library for examining various printed sources, which yielded no information about Lewknor Markham. What is of prime importance to the present argument is the likelihood that Lewknor was an elder son of the poet and dramatist Gervase Markham, who also came from Nottinghamshire. If this were the case, the reasons for Mary Frith's appearance at the Fortune Theatre would assume a new dimension.

19. For the legal position of women see Kermode and Walker, *Women, Crime, and the Courts*, 6. For a comprehensive analysis of the patriarchal doctrine of coverture see Amy Louise Erickson, *Women and Property in Early Modern England* (London: Routledge, 1993). Her research has brought to light that women of the lower class also used to make arrangements at marriage to circumvent legal discrimination due to coverture.

20. For Moll's conservative view on marriage see Jo E. Miller, "Women and the Market in *The Roaring Girl*," *Renaissance and Reformation* 26 (1990): 11–23.

21. For women and the market of stolen goods in Cheshire see Garthine Walker, "Women, Theft, and the World of Stolen Goods," *Women, Crime, and the Courts*, ed. Kermode and Walker, 81–105. Kay E. Lacey has shown that Englishwomen operating as brokers in the Middle Ages were accepted as citizens in their economic capacity provided they declared themselves *sole.* See her paper "Women and Work in 14th and 15th Century London," in *Women and Work in Pre-Industrial England,* ed. Lindsey Charles and Loma Duffin (London: Croom Helm, 1985), 24–82. Jodi Mikalachki in "Gender, Cant, and Cross-talking in *The Roaring Girl*," *Renaissance Drama* 25 (1994): 119–43, has focused his attention on the paralegal activities of the stage Moll.

22. Surprisingly, the crucial confession that she has come to be called Mall Cutpurse is missing in the document as published by Mulholland in Appendix E and by Spearing in the introduction to *Counterfeit Ladies* (xv); I am therefore quoting from the text edited by Mulholland in "The Date of *The Roaring Girl*," *Review of English Studies* 28 (1977): 31.

23. See Marjorie Garber, *Vested Interests: Cross-Dressing and Cultural Anxiety* (London: Routledge, 1992), 30; Rudolf M. Dekker and Lotte C. van de Pol, *The Tradition of Female Transvestism in Early Modern Europe* (London: Macmillan, 1989).

24. The scandal mounted by the four lessees and Mary Newborough in converting Bridewell into a brothel in 1602 will be dealt with in a forthcoming paper.

25. Susan E. Krantz in "The Sexual Identities of Moll Cutpurse in Dekker and Middleton's *The Roaring Girl* and in London," *Renaissance and Reformation* 31 (1995): 5–20, notes that the real Moll Cutpurse rejected "her fictional rehabilitation as . . . a non-threatening androgynous ideal" (17).

26. This point is made by Stephen Orgel in "The Subtext of *The Roaring Girl*" in *Erotic Politics: Desire on the Renaissance Stage,* ed. Susan Zimmerman (London: Routledge, 1992), 12–26.

27. Jean Howard, "Cross-dressing, the Theatre, and Gender Struggle in Early

Modern England," *Shakespeare Quarterly* 39 (1988), 418–40. Roman courtesans took to dressing up in male attire. Some of them were fined for their cross-dressing: Imperia (1570), Doralice de Sigillo (1581), Anastasia Spagnola (1582), Leonora Magna da Parma (1582), Laura (1583). See Monica Kurzel-Runtscheiner, *Töchter der Venus. Die Kurtisanen Roms im 16. Jahrhundert* (München: C. H. Beck, 1995), 77 and 291, nn. 137, 138.

28. Quoted from Charles Read Baskervill, *The Elizabethan Jig and Related Song Drama* (Chicago: University of Chicago Press, 1929; rpt. New York: Dover Publications, 1965), 116.

29. The point I am making about Mary Frith's breach of the sumptuary laws is corroborated by Stephen Orgel, who in *Impersonations: The Performance of Gender in Shakespeare's England* (Cambridge: Cambridge University Press, 1996) argues that the sumptuary laws said nothing about what were sexually inappropriate garments. Women dressing in male attire committed no legal offense (96–98, 107). For Orgel's reading of the case history of Mary Frith see pages 139–53.

30. For Shank's career as comedian and author see Baskervill, *The Elizabethan Jig*, 114, 118–19, 301.

31. For Tarlton's career and art see David Wiles, *Shakespeare's Clown. Actor and Text in the Elizabethan Playhouse* (Cambridge: Cambridge University Press, 1987, 1990), chap. 2.

32. Cross-dressed women are recorded as being "in service" to various London tavern-keepers. See Howard, "Cross-dressing," 421.

33. Gabriel Harvey found fault with the newfangled tavern phrases that Thomas Nashe coined in imitation of Tarlton's style. The quotation is taken from Robert Weimann, *Shakespeare und die Tradition des Volkstheaters: Soziologie, Dramaturgie, Gestaltung* (Berlin: Henschelverlag, 1967), 209, 305. The Roaring Girl in Middleton and Dekker's play sings two drinking songs (5.1.214ff and 256ff) and a bawdy song (4.1.102–23).

34. A perceptive analysis of costume change is given by Jean MacIntyre and Garrett P. J. Epp, " 'Clothes worth all the rest': Costumes and Properties," in *A New History of Early English Drama*, ed. John D. Cox and David Scott Kastan (New York: Columbia University Press, 1997), 269–85.

35. C. H. Herford and P. Simpson, *Ben Jonson* (Oxford, 1927, rpt. 1966), 3:526, 3.9.78ff.

36. A. H. Bullen, ed., *The Dramatic Works of Thomas Middleton* (Boston, 1885), 3:2.3.91–92.

37. Craig Rustici, in "The Smoking Girl: Tobacco and the Representation of Mary Frith," *Studies in Philology* 96 (1999), 159–79, has addressed the gender and dramatic issues of Moll Cutpurse as a smoker in *The Roaring Girl*.

38. There is no reference to Mary Frith as a smoker in Sarah Augusta Dickson, *Panacea or Precious Bane: Tobacco in 16th Century Literature*. Arents Tobacco Collection Publication 5 (New York: New York Public Library, 1954), nor is there in Jerome E. Brooks, ed., *Tobacco: Its History Illustrated by the Books, Manuscripts, and Engravings in the Library of George Arents, Jr.* (New York: Rosenbach, 1937–52), 5 vols.

39. Quoted from Jeffrey Knapp, "Elizabethan Tobacco," in *New World Encounters*, ed. Stephen Greenblatt (Berkeley: University of California Press, 1993), 273–312. Andor Gomme in his introduction to *The Roaring Girl*, The New Mermaids series (London: E. Benn, 1976), notes that Mary Frith is said to be the first woman to vindicate "for her sex the right of smoking" (xiv).

40. E. J. Burford and Joy Wotton, *Private Vices—Public Virtues: Bawdry in London from Elizabethan Times to the Regence* (London: Robert Hale, 1995), 23.

41. Henry Killigrew was a major in the king's army when he was killed at Bridgewater in 1644 while defending a magazine of provisions against an attack by the Parliamentary troops. His uncle William was a groom of the Privy Chamber to James I. See Walter H. Tregellas, *Cornish Worthies: Sketches of Some Eminent Cornish Men and Families* (London: Elliot Stock, 1884), ii, 153.

42. Obviously, he was Edward Florio, son of John Florio, the eminent lexicographer, grammarian, author of language manuals, and translator. Edward was christened on 19 June 1588. See Frances Yates, *John Florio: The Life of an Italian in Shakespeare's England* (Cambridge: Cambridge University Press, 1934), 68.

43. For more information on Sheppard's mock almanacs see Bernard Capp, *English Almanacs 1500–1800: Astrology and the Popular Press* (Ithaca: Cornell University Press, 1979).

44. Appendix 2, pp. 323–67, in Judith Petterson Clark's dissertation offers a meticulously researched acount of the portraits and eighteen reproductions, among them Jan Barra's "Five Senses." I have pursued a different line of investigation and interpretation.

45. The three couplets are also given in James Granger's *A Biographical History of England from Egbert the Great to the Revolution,* vol. 1, pt. 2 (London, 1769), 658–59. I quote the text from the print in A. H. Bullen's edition of *The Works of Thomas Middleton,* vol. 4 (Boston, 1885), modernizing the punctuation. The term "Presidesse," which has gone unnoticed in modern lexicography, was obviously prompted by James Hind's status as "president" in George Fidge's *Hind's Ramble* (1651).

46. For the emblematic use of the ape as sinner and devil see Horst Waldemar Janson, *Apes and Ape Lore in the Middle Ages and the Renaissance* (London, 1952), 109.

47. Judith Petterson Clark, Ph.D. dissertation, 328.

48. I owe this information to Catharine MacLeod, Curator of Sixteenth and Seventeenth Century Collections of the National Portrait Gallery, London.

49. Clark notes that the early owner of the Plymouth copy of the criminal biography had the text bound together with five different versions of the "Presidesse" portrait. See Clark, 328.

50. The Folger print has been reprinted by Spearing in her modern edition of the biography. A poor reproduction of the "Presidesse" portrait without the caption and with a feminized face, obviously a recent photomontage, is displayed in Sara Mendelson and Patricia Crawford, *Women in Early Modern England 1550-1720* (Oxford: Clarendon Press, 1998), fig. 3.

51. The text and information has been supplied by Catharine MacLeod, to whom I am heavily indebted for her collaboration.

52. A. M. Hind, *Engraving in England in the Sixteenth and Seventeenth Centuries,* part 3. *The Reign of Charles I* (Cambridge: Cambridge University Press, 1964), 95–99.

53. W. A. Thorpe, "Portrait of a Roaring Girl," *Country Life,* vol. C (6 December 1946), 1070–72.

54. It has been reproduced in Mulholland's edition of the play and in Rustici's article on smoking.

55. Andrew Gurr, *Playgoing in Shakespeare's London* (Cambridge, 1987), 63; the woodcut is reproduced on p. 62.

56. For the man/woman debate see Barbara J. Baines, ed., *Three Pamphlets on*

the Jacobean Antifeminist Controversy, Scholars' Facsimiles & Reprints (New York. Delmar, 1978).

57. The original woodcut representing the cross-dressed Mary Frith has been reproduced in Rustici's article (fig. 1) and in Clark's diss. (fig. 12, p. 361).

58. For the "Satire on Censorious Old Maids," see William Lee, *Daniel Defoe: His Life, and Recently Discovered Writings Extending from 1716 to 1729* (London: John Camden Hotten, 1869), iii, 125–27. No portrait of Mary Frith is listed in C. H. Collins Baker's *Lely and the Stuart Portrait Painters* (London, 1912); none is registered in the Courtauld Institute of Art or in the National Portrait Gallery.

Rethinking the Discourse of Colonialism in Economic Terms: Shakespeare's *The Tempest,* Captain John Smith's Virginia Narratives, and the English Response to Vagrancy

Paul A. Cefalu

> The strategy of transition forms the essence of Shakespeare's work.
> —Kenneth Burke, *Attitudes Toward History*

Recent criticism of *The Tempest* and early modern travel narratives has discussed the various ways in which these texts are implicated in a larger discourse of colonialism. Anticolonialist critics have sought to "demystify the national myths"[1] of empire and to write an alternative history of the colonial encounter. Typically, in their desire to delegitimate colonialist self-representation and restore agency to a native countervoice, critics have drawn out moments of textual rupture and contradiction in early modern texts such as *The Tempest* and John Smith's Virginia narratives.[2] Undoubtedly, recent ideology critiques of early modern texts have done much to unmask Western incorporation of new world, peripheral cultures; however, while anticolonialist critics have paid much attention to the politics of the early modern English–Native American encounter, they have generally overlooked the extent to which some central early modern "colonialist" texts, including Smith's writings and *The Tempest,* are primarily concerned with describing or allegorizing embattled economic relationships among the European colonists themselves.[3] Much of Smith's concerns in the Virginia narratives, for example, center on issues of English idleness, unproductive labor, and exploitation of the early Virginia labor force by merchant capitalists, economic topics that have been largely passed over in the more sociopolitical, colonialist readings of early modern travel writing.[4]

Because so much effort has been devoted to exposing Western oppression of New World cultures, critics have also neglected to consider the forms of class division prevalent among the early Virginia settlers, particularly the ways in which the English response to vagrancy and "masterlessness" shaped the New World labor force in the short term and inadvertently halted the transition to distinctly capitalist forms of wage-labor in the long term. This neglect is itself the product of the mythologization of the figure of the masterless man by literary critics, who have connected masterlessness with misrule, "topsy-turveydom," and any number of cultural anxieties, often abstracting masterlessness from its socioeconomic origins and connections with the dissolution of feudalism and the long and uninevitable path toward the proletarianization of labor.[5]

In the following pages, taking into account revisionist positions on early modern employment and the so-called doom-and-gloom school of British history, I raise a question that has been often asked, but not sufficiently answered: Why were masterless men subject to such widespread demonization in early modern England? What motivated the Tudor and Stuart regimes to pass the Statute of Artificers (1563) and the Act of Settlement (1662), paternalistic statutes that, in a later age, classical economists were to denounce as neofeudal, "parish serfdom"? The answer that I offer is that Tudor and Stuart orthodoxy reveal a horror of movement, broadly construed, that is projected onto the vagrant underclass: this in turn has a profound but unanticipated effect on the development of capitalism, to the extent that the free circulation of labor is immobilized until the Elizabethan poor laws are repealed on the eve of the industrial revolution.[6]

In the second section of my argument, I show how the English anxieties over unauthorized movement and vagabondage are reproduced in the New World, specifically how the Virginia Company attempts (but fails) to set England's landless poor to productive labor in the Chesapeake. Not simply representations of the manner in which the European "metropole" encounters the native "periphery," the Virginia texts show the extent to which England exports its own, domestic periphery to the colonies, superimposing a drawn-out confrontation between official power and vagabondage onto the European-Native encounter.[7] We see in these texts principally *three* interacting cultures, an official metropolitan culture, a culture of European vagabondage and poverty, and the native culture, all part of an historical conjuncture or "contact zone,"[8] in which the fears of unauthorized movement that halt colonial economic advancement are counterposed to the native culture's self-confident appropriation of the power of movement.

If English culture attempts to solve its masterless problem by exporting the poor to the New World, and the Virginia texts record the failure of that effort, *The Tempest,* I argue, reveals the consequences of a *repression* of masterlessness. *The Tempest* intervenes in the unproductive historical contradiction stemming from the confinement of vagabondage and consequential arresting of capitalist development; it offers an alternative or ideal history, one that obsessively denies the emergence and protraction of masterlessness and imagines a chronologically overlapping succession of pre-capitalist master-servant relations to the commercialization of labor. Rather than reveal its own textual ruptures that agitate historical and ideological illusions of continuity, *The Tempest* offers a continuous narrative to resolve historical contradictions. The play's utopianism lies in its idealization of diachronic process, not in its Gonzalo-like imaginings of a timeless, synchronic land of Cockaigne.

The larger aim of the paper is to suggest that typical "transitional" arguments of early modern texts have been under thrall to a too linear and symptomatic conception of the decline of feudalism and rise in capitalism. As I describe below, economic historians have recently argued that the historical passage from feudalism to capitalism is shaped more by historical accidents than purposive-rational choices of entrepreneurial forces during the early modern period. The tortuous and near-accidental transition to capitalism can be ascribed to a series of unintended effects operating at multiple levels of the early modern social formation. Recent scholarship has abandoned the use of organic metaphors that describe capitalism as embryonic in the womb of the feudal mode of production, and it has discredited not only Althusserian structuralism, but also the assumptions that either bourgeois revolutions or historical materialism act as natural, unilinear forces of social change.[9]

Thus after suggesting that the complex interaction of the poor law regime and English response to masterlessness (in England and in the colonies) helps us understand why capitalist wage-labor did not advance in a unilinear way following the decline of medieval serfdom, I argue finally that *The Tempest,* in its reconstruction of unilinear transformation—from feudal relations of coercion to early capitalist forms of labor (which historically precede so-called bourgeois individualiam)—looks retrospectively at history and attempts to rejoin history at pregnant moments prior to systematic encroachments by social actors (the encroachments in this case being the ill-fated implementation of the Elizabethan poor-law regime and the confinement of a segment of England's labor force). To the extent that *The Tempest* telescopes and rewrites history, representing unobstructed and productive change, recrafting a sense of history *foregone* or as it *might have happened,* it in many ways offers a philosophy of history. The pre-Enlightenment period did indeed have an evolved sense of progress in spite of its preoccupation with decay and cyclical change, but one finds it in the narratives of process unfolding in dramatic texts like *The Tempest* more so than in historical writing proper, for instance in Raleigh's *History of the World.*

English Paternalism and the Threat of Masterless Migration

Throughout the sixteenth and early seventeenth centuries, contemporaries offered principally two arguments to explain the rise of unprecedented vagabondage. The argument of the Puritan divines (and of the poor laws for the most part) employ what Richard Halpern has called a "discourse of capacities": vagabondage is often equated with the neglect of a productive calling and a predisposition among the poor toward idleness and sloth.[16] In *A Description of England,* William Harrison offers the usual charge against vagrants: "[vagrants] are thieves, robbers, despisers of all laws, and enemies to the commonwealth and welfare of the land. What notable robberies, pilferies, murders, rapes, and stealings of young children . . . I need not to rehearse; but for their idle roguing about the country the law ordaineth this manner of correction."[11] The alternative argument, not voiced until the mid-seventeenth century in any sustained way (with the exception of Thomas More's *Utopia*), was a humanitarian one, which attributed rising vagrancy to enclosures, unemployment, inflation, and a population explosion.[12] During the Commonwealth years, for instance, Samuel Hartlib and Peter Chamberlen went so far as to blame poverty and vagabondage on inefficient bureaucratic planning, envisaging labor exchanges similar to modern unemployment offices where "employers, labourers, servants, and apprentices might converge to supply each other's needs."¹³

The argument for unemployment rather than idleness to explain the rise of vagabondage makes more sense to modern ears, and until recently, historians have linked the rise of masterlessness to economic upheaval and unemployment in the sixteenth and seventeenth centuries. By most traditional accounts, dispossessed peasants, casualties of the disintegration of feudalism and the dissolution of the charitable monasteries, were forced into vagabondage because unemployment prevented their reabsorption into the economy as wage laborers or petty producers.¹⁴ One study claims that "chronic unemployment obliged many urban poor to roam from place to place in search of subsistence."¹⁵ Beier, discussing the state of vagrancy during the civil war period, writes, "This period was the grand finale of a disastrous century marked by rising population, rents and food prices, and declining real wages. . . . The result for the poor was a deepening crisis; it is no coincidence that parish poor relief was first widely enforced, and that large-scale emigration overseas began then."¹⁶

Recently, revisionist history has provided new arguments that question the extent of unemployment and economic recession in early modern England. Historians have forced us to rethink the so-called doom-and-gloom tradition of early modern economic history—a tradition headed by R. H. Tawney and W. G. Hoskins—according to which England suffered a century-long economic retrogression attributed to, among other things, a "little ice age," continental religious wars, and civil wars appearing on the eve of absolutism. Steve Rappaport writes, "That the Elizabethan decades were to some degree years of economic hardship in London seems undeniable, but the case for economic decline should not be overstated. . . . It is likely . . . that during the reign of Elizabeth employment expanded considerably."¹⁷ Ian Archer writes of the late sixteenth century, "We have no way of telling, for example, whether the number of productive niches expanded at the same rate as the city's population, and therefore we have no measure of the extent of unemployment or underemployment."¹⁸ With respect to the oft-noted sloth and criminality of the vagrant underclass, Archer has also shown that vagrant delinquency and subversion has been inflated by historians, who have often collapsed stylized literary representations of a criminal fraternity with historical reality: "there was a criminal underworld in the sense of people for whom criminal activity was regular, but it is arguable that its rapidly shifting allegiances made it somewhat easier for the authorities to penetrate it."[19] And against Beier's claim that London faced "large scale juvenile delinquency," Rappaport tells us that even five hundred vagrants appearing in Bridewell in 1600 represented a tiny portion of the population and should not have been as threatening as contemporaries had supposed.[20]

In the same vein, although less concerned with vagrancy specifically, D. M. Pallister has argued that early modern England was not overpopulated, nor subject to Malthusian positive checks, falling wages, and harvest failures, as has been traditionally assumed.[21] Robert Brenner has claimed that England managed to escape the economic hardship of the general crisis of the seventeenth century: "agricultural demand made possible the emergence of a growing home market, not only for industrial goods and products for general consumption, but also for agricultural means for production . . . which provided the indispensable basis for the development of the English economy through the period of the general crisis of the seventeenth century, when elsewhere industry was contracting."[22]

Undoubtedly many vagrants were a wayward, threatening presence during the period, some of whom were delinquent, nonproductive, and "congenitally" idle (rogues by birth, Timon suggests in *Timon of Athens*), but when we no longer make the too easy assumptions that unemployment created vagrancy, that vagrants were part of an insidious criminal underworld, or that masses of landless peasants took to vagabondage because of refractory delinquency, we can no longer easily explain the establishment of the Elizabethan poor laws, or at least the many persecutory vagrancy acts that were an integral part of poor law legislation. We should be wary, I think, of accepting Marx's famous analyses of vagrancy in *Capital* and elsewhere, where he suggests that the newly free labor force was forced into vagabondage and crime because it could not be reabsorbed into the economy as fast as it had been created. Nor should we uncritically accept (at least as it relates to England), Foucault's assertion in *Madness and Civilization* that the repressive confinement of vagrants and the impotent poor followed from an "economic crisis that affected the entire Western world: reduction of wages, unemployment, scarcity of coin."[23] If revisionist history suggests that the fugitive poor were not necessarily criminal, and if it were possible that a good number, given freedom to migrate, could have found employment, we should perhaps reconsider why the Elizabethans were preoccupied with restricting their poor from freedom to move outside parish boundaries, and what consequences these measures had in the long term.

Drawing on official documentation, humanist polemic, and Protestant theology, historians have traditionally argued that vagrancy threatened to subvert the entire fabric of society. A. L. Beier writes, "Vagrants were not ordinary criminals; they were actually menaces to society. They posed this threat because they were corrupt and social outcasts."[24] Derek Hirst writes, "The 'masterless man' . . . threatened society's image of itself as an organic whole, an interdependent family, and was denounced as the source of all disorder, whether criminal or political."[25] David Underdown notes, "The vagrant was the extreme case of that much-feared menace, the 'masterless' man or woman. . . . Poverty, vagrancy, masterlessness, landlessness: all seemed to strike at the very foundations of order."[26] And C. B. Macpherson remarks, "The sturdy vagrant beggars were commonly thought to have put themselves outside society by their refusal to labour usefully . . . they were masterless men, and Puritan society had no place for them."[27]

What remains unstated, but what can supplement and unite all of the above accounts of masterless demonization, is the pervasive fear of unauthorized travel and movement that English culture expresses when it describes the problem of masterlessness. Masterless men not only show up in Puritan sermons or the Elizabethan poor laws, but also in some unexpected places, in Hobbes's *Leviathan,* for example, where Hobbes, after outlining his Democritean-atomistic theory of self-moving objects and bodies, determines that "corporations of beggars, Theeves and Gipsies," constitute "Private Bodies, Regular, but Unlawful, who unite themselves into one Representative without any publique authority at all."[28] A few pages earlier Hobbes describes the masterless man as the embodiment of the state of war *within* civil society: "amongst masterlesse men, there is perpetual war, of every man against his neighbor . . . no propriety of goods, or Lands, no security; but a full absolute Libertie in every particular man."[29] According to Hobbesian materialism, a "private body" enjoying absolute liberty is like an unconstrained, wayward atom, which wanders uncontrollably toward its own self-preservation.

The related concepts of "absolute liberty" and masterlessness also dovetail nicely, if implicitly, in Thomas Carew's well-received mask, *Coelum Britannicum.* After Mercury purges the heavens of the vices, which have been exiled there as a result of Jove's penance for adultery, Momus worries, "in my judgement it is not safe that these infectious persons should wander here to the hazard of this island, they threatened less danger when they were nay'ld to the

Firmament: I should . . . send them to New England, which hath purg'd more virulent humors from the politique body."[30] Carew expresses the familiar fear of wandering from a fixed point of origin, connecting the loosening of cosmological fixity with a subsequent pernicious aimlessness on Earth. While he does not attach the term masterless or vagrant to these unfixed spirits, he does suggest that they should be sent to the new world. And we know of course (and will have occasion to discuss later) that the most common remedy for masterlessness throughout the seventeenth century and beyond was exile or voluntary emigration to the colonies.

A brief look at the Elizabethan poor laws shows that the statutes themselves repeatedly express a fear of unauthorized movement. The most comprehensive vagrancy acts and proclamations, the 1598 and 1601 Poor Laws, the 1607 Stuart Proclamation, and the Act of Settlement (1660), comprise what Karl Polanyi called a fateful "code of labor," one that controlled economic expansion for more than two centuries.[31] The hallmark of these acts was not their specificity of crimes or punishment thereof, nor their establishment of charitable doles and work-projects, although these features were integral. While placing the burden of relief squarely on decentralized parish authorities, these acts were above all concerned to restrict any unlicensed movement and migration outside parish boundaries or the individual's birthplace. The Statute of Artificers (1563), not concerned with vagrants specifically, set the tone for the restrictive hysteria against unauthorized mobility that became the centerpiece of most of the later acts and proclamations. The statute stipulated forced labor, seven-year apprenticeships, and wage assessments by public overseers, and it placed burdens on masters and overseers to monitor any travel of their apprentices or laborers.

In 1598 an Elizabethan statute declared that "any rogue, vagabond or sturdy beggar who shall be taken begging, wandering or misordering themselves . . . should be openly whipped and sent from parish to parish . . . the next straight way to the parish where he was born . . . and if the same not be known, then to the parish where he or she had last dwelt by the space of a whole year . . . or if it be not known where he or she was born or last dwelt, then to the parish through which he or she last passed without punishment."[32] One notes in this act an obsessive desire to locate a place of origin and to fix movement. Jacobean politics reinforced the Elizabethan constraint on unauthorized wandering. A 1606 Proclamation demanded that all "idle persons and masterless men depart and avoid themselves from the city of London . . . and from thence to repair to the Counties and places where they were borne, and there to tary and abide in some lawfull worke."[33] This concern to hinder unsupervised movement is concisely expressed in Shakespeare's *Coriolanus*, when the first citizen complains that the patricians "repeal daily any wholesome act established against the rich, and provide more piercing statutes daily to chain up and restrain the poor."[34]

The preoccupation with restrictions on unlicensed travel becomes more pronounced under the Commonwealth. In 1656 the Master-General appointed a committee to revise existing laws on vagabondage. The committee recommended that all individuals found wandering outside a ten-mile radius from their residences should be classified as fugitives. One member of the committee objected to the overly general nature of the mandate, claiming, "if you leave it in the power of the justices to judge who shall be a wanderer, for aught I know I myself may be whipped, if I be found but ten miles from my house. . . . In this statute . . . any man may be adjudged by the justice to be a vagrant."[35] A number of years later the Act of Settlement (1662) also expressed a fear of unauthorized travel: "by reason of some defects in the law, poor people are not restrained from going from one parish to another . . . and then to another parish, and at last become rogues and vagabonds."[36]

While we can speculate as to the particular causes of the early modern fear of unlicensed and unauthorized movement—Deleuze and Guattari argue, for example, that "it is a vital concern of every state not only to vanquish nomadism but to control migrations and, more generally, to establish a zone of rights over an entire 'exterior,' over all the flows traversing the ecumenon"[37]—I am more interested in the *consequences* rather than the origins of masterless confinement. In terms of the consequences, the historical conjuncture becomes more complicated. The restrictions on vagrant mobility and migration had profound, although unintended, long-term effects on the rise of capitalism. The Enlighteners inveighed against the entire English poor law apparatus on the grounds that it immobilized the free circulation of labor. Adam Smith remarked, "The very unequal price of labor which we frequently find in England in places at no great distance from one another, is probably owing to the obstruction which the law of settlements gives to a poor man who would carry his industry from parish to parish without a certificate."[38] Malthus recommended the "total abolition of all the present parish-laws," in order that the poor "would be able to settle without interruption . . . [and] the market of labour would then be free."[39] Not just the classical economists, but also modern historians railed against the English poor law system. Paul Mantoux wrote of the Act of Settlement: "The law safeguarded the interests of the parishes. But at what a cost! The whole working class found itself deprived of one its most valuable rights: the right to move about freely."[40] Karl Polanyi, impassioned defender of liberalism and the free market, writes, "The two great Elizabethan statutes of The Act of Settlement together were a charter of liberty to the common people as well as a seal of their disabilities."[41] Another economist, not as stridently liberal as Polanyi, writes simply, "In short, the effect of the Law of Settlement was to keep people where they were and to restrict greatly the opportunities for employment available to the man who was out of a job."[42]

There is some evidence that the Enlightenment critique of the restrictive nature of the settlement laws had been anticipated in the mid-seventeenth century. In *The Office of Addresses and Encounters* (1650), Henry Robinson realizes that the conditions of poverty are not simply created by idleness and sturdy beggary, but that the idle poor remain unemployed because they have no access to potential employers and thus cannot offer their labor where it is in demand: "poore people are not acquainted with other peoples wants, besides their own; they have hitherto had no meanes to come to the speedy knowledge of such persons as stand as much in need of poore man's labours, as the poor people doe of rich mens moneyes . . . but when the rich, as well as the poore men's occasions, and necessities, are equally known to one another, the poor will be able to treat with more reputation, and get more indifferent and advantageous prices."[43] Robinson goes on not to recommend the free circulation of labor, but, in keeping with the still-paternalist nature of early modern culture, the establishment of a registry and centralized employment agency that would facilitate communication between the poor and prospective employers. But the implication is that compulsory poor rates and the confinement of the poor in workhouses are inefficient antipoverty measures, given Robinson's belief that a simple improvement in open communication between employer and laborer could provide gainful employment for the available labor force.

We see a series of ungovernable events, then, neither sequentially unfolding nor anticipated by individual agents or the conscious efforts or prejudices of ascending or descending ruling power, in which vagabondage, the poor law system, and the rise of capitalism are all deeply and contradictorily interwoven. Clearly this provides evidence against old-fashioned historical materialism, since immanently expanding productive-economic forces or relations are not primary catalysts in the rise, protraction, and dissolution of masterlessness. What I have been trying to bring out in the above argument is the unforeseen and unplanned nature of the consequences that the limitations on vagabondage and establishment of poor laws had on capitalist development. The unintentional aspect of these developments is consistent with recent arguments on the transition between feudalism and capitalism, which a brief detour into one of the more influential of these arguments will bear out.

Robert Brenner has argued that most of the theories of the transition—from Wallerstein's and Frank's world-systems theory and market-model approach, to Maurice Dobb's earlier productive forces model—all resemble in basic outline Adam Smith's explanation of economic development, which emphasized a rise in trade, division of labor, and the underlying belief in the importance of *homo economicus* in guiding capitalism toward a naturally unfolding end. As Brenner notes, the neo-Smithians believe that capitalism was caused by the instrumental rationality of individual profit-maximizers. Brenner's argument cannot be summarized in brief compass, but he has argued that relatively autonomous class structures and class conflicts determined the different ways that ruling classes were forced to carry out practices of surplus extraction following the decline of serfdom. A relatively mobile and free peasantry in England, coupled with scarcity of land available to the lower orders, led to accumulation, innovation in agriculture, and the establishment of what Marx described as the classic triadic structure of agrarian capitalism (landowner, tenant-farmer, and laborer).[44]

The important point in Brenner's argument for our purposes is the following: "the methods applied by the ruling class . . . are thus incomprehensible simply as their own choice. These were given as it were by the class structure; by the system of surplus extraction relations with the direct producers in which the ruling class found itself." The ruling classes "were not free to choose the manner in which they exploited the direct producers."[45] According to such an argument, capitalism was an unintended effect of structural conflict. As Eileen Meiksins Wood has recently written. "Capitalism is no longer a presupposition, whose unexplained existence in embryo must be assumed in order to account for its being. Instead it emerged as an unintended consequence of relations between non-capitalist classes."[46]

Brenner's argument for ruling class unintentionalism is mostly concerned with explaining the onset of capitalism following the decline of the feudal mode of production. The argument I have been making with respect to masterlessness and the poor laws shows how the same logic applies but in the opposite direction: just as we find little ruling-class choice in propelling capitalism forward, so we see no ruling-class agency in obstructing that movement once underway. This argument for the indeterminate nature of capitalist development and for the limitations on ruling class agency to influence that development impacts literary criticism concerned with representations of economic change in Tudor and Stuart literature. Because we can no longer argue for capitalist inevitability, bourgeois revolutions, and market forces willfully speeding capitalist advancement to a preordained end (what Conrad Russell and English civil war historians have been arguing for some time now), we should be wary of offering, as some recent criticism has, symptomatic or anticipatory readings of early modern texts, according to which bourgeois writers and an official culture inscribe their own voluntarist capitalist ethic in advance of the realization of entrenched capitalist relations.[47]

The following pages will show how the contradictions inherent in the Tudor and Stuart reaction toward masterlessness are reproduced (and the consequences of that contradiction realized) in colonial Virginia. Following this exposition is a discussion of the repression of masterlessness in the *Tempest,* and the attempt in the play to undo the contradictions revealed in the poor law history (those which are made more manifest in the Virginia texts). Needless to say, in neither John Smith's texts nor *The Tempest* do dominant cultural forces (seigneurial or bourgeois) intentionally or unidirectionally shape the representation of economic advancement in *The Tempest* or economic retrogression in Virginia.

New World Vagrants, Old World Anxieties

Seventeenth-century reformers and propagandists frequently argued that the New World could absorb England's postfeudal landless population. A 1603 proclamation called for the banishment "beyond the seas" of any "incorrigible or dangerous Rogues."[48] Hakluyt thought the colonies could provide a haven for "condemned English men and women, in whom there may be founde hope of amendment,"[49] and the author of *Nova Britannium* recommended exportation to the new colonies on the grounds that it would be "most profitable for the state to rid our multitudes of such as lie at home, pestering the land with pestilence and penury, and infecting one another with vice and villanie, worse than the plague itself."[50] Similarly, the author of *The Reformed Virginian Silk-Worm* wrote that emigration to the colonies would "disburthen this nation of many indigent persons, who having formerly perhaps enjoyed a fulnesse of abused or forfeyted plenty . . . are prompted by their owne and other mens ruine by making the highways . . . an ambuscado of innocent Travellers."[51] Captain John Smith argued that the establishment of a colony in Virginia would "so employ and encourage a great part of our idlers . . . that could they but once taste the sweet fruites of their owne labours, doubtlesse many thousands would be advised by good discipline, to take more pleasure in honest industrie, then in their humours of dissolute idlenesse."[52] One modern historian has concisely summed up the propaganda campaign: "practically everyone who had anything to say on the subject of colonial development recommended that beggars, delinguents, 'all such as lie on the parishes,' all 'lewed and lazy fellowes,' be forthwith collected and sent off."[53]

After repeated failure to establish a stable and productive colony throughout the first decades of the seventeenth century, and after a withdrawal of investments in the colonial venture, the same propaganda that championed the emigration of delinquency to the new world took an about-face, and blamed the failures of the colony on the preponderance of an idle and delinquent labor pool. William Strachey describes the early colonial laborers as unskilled and unhallowed "scum of men," and importunes England to send over "men of rank and quality," "carpenters and workmen, and skillful vignerons."[54] The author of a *New Life in Virginia* recommends emigration for those "of honest minds and better sort," instead of those who "cannot live at home, nor lay their bones to labor."[55]

The arguments against the immigration of delinquents run throughout all of John Smith's writings. In the *Proceedings* Smith (and his collaborators) note that their men are "little better than atheist,"[56] "whose mischiefs" daily spring from their ignorant (yet ambitious spirits)" (207); they are variously described as "mutinous prisoners" (271); "untoward gallants" harboring "childish fears" (226–78). At one point, threatening coercive measures and forced labor, Smith warns his men, "and thinke not that either my pains, or the adventurers purses, will ever maintaine you in idlenesse and sloth" (259). Smith compares the planters of Virginia to those in England who "lie under windows and starve in Cheapside, rot in Gaoles, doe in the street, high-waies, or any where, and use a thousand devices to maintaine themselves in those miseries, rather than take any paines, to live as they may be honest labour."[57] In response to King James's question how misery in Virginia can be mitigated, Smith writes "with sufficient workmen and meanes to maintain them, not such delinquents as here cannot be ruled by all the lawes in England . . . to rectify a Commonwealth with debauched people is impossible" (*Generall Historie*, 330).

We see in these passages more than the casual recognition of a failed endeavor to establish Virginia as an outpost for England's idle or criminal fringes. Smith's and the other's recriminations against the Virginia laborers are excessive and borderline-paranoid. If we set a more or less monological or unified official culture against an alien native culture we fail to register the internal divisions within the European culture itself, and the extent to which the English attitudes toward their own are part of the bad faith endemic to the colonial experience generally. The about-face the official culture makes, and the inflated rhetoric of their explanations for colonial hardship, should perhaps make us as wary of accepting colonial representations of idle (English) labor as we are of accepting the European representations of the inferiority of the native culture. In the following pages, resisting the colonist's ascription of colonial failure to masterless unproductivity, I will show how the New World English laborer is the most available scapegoat for economic ruin. I will also argue that such ruin is itself caused by a number of economic and ideological contradictions stemming from the reproduction in Virginia of an unresolved poverty problem that had originated in England.

Historians have traditionally described Virginia as a haven for economic individualism and free competition. One historian writes of the Virginia company: "The self-interest of the company was to be assured by giving a free rein to the economic self-interest of individual colonists and groups of colonists."[58] Another historian writes that the headright system "was supposed to involve the free play of economic opportunity within the context of an industrious society."[59] Recently, Jack Greene has argued that Virginia's entrepreneuralism was coextensive with the secularized market values prevalent in England. Greene describes seventeenth-century England, and by implication early Virginia, as "dynamic, loose, open, individualistic, competitive, conflicted, acquisitive, highly stratified, and market-based. . . ."[60]

How can we reconcile this oft-noted bourgeois and opportunistic outlook of the early colonial leaders with the backlash against that free-market ethos running throughout John Smith's writings? Such a backlash is evident in, for example, the Virginia Company's concern to reoccupy the private land; their pejorative comments regarding the self-interest of the planters; their claim that individualism sacrifices the "common benefit"; the retention of traditional economic relations and belief systems, particularly, classical republicanism, indentured servitude and coerced labor among the governors; and the overall persistence of feudal values within an assumed capitalist setting. It can perhaps be argued that all these elements are consistent with the company's opportunism, that faced with the threat of declining profits and self-interested investors, it was merely strategic and not backward-looking for the company to reinstate the old world value system it did; or that the company merely paid lip-service to classical republican arguments and georgic ideals. But against these views one could argue that a commitment to a capitalist ethos might have compelled the adventurers to ignore the privateering, once-indentured producers or to fit them into a market framework that saw utility in most private endeavors.

Rather than take sides in a debate that sets self-interest on the one hand against traditional, communitarian values on the other, I suggest an alternative argument. We may begin with the premise that the structure of the relationships between the governors and their (white) laborers bears a striking resemblance to that which inhered between English culture and their destitute poor, in which a philanthropic temper is interwoven with a fear of dispersal and migration. In Smith's writings the problematic of movement becomes more complex, since the power of movement that is denied to the Euro-American poor is acknowledged in the text to be a primary support of power of the native culture. Simply put, power and authority in these texts resides in the ability either to migrate or to prevent the migration of another.

When Smith and the governors adopt the authoritarian tone we have noted above, it is usually directed at the economic opportunism of those laborers who, after their indenture had been fulfilled, dispersed from the central plantation and sought a life outside the ambit of the common stock and company settlement. Wesley Craven writes of the governor's reaction against the felt break-up of the company's plantation into individual holdings, "The first step toward the decline of the company's plantation, or 'publique' as it was known, had come in 1614. The seven-year term of service of the oldest inhabitants expired in that year, and there were present for the first time in that colony free laborers."[61] Sandys, the governor of the colony at the time, reacted to the disperson, warning "as the Private Plantation began thus to increase so contrary wise the estate of the Publique . . . grew into utter consumption."[62] Eventually, Sandys, in an effort to force colonists to grow diverse food crops and to thwart the reliance on tobacco as a single cash crop, convinced the Virginia Company to reoccupy much of the once-common land and to strictly control the granting of patents to individual, semi-independent plantations. A need for more labor forced Sandys to promote large-scale immigration, doubling the population of the colony, but in the process only making conditions worse than prior to 1618, because the colony could not absorb the rapid influx of laborers.

Sandys suggests that disperson among the colonists threatens the well-being of the colony as a whole. This in itself sits oddly with any notion of the "free play of economic opportunity," but eventually another seemingly more plausible argument was made by the colonial leaders against colonial dispersion, namely that the colonists became susceptible to native attack when settlements were separated one from another. When Smith was asked by the "Majesties Commission" to explain the cause of the massacre in 1622, in which more than three hundred colonists had been killed, he explained: "the cause of the Massacre was the want of marshall discipline, and because they would have all the English had by destroying those they found so carelessly secure, that they were not provided to defend themselves against any enemy, being so dispersed as they were" (*Generall Historie,* 328).

For our purposes, it is important to note that interspersed throughout the passages in which Smith narrates the events leading up to the massacre, he invokes masterlessness and vagrancy, as if it were somehow connected with the colonial susceptibility to attack in the first place. After Smith offers his explanation for the massacre, a commission organized by James I asks Smith how the problems in the colony could be rectified. Smith uncharacteristically argues that part of the problem is that many of the adventurers exploit and abuse their laborers because, "God forbid . . . that masters there [Virginia] should not have the same privilege over their servants as here" (330). This is an important line in the *Historie* and shows how Smith occupies two positions throughout his writings. On the one hand, he speaks as the mouthpiece for the Virginia

Company; on the other hand, he champions the laboring poor. Rather than suggest that vagrancy created the conditions that enabled the massacre, Smith pushes the argument back a step further and locates the causes of vagrant dispersion and idleness in the harsh treatment the laborers received under the authoritarian adventurers, those who, we have seen, oscillate wildly between solicitude and outright oppression. Thus, if on the manifest level, dispersion leaves the plantations open to native attack, dispersion is perhaps more latently dangerous, Smith implies, because it undermines master-servant bonds and creates disunity and a threat to synoptic order at Jamestown. Not surprisingly, the one native tribe well-respected among the colonists is the Pawtuxunt, "who inhabit together, and not so dispersed as the rest. These of al others were found the most civill to give intertainment."[63] And if one good thing came out of the massacre, Smith adds (reverting back to his usual campaign against idleness) it forced the company to replace those vagabonds who contributed to the massacre with more responsible, upstanding citizens: "since I came form thence, the honorable Company have bin humble suiters to his Majestie to get vagabonds and condemned men to go thither . . . yet for all the worst of . . . this lamentable massacre, there is more honest men now suiters to go, then ever hath been constrained knaves."[64]

We can see in these developments the same double bind that we saw earlier in the response to masterlessness in England. If dispersion of the undesirable second-generation vagrants Smith describes (those who became free of seven-year indentures beginning around 1614) had made them susceptible to native invasion, Sandys and others might have let self-interested migration run its course and burn itself out. If native invasion had not been a threat to scattered private plantations, then Sandys *still* should have left individual initiative to its own devices, in keeping with the colonist's vaunted free-enterprise outlook. But because the company held fast to a paternalistic conception of its laboring force which was conditioned no doubt from stubborn fears of masterlessness and vagabondage originating in England, the company's leaders attempted to force unity and prohibit unauthorized planting outside the perimeter of the main settlement. The very concern that masterlessness and migration obstructed order and productivity only ended up forestalling productivity; without uninhibited expansion and free enterprise, the company and colony could not support each new wave of immigration, a principal cause of its dissolution of 1624.[65]

One of the ironies in Smith's texts is that the very power of a nomadic lifestyle that is denied to the planters in the Virginia Company is the defining feature of the power the natives hold over the colonists. On a number of occasions Powhatan warns Smith that the natives can migrate to another culture without much readjustment, an act that would devastate the colonists. Powhatan warns that if the Europeans attempt to destroy the native culture, they "will have worse by our absence; for we can plant anywhere, though with more labour, and we know you cannot live if you want our harvest . . . if you proceed in revenge we will abandon the country" (*Generall Historie,* 210). In another exchange, recorded in *The Proceedings,* Powhatan repeats the similar threat: "what can you get by war, when we hide our provision and flie to the woodes, whereby you must famish by wronging us your friends" (247). Smith advises his men against unnecessary antagonism of the natives because, "If we should each kill our man and so proceede with al in this house; the rest will all fly, then shall we get no more, then the bodies that are slaine, and then starve for victuall" (*Proceedings,* 251–52). And Smith recognizes the advantages the natives enjoy because of migration and a nomadic lifestyle: "by their continuall ranging, and travell, they know all the advantages and places most frequented with Deer, Beasts, Fish, Foule, Roots, and Berries" (*Generall Historie,* 118).

One encounter between the Natives and Smith that brings out the importance of the power of movement occurs when Smith is captured by the Natives and offers his compass as barter for his liberation:

> He [Smith] demanding for their Captaine, they shewed him Opechankanough, King of Paumankee, to whom he gave a round ivory double compass Dyall. Much they marvailed at the playing of the Fly and Needle, which they could see so plainely, and yet not touch it, because of the glasse that covered them. But when he demonstrated by that Globe-like Jewell, the roundnesse of the earth, and skies, the spheare of the Sunne, Moone, and Starres, and how the Sunne did chase the night round about the world continually; the greatnesse of the Land and Sea, the diversitie of Nations, varietie of complexions, and how we were to them Antipodes, and many other such like matters, they all stood as amazed with admiration. (*Generall Historie,* 147)

While Smith describes the compass as a signifier for so much by the way of analogy, specifically its spherical resemblance to the sun and "roundness" of the earth, the compass is for the most part separated from its most important function; its power to provide direction when traveling. Since the freedom of movement is severely constricted for the colonists, the compass *as compass* becomes alien to or no longer functional for Smith and the Europeans. It is as if the transference of the compass to the natives represents Smith's acknowledgment that in the New World the natives hold the power associated with migration and travel, and therefore should rightfully possess the greatest symbol of that power. Opechankanough merely needs to hold up the compass, letting it represent itself, and by extension the natives' natural claim over it; he does not need to recode or reinvent the compass as a symbol for so many things over and above its principal use value. If in England, and during the passage to the New World, the European adventurers could claim a symbolic attachment to the instrument, once in the New World the power of the compass belongs to the natives.

The Tempest and the Transition from Feudalism to Capitalism

We have seen thus far that English culture exported its anxieties over masterlessness to the New World. Such a phenomenon provides a partial explanation for the failure of the colonists to set up a prosperous colony in Virginia during the first half of the seventeenth century. If the rise of masterlessness explains why history only fitfully develops, and history itself cannot conceal the obstacle of masterlessness to diachronic process, then *The Tempest* works to obscure and suppress that unsettling reality. Obsessively reimagining and reinforcing master-servant relations, the play does not tolerate any unsubordinated relationship. But *The Tempest* is not static, and if not within history, then within the play world does a dialectic motor itself toward a higher unity. Straddling both feudalism and capitalism, *The Tempest* performs a bypass on diseased history, clearing from its path any masterless impediment that might halt seamless economic transformation.

We can begin with a discussion of the many forms of mastery and servitude one finds in the early scenes, particularly in the exchanges among Ferdinand, Prospero, and Miranda. Ferdinand, "released" from a prior condition of subordination to his father, invents himself as the newly installed King of Naples upon meeting Prospero: "single thing, as I am now, that wonders / To hear thee speak of Naples. . . . Myself am Naples."[66] Prospero intervenes almost immediately, compelled to reimpose mastery over Ferdinand:

"The Duke of Milan / And his more braver daughter could control thee" (1.2.439–41), and later, "I'll manacle thy neck and feet together" (1.2.463). Prospero at this point has not imagined an alliance between Ferdinand and Miranda; he is motivated, it seems, by his own will to punish Ferdinand for the latter's audacity in claiming any sense of "freedom." Prospero then promises Ariel his freedom in exchange for the newly enslaved or enserfed Ferdinand: "Delicate Ariel, / I'll set thee free for this" (1.2.443–44). Prospero's means of compensation to Ariel for Ariel's labor of enslaving Ferdinand is an avowal of Ariel's liberty. Not only all isolated relations between individuals, but also the entire system of exchange is founded on a tightly supervised economy of lordship and domination. These relationships—indentured servitude, outright slavery, reciprocal gift-exchange and barter—represent precapitalist relations with a vengeance. The value of Ariel's service is measured more by canons of proper obedience and deference to a capricious master than it is by productivity. Ariel reminds Prospero, "I have done thee worthy service, / Told thee no lies, made thee no mistakings, serv'd / Without or grudge or grumblings" (1.2.246–48). And we should note just what kind of power Prospero wields over Ariel and everyone else: the power to immobilize, to "stow" the Mariners under "hatches" (1.2.230), to "rend an oak and peg in his [Ariel's] knotty entrails" (1.2.294–95), to "sty" Caliban in the "hard rock" (1.2.344–45), to maintain the spirits in "their confines" (4.1.121), and to tie Ferdinand's arms in a "sad knot" (1.2.223). In his obsession with practices of ritual bondage and immobilization, Prospero is figured as a vigilant overlord, as if in a neofeudal repetition-compulsion he unceasingly suppresses a flight from serfdom among his unfree dependents. Of the immobilizing tendencies of the feudal state, Michael Postan tells us that the "miscellaneous rights or 'freedoms' which a free man could claim as his own—the right to move away . . . could not be exercised by the lord's dependent tenants except with his permission."[67] Erik Olin Wright notes that feudal culture described these flights as "moments in which the peasant was stealing part of the labor power owned by the lord."[68] In a seventeenth-century extension of these feudal practices of migratory constraint, Prospero's magic stands in for the legislative power of the poor laws to hinder movement; the difference, of course, is that while the poor laws restrict freedom to labor, Prospero's magic overcompensates, sending Ferdinand, for example, into potentially interminable hard labor.

Once under Prospero's mastership, Ferdinand, like Caliban, is forced to gather logs. Ferdinand labors in a rite of passage in order to gain the affection of Miranda and the support of Prospero, who finally informs him "All thy vexations were but my trials of thy love, and thou / Hast strangely stood the test" (4.1.7–10). We recall also that Caliban is forced to work under Prospero's dominion in atonement for his earlier advances upon Miranda. It goes without saying that this is unproductive work, without a division of labor and any sense of a social order based on rationalization, efficiency, or productivity. When Prospero tells Miranda that Caliban "serves in offices that profit" (1.2.314–15), "profit" denotes subsistence, not accumulation. It is even unclear whether all this work is required for anyone's livelihood. (Just how many thousands of logs does Prospero need to maintain himself and Miranda?) Prospero is an inversion of Weber's precapitalist charismatic magus, whose near-demonic power relies on unmitigated will, persuasion, and coercion operating in the absence of any legitimating norms, values, or institutions. He is quite unlike *King Lear*'s Edmund for instance, whose argument for self-interest and rationalization is of a piece with his comprehension of a new world order and a rift between man and nature.

Yet *The Tempest* does not honor Prospero's magic, and one of the most striking aspects of the play is the way in which the precapitalist relations of unmasked coercion and servitude seem to silently pass over into naturalized relations of capital and commodity worship. The moments of textual rupture occur when the play extends its own diffuse but unsourced magic over Prospero's charismatic precapitalist magic. We can see this occur in the various metamorphoses Miranda undergoes in her development from primitive barter object to commodity fetish. Initially, Prospero offers her as a "gift" to Ferdinand: "Then, as my gift, and thine own acquisition / Worthily purchased, take my daughter" (4.1.13). Miranda is doubly inscribed here, at once Prospero's gift, as if she is an exchange-object in a primitive potlatch, in which the countergift offered to Prospero will be his restoration and liaison with Alonso. But on the other hand, she is an item "purchased" by Ferdinand, no longer a gift or reward freely tendered, but a compensatory object.

Later in the play, the double-coding of Miranda is displaced by coding of a new order: in response to Alonso's question, "What is this maid with whom thou wast at play?" Ferdinand responds, "Sir, she is mortal; / But by immortal providence she's mine. / I chose her when I could not ask my father / for his advice . . ." (5.1.189–91). Miranda's status has changed from a gift given by

Prospero to Ferdinand, to a purchase of Ferdinand's, to a providential windfall, to finally an object-choice of Ferdinand's. But Miranda is not merely overdetermined; her status as an object in a natural economy is transformed into an object of exchange circulating among allegorically described market-type relations. Ferdinand recognizes that he labors for Miranda as her "patient log-man." Yet Ferdinand's laboring past is soon forgotten, rendered invisible, and he begins to acknowledge only the mystified presence of Miranda, divorced from the labor undergone in her "acquisition," and now granted to him by "immortal providence." Ferdinand mistakes the result of hard labor for a natural endowment, and Prospero as overseer recedes in the background, displaced by a higher power. "Immortal Providence," then, need not simply mean divine providence here; it suggests the power of a secularized providential materialism, in which Miranda comes to represent, among other things, the detached and congealed labor of Ferdinand. When Alonso mistakes Miranda for a goddess, he is bowing to a new capitalist-type goddess, not a sacred one.

The silent, unobstructed passage from precapitalist values to capitalist relations is brought out more clearly in the relationship between Caliban and the Europeans. Caliban learns not one, but two languages in the play (or he learns one prior to the beginning of the play and another as the play unfolds): the language taught to him by Miranda is the language of a natural economy and precapitalist values; the language he internalizes by the end of the play (one that he teaches himself) approximates the language of instrumental labor and capital. Early in the play he worries that Prospero could "make a vassal" of his God Setebos (1.2.375). Unlike the commodities Harriot and colonial propagandists held up to colonialist investors, Caliban is not initially described as a valuable commodity transferable to England. Instead he is merely a spectacle, one not to be bought and sold, but more of a display item, like an artifact or ornament. Stephano describes him as a potentially valuable "present for any Emperor that ever trod on neat's leather" (2.2.69–72). And Caliban, of course, is no free laborer for much of the play; he works under coercion as Prospero's "slave."

Yet the crucial moment in Caliban's transformation comes when he supplants Prospero as master with, not simply Stephano, but the "celestial liquor." He does so by promising that in return for the bottle, he will show the "best springs" to Stephano and Trinculo, and "dig pignuts," and reveal to them a "jay's nest," and "snare the nimble marmoset" (2.2.168–69). After contracting himself to Stephano and Trinculo by swearing upon the bottle, Caliban announces he will be their "true subject, for the liquor is not earthly" (2.2.126–27). Self-fashioned as an altered, "true" subject, putting his labor-capacity to a self-interested end, Caliban has not merely substituted one master (Prospero) for another (Stephano). He has replaced both masters with the more amorphous master that is capital, effecting the substitution by exchanging his own alienable energies for the phantasmagoric, unearthly "bottle." If under Prospero he was enslaved or enserfed, under Stephano and Trinculo he has attained at least a precarious and ironic degree of freedom. He has discovered, or rather stumbled upon, the perverse logic of possessive individualism. He has become, as Antonio asserts, a "plain fish and no doubt marketable" (5.1.265).

Of course, what I am describing as the scene of Caliban's self-alienation, one might describe as the simple pursuit of base desires among low characters in a comic mode. But the scene is remarkable, I think, because, like Miranda's shifting status and the recoding of Ferdinand's labor form, Caliban's relations with Stephano and Trinculo are so essentially different from his prior relations with Prospero. Caliban is not simply, as George Lamming suggests, "the excluded, that which is eternally below possibility . . . an occasion which can be appropriated and exploited to the purposes of another's own development."[69] Under no compulsion by an overlord, freely discoursing in a new version of the language he had hitherto cursed, Caliban sets the terms of the bargain, instrumentalizing his labor capacity in order to attain a desired end. When Caliban says "Caliban Has a new master" (2.2.192–93), the meaning is not entirely clear. If Stephano is Caliban's new master (the most likely signification), then mastery does not imply refeudalization, since Prospero-like compulsion is not readily apparent: in place of Prospero's spirit-induced bodily persecution of Caliban, Trinculo's method of persecution is verbal taunting and "mocking," an affront, Stephano self-righteously declares, to Caliban's "dignity" (3.2.28–35). "Master" could equally refer either to the bottle, suggesting reification, or Caliban himself, suggesting a newly conceived, if momentary, form of alienable self-mastery.

Not only is Caliban a different servant to Stephano than he is to Prospero, but Stephano is also a different master to Caliban than is Prospero. Stephano boasts that he has made the bottle "with his own hands" (2.2.124) after escaping from the shipwreck "upon a butt of sack" (2.2.122), and he assures Caliban that he has a household supply of the celestial liquor in a cellar "in a rock by the seaside, where my wine is hid" (2.2.134–135). Whereas Prospero possesses an overflow of subsistence goods (surplus logs) but only one desirable and exchangeable commodity (Miranda), the surprisingly resourceful Stephano harbors a commodity surplus, potentially exchangeable, in this comically inverted world, for more worthwhile commodities proper, including not simply the knowledge of Prospero's whereabouts and elusive books (which only Caliban's specialized labor can provide) but the valuable rarities Caliban will furnish as recompense for the bottle. Caliban exclaims, "I with my long nails will dig thee pignuts; / . . . bring thee . . . clustering filberts, and sometimes I'll get thee / Young scamels from the rock" (2.2.168–72). Unlike the labor he ungainfully performs for Prospero's subsistence—"fetch in firing" (2.2.181), "scrape trenchering" (2.2.183), and log-gathering—Caliban offers Stephano the sorts of commodities that would have stirred the imagination (and purses) of colonialist merchants and investors: "clustering filberts," "young scamels," and "nimble marmosets." In William Strachey's *True Repertory of the Wracke,* as Frank Kermode notes, "scamels," or "seamels," are described as exotic commodities and delicacies.[70] While Stephano and Trinculo enlist Caliban's talents with a manifest view to conquest and consumption, the items Caliban invokes are potentially convertible to further commodity and gain; indeed part of the irony in the scene lies in the fact that Stephano, the depraved and "poor drunkard," would hardly have cultivated the refined palate and tastes required to appreciate the nonpareils Caliban is offering, and the use or exchange to which Stephano would put these commodities if ever furnished is an open question. The important point is not that these relations are so firmly, if allegorically capitalist, but that inasmuch as Marxist critics such as Walter Cohen principally focus on Prospero (who I have suggested acts like a customary, paternal overlord) as the exemplar in the play of postfeudal, "perhaps bourgeois,"[71] individualism, they fail to consider the more materialist forms of flexible, uncoerced self-interest and forms of labor distributed among these low characters in this allegorically rich comic mode.

Critics have labored over Prospero's disturbance when he realizes he has momentarily forgotten the subplot and Caliban's conspiracy. Hulme and Barker have seen this disturbance as a "textual excess," one that almost shakes Prospero's power, but because Shakespeare relegates the subplot to the comic mode, "in the end his version of history remains *authoritative,* the larger play acceding as it were to the containment of the conspirators in the safely comic mode."[72] Hulme and Barker fail to note that the moment of "slippage" in the text—the moment when Prospero's power is deauthorized—occurs during the all-important allegorical metamorphosis of Caliban into a possessive individualist, managed by his own impulses and outside the jurisdiction of Prospero's magic. This is the more remote or long-term consequence of Prospero's neglecting to monitor closely events in the subplot. If *The Tempest* aims to represent the historical change from feudal forms of labor to early capitalist forms of labor (and I am assuming it makes that attempt, given its extended discussion and transformation of different forms of labor and servitude), and the beginnings of that transformation occurred the way revisionist history has suggested (and I am assuming this is the most compelling argument available), then Prospero's influence or agency in realizing that transformation needs to be negated, and the onset of postfeudal labor forms need to be allegorized in the absence of any ruling power underwriting that transformation. Prospero's history is not authoritative, as Hulme and Barker would have it, but rather subordinate to the play's insistence on duplicating the formal logic or structure of economic transformation that had earlier begun (but then was saddled by authoritarian antivagrancy measures) in historical reality.

But how can we reconcile the crucial negation of Prospero's power with the emphasis the play places on the prodigiousness of his power to control all forms of labor, movement, mastery, and servitude? We can explain these strands if we see that Prospero has a twofold responsibility or role in the play. His project (the play's project) is, on the one hand, to repress any notion of masterlessness if the play is to represent an undisturbed transformation from precapitalist to capitalist relations; yet after having done so, he needs to recede or relinquish his power at the very moment of that transformation, to vanish as a ruling force or influence if the play is to be consistent with the logic of actual history (history as told by Brenner, Wood, et al.) that was momentarily submerged with the advent of masterlessness. In other words, the play relies on Prospero's ruling agency to undo a historical contradiction (masterlessness) but then negates that agency in order to recapture the history that masterlessness had subsequently precluded, to represent the continuation of capitalism divested of any ruling coordination or planning. In semiotic terms, following from Fredric Jameson's appropriation of Propp and Greimas, Prospero serves as an actant or donor, a mediator or catalyst bridging two "semes," a feudal labor form and its uncoerced but still exploitative successor form.[73]

But this in itself seems to beg the question of how, if at all, the play deals with the question of masterlessness; that is, Prospero's obsession with mastery doesn't necessarily entail an obsession against masterlessness or the repression thereof. We can understand the curious *nonrepresentation* of masterlessness in the play through a discussion of Prospero's compulsion to repeat the events that led up to his exile. Of the series of repetitions in Prospero's play—the restaging of the storm, the planned conspiracies, Prospero's comments to Alonso on the loss of his daughter—Hulme writes, "Prospero stages a fantasized version of the original conspiracy with the difference that, this time, he will defeat it. . . . His pastoral romance is a dream of wish-fulfillment, a fantasy of dreams come true."[74] Hulme refers to Erik Erikson's account of repetition, in which an individual "constructs a model of his past experiences which will allow him to 'play at' doing something that was in reality done to him."[75] While it is commonsensical enough to assume that Prospero's compulsion to repeat is attached to a desire for revenge and wish fulfillment, Hulme for the most part elides the importance of repression in the repetition-compulsion. For Freud the compulsion to repeat is the manifestation of the power of the unconscious repressed. Repetition expresses a partial return of the repressed, in which the subject repeats distortions of events rather than directly reencountering them.

If we believe that repetition stems from repression, how can we reconcile Prospero's repetition of the events of his exile with his tendency to explain and reexplain those very events at opportune moments throughout the play? If the aim of repetition is to prevent the emergence of past displeasure that would accompany the return of the repressed, why would Prospero repeat and restage events if those events are so patently *unrepressed,* if they are such a manifest part of his conscious explanatory power and identity? Narrative repetition (Prospero's narration of past events to Miranda, Ariel, and Alonso) would perhaps obviate the functional importance of repetitive action. The reasons motivating Prospero's compulsion to repeat should therefore be latent throughout the text, and we can only understand the root causes of Prospero's neurotic symptoms if we look beyond the manifest level of the events in the subplot or the play itself.

Given the disjuncture between on the one hand the all-pervading threat of masterlessness in early modern England, and on the other hand the play's near-miraculous displacement of servitude built upon personal relations to an allegory of servitude structured around the phenomenology of the commodity, we can suggest that what Prospero mostly represses is masterlessness itself and its contradictory influence on historical development. *The Tempest* rewrites undisturbed history by imagining history without masterlessness, or it allows masterlessness to emerge only momentarily, only insofar as masterlessness can effectively transmute into post-feudal labor forms. The play achieves this end by offering discrete moments of *transformation* without offering an extended space of *transition,* and in the process it omits the entire historical record of "subversive" masterlessness and the constraining poor law countermeasures. In order to fuse the two ends of the transitional period, the play offers history with an excluded middle.

The argument I have been making above runs counter to Paul Brown's claim that the play relies on masterlessness as an archetype for subversion. Brown argues, in a paradigmatic new historicist essay, that the official culture represented in the play relies on the subversive power of masterlessness to reinvent or bolster its own sense of mastery over disrupting forces. *The Tempest* aims to produce masterless subversion in order to (re)confirm courtly authority, but this "orientalist" project partially fails because it inadvertently reveals internal contradictions and "produces the possibility of resistance."[76]

One problem here is that Brown never offers a precise definition of the masterlessness he claims to have found in the play. He makes reference to Stephano and Trinculo's "masterless aping of the aristocrats" during which they steal clothes off a line, an action that "draws attention to their bestiality."[77] Later he notes that Ireland and the island are "peopled with a strange admixture of the savage and masterless other, those who are fully controlling and malcontentedly lapsed civil subjects."[78] For Brown, masterlessness includes within its wide horizon the Irish, malcontentedness, and bestiality; in other words, anything that hegemony or orthodoxy deems alien, subversive, criminal, and so on. This catch-all definition divorces masterlessness from the specificity of the connections among vagrancy, poverty, and labor. As a term describing subversion generally, Brown's use of "masterlessness" is reasonable, but if we define the masterless man as the landless vagabond who for various reasons does not labor and is subject to restrictions on movement and severe poor law penalties, we will not find that figure allegorized in *The Tempest* (although we will in *Timon of Athens, King Lear,* and *The Winter's Tale*). On the contrary, we will find an intensification of nonmasterlessness as a counterpoint to historical reality.

I should perhaps note the larger strategy underlying Brown's argument, and the point at which my argument differs not only from his, but also from new historicist arguments generally. Brown implicitly argues that a kind of abortive contract exists among history, colonialism, and *The Tempest,* in which the text sets out to rescue history from its internal contradictions with the goal of legitimizing ruling class power. He shows how the text fails to deliver on that promise and instead points up "problems which it works to efface or overcome."[79] Accordingly, since *The Tempest* ultimately cannot "harmonise disjunction" and "transcend irreconcilable differences," it thus exposes a moment of "historical crisis." But we have seen in the earlier discussion of masterlessness and the poor laws that historical events and reigning ideologies point up their own arbitrariness and noncausal sequencing of events. The history of masterlessness shows its own contradictions with or without *The Tempest* revealing those contradictions. *The Tempest* is history after the fact (to invert a coinage of Myra Jehlen's),[80] or history *against* the fact, history as an alternative or corrective to the discordant poor law history with which it is engaged. The important point is that Prospero's magic is not enlisted in the service of any ruling power passing itself off as eternal, nor is his power even antagonistic to vagabondage and the threat of "courtly disorder." Rather, Prospero and the entire play is antagonistic to the *effect* the intersection of a number of discourses—masterlessness, the new science, Puritanism, poor law legislation—has had on the course of historical development. That effect is simply the slowing down of the development of capitalism. History has already revealed the danger of direct confrontation or containment of masterlessness. As I have already suggested, Prospero's task is to repress the consequences of that confrontation, to reimagine a history of which masterlessness was never a part.

The argument I have been making, that *The Tempest* represses the inadvertent consequences of ruling class confinement of masterlessness in order to re-instate the already begun development of capitalism (without in itself acting on the behalf of any particular cultural or political dominant) implies that *The Tempest* is curiously nonideological in assisting the advance of capitalism; this need not sound contradictory if we assume that the rise of capitalism itself was not the product of any rational human propensity toward progress, but rather that it forced itself upon England (producers and owners alike) following the decline of medieval serfdom. In this sense, *The Tempest* works for capitalism and for no class in particular, or it works against masterlessness (and the ruling class interference thereof) for history in general.[81] Masterlessness becomes a mutation and a threat to the development of English society only after it is contained by those who had mistaken it for a threat in the first place.[82]

I have not fully explained *why The Tempest* sets out to reconstruct potential historical immanence (to use a structural modification of Lucien Goldmann's belief in the stirring of "potential class consciousness" by the artistic work),[83] or why an early modern text would elevate a depersonalized historical consciousness above (on the level of intention but not effect) the forces of rational human agency. A provisional answer would be that, while we do not need to fully endorse Robert Nisbet's or J. B. Bury's one-sided view that the early modern period could not sustain a belief in uncylical, nondegenerative progress, the period could not easily reconcile an enthusiasm for social development with its antidevelopmental ideological commitments, including classical exemplarity, common law immemorialism, golden-age sentimentalization, the still-prevalent fetishization of *Fortuna,* and versions of irrationalism in its partial retention of magical and supernatural ritual forms.[84] Certain early modern texts like *The Tempest* perhaps function to omit or self-consciously negate these constraining ideological commitments. As such, the developmental logic they imagine follows from a more primary-order imagining: that once stripped away of widely held belief systems as schematized above, history would resume a steady, unimpeded march forward. This is the sense in which I have described *The Tempest*'s overall project as nonideological: its progressive vision seems to be more of a discovery than a prescription, one constructed negatively and without a partisan objective, in a sense the inadvertent consequence of the text's negation of its own historical horizons.

I have discussed in this paper the impact of two historical class struggles on textual representations of early modern economic development. The first, foundational struggle, one I have assumed in advance, occurs between a feudal peasantry and a surplus-extracting landowning class, out of which is produced the structure of agrarian capitalist relations and a newly dispossessed masterless underclass. The second struggle occurs between that masterless underclass and Tudor orthodoxy, out of which arose the historic Elizabethan poor laws. The Virginia texts show the effects of the second struggle, the consequences of a wildly unresolved poverty problem and anxiety over masterlessness after it is exported to the New

World. *The Tempest,* on the other hand, tries to represent the effects of the first class struggle, that effect being simply nascent capitalism *prior* to the impact of the second struggle, and even in the absence of the conditions of masterlessness that were an unforeseen consequence of that first struggle.

Thus, if the Virginia texts represents masterlessness without capitalism, *The Tempest* represents capitalism without masterlessness. *The Tempest* is a curious oddity: a relatively autonomous literary artifact that allegorically figures as a mode of production. The Virginia texts and colonial venture, by contrast, seem to primarily represent economic relations, but we have seen that colonial relations are partially determined by deep cultural anxieties about vagabondage. In a sense, we have ended up with an economic understanding of a literary text (*The Tempest*) but a literary understanding of a group of arguably economic texts (Smith's writings). Finally, if struggles between power and subversion have at all factored into my argument, they do not describe relations between dominant interests and potentially subversive others, as new historicism would have it. Literary texts like *The Tempest* can record or allegorically undermine the *effects* of prior class struggles, the in-betweeness of determinative conflicts or ruling interests, without having to record those actual struggles.

Notes

1. See Myra Jehlen's "History Before the Fact; or, Captain John Smith's Unfinished Symphony," *Critical Inquiry* 19, 4 (Chicago: University of Chicago Press, 1993); 677–92.

2. See, for example, Peter Hulme, *Colonial Encounters: Europe and the Native Caribbean, 1492–1797* (London: Routledge, 1986); Peter Hulme and Francis Barker, "Nymphs and reapers heavily vanish: the discursive con-text of *The Tempest,*" in *Alternative Shakespeares,* ed. John Drakakis (London: Routledge, 1985), 191–205.

3. Some of the recent influential arguments that either make cursory reference or omit entirely questions of economic relations in their discussion of *The Tempest* include Hulme, *Colonial Encounters;* Hulme and Barker, "Nymphs and reapers heavenly vanish"; Thomas Cartelli, "Prospero in Africa: *The Tempest* as Colonialist Text and Pretext," in *Shakespeare Reproduced: The Text in History and Ideology,* ed. Jean E. Howard and Marion F. O'Connor (New York: Methuen, 1987), 99–115; Alden T. Vaughan, "Shakespeare's Indian: The Americanization of Caliban," *Shakespeare Quarterly,* 1988 Summer, 39:2, 137–53; Ronald Takaki, "*The Tempest* in the Wilderness: The Racialization of Savagery," *The Journal of American History (December 1992);* 892–911.

4. In addition to Myra Jehlen's essay mentioned above, some recent essays on Smith's writings and the discourse of colonialism include: Hulme's *Colonial En-*

counters; and David Read's "Colonialism and Coherence: The Case of Captain John Smith's *Generall Historie of Virginia, Modern Philology* May 1994, 91:4, 428–48.

5. One notable example is Paul Browne's essay " 'This thing of darkness I acknowledge mine': *The Tempest* and the Discourse of Colonialism," in *Political Shakespeare: New Essays in Cultural Materialism,* ed. Jonathan Dollimore and Alan Sinfield, Ithaca, NY, Cornell Univ. Press, 1985, 59. See also the brief discussion of vagabondage in Stephen Greenblatt's *Shakespearean Negotiations: The Circulation of Social Energy in Renaissance England* (Berkeley: University of California Press, 1988), 47–56.

6. The rise of masterlessness also complicates an already counterintuitive post-structural understanding of historical process without a subject. Outside the parameters of any discursive understanding of what would constitute a Renaissance subject, but yet also deeply connected with the vicissitudes of history, the masterless man is in one sense the perfect metaphor for antihumanist history; yet on the other hand he is also a very real, very oppressed historical presence during the early modern period. He is, paradoxically, the *embodiment* of history without a subject.

7. I borrow these terms from Mary Louis Pratt's *Imperial Eyes: Travel Writing and Transculturation* (London: Routledge, 1992).

8. Pratt uses the term "contact zone" "to invoke the spatial and temporal copresence of subjects previously separated by geographic and historical disjunctures, and whose trajectories now intersect." See *Imperial Eyes,* 7.

9. Important revisionist accounts of the transition from feudalism to capitalism include: Ellen Meiksins Wood, *The Pristine Culture of Capitalism* (London: Verso, 1992); Colin Mooers, *The Making of Bourgeois Europe* (London: Verso, 1991); and Robert Brenner, "The Origins of Capitalist Development: a Critique of Neo-Smithian Marxism," in *New Left Review* 104 (1977), 25–92.

10. See Richard Halpern, *The Poetics of Primitive Accumulation* (Ithaca: Cornell University Press, 1991), chapter 2.

11. William Harrison, *A Description of England,* ed. George Eden (London: Dover Publications, Inc. New York, 1994), 185.

12. The classic account of enclosures and the decline in villeinage is R. H. Tawney's *The Agrarian Problem in the Sixteenth Century* (New York: Harper and Row, 1967).

13. Cited in Margaret James, *Social Problems and Policy During the Puritan Revolution 1640–1660* (New York: Barnes and Noble, 1966), 281.

14. Marx was inclined toward this view, although his opinions on vagabondage seemed to have changed throughout his writings. In *The German Ideology* Marx writes, "These vagabonds, who were so numerous that, for instance, Henry VII of England had 72,000 of them hanged, were only prevailed upon to work with the greatest difficulty and through the most extreme necessity. The rapid rise of manufactures, particularly in England, absorbed them gradually." Karl Marx, *The German Ideology,* ed. C. J. Arthur (New York: International Publishers, 1993), 74. It is difficult to tell in this passage whether Marx believes vagabonds were reluctant to work, or whether Tudor culture was reluctant (or able) to employ them. In *Precapitalist Economic Formations,* Marx writes of the newly dispossessed peasants: "such a mass would be reduced either to the sale of its labour power or to beggary, vagabondage or robbery as its only source of income. History records the fact that it first tried beggary, vagabondage and crime, but was herded off this road on to the narrow path which led to the labour market by means of gallows, pillory and whip." Karl Marx, *Pre-capitalist Economic Formations,* ed. E. J. Hobsbawm (New

York: International, 1989), 111. Marx seems to be invoking history or an immanent, materialist dialectic as an agent here, rather than idleness of the vagabonds themselves. In *Capital* Marx writes of the new proletariat: "these men, suddenly dragged from their wonted mode of life, could not as suddenly adapt themselves to the discipline of their new condition. They were turned en masse into beggars, robbers, vagabonds, partly from inclination, in most cases from stress of circumstances." Karl Marx, *Capital,* vol. 1, ed. Frederick Engels (New York: International, 1967), 686. Marx offers here a compromise: on the one hand, the feudal peasantry was not immediately convertible into a wage-laboring proletariat; on the other hand, "stress of circumstances" (unemployment?) created the conditions of vagabondage.

15. C. Lis and H. Soly, *Poverty and Capitalism in Pre-Industrial Europe* (Atlantic Highlands, N.J.: Humanities Press, 1979), 48.

16. A. L. Beier, *Masterless Men: The Vagrancy Problem in England, 1560–1640* (London: Methuen & Lo, 1987), 16.

17. Steve Rappaport, *Worlds Within Worlds: Structures of Life in Sixteenth-Century London,* (Cambridge: Cambridge University Press, 1989), 120.

18. Ian Archer, *The Pursuit of Stability* (Cambridge: Cambridge University Press, 1991), 13–14.

19. Ibid., 210.

20. The revisionist economic history suggests that W. K. Jordan's classic description of vagrancy was dogmatic, to say the least. Jordan writes, "There is no doubt whatever that vagabondage was widespread, that it was organized, and that it imposed on rural village communities burdens and dangers with which they could not cope. The evidence is abundantly clear that this class was feared by all elements in the society and that the incredibly harsh penalties against it were to a large degree justified." See W. K. Jordan, *Philanthropy in England: 1480–1660* (London: Allen and Unwin Ltd.), 78.

21. See D. M. Pallister, "Tawney's Century: Brave New World or Malthusian Trap?" *Economic History Review,* 2nd series, 35 (1982). Pallister is referenced in A. L. Beier's article "Poverty and Progress in Early Modern England," in *The First Modern Society: Essays in English History in Honour of Lawrence Stone* (Cambridge: Cambridge University Press, 1989), 201–40.

22. Robert Brenner, "The Origins of Capitalist Development," 77.

23. Michel Foucault, *Madness and Civilization* (New York: Vintage Books, 1965), 49.

24. Beier, *Masterless Men,* 6.

25. Derek Hirst, *Authority and Conflict* (Cambridge: Harvard University Press, 1986), 51.

26. David Underdown, *Revel, Riot and Rebellion* (Oxford: Oxford University Press, 1985), 37.

27. C. B. Macpherson, *The Political Theory of Possessive Individualism* (Oxford: Oxford University Press, 1962), 147.

28. Thomas Hobbes, *Leviathan,* ed. C. B. Macpherson (London: Penguin, 1968), 285.

29. Ibid., 266.

30. Thomas Carew, *Coelum Britannicum,* in *The Poems of Thomas Carew,* ed. Rhodes Dunlap (Oxford: Clarendon Press, 1949), 163.

31. See Karl Polanyi, *The Great Transformation: The Political and Economic Origins of Our Time* (Boston: Beacon Press, 1944).

32. See Sir Henry Nicholls, *A History of the English Poor Law* (New York: G. P. Putnam's Sons, 1898), 1:183.

33. *Stuart Royal Proclamations,* ed. James F. Larkin (Oxford: Clarendon Press, 1973), 1:361.
34. William Shakespeare, *Coriolanus* (Oxford: Oxford University Press, ed. R. B. Parker, 1994), 1.1.80–81.
35. Cited in James, *Social Problems and Policy,* 287.
36. Nicholls, *A History of the English Poor Law,* 159.
37. Gilles Deleuze and Felix Guattari, *A Thousand Plateaus,* trans. Brian Massumi (Minneapolis: University of Minnesota Press, 1987), 385.
38. Adam Smith, *An Inquiry into the Nature and Causes of the Wealth of Nations,* ed. Edwin Cannan (Chicago: University of Chicago Press, 1976), 157.
39. Thomas Malthus, *An Essay on the Principle of Population,* ed. Anthony Flew (London: Penguin Books), 101.
40. Paul Mantoux, *The Industrial Revolution in the Eighteenth Century* (New York: Harper and Row, 1962), 433.
41. Polanyi, *The Great Transformation,* 88.
42. Karl de Schweinitz, *England's Road to Social Security* (Philadelphia: University of Pennsylvania Press, 1943), 42.
43. Henry Robinson, *The Office of Addresses and Encounters* (1650), *Short-Title Catalogue.*
44. See Brenner, "The Origins of Capitalist Development," 25–92.
45. Ibid., 78.
46. Wood, *The Pristine Culture of Capitalism,* 10.
47. This is Halpern's argument in *The Poetics of Primitive Accumulation,* 13: "My project in this book is to locate those regions within English Renaissance culture where the elements of a specifically capitalist culture began to emerge in nascent or anticipatory forms from within the context of a late feudal society. Their emergence in advance of capital itself is made possible by the relative autonomy of culture."
48. *Stuart Royal Proclamations,* 53.
49. Edmund S. Morgan, *American Slavery, American Freedom: The Ordeal of Colonial Virginia* (New York: Norton, 1975), 17.
50. *Nova Britannia,* in *Tracts,* ed. Peter Force (Gloucester, Mass.: Peter Smith, 1963), vol. 1, part 6, 19.
51. *Tracts,* vol. 3, part 13, 4.
52. Captain John Smith, *Description of New England,* in *The Complete Works of Captain John Smith,* 3 vols., ed. Philip Barbour (Chapel Hill: University of North Carolina Press, 1986), 1:338.
53. Ibid., 138.
54. William Strachey, *A True Repertory of the Wreck and Redemption of Sir Thomas Gates, Knight in A Voyage to Virginia in 1609,* ed. Louis B. Wright (Charlottesville: The University of Virginia Press, 1964), 68–69.
55. Colonel Norwood, *A Voyage to Virginia,* in *Tracts,* vol. 3, part 10, 15.
56. Captain John Smith, *The Proceedings of the English Colonie in Virginia* (1612), in Barbour, Vol. I.
57. Captain John Smith, *The Generall Historie of Virginia* (1623) in Barbour, vol. 2.
58. James Lang, *Conquest and Commerce: Spain and England in the Americas* (New York: Academic Press, 1975), 115.
59. David Bertelson, *The Lazy South* (New York: Oxford University Press, 1967), 29.
60. See Jack P. Greene, *Pursuits of Happiness* (Chapel Hill: University of North Carolina Press, 1988), 25.

61. Wesley Craven, *The Dissolution of the Virginia Company: The Failure of a Colonial Experiment* (Gloucester, Mass.: Peter Smith, 1964), 35.
62. Ibid., 38.
63. Captain John Smith, *A Map of Virginia,* in Barbour, vol. 1, 148.
64. Captain John Smith, *New England's Trials* (1622), in *Captain John Smith: A Select Edition,* ed. Karen Ordahl Kupperman (Chapel Hill: University of North Carolina Press, 1988), 197.
65. See Craven, *The Dissolution of the Virginia Company,* chapter 2.
66. All citations from *The Tempest* taken from the Signet edition, ed. Robert Langbaum (New York: Signet, 1964).
67. See Michael Postan, *The Medieval Economy and Society* (London: Pelican, 1975), 82. Feudal exploitation traditionally aimed to restrict peasant movement across the land, particularly during the High Middle Ages, when rents in kind were commuted to money rents. Faced with increasingly coercive feudal tenures, discontented serfs attempted to flee manorial life in search of independence in the expanding towns. The earliest "masterless" movement was thus the well-known flight of the serfs.
68. Erik Olin Wright, *Classes* (London: Verso, 1985), 78.
69. Cited in Edward Said, *Culture and Imperialism* (New York: Random House), 1993.
70. See William Shakespeare, *The Tempest,* ed. Frank Kermode (London: Routledge, 1988), note 172, act 2, sc. 2.
71. See Walter Cohen, *Drama of a Nation* (Ithaca: Cornell University Press, 1985), 401.
72. See Hulme and Barker, "Nymphs and reapers heavily vanish," 203.
73. See Fredric Jameson, *The Political Unconscious* (Ithaca: Cornell University Press, 1981), chapter 2.
74. Hulme, *Colonial Encounters,* 122.
75. Ibid., 296, n. 65.
76. Paul Brown, "'This thing of darkness I acknowledge mine': *The Tempest* and the Discourse of Colonialism," in *Political Shakespeare,* 59.
77. Ibid., 55.
78. Ibid., 57.
79. Ibid., 49.
80. See Jehlen, "History Before the Fact," 677–92.
81. When Walter Cohen suggests that Prospero shares with Hamlet "his contact with the audience, his humanism, and perhaps even his bourgeois traits," or that the utopianism of the play hints "at the antithesis of capitalism and the abolition of class society, at the formation of a post-bourgeois world," the assumption is that the play focalizes a series of class antagonisms, much the way Brown suggests the play tests the bearings of a dominant ideology. But I have suggested that the play is belated, in the sense that the play works through and offers a reversal of the unintended effects of prior class antagonisms and social conduct. See Cohen, *Drama of A Nation,* 401–2.
82. In a recent essay Slavoj Zizek describes the transformation of the precapitalist master-servant relationship (in which the determination "being-a-king" is naturalized, and relations between a king and subject are founded upon fetishistic misrecognition) to the capitalist commodity fetish which is built upon relations between things: "it is as if the retreat of the Master in capitalism was only a displacement: as if the de-fetishization in the 'relations between men' was paid for by the emergence of fetishism in the relations between things—by the commodity fetish" (See Slavoj Zizek, *The Sublime Object of Ideology* (London: Verso, 1989),

25–26. For Zizek, one fetish immediately succeeds another, the interpersonal relations of feudal fetishism are repressed, and the persistence of domination and servitude emerges under capitalism as a "symptom which subverts the ideological appearance of equality, freedom and so on" (Zizek, 26). What Zizek fails to consider is the long transitional period between the two forms of fetishism, and the wrenching apart by masterlessness of the otherwise continuous but displaced fetishistic relations of mastery and servitude. The commodity fetish is not the displacement or repressed symptom of the fetishization of feudal relations between men: it is the historical displacement of the masterless man, the symbol of the defetishization of those relations. What Zizek describes is not early modern reality but history as imagined by *The Tempest:* a simple displacement between two forms of relations of mastery without a defetishized masterless intermission.

83. Lucien Goldmann, *Cultural Creation in Modern Society,* trans. by Bart Grahl (St. Louis, Mo.: Telos Press, 1976), 76–78.

84. See Robert Nisbet's *History of the Idea of Progress* (New York: Basic Books, 1980), and J. B. Bury's *The Idea of Progress: An Inquiry into Its Origin and Growth* (New York: Macmillan, 1932). For a more balanced assessment of Renaissance views on progress see Hans Baron, "Querelle of Ancients and Moderns," in *Renaissance Essays,* ed. Paul O. Kristeller and Philip P. Wiener (New York: Harper and Row, 1968).

SYMPOSIUM
Material Culture

Material Culture: Introduction

Peter Stallybrass

"Material culture": the concept is a commonplace in anthropology. Yet its present attraction for literary historians is surely because it retains for them an air of perversity. It sounds like an oxymoron. However much literature departments have changed over the last decades, they emerged out of two very different concepts of "culture": national culture; culture as the "best" artistic production of the past and present (Shakespeare, Beethoven, Picasso). These latter concepts of "culture" seem to rise above—even to be in opposition to—the "merely" material. "Materials" like paper and ink and binding used to be incidental to "Shakespeare," for instance. True, they were minutely and illuminatingly examined by bibliographers at the beginning of the twentieth century, but primarily so that they could find the traces of Shakespeare himself behind the materials that both hide and deform him.

The process of divorcing a supramaterial "culture" from its "mere" material supports begins in the Renaissance. Alberti, for instance, advocated that artists should forego the use of gold leaf in their paintings so as to emphasize their skill rather than the value of the materials they were using. Cultural value here begins to emerge in opposition to economic value (although, paradoxically, the cheapness of the pigments might be more than compensated for economically by the added value of the artist's genius). The attempt to elevate cultural objects above material or economic value finds a curious analogy in the changing meanings of the English words "priceless" and "valueless." Prior to the fifteenth century, "price" (from the Latin *pretium*) meant not only "price, value, wages," but also "reward" and "honor, praise." But "pris"/"preis" split during the fifteenth and the sixteenth centuries into three differentiated words: "price," "praise," "prize." Increasingly, "praise" and "prize" were distinguished from mere "price." Praise is above price; it is "priceless"—a word the *OED* first records in Shakespeare's work.

Here we confront a paradox. For something to be "priceless," it must be worth more than its financial value. "Valueless" has the same semantic form as "priceless": to be without value, to be without price. But whereas the "priceless" is raised above economic valuation, the "valueless" sinks below it. "Valueless" is also first recorded in Shakespeare in the last decade of the sixteenth century, where its sense, in opposition to "priceless," is "destitute of value, having no value" ("You Haue beguil'd me with a counterfeit / Resembling Maiesty, which being touch'd and tride, / Proues valuelesse," *King John* [3.1.101]). The "culture" of literary departments will emerge as the culture of a price that has no price, opposed to an economic value that (from the perspective of the "priceless") has no true value. This priceless culture is elevated to a transcendental heaven; the materials of culture will be relegated to a valueless hell.

"Priceless" culture (with its prices nonetheless attached) is related to the Renaissance separation of the liberal from the mechanical arts, which Rayna Kalas illuminatingly explores below. By suppressing the mechanical craft of the application of gold leaf, Alberti attempts to produce the painter as a liberal artist rather than a manual craftsman. But the separation of the liberal from the mechanical was not accomplished at a single theoretical blow. In Venice, for instance, it was only in 1682 that painters established a separate *Collegio dei Pittori;* prior to that, they were coworkers in the guild of *depentori* along with "gilders, textile designers and embroiderers, leatherworkers, makers of playing cards, mask makers, sign painters, and illuminators."[1]

It was also in the seventeenth century that the author was increasingly distinguished from the scribe or writer. Value, from the perspective of authorship, could no longer be found in the material surface of parchment or vellum, in the expensive pigments of illuminations, or in the added marginalia that made a book usable; it lay behind the materials in the imagined workings of the author's mind. The book itself was waste matter. One learned now to read *through* a book, no longer conscious of its material surface. What is the later "page turner" if not an invisible book that turns its own pages? The book becomes the immaterial support above which the mind of the reader communes with the mind of the author. And the author becomes a transcendental value who has no place in the material world. In this new cultural regime, Byron will insist that he never be painted with books or pens around him because inspiration is immaterial.

Material Culture: Introduction

This symposium attempts to accomplish three purposes: to reemphasize the materiality of Renaissance textual culture ("Material Texts"); to set material texts in the broader context of the production and circulation of material goods ("Clothes, Properties, Textiles"); to reexamine some of the Renaissance concepts that produced or resisted the oxymoronic feel of "material culture."

The first section, "Material Texts," explores some of the material forms that shaped Renaissance culture. Paper was, as several of the discussions below note, expensive, and it was by no means the only, or even the main, textual material. Walls, furniture, plates, cutlery, rings, jewels, buildings themselves (as the "ES"s on top of Hardwick Hall remind us) could be and were written on. Juliet Fleming shows both here and elsewhere that our own sense of "legitimate" and "illegitimate" writing surfaces (walls being usually of the latter kind) was familiar to neither Montaigne nor Luther, who advocated and practiced what we would now call the "illegitimate" form of "graffiti." Moreover, there was a particular value to the erasable qualities of wall writing (that could be whitewashed) and slates (that could be wiped clean), even if whitewashing, as Fleming shows, preserved what was covered over, or writing on slates, as Jessie Owens notes, might be preserved to check later versions on paper.

Owens's piece powerfully reminds us, too, of the resistance of so much Renaissance culture to our notions of the "artistic whole," of which the composer's score later emerged as a privileged example. The Renaissance music that Owens examines was written in separate parts, often on more than one slate. The parts are only added together in performance. The musical piece is thus piecemeal, requiring the work of singers to piece it together. (In the next section, Lena Orlin will note how the process can also work in the other direction: what we would think of as Richard Belassis's single house is disassembled by his will into separate rooms and even parts of rooms that can be bequeathed to different people.) The other papers in this section equally emphasize the material transformations of Renaissance texts. Books are marked up by readers to make them more usable, or, given the scarcity of paper, the margins of a book are used for a recipe or to document family history. "The" text is transformed as it is annotated and emended; as it is printed in large or small format; as it is sold at the sign of Adam and Eve or at the sign of Ben Jonson's head; as it is bound and unbound with other texts; as "*guyana*" is turned into "Vienna." Visually, as Stephen Orgel shows, a depiction of Athena becomes a woodcut of Alexander; Claudius becomes Julius Caesar's supposed wife, Cossutia, although the woodcut is used again for Claudius himself. No doubt this is partly the material principle of thrift that, as it can transform funeral bakemeats into a wedding banquet, can transform male into female. As Ana Armygram observes, Willem van der Passe does not make a new engraving of the royal family when James dies and Charles becomes king. He simply adds a crown to Charles's head. And since Charles has married, Henrietta Maria is added, a table carpet being transformed into her dress. New children are added in later states of the engraving, but, as others have died, the survivors are redistributed among the previous figures. The previous figures now assume new names and even new genders: Louisa Hollandina becomes Lodovicus.

The second section, "Clothes, Properties, Textiles," moves further away from the narrow definition of "culture" (literature, music, painting, etc.) to the way in which social meaning is materialized in other objects. As Evans-Pritchard wrote in 1940, "material culture may be regarded as part of social relations, for material objects are the chains along which social relations run."[2] The eccentric William Reynolds, a letter of whom Katherine Duncan-Jones edits, maps his relation to England and to his religion through the clothes he wears. Even in his second suit of tawny, signifying "the darkness of my country England," he is still protected from the wiles of foreign Catholicism by his sea-colored stockings, as the English Channel separates him from damnation. If Reynolds is eccentric, Foxe is normative, and Laurie Shannon shows how even those Protestants who want to eschew the gross materiality that they believe characterizes Catholicism can only define their resistance through the clothes they wear or refuse to wear. Similarly, Will Fisher notes how much can depend upon a handkerchief, which may condense the body of its owner as a memorial object, even as it circulates and is potentially "contaminated" by its recipient.

The pieces by Maureen Qulligan and Susan Cerasano are concerned with contradictory aspects of circulation: the gift as "inalienable possession," in the case of Elizabeth's prayer book, given to Katherine Parr so as to knit together a Protestant royal family; the gifts and loans that businessmen and actors like Henslowe and Alleyn, as well as aristocrats, made to the monarchy so as to assert their exogamous absorption into an extended royal "family." Lena Orlin's piece brings together these two contradictory aspects of the circulation of things. In the absence of a son and heir, Richard Bellasis both remembers his family through the dismemberment of his house and dislocates the very meaning of "family" by leaving major legacies to, and sharing financial secrets with, his servant, Margrett Lambert. Linda Levy Peck returns us to the concerns with which this section began: the connection between material and national "culture." William Reynolds used his clothes to map out the relations between England and its spiritual and temporal enemies. But the very textiles of fashionable clothing materialized the dependence of England upon foreign trade. For England to produce an elite that was both "homespun" and fashionable, it needed to develop a native silk trade. Ironically, the development of this trade depended upon the immigration of skilled French workers. The "national" body thus remained dependent upon the "culture" of immigrants.

The final section, "Languages of Materiality," examines some of the Renaissance terms that resist or facilitate the emergent opposition between "culture" and "materiality." Margreta de Grazia argues that in trying to link words referentially to things, the Royal Society erased what was so central to the whole rhetorical tradition: namely, that words were themselves particular kinds of things (oral, aural, visual). "Things" came to include "things to be discussed" only through a weak metaphor; "real" matter became "physical" matter, not "subject matter." In other words, the very notion of materiality is radically reduced. Gary Tomlinson, from a very different perspective, also argues that sound, along with spirit, becomes transcendental only in a post-Cartesian epistemology that erases the imprint of image upon imagination and phantasm upon phantasy that Ficino insisted upon. "Significant" sound comes less and less to include the "noise" of thunder, hummings, buzzings, and twangings—the signifying sounds that Caliban hears. Rayna Kalas looks at how the powerful sense of "framing" as an act of making and structuring (God "frames" the universe) is only belatedly reduced to the "frame" as external/extraneous material. In thinking of the "frame" of language, Lyly points both to the abstract principles that order it and to the material substance that rhetoric deploys. In the Renaissance, the liberal art of rhetoric cannot be detached from the mechanical art of crafting.

Jonathan Goldberg's *Writing Matter* has been a formative influence upon the study of the materiality of culture. But he reminds us here that the materials of culture are not locked into place once and for all. If objects have provenances and histories, these are made and remade as objects circulate, and as they acquire and lose meaning. This is nowhere more striking than in the props of the professional theaters, which appear and disappear, are given radically different meanings, or are forgotten. To emphasize the materiality of culture is not to give it a fixed grounding.

Indeed, the renewed attention to materiality needs to reexplore the very terms by which we separate the material from the immaterial, subject from object, person from thing. It is this latter relation or opposition between person and thing that Ian Smith and Jim Kearney explore. Smith shows how the concept of "barbarism" (a Greek concept referring to the inarticulate mutterings of "aliens") was mapped onto the unrelated concept of "Barbary" (a geographical location in North Africa). It was in this context that slavery violently rearticulated the speaking subject ("person") in relation to the mute commodity ("thing," "slave"). To be a thing in this new ontology was to be bought and sold. But the violence of this hierarchy depends, Kearney suggests, upon a newly emergent notion of the "thing" as different from, and in opposition to, the "person." Aristocratic possessions (lands, armor, heraldry, and so on) are certainly things but they have the power to transform and elevate a person into a more powerful social being. Similarly, in Catholicism, a saint's bones or a venerated statue are things, but they are anything but mute or "mere" things. If it becomes a form of disempowerment to categorize a person as a thing, the concept of the thing must itself first be disempowered. By contrast, Marcel Mauss suggests that in precapitalist societies, things are often "personified beings that talk and take part in the contract." Such things are not "indifferent"; they have "a name, a personality, a past."[3]

Kearney argues that English Protestants employed two very different concepts to destroy the power of the Catholic "thing": the "idol," which registered the demonic power of the object, even as it invalidated the object; the "trinket," which treated the object as a trivial innovation, which could be discarded with ease. The concepts of the idol and the trinket were later absorbed and displaced by the concept of the "fetish," a concept that, Bill Petz has argued, developed on the boundaries of capitalism.[4] The fetish came to point to demonized forms of materialization.

The fetish as posited by the new language of fetishism was simultaneously all-powerful (an external organ of the body) and trivial (since the emergent regime of the "individual" would deny that the body could have any such external organs). In this emergent regime, dependency upon "mere things" invalidated the individual's supposed autonomy. The theory of the fetish produced by back-formation the subject of modernity: the individual who, detached from the supposed fetishism of things, attempts to rise above material forms. As the subject was dematerialized, so was the "culture" that was supposedly the subject's finest expression. If the individual was imagined as prior to the cultural markings of labor, land, clothes, so the text, for instance, appeared to detach itself from the material supports of papyrus, parchment, rag paper, wood pulp, ink, typeface. The printed book would finally become the material embodiment of the immateriality of culture. Shakespeare is priceless; the material forms that inscribe him are, from this cultural perspective, valueless.

The final section of this symposium thus attempts to show how the oxymoronic quality of "material culture" emerged, while reemphasizing the ways in which Renaissance forms of making continued to register the materials of words, of sounds, of images.

Notes

1. David Rosand, *Painting in Cinquecento Venice: Titian, Veronese, Tintoretto* (New Haven: Yale University Press, 1982), 11–14.
2. E. E. Evans-Pritchard, *The Nuer* (Oxford: Clarendon Press, 1940), 89.
3. Marcel Mauss, *The Gift: Forms and Functions of Exchange in Archaic Societies,* trans. Ian Cunnison (New York: Norton, 1967), 22, 55.
4. See William Pietz, "The Problem of the Fetish, I," *Res* 9 (1985): 5–17; "The Problem of the Fetish, II," *Res* 13 (1987): 23–45; "The Problem of the Fetish, IIIa," *Res* 16 (1988): 105–23. Kearney suggests that the distinction between idolatry and fetishism is less clear-cut than Pietz argues.

I
Material Texts

Whitewash and the Scene of Writing

Juliet Fleming

> What is a text, and what must the psyche be if it can be represented by a text?
> —Jacques Derrida

In "A Note Upon the 'Mystic Writing Pad'" (1924) Freud remarked that, as *aides memoires,* writing surfaces are always limited in one of two ways. A writing surface that retains indelible marks (such as ink on paper) is "soon exhausted," and will, moreover, store information long beyond the point at which it might be required again. A writing surface that may be wiped clean, such as chalk on slate, has neither problem, since it "retains its receptive capacity for an unlimited time," while the notes upon it "can be destroyed as soon as they cease to interest me, without any need for throwing away the writing-surface itself." Its disadvantage, however, is that it cannot preserve a permanent trace: "If I want to put some fresh notes on the slate, I must first wipe out the ones which cover it."[1] As Derrida redacts Freud's argument: "A sheet of paper preserves indefinitely but is quickly saturated. A slate, whose virginity may always be reconstituted by erasing the imprints on it, does not conserve its traces. All the classical writing surfaces offer only one of the two advantages and always present the complementary difficulty."[2]

The purpose of Freud's meditation is to discover a writing apparatus he can use to model the relations between perceptions, consciousness, and memory in the *Pcpt.-Cs.* system.[3] He found what he was looking for in the "mystic writing pad," a child's writing tablet from which notes could be magically removed by the simple expedient of lifting a sheet of semitransparent paper from (and thus ending its contact with) a block of dark wax beneath it. Of particular interest to Freud is the fact that the writing that disappears easily and permanently from the paper "is retained on the wax slab itself and is still legible in suitable light." Combining the two incommensurable functions of receptivity and retention "by dividing them between two separate but interrelated component parts or systems," the mystic pad thus models the relation between perception and memory as these function within "the inexplicable phenomenon of consciousness."

Derrida has much to say about Freud's argument, and the way in which it works toward, but stops short of, "what might be called a new *psychoanalytic graphology*"—an analysis of the ways in which writing instruments hypercathect (call attention to), and so produce, *as objects of consciousness,* particular perceptions and memories.[4] Keeping in play the status of the mystic pad as psychical model or exemplum—that is, as something that is itself an aid to those processes of consciousness it would describe—Derrida's essay finds in *writing* (in a *techne* or verbal trace that is at once a machine and an idea) that interface between the neurological and the psychical that both founds and escapes the project of psychoanalysis.

It is my concern to argue for the existence and consequence of a writing apparatus that fulfilled the functions of receptivity and retention long before Freud found them combined in the mystic pad. I have proposed elsewhere that a significant quantity of Elizabethan writing was written not with ink on paper, but with charcoal, chalk, and other marking stones on whitewashed walls: a proposition that invites us to imagine, as characteristic of sixteenth-century English culture, a representational economy within which writing and drawing were not fully distinguished, and within which the production and circulation of texts was markedly less constrained by market and author-functions than it has since become.[5] But as a writing practice that is tied to neither the spatial decorums (including those of defacement and erasure), nor to the mnemic capacities, of the paper page, wall-writing may be further considered, both as an instrument of knowledge, and as the object of an historically inflected "psychoanalytic graphology."

Early modern wall-writing was, in both theory and in practice, ephemeral. Then as now it was written in marking media that were *in effect* (though not necessarily) less permanent than ink on paper; it made its appearance on surfaces from which it could be either wiped clean or overwritten; and its functions were in large part occasional. Documenting the occurrence of fifteenth- and sixteenth-century church graffiti, one local historian has recently suggested that part of the church wall was sometimes set aside to serve as the parish notice board, from which erasures could be made by water, scraping, or successive coats of limewash.[6] I imagine that similar procedures were followed with domestic walls, the occasional or regular deletion of whose contents allowed them to retain both their receptive capacities, and their ability to display information in such a way as to catch the eye, and activate attention or memory.

It is true, of course, that writing, even in ink, can be "erased" ("scraped out") from paper (for that matter, any writing that was not finally erasable would not be writing at all). As Jonathan Goldberg has demonstrated, early modern writing instruments included a knife that might be used to remove ink from vellum or paper by scratching.[7] But such erasures are neither readily effected nor infinitely repeatable: they are possible, but not practical. The cutting or burning of pages aside, marks left by ink on paper are more easily erased by being crossed or blotted out. These techniques are not fully distinct from one another; and each may be said to preserve what it deletes. For while, as Calvin's translator Thomas Norton puts it, the blot seeks "utterly . . . to deface" writing "out of mennes remembrance," to systematically blot the name of the pope from the pages of a book is to produce a blot *as* that name.[8] Again, to cross or "expunge" ("prick out") writing is to mark it, more or less memorably, for erasure: it is, in effect, to *write it again*. Clearly, then, paper does preserve writing that has been effaced from it. But neither blotting nor crossing can restore a clean writing surface, each, indeed, operates at the expense of its further receptivity. It seems that we are back at the problem outlined by Freud as the Achilles' heel of the mnemic apparatus: writing can be permanently retained, or regularly erased—but not on the same surface.

But the whitewashed wall is a writing apparatus not entirely governed by the tension between those two functions. Whitewash is a composition of lime and water: in the sixteenth century its cognates include "whiting," "white-lime," "size" (lime and water to which glue has been added), and plaster or "pargett" (a mixture of water and gypsum used to cover walls and also, when mixed thickly, for work in relief). To "wash" a wall in the period is to clean it not by removing what was on it, but by covering it with a fresh surface—whitewash. Limewash does not restore the original writing surface, but creates a new one in the act of obliterating the old. And, crucially, beneath the new surface and whatever contents it may acquire, the original writing remains—which is why the whitewashed or pargetted wall is an emblem for hypocrisy.

That such writing can be recovered is demonstrated by the work of today's conservators, who can now retrieve pre- and post-Reformation paintings from the whitewash, plaster, and paneling that obscures them. I and others have already argued that early modern wall-writing was a practice that materially informed not only memory systems based on imagined interior "places," but also the mental topography of the intellectual system that manifested itself in the keeping of commonplace books.[9] But we can add to this that its practitioners had at their disposal a writing apparatus that gave specific material form, not only to such artificial memory aids, but also to that marking (for attention) of memories and perceptions that is consciousness itself. At least at the level of analogy at which Freud deployed the mystic pad, this would be the case whether or not the early modern English knew or intended that their graphic and pictorial work would one day reemerge from the surfaces behind which it was hidden. In fact, however, the retentive, protective, and reversible properties of plaster and whitewash (which today's conservators may use to recover, and so protect, fragile wall-paintings) were fully understood in Reformation England, where they could be used by priests, parishioners, and householders to preserve, rather than to deface, prohibited images.[10]

Eamon Duffy has already suggested that "the reversability of whitewashing was an established fact," both among iconoclasts, and among those who resisted them: in the early 1580s "some well wishers" of the older tradition had rubbed at the whitewash covering a painting of the Passion of Christ in Chichester Cathedral so that it was now "almost as bright as ever it was"; while the curate of Ashford in Kent was accused of having improperly destroyed a wooden font cover painted with popish images by causing it to be merely "slubbered over with a white wash that in an hour may be undone," so that it stood "like a Dianae's shrine for a future hope and daily comfort of old popish beldames and yong perking papists."[11] The whitewashed font cover suggests to its detractors the presence of a representational logic that could reattach the affect of an image to the marks left behind by its destruction. But the "daily comfort" of the old extends to become "the future hope" of the young: the old are comforted not only by the continued, though hidden, presence of the object of their veneration; but also by the thought that current preservation may lead to future restoration.

Whitewash is not the only method of reversible erasure designed to meet the exigencies of the English Reformation: prohibited passages in books were lightly pasted over, or scored through so lightly that their original contents were unaffected; altar stones and holy-water stoups were buried; saint's images were deprived of their identifying marks and asserted to be portraits of local benefactors.

But as a surface from which data could be both erased and retrieved, the whitewashed wall subtends and improves on these methods, while its scope extends beyond moments of state or even self-censorship. To the extent that a wall can reproduce ("from within") writing that has once been erased from it, it provides a better model for consciousness than Freud's mystic pad.[12] Beyond this, however, it constitutes a writing apparatus the relation of which to consciousness is more than analogical in early modern England. For the scriptural precedents that underpinned the practice of wall-writing there—Deuteronomy 6:4–9 and 11:18–21; Deuteronomy 27:2–3; and Daniel 5:5–30—all understand the wall as the site of a hypercathexis (a writing) that draws attention to things already known.[13] (It is for this reason that both Luther and Calvin recommended householders write "God's law" on their walls, even while that law can be properly held only in the heart.)[14] The whitewashed wall "represents" consciousness (to use a term that vexed Freud) as the reactivation of memories and perceptions that have been stored within writing: it may be considered as the mystic but practical apparatus through which early modern consciousness appears to itself in an historically and psychically specific form.

Notes

I am grateful to Muriel Carrick and Tobit Curteis for providing me with technical information about the recovery of early modern wall-painting; and to Margaret Aston, Christopher Cannon, Brian Cummings, and James Simpson for allowing me to discuss the claims of this paper with them.

1. *The Standard Edition of the Complete Psychological Works of Sigmund Freud* (London: Hogarth Press), 19:227.

2. Jacques Derrida, *Writing and Difference,* trans. Alan Bass (Chicago: University of Chicago Press, 1978), 222

3. In Freud's work, the perception-consciousness system (*Pcpt.-Cs.*) receives information both from the outside world (in the form of sensations that impress themselves on the pleasure-unpleasure scale) and from internal sources (in the forms of memories revived from the unconscious).

4. Jacques Derrida, *Writing and Difference,* trans. Alan Bass (Chicago: University of Chicago Press, 1978), 231

5. Juliet Fleming, "Graffiti, Grammatology, and the Age of Shakespeare," *Criticism* (winter 1996), 1–30. Reprinted (enlarged) in *Everyday Life in Early Modern England,* eds. Patricia Fumerton and Simon Hunt (Philadelphia: University of Pennsylvania Press, 1998) 315–51.

6. Doris Jones-Baker, "English Medieval Graffiti and the Local Historian," *The Local Historian* 23:1 (February 1993): 3–19.

7. Jonathan Goldberg, *Writing Matter: From the Hands of the European Renaissance* (Stanford, Calif.: Stanford University Press, 1990), 63–80.

8. Cf. 34 and 35 Henry VIII: "Persons, having anie bibles . . . whith anie suche annotacions or preamble shall . . . cutte out or blotte the same, in such wise, as they cannot be preceived nor red."

9. See Fleming, "Graffiti, Grammatology, and the Age of Shakespeare," 10 (*Criticism*) 329 (ed. Fumerton.)

10. Early modern wall-paintings that survive today do so *because,* rather than in spite of, the fact that they were covered. Paintings are destroyed by the application of covering materials whose chemical properties are close to their own. But lime wash will remain distinct from paint that has been prepared with glue (distemper) or with oil, while plaster can be mixed to a density that will not penetrate the painted surface. In *The Guild Chapel Wall Paintings at Stratford-upon-Avon* (New York: AMS Press, 1988) Clifford Davidson describes the less-than-vigorous iconoclasm with which, in 1563, Shakespeare's father, John, undertook to "remove" the chapel wall-paintings: those in the chancel were partitioned off behind a temporary wall or screen; those in the nave were whitewashed (and rediscovered in 1804 when the whitewash was taken off); while the Dance of Death on the north wall of the nave was allowed to remain uncovered at least until 1576 (when it was seen by John Stow), and subsequently covered by paneling.

11. Eamon Duffy, *The Stripping of the Altars: Traditional Religion in England c. 1400–1580* (New Haven: Yale University Press, 1992), 583; quoting from Albert Peel, ed., *The Second Part of a Register* (Cambridge: 1915), 1:239, 2:191.

12. Cf. Freud: "It is true, too, that once the writing has been erased, the mystic pad cannot 'reproduce' it from within: it would be a mystic pad indeed if, like our memory, it could accomplish that" (230).

12. Deuteronomy (6:4–9 and 11:18–21) instructs the Israelites to "write . . . uppon the postes of thy house and uppon thy gates" the injunction to remember to "love the Lorde thy God with all thyne hearte"; Deuteronomy 27:2–3 contains Moses's command to the people to set up an altar of stones, "and plasiter them with plaister: and . . . write upon them all the words of this law"; Daniel 5:5–30 recounts the appearance of the feckless Belshazzar's doom "upon the plaister of the wall."

14. See Calvin, *Sermons on Deuteronomy,* trans. Arthur Golding (London: Henry Middleton, 1583), 473: "Let us have Gods lawe written, let us have the sayings of it painted on our walles as in tables, and let us have things to put us in minde of it early and late." Luther was also pleased to imagine "the whole Bible to be painted on houses, on the outside and the inside, so that all can see it": see Ernest B. Gilman, *Iconoclasm and Poetry in the English Reformation: Down went Dagon* (Chicago: University of Chicago Press, 1986), 35.

Erasable Tablets as Tools for Musical Composition

JESSIE ANN OWENS

IN AN ERA WHEN PAPER was very expensive, reusable surfaces of various kinds—slate, plaster, varnished parchment—served a variety of functions, in schools, in business, even for recording gambling debts. Their use for music is a recent discovery.[1]

Tablets have been unearthed in archeological excavations all over Europe, mostly associated with cathedral schools and presumably used for pedagogical purposes.[2] They consist of slates, mostly small fragments, with musical staves and some with musical notation.

The ephemeral nature of these tablets means that most of them have not survived. As a result, information about their size, makeup, and use must be drawn from documents, books about music, and visual representations. We know that they were used by composers as well as by students,[3] and that they came in different sizes and shapes, to suit the various functions they filled. For example, the composer, music theorist, and choir director Giovanni Spataro, who lived in Bologna, asked his friend, the music theorist Giovanni del Lago, who lived in Venice (which would become a great commercial center for music books), to buy two different tablets (his word was *cartella* or *tabula de abaco,* abacus tablet) in 1529 and 1533. One was to measure roughly 6 by 9 inches (half the size of standard letter-size paper), the other roughly 12.5 inches on all sides.[4] Although none of the composers' tablets has survived, the evidence suggests that composers used them for all stages of composition, from the initial rough sketches to drafts of extended portions to fair copies neat enough to be performed from.

With so few surviving exemplars, visual evidence concerning tablets becomes extremely valuable, even though it requires cautious interpretation. Thus, the representation of two large musical

Maarten de Vos's "Mary's Song of Praise" ("Madonna with Angel Musicians"), engraved by Jan Sadeler the Elder. Reproduced by permission of The Metropolitan Museum of Art, Harris Brisband Dick Fund, 1953. [53.601.16(163)]

tablets in Martin de Vos's "Mary's Song of Praise" ("Madonna with Angel Musicians"), engraved by Jan Sadeler the Elder is a notable find.[5] This engraving, known to music historians since the beginning of the nineteenth century, is the only surviving source of a five-voice Magnificat by the Flemish composer, Cornelis Verdonck (1563–1625).[6]

Max Seiffert recognized that "Mary's Song of Praise" was one of a series of Flemish engravings of biblical scenes that contain complete musical compositions.[7] These folio prints, the earliest of which dates from 1584, are significant in part as early instances of the use of engraving rather than moveable type for polyphonic music. Seiffert used them primarily as a source of information about performance practice, particularly the use of instruments in sacred music. But they also provide valuable information about the kinds of objects employed for transmitting music—books, scrolls, sheets, tablets—and about the kinds of musical formats or layouts current at the time.[8]

Two of the engravings contain representations of musical tablets. Maarten de Vos/Jan Sadeler's "Adoration of the Shepherds" has three tablets, for three of the nine voices of Pevernage's *Gloria in excelsis* (each tablet has the music for one part); the six other parts are written on long, thin strips of paper.[9]

"Mary's Song of Praise" has two tablets, similar in size to those in "Adoration of the Shepherds," that between them contain all the music for Verdonck's five-voice Magnificat. The music, written in the standard musical notation of the time,[10] is notated in separate parts in "choirbook" format.[11] Although the tablets are two separate objects, in most respects they look just like the opening of a book, except that the two "leaves" are separated by the image of the Virgin. The tablet on the left has music for the highest voice (superius or soprano) on the top half, the tenor on the bottom; the one on the right has the altus on top, the bass on the bottom. A fifth voice (quinta pars) is not notated (written down in musical notation), but would have been derived from/sung from the tenor; this voice is in "canon," and the singer is given the "canon" or rule for deriving it from a notated part. At the *signum congruentiae* or sign of congruence, the canonic voice enters "in diapason," that is, an octave higher.

The two tablets each have a hole at the top, which suggests that they could be hung from a wall; the hole can also be used for attaching a slate pencil with a string. They seem to be at least two feet tall by one foot wide, extending from the waist to above the head of the angel on the left. The size, of course, may have been determined in this case by the need to fit a particular musical composition into the space delimited by the tablets, or by artistic considerations. The tablets act as a counterbalance between the central image of the Virgin and two candelabras on either side, thus creating an inverted arch that runs—left to right—from candle to tablet to halo to tablet to candle, in parallel to the concentric semicircles formed by the clouds and the sun.[12]

Sadeler's engraving of de Vos's painting enacts its subject. Mary, accompanied by four angel musicians, "performs" her song: "My soul doth magnify the Lord, And my spirit hath rejoiced in God my Saviour. For he hath regarded the low estate of his handmaiden: for, behold, from henceforth, all generations shall call me blessed" (Luke 1:46–48, King James translation).[13] The angel musicians, all of whom are instrumentalists (playing the viola da gamba, cornetto, and flute), read from the tablets, with their backs to the viewer. Mary kneels in front of the tablets, as though she had no need to read the music.[14]

In this engraving the tablets contain the final, complete version of the Magnificat, written out neatly and with sufficient detail to be used in performance, in other words, the "fair copy." It may seem counterintuitive that a temporary surface like slate would be used for the final stage of writing out a composition, but there is evidence to support this function. Giovanni Spataro, in order to defend himself from Pietro Aaron's accusations about errors in a composition Spataro had sent him in a letter, looked back over his tablet (*cartella*) and found the mistake, which he had not noticed because he had simply copied the music from the tablet and sent it to Aaron without testing it first in performance. Perhaps this engraving suggests what the writing on Spataro's tablet could have looked like.[15]

There are clear limits to the weight that this engraving will bear as evidence of compositional practice. Still, the tablets it contains conform in many respects to other evidence—composers' autograph manuscripts, documents, etc.—and may allow us a glimpse of one of the implements a composer had to work with. This visual representation is one more instance of music being written on an object associated with composition in choirbook format, that is, in separate parts, and not vertically aligned in score. It serves as a reminder that the core format in which we normally look at Renaissance music is a modern translation that distorts important elements of the musical language.

Notes

1. A detailed account can be found in my *Composers at Work: The Craft of Musical Composition 1450–1600* (Oxford, 1997), ch. 5. My thanks to Peter Stallybrass, colleague extraordinaire and fellow fellow at the Folger Shakespeare Library in 1998–99, for helping me understand some of the implications of my research for the study of material culture. I am grateful to the National Endowment for the Humanities and Brandeis University for funding, and to the Folger Shakespeare Library and Institute for creating such a nourishing environment for research and collaboration.

2. In addition to those listed in *Composers at Work*, I recently came across slates with musical notation preserved in the newly renovated archeological museum of the Cathedral in Reims, housed in the Palais du Tau.

3. The names include: Cipriano de Rore, Sigmund Hemmel, Adam Gumpelzhaimer, Giovanni Spataro, and Francesco Corteccia. In addition, Arnaldo Morelli has recently found evidence of a "composing stone" among Ghiselin Danckert's possessions.

4. Bonnie J. Blackburn collected and interpreted the important evidence concerning tablets contained in the massive volume of letters and theoretical writings, Vatican City, Biblioteca apostolica vaticana, Vat. lat. 5318 (and related sources). See the edition, *A Correspondence of Renaissance Musicians,* ed. Bonnie J. Blackburn, Edward E. Lowinsky, and Clement A. Miller (Oxford, 1991), and especially ch. 5, "The Art of Composition." I also discuss this evidence in *Composers at Work,* ch. 5.

5. On Jan Sandeler's engraving, see *Hollstein's Dutch and Flemish Etchings, Engravings and Woodcuts ca. 1450–1700* (Amsterdam, 1980), vol. 21, no. 304. On Maarten de Vos's design, see, in the same series, vol. 44, no. 726 (Amsterdam, 1996), with a listing of exemplars of the engraving as well as copies; and the facsimile in vol. 45 (Amsterdam, 1995) which should probably be listed as "726/II" rather than "726/I." My thanks to Larry Silver and Armin Zweite for assistance.

6. It was first described by Ernst Ludwig Gerber in his *Neues Historisch-Biographisches Lexikon der Tonkünstler* (1812–14, facsimile edition, 1966), vol. 4, col. 437. On Verdonck, see the entry by R. B. Lenaerts in *The New Grove Dictionary of Music and Musicians,* ed. Stanley Sadie (London, 1980).

7. Max Seiffert, "Bildzeugnisse des 16. Jahrhunderts," *Archiv für Musikwissenschaft* 1 (1918), 49–67. Seiffert published a modern edition of the Magnificat and nine other compositions preserved in engravings in his *Niederländische Bildmotetten aus dem 16. Jahrhundert,* Organum, erste Reihe, 19–20 (Leipzig, 1929); the edition includes a facsimile of each engraving. An excellent facsimile (with helpful commentary) of "Mary's Song of Praise" is found in Robert Wangermee, *Flemish Music and Society in the Fifteenth and Sixteenth Centuries* (Brussels, 1968), 106, from the copy in Paris, BN, Print collection, Cc 20 fol., no. 118.

8. Including separate parts on single sheets, separate parts in partbooks, separate parts stacked one after another on a single page, choirbook, etc. The absence of score, a format that became standard after 1600, is noteworthy. On formats, see *Composers at Work,* 34–48.

9. Facsimile, *Composers at Work,* 86.

10. White mensural notation. "White" because most of the notes are white, though the smaller values are black. "Mensural" because in theory the individual notes take their value not from an absolute relationship defined by different shapes as is the case today but from context; in practice the notation is virtually

identical to ours. Except, of course, that there are no barlines, a feature associated with score format.

11. "Choirbook" format refers to the layout found in large volumes propped on lecterns, used by choirs for musical performance. A choir of ten to fifteen singers, arranged by height with the short singers in front, can read from a single choirbook. For a representation of a choirbook, see "Encomium musices" with the six-voice *Nata et grata* by Pevernage; for a choir singing from a choirbook, see Philippe Galle (after Johannes Stradanus), "Harmony, Music, and Measure," in facsimile in Wangermee, figures 30 and 36.

12. It would of course be interesting to know what de Vos's original painting looks like. According to Seiffert, the painting is in Cannstatt, near Wurttemburg. It is not listed by Armin Zweite, *Marten de Vos als Maler: ein Beitrag zur Geschichte der Antwerpener Malerei in der zweiten Halfte des 16. Jahrhunderts* (Berlin, 1980).

13. Many Magnificat settings are *alternatim,* providing polyphony for alternate verses (odd or even), and alternating with chant. This setting is unusual in setting all three of the opening three verses in polyphony and omitting the rest.

14. Seiffert is so determined to derive evidence about performance practice from this print that his edition of specifies *Zinke* (modern substitute, oboe), *Altflöte* (English horn), and two violas da gamba, and leaving the fifth (canonic) voice, Mary's part, to be sung. The edition notates the tenor part an octave too high.

15. See note 4.

Used Books

William H. Sherman

On every desk in the Cambridge University Library there is a sign warning readers that MARKING BOOKS IS FORBIDDEN. A glance at the volumes that have come down to us from the past, however, will suggest that writing in books (even library books) has not always been forbidden. At times marking books has been encouraged and even taught as a way of making them more personal and more useful for present and future needs: in the early modern period, writing in books played a central role not only in pedagogical theory and practice but in the management of information in a wide range of social and professional settings—from making legal cases and giving sermons to planting crops and keeping household accounts.

In *Marks in Books, Illustrated and Explained*—a catalogue of the kinds of marks left in books as they move through the hands of printers, censors, sellers, and readers—Roger Stoddard explains that "When we handle books sensitively, observing them closely so as to learn as much as we can from them, we discover a thousand little mysteries.... In and around, beneath and across them we may find traces... that could teach us a lot if we could make them out."[1] In recent years, scholars of the early modern period have been especially concerned with making out, and making sense of, the most visible traces of interaction between books and readers: "marginalia," or notes written in the margins and other blank spaces of texts.

There is now a growing body of scholarship on marginalia in early modern books;[2] but the rise in the stock of marginalia has been most clearly marked in the attitudes of collectors. A particularly telling example is that of James R. Page, a businessman and trustee of the Huntington Library, who assembled a remarkable collection of rare prayer books. One of his volumes, a 1586 *Book of Common Prayer,* has the catalog entry from the sale at which Page bought it pasted onto its front flyleaf, where it is described as "rather soiled by use." The soil, as it turns out, is a thorough set of contemporary marginal annotations; and, for Page, they added to rather than detracted from the value of the volume.³ Another savvy collector of early annotated books was the book dealer Bernard M. Rosenthal, who recently told this story when his collection was acquired by the Beinecke Library at Yale:

> early printed books stained with occasional fingerprints of a fifteenth-century pressman, or filled with scribblings by a contemporary student, or still hanging by a thread in their original limp vellum covers battered by constant use, did not have the same appeal to the bibliophiles as the flawless, virginal copy—even now one sometimes finds dealers' and auction catalogues in which the presence of manuscript annotations is mentioned in the same breath with the defects, e.g. "some waterstains, occasional manuscript notes, else fine." . . . Yet I [became] completely captivated, not to say, obsessed, by the idea of some day . . . producing a catalogue of books in which the presence of annotations would not merely be mentioned, but in which the manuscript portions would be ranked on the same level as the printed text and dignified by proper descriptions which would call attention to and emphasize their importance as primary sources for a great variety of topics.⁴

The topic for which the evidence of marginalia has been most important is the study of reading practices. Marginalia do, indeed, allow us to recover an extraordinary range of textual responses and strategies, both individual and collective. But it has become increasingly clear that marginalia do not simply provide evidence of reading: the evidence they provide is rarely simple, raising as many questions about reading as they answer and, moreover, often testifying to uses that take us well beyond what is normally understood as "reading."

Readers' marks provide some of the most interesting links between books as texts and books as artifacts of material culture: they provide evidence of a wide variety of reading and writing practices as well as pointing to the disparate ways in which books could be used. Instead of seeing the study of marginalia as a branch of the history of reading, it might therefore be more appropriate to emphasize their use in exploring the interface between the "text itself" (the words on the page) and the broader social and material matrix of what has been referred to as "the extended work"⁵ (the contexts and collaborative efforts involved in creating meaning), or—more simply—in exploring the place of books in the lives of readers. After all, a significant proportion of the notes in books have more to do with the life of the reader than the content of the text: the blank spaces of Renaissance books were used not just to digest or comment on the printed text but to document family histories and financial obligations, to record prayers, poems, and recipes (both culinary and medical), and sometimes just to scribble in. This is not only true of almanacs, which were the conventional repositories of this sort of information: I have found notes on the weather in books on rhetoric, instructions for poisoning birds in works of literature, and bawdy sketches in Bibles. An important factor was, of course, the price of paper: it was extremely expensive in the early modern period, which meant that, unlike today, printed paper was a more affordable place for miscellaneous notes than blank paper. It is also possible that these spaces would have provided a more "archivable" place in which to store important memoranda.[6]

G. Thomas Tanselle has suggested that "All artifacts can be read, once their language is learned, for what they have to tell about their own production and about the place they held in the lives of those who previously possessed them. All are evidences of human activity, manifestations of the physical basis of culture. Books, since they are manufactured objects, can be read in this way."[7] But we must be wary of making either the artifacts or the reading sound more straightforward than they are. Once we have learned the language of marginalia we have only begun to solve their mysteries.

Notes

1. Roger Stoddard, *Marks in Books, Illustrated and Explained* (Cambridge, Mass.: Houghton Library, Harvard University, 1985).

2. See, for a start, William H. Sherman, *John Dee: The Politics of Reading and Writing in the English Renaissance* (Amherst: University of Massachusetts Press, 1995); Lisa Jardine and Anthony Grafton, " 'Studied for Action': How Gabriel Harvey Read His Livy," *Past and Present* 129 (1990); Lisa Jardine and William Sherman, "Pragmatic Readers: Knowledge Transactions and Scholarly Services in Late Elizabethan England," in Anthony Fletcher and Peter Roberts, eds., *Religion, Culture and Society in Early Modern Britain: Essays in Honour of Patrick Collinson* (Cambridge, Eng.: Cambridge University Press, 1994); Anthony Grafton, "Is the History of Reading a Marginal Enterprise? Guillaume Budé and His Books," *PBSA* 91 (1997); and Kevin Sharpe, *Reading Revolution: The Politics of Reading in Early Modern Europe* (New Haven: Yale University Press, 2000).

3. The James R. Page Collection has not yet been catalogued: I am grateful to Alan Jutzi, at the Huntington Library in San Marino, California, for bringing this volume to my attention and providing access to it.

4. Bernard M. Rosenthal, *The Rosenthal Collection of Printed Books With*

Manuscript Annotations: A catalog of 242 editions mostly before 1600 annotated by contemporary or near-contemporary readers (New Haven: Yale University Press, 1997), 9.

5. Stephen G. Nichols, "On the Sociology of Medieval Manuscript Annotation," in Stephen A. Barney, ed., *Annotation and Its Texts* (Oxford: Oxford University Press, 1991), 48.

6. It was Peter Blayney who first suggested this to me.

7. "Libraries, Museums, Reading," in his *Literature and Artifacts* (Charlottesville: Bibliographical Society of Virginia, 1998), 7.

Size Matters

David Scott Kastan

Whatever else people know about *Acts and Monuments,* they know it is a big book. Its massive physical presence, along with its spectacular woodcuts, carry its message as powerfully, and more memorably, than its carefully crafted narratives of the faithful witnessing to and suffering for Christ's true church. "The sheer size of the *Book of Martyrs* staggers the imagination," writes John King.[1] And in a sense that is the very point; what might be merely cliché is an exact formulation, for the book is clearly designed in some literal sense to stagger the imagination with the accumulated evidence of the persecution and resilience of the faithful.

Certainly the written text matters, but the book's imposing physicality is unquestionably part of its polemical strategy, overwhelming resistance to its historical vision by the sheer magnitude of the demonstration, "a Club able to beate down the Popish Tower of Babell,"[2] as Thomas Mason said in 1615. Even its critics recognized its extraordinary size; Thomas Harding, for example, mocked, in the course of his debates with John Jewel, the "huge donghill of your stinking martyrs."[3] In its fullest Foxean form, the two volumes of the 1570 edition, the *Book of Martyrs* run to approximately two and a half million words printed on somewhat more than 2,300 large folio pages ($14^{1}/_{2}$ by $9^{1}/_{2}$ inches), the most extensive book project undertaken in England in the hand press period. (Indeed, sizable enough that it completely exhausted the available supply of large paper and forced Day to paste together smaller sheets of cheaper writing paper on which he printed the last 150 pages.)[4]

Committed to the presentation and preservation of the records of a heroic past that had been lost to written history, what Foxe calls "precious monuments . . . meet to be recorded [rather than] buried . . . under the darkness of oblivion" (1570, sig. [hand]2v), the book stands in two senses as a *monumental* witness to what Foxe calls "the secret multitude of true believers." It is monumental both in size and in intent, an imposing memorial to the "milde and constant Martyrs of Christ." Foxe's own remarkable comparison of the seven years spent in his revision of the first English version with Solomon's seven-year effort building the Temple in Jerusalem (1570, sig. [hand]2r) marks the book as a much as a material accomplishment as a literary one.

Though there is undeniable evidence of how eagerly the book was in fact read (Nicholas Ferrar, for example, having a chapter read in his household every Sunday evening),[5] there is equally persuasive evidence of how aggressively the book was displayed. In 1571 the Court of Alderman mandated that it be "set up" and "fast chained" in the Orphans' Court and in each of the "City companies that is of ability" to afford it.[6] According to the canons published by John Day in 1571, it was ordered to be placed, along with the "The Hollie Bible in the largest volume, as it was lately printed at London," in either the hall or the great chamber of the house of every "Archbyshop and byshop." Deans were to bestow both books in their cathedrals, and, along with other "dignitaries of the churche," were to set them out in their own houses "in some fitt place."[7] Foxe himself speaks of his desire that Kings and princes, as well as their subjects, "would diligently peruse suche monumentes of martyrs, and lay them alwayes in sight" (1570, sig. *3r); and, indeed, according to William Harrison writing in 1577, "Every office at court had either a Bible or the books of the *Acts and Monuments of the Church of England* or both."[8] Though seemingly there was no order requiring the book to be placed in parish churches (in spite of William Prynne's claim that the book was "enioyned to be kept in euery Church for the people to read in"), clearly many churches did have the book prominently displayed, chained next to the Holy Bible.[9]

Though these volumes of *Acts and Monuments,* when in fact they were set out in public, were certainly available for reading, unquestionably their function was as much iconic as discursive, their substantial presence in places of authority testifying to the triumph of the faithful every bit as compellingly as what was promised by the narratives within. The "Hollie Bible in the largest volume" and the impressive, two folio volumes of Foxe's *Acts and Monuments* stood together in both secular and sacred institutions as powerful confirmation of the triumph of God's Word in Elizabethan England.

Nonetheless, retailing at something around 30s. the book would have been affordable by only a few individuals, and most of its sales therefore must have been institutional. Indeed, if, by 1646, even 25 percent of the more than eight thousand parish churches had a copy, then most of the print runs of the first seven editions would have been taken up by this and other institutional demands. William Turner, Dean of Wells, angrily wrote Foxe about the price of the first English edition of the book.

> Printers generally prefer their books to be big for the sake of the big profit they can make from them, rather than small and easily available to the small and wretched flock of Christ. I wish that your means were ample enough to save you from having to work for miserable, greedy, vainglorious, and ignorant booksellers. . . . Please consider for whose benefit, in particular, your book is written. If you do so, I am sure that you will produce one which better serves the interests of the Church, though it may disgrace the printer; for if it were shorn of what is needless and superfluous, its price would not be more than 10 shillings.[10]

But if Turner, in his letter to Foxe, has ungenerously misjudged Day, he has correctly seen that the large and expensive book did not fully serve the needs of the "small and wretched flock of Christ." In part, of course, the various orders to have it set out in public were efforts to make it available to readers who could not afford to own it, but the book was not easily accessible to the godly. Various abridgments were undertaken, but unquestionably the most extraordinary appeared in 1616. That year John Taylor's redaction, entitled *The Booke of Martyrs,* was published by John Hammon. A 64mo volume in sixteens, its pages measuring $1^{5}/_{8}$ by $1^{1}/_{4}$ inches, the book improbably reduces the *Acts and Monuments* to 238 couplets. The 1616 edition, surviving in a unique copy in the Bodleian, carefully replicates the structure of Foxe's original, similarly dividing the history into two books, with the break also coming at the reign of Henry VIII, each with its own dedication (the dedications in turn to Philip and William Herbert, earls of Pembroke and Montgomery respectively, and better served seven years later as dedicatees, it might be said, with Heminge and Condell's dedication to them of the 1623 Shakespeare folio). Each book is printed on a single sheet, imposed in 16s. Though the printing itself is inelegant, the Bodleian's copy is an ingenious object, the two books bound together in an "S" binding, so each can be read from the beginning of the book by turning it upside down. The 64mo printing of Taylor's *Book of Martyrs* unquestionably was conceived as a curiosity piece, not least because each book seems so clearly to have been designed to fit on a single sheet; and indeed it successfully piqued the curiosity of the public, five editions in 64mo appearing by 1633, and two additional octavo editions in the four subsequent years.

If Taylor's book is remarkable neither for its poetry nor its historiography, it is undeniably remarkable in its physical presence—the very conception outrageous in its complete reversal of the logic of "old Monumentall Foxe," in Taylor's own phrase (*Workes,* sig. EeG[r]). The largest book in the hand-press period is reduced to one of the smallest, in part of course a delicious joke appropriate to one of the inventors of English nonsense verse,[11] but a joke that reinforces the fundamental promise of Christianity for the exaltation of the humble. Though small-format books had become popular in the seventeenth century, and so called "penny godlies" among these, these were almost all octavos of about twenty-four pages, small of course, usually measuring about $5^1/_2$ by $3^1/_2$ inches, but hardly the extraordinary miniature of Taylor's *Book of Martyrs*.[12] Much of Taylor's own work was printed in these popular formats, but only two of his more than 140 publications appeared in 64mo: *The Book of Martyrs* and, in 1614, a book first titled *Verbum Sempiternae* and then corrected that year to *Verbum Sempiternum.*

The *Verbum Sempiternum* is in fact what later would be called a thumb Bible,[13] an abridgement in verse of each biblical book. Taylor's dedication affirms that "with great reverence I have cul'd from thence, / All things that are of greatest consequence. / And though the Volume and the Work be smal, / Yet it contains the sum of All in All." Taylor's short verse summaries are poetically undistinguished but not unintelligent; Paul's Letter to the Romans, for example, is rendered:

> Th' Apostle *Paul* from *Corinth* writes to *Rome,*
> To strength their faith, and tell them Christ is come.
> He shewes how high and low, both Iew and Greeke*
> Are one with God, who faithfully him seeke.
> He tels how sinne in mortal bodies lurkes,
> How we are sau'd by faith, and nor by workes.
> In louing tearmes, the people he doth moue,
> To faith, to Hope, to Charity, and Loue.

Taylor's thumb Bible was incredibly successful, requiring five editions by 1631 (and dignified by Joseph Hall, Bishop of Norwich, carefully copying it into his commonplace book),[14] but also being continuously reprinted with little if any alteration, often without Taylor's name, hundreds of times well into the nineteenth century on both sides of the Atlantic.

Size Matters 153

The two defining books of English Protestantism, the Bible in English and Foxe's *Acts and Monuments,* two books that in their monumental form were often chained together in English churches, have in Taylor's summaries found no less iconic versions, though here, of course, in miniatures that would permit English Protestants to hold both their sustaining texts in the palm of their hand. In both cases the miniaturization is the very point, exactly as the monumentality was the point both of the 1570 Foxe and "the holy Bible of the largest volume" that it was often found next to. These miniatures were, like their larger versions, books to be wondered at every bit as much as books to be read, if not exactly icons, as the large folio volumes were, of Protestant triumphalism, at least serving as fetishes of the faith.

Notes

1. John King, "Fiction and Fact in Foxe's Book of Martyrs," in *John Foxe and the English Reformation,* ed. David Loades (Aldershot: Scolar, 1997), 13.
2. Thomas Mason, *Christs Victorie over Sathans Tyrannie* (London, 1615), sig. A3r.
3. Thomas Harding, *A Confutation of a Booke Intitled an Apologie of the Church of England* (Antwerp, 1565), sig. 14r.
4. Paul S. Durkin, "Foxe's *Acts and Monuments,* 1570, and Single-page Imposition," *The Library* 5, 2 (1947): 159–70.
5. See J. F. Mozley, *John Foxe and His Book* (London: Society for Promoting Christian Knowledge, 1940), 180.
6. W. W. Greg, *A Companion to Arber* (Oxford: Oxford University Press, 1967), 13.
7. *A Booke of Certaine Canons* (London, 1571), sig. A3v–A4r.
8. William Harrison, *The Description of England,* ed. Georges Edelen (1968; New York: Dover, 1994), 230.
9. It is William Prynne, in his *Canterburies Doome* (London, 1646), who seems to be the source of the idea that the book was "enioyned to be kept in every Church for the people to read in" (88). See Leslie M. Oliver, "The Seventh Edition of John Foxe's *Acts and Monuments,*" *Papers of the Bibliographic Society of America* 37 (1943); 245–47.
10. C. L. Oastler, *John Day, the Elizabethan Printer* (Oxford: Oxford Bibliographic Society, 1975), 27.
11. See Noel Malcolm, *The Origins of English Nonsense* (London: HarperCollins, 1997).
12. See Tessa Watt, *Cheap Print and Popular Piety, 1550–1640* (Cambridge: Cambridge University Press, 1991), esp. chap. 8.
13. On thumb Bibles, see Ruth Elizabeth Adomeit, *Three Centuries of Thumb Bibles* (New York and London: Garland Publishing, 1980).
14. Folger Library, MS V.a.339, fos. 24v–29.

Vox Piscis: Dead Men Shall Ryse Agayne

KATHLEEN LYNCH

SMALL BOOKS WERE GENERALLY sold unbound in the early modern period. This might well make them among the cheapest, most portable, and even most easily concealed of printed materials. But without the benefit of binding, small size just as surely increased a book's vulnerability to damage and eventual loss—the artifactual equivalent of death and erasure from communal memory. In the story of *Vox Piscis: or, The Book-Fish,* we have one of the more curious instances of the preservative character of bookbinding assuming a revitalizing and even transformative role in the history of a book.

On Midsummer's Eve in 1626, a fisherman brought a cod to the market in Cambridge. When it was cut in preparation for sale, as was the practice, a tiny book printed in *decimo sexto* was discovered wrapped in canvas, "in the depth of the mawe of the fish"[1]. The book was brought to the vice-chancellor of the university, "who took special notice thereof. . . . Whereupon by Daniel Boys, a Book-binder, the leaves of the Booke were carefully washed and cleansed" (10). The book proved to contain three treatises bound together, and the treatises were determined to be three devotional works by John Frith, an early protestant martyr. In the course of the next year, two London booksellers reprinted the treatises, prefaced by a description of the marvelous (though not miraculous, they were careful to say) preservation of the works in the Book-Fish. Alluding to the religious contestations of their own day, James Boler and Robert Milbourne published *Vox Piscis* to deliver, as they explained, Jonas's words from the belly of the whale.

Three treatises bound together, wrapped in canvas, further encased in the digestive organs of a fish, retrieved in Cambridge, and repackaged for a wider reading audience in London. As unusual a story of materials, methods, and provenance as it is, there is at least this much of the routine about the Book-Fish: the act of binding,

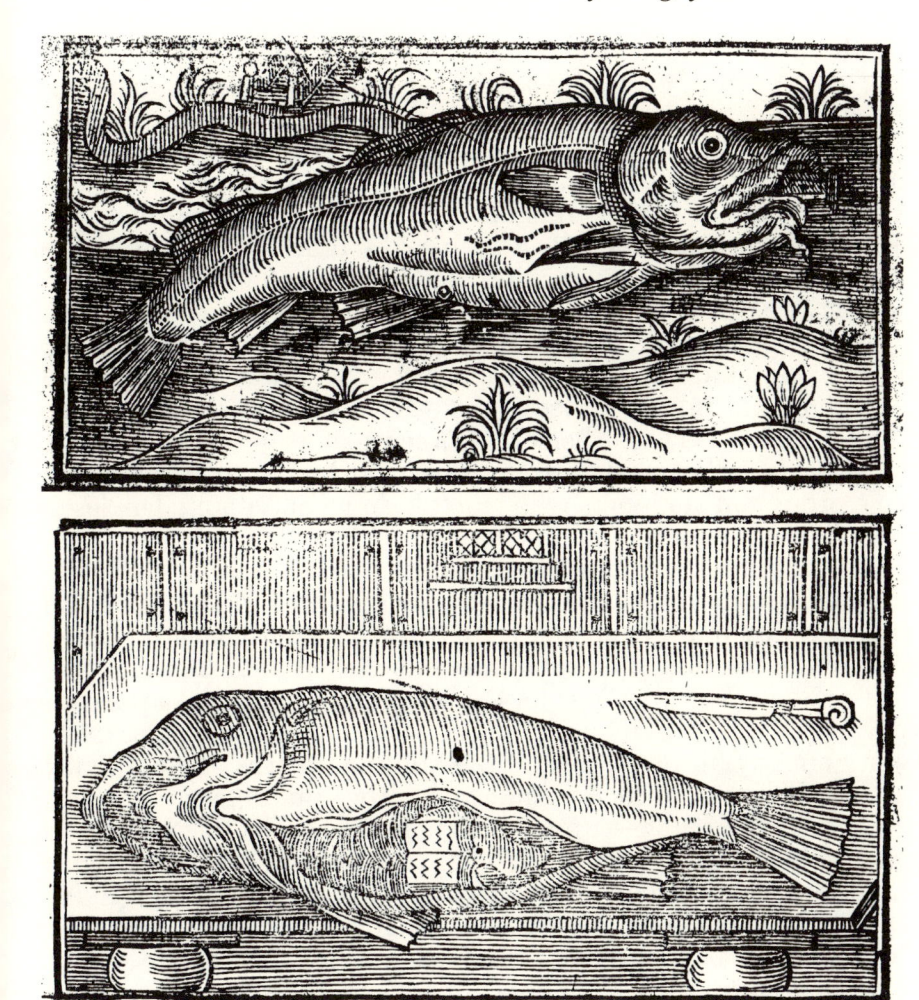

Two views of the Book-Fish in John Frith, *Vox Piscis* (London, 1627). By Permission of the Folger Shakespeare Library.

ostensibly the final act of demarcation and stabilization in the book trade proves to be the most variable. A transactional and liminal moment, binding is as much the first act of reception as the final stage of production.

I leave aside for the moment questions of attribution and identification to posit that in this particular act of reception, the prophecy of the epigraph of one of Frith's works is fulfilled: a dead man rises again.[2] *The Book-Fish* is not Frith's only moment of resurrection. The first publications of the treatises found in the Book-Fish were posthumous. Fifteen years after his death, *A Mirror to Know Thyself* and *A Proper Instruction* were republished in *The Contents of thys boke*, a volume with a "caption title," that is without a title page proper (and so without the details of place, publisher, or year of publication). *The Preparation to the Crosse* was then published as a companion piece (similarly lacking publication information).[3] Three-quarters of a century after that, the prophecy would be fulfilled again with the publication of *Vox Piscis,* the treatises bound in *The Book-Fish.*

To a certain extent, in claiming a transformative role for binding, I am using binding as a synecdoche for the whole printing—and especially reprinting—process. More generally still, the case of the Book-Fish speaks to the book trade's sense of itself as very much in service of God's revealed truth. Boler and Milbourne are respectable protestant stationers who won't indulge in Catholic fancies of miracles and apparitions. But they do believe that the book of nature is intended to be read with care. As a public service, they record the testimony of strange occurrences, thus legitimating and broadcasting the proclaimed truths. They are fully aware of their role in the creation of a community of believers as readers.[4]

The Book-Fish summons for those readers an image of a purportedly simpler time of reformation. And it largely achieves its exhortatory effect with one aspect of the binding process, the particular and final act of collection and assembly—the determination of what to bind together—from which may flow such other choices as what title to impose and what author to credit. In other words, what identity and commemorative power to invest in the object. In the case of *The Book-Fish,* these are commercial decisions, not the acts of individual ordering that reveal the interests of a single reader, but the framing of a large number of readers' experiences by a trade practice.

A closer look at the five parts of *The Book-Fish* makes it clear that the work of association and ascription depends on binding practices. Four separate printing jobs are bound together: *Vox Piscis,* a forty-six page introduction, contains the history described above and is sandwiched or bound between two engravings, one of the uncut and the other of the cut fish; *The Preparation of the Crosse* is a treatise in two books; *A Mirror of Glasse to Know Thyself* is printed together with *A Brief Instruction*; and finally *The Treasure of Knowledge* completes the set of treatises. With the exception of *A Brief Instruction,* each section of the book has its own title page, is separately paginated, and starts with a new signature sequence. No author's name graces any of the title pages.[5]

It is not so much the printing per se, then, that constitutes the act of reclamation, as the gathering together and labeling that summons the reformation martyr John Frith to counsel his English progeny. The appearance of the Book-Fish was a sensational event in Cambridge that summer. In a newsletter to Sir Martin Stuteville, Joseph Mede wrote of the "accident . . . rare, if not strange, whereof I was yesterday morning an eye-witness myself." Samuel Ward also mentioned the event in a letter to Archbishop Ussher in County Armagh, Ireland. Mede examined the contents, and, as Ward wrote, "now it is found to have been made by Richard Tracy, of whome Bale maketh Mention. He is said to flourish then MDL. But, I think the book was made in king Henry the eighth's time, when the six articles were a-foot."[6]

The *STC* agrees with the Tracy attribution of the longest of the treatises, *A Preparation to the Crosse,* giving the title an unnumbered listing as a translation under his name.[7] Similarly, the *STC* challenges the attribution to Frith of *The Brief Instruction* (printed together with *A Mirror* in both the sixteenth and the seventeenth centuries) and *The Treasure of Knowledge* (which Boler and Milbourne seem to have added to the collection as a bonus).

Nevertheless, the claim for Frith held. Indeed, Frith was an eminently resurrectable martyr, having been burned at the stake in the summer of 1533 and memorialized in John Foxe's *Actes and Monuments* in 1563.[8] *Vox Piscis* nostalgically celebrates Frith's English mode of reformation as one untinged by German models. But in his own day, Frith was part of a Cambridge study group that gathered at the White Horse tavern which came to be known as "little Germany." If that moniker didn't have much authority as a description of the motives and influences of the individual members (who included Stephen Gardiner, for instance), it still indicated an underlying parochial fear about reformed thinking. Frith himself would soon come to be more closely associated with Continental influences. Following a brief imprisonment, he joined Tyndale in exile in 1528. Specific titles of his were proscribed in a 1530 royal proclamation against the importation of heretical books from abroad. The next year, he achieved instant fame with *A Disputation of Purgatory* (Antwerp, 1531), his entrance into a polemical dispute among Simon Fish, Thomas More, and John Rastel. Late in his short life, he resisted Henry VIII's attempts to draw him into a scriptural defense of divorce. Neither wholly homegrown nor wholly imported, Frith's beliefs were grounded in the theology of grace, predestination, and the authority of the Bible over the church.[9]

The trace of his engagement with foreign thought is marked in the printed volume. The *decimo sexto* editions found in the fish were English editions. But at least one is a domestic version of an earlier edition published in Antwerp for an English market. Nearly one hundred years later, in another time of heightened sensitivities to the influence of foreign affairs on English politics and religion, the Book-Fish would once again import potentially dangerous intellectual goods to the marketplace in Cambridge. Dedicated as it is to the establishment of boundaries and identities, bookbinding has a stabilizing role in the delivery of those goods. But the work of the binder is easily disassembled, reassembled, and differently attributed. For that reason, while making for greater material permanence, bookbinding may also transform texts through its acts of ordering and disordering.

Notes

1. *Vox Piscis: or, The Book-Fish*. London: James Boler and Robert Milbourne, 1627 (parts three and four dated 1626) (*Short Title Catalogue* number 11395), 8. Additional references to this edition are incorporated into the text. Further references to the catalogue numbers will be abbreviated *STC*.

2. From the title page of *A Boke Made by John Frith,* which contains a treatise written in the Tower of London. It was first published in Antwerp shortly after Frith's death in 1533 (*STC* 11381) with the epigraph in Latin. The epigraph appears in English in the two London editions published in 1548 (*STC* 11383 and *STC* 11384).

3. *STC* 11385.5 and *STC* 11393.5. The Folger has exquisitely rebound unique copies of *STC* 11386 (another edition of 11385.5) and *STC* 11393.5 (with a Folger shelf mark keyed to the original *STC* number, 11392). Both come from Sir Leicester Harmsworth's collection.

4. Alexandra Walsham considers the nuanced political and religious motivations of the revival of these texts in "*Vox Piscis: or, The Book-Fish*; Providence and the Uses of the Reformation Past in Caroline Cambridge," *The English Historical Review* 114 (1999): 574–606.

5. The author is an absent presence (at least at the front of the book) in the sixteenth-century domestic printings, as well. Neither of the two editions of *The contentes of thys boke* (*STC* 11385.5 and *STC* 11386, both in *decimo sexto* format) has a traditional title page. The leaf on which Frith's name might appear is lacking in the unique copy of *STC* 11385.5. It's conceivable, though, that Frith might have been identified at the end of that edition as the author, as he is at the end of *STC* 11386. Only one copy of *The Preparation of the Crosse* (*STC* 11393.5) is extant. It has a faked title page, which nevertheless does not identify Frith as the author.

6. Mede's letter can be found in *The Court and Times of Charles the First,* ed. Thomas Birch (London: Henry Colburn, 1848): 1.114–6. Ward's letter is numbered CXI in *The Whole Works of the Most Reverend James Ussher*, 15.345. I am grateful to Sabrina Baron and Suellen Towers for calling my attention to the respective letters. Dr. Towers has also saved me from numerous bibliographical slips.

7. See Christopher Haigh's *English Reformations* (Oxford: Clarendon Press, 1993), the end of chapter 3, on the inflammatory impact of the reformed last will and testament that Tracy's father William wrote. For the offense, the elder Tracy's body was exhumed and burned.

8. Foxe also edited Frith's works, which were sold bound together with Tyndale and Barnes's (John Day, 1573) (STC 24436).

9. John Guy, *Tudor England* (New York: Oxford University Press, 1988), 119–20. See also Guy's *The Public Career of Thomas More* (New Haven: Yale University Press, 1980), 171–73; Richard Marius, *Thomas More* (New York: Alfred A. Knopf, 1984), 390–91 and 428–30; Christopher Haigh, *English Reformations* (Oxford, Eng.: Clarendon Press, 1993), 56–71.

Ben Jonson's Head

Jeffrey Masten

I'M TRYING TO IMAGINE what it might mean to buy a book "at the *Ben Johnson's* Head in Thredneedle-street" in 1656. I stumble upon this shop sign in reading a list of plays available in print—a list published at the end of *The Old Law,* a play attributed on its title page to Middleton, Rowley, and Massinger. Advertised as "An Exact and perfect CATALOGUE of all the PLAIES that were ever printed; together, with all the Authors names; and what are Comedies, Histories, and Interludes, Masks, Pastorels, Tragedies,"[1] and running to sixteen pages and 622 titles, this list groups plays alphabetically by title and includes a column noting the genre of each play—comedy, tragedy, interlude, masque—by abbreviation (C, T, I, M), and a column that sometimes attributes authorship. "All these Plaies," the catalogue promises, "you may either have at the Signe of the *Adam and Eve,* in Little Britain; or, at the *Ben Johnson's* Head in Thredneedle-street, over against the Exchange."[2] The Jonson's Head was the sign for Robert Pollard's shop from 1655 until at least 1658;[3] a later list, published in 1661 by Francis Kirkman, advertises as one of its locations for the buying and selling of plays "the *John Fletchers Head.*"[4] I want to ask what it means to place a playwright's head on a shop sign—to sell under its sign, or to read it, in an advertisement or in the street. What kind of sign do these head signs represent?

Part of an answer lies in the formatting of the play catalogues themselves. As they emerge in the 1650s, '60s, and '70s, the catalogues seem to me to trace the rising (though still tentative) importance of authorship as a visible category for organizing printed drama. To the extent that they engage authorship (and they do so to different degrees), the catalogues seem not as interested in consistency with even the other available printed attributions as they are in promoting a growing interest in plays associated with recognizable names.[5]

The first extant list, published with *The Careless Sheperdes* in 1656, is organized to facilitate locating plays alphabetically by *title,* with occasional authorial identifications following in italics. There is no separate column for authors.[6] The *Old Law* catalogue likewise lists plays alphabetically by title, with a column for genre, and then a column with more frequent notation of authorship in italics.[7] A 1661 list—Francis Kirkman's initial effort, published in an old interlude—places an author column first ("Names of the Authors"), but continues to arrange/group the plays alphabetically *by title* ("Names of the Playes").[8] In the layout of Kirkman's page, authorship is thus marked more prominently than in the earlier catalogues, but title remains the organizing principle. Kirkman's second list, published with a translation of Corneille's *Nicomede* in 1671, uses the same column arrangement, but in its "Advertisement to the Reader," the publisher bestows great attention on what he calls "the placing of names," which system he presents as an innovation.[9] Kirkman explains that in the 1671 catalogue he has grouped the plays of the most prolific playwrights together at the beginning of each letter in the alphabetical list of titles:

> Although I took care and pains in my last Catalogue to place the Names in some methodical manner, yet I have now proceeded further in a better method, having thus placed them. First, I begin with *Shakespear,* who hath in all written forty eight. Then *Beaumont* and *Fletcher* fifty two, *Johnson* fifty, *Shirley* thirty eight, *Heywood* twenty five, *Middleton* and *Rowley* twenty seven, *Massenger* sixteen, *Chapman* seventeen, *Brome* seventeen, and *D'Avenant* fourteen; so that these ten have written in all, 304. The rest have every one written under ten in number, and therefore I pass them as they were in the old Catalogue.[10]

Kirkman's system is a significant innovation in the emergence of the dramatic author as a category: at the moment of an emergent bibliophilic culture interested in the collection of printed drama,[11] he becomes absorbed in discovering/producing authors who have a discernible, definable corpus—writers whose plays can be grouped. Like the innovation of printing collections of drama in the Jonson, Shakespeare, Beaumont and Fletcher, and (by 1671) Margaret Cavendish folios,[12] this is a new way to imagine, indeed, to materialize, the complete corpus of printed drama that Kirkman, as his advertisement notes, aspires to catalogue: a corpus that is now beginning to be imagined not as a mass of plays with titles one can arrange alphabetically, but rather as a corpus divisible into ten major authors and then all the rest. It's noteworthy both that the collaborative pair begins here to function, in effect, as a single unit *and* that, simultaneously, the pair seems devalued, displaced, from its apparently rightful place in a numerical order within Kirkman's "better method." (Shakespeare's forty-eight plays precede Beaumont and Fletcher's fifty-two; Heywood's twenty-five precede Middleton and Rowley's twenty-seven, etc.) It is also not insignificant, in this context, that women writing plays begin to signify prominently, something Kirkman again highlights, noticing "not only Male, but Female Writers; there being seven of them in all, four whereof in these last hundred [printed]."[13] With the emergence of authorship—that is, of the linkage of these texts *to persons,* rather than to acting companies or particular performance locations, as earlier quarto title pages emphasize—comes the identification of singular authorial traits, authorial difference.

In this context, the Jonson's Head, like the Fletcher's Head, may be a particularly interesting piece of material evidence for rethinking authorship and collaboration culturally (that is, as a *sign,* rather than as a *fact*). To be sure, like so many of the booksellers' signs indicated on title pages of early modern plays and other books—like the playwrights' names that also appear there—the Jonson's Head looks like it could hardly be more factual, more solid as a material artifact: it is an address, a definitive, mapable place, a denotation of location in a culture that had not yet invented street numbers or postal codes.[14] But, as I have been suggesting, I think that it *is* culturally significant that plays should, in 1656, be sold at the sign of a playwright's head. As far as I have been able to learn (and I am grateful to Peter Blayney for his assistance with this), it seems that the idea of a playwright's head as a sign arrives on the scene only *after* the closing of the theaters. There are King's Head signs earlier (for example, 1566, 1606, 1617–40 and thereafter), even a Pope's Head (1584–90, 1598, 1633), a Saracen's Head (1577?, 1615–40+), and a Turk's Head (1602–3, 1626–71),[15] as well as various animal heads (Bull, Boar, Tiger), but there is no trace of the Ben Jonson's Head prior to 1655.[16] Fletcher's Head is even more belated; Kirkman sells at this sign from 1661–62.[17] This may mean simply that no one had yet thought to post Jonson or Fletcher; if, as several critics have argued, the relation of the playwright to the theater is not the same as that of author to printed text,[18] it may also raise the possibility that a playwright's head is not thinkable under the sign of the working theater.

More broadly, Jonson's head may indicate that we can usefully begin reading inscriptions on title pages—including bookselling locations—not as (or *only* as) publication facts, but as information located more thickly within the cultural codes that, first, connect them to other rhetorics, social structures, and practices in the culture that produced them, and, second, make them important *as information,* bring them into legibility in the first place.[19] The sign of a King's Head might have read somewhat differently in 1606, just a few years after James succeeded Elizabeth, or in 1649, after the decapitation of Charles—especially since, as Nigel Smith has pointed out, "bookshops became important meeting places for those attached to religious or political causes" during the English civil wars.[20]

What would it mean to read Jonson's or Fletcher's Head within such rhetorics, conventions, and structures? Why post, for example, a playwright's *head* rather than his *hand*? "His mind and hand went together," says the actors' preface to the Shakespeare folio,[21] but this is not the case here in these signs: though the material signs, to my knowledge, don't survive, Jonson and Fletcher are apparently just handless, disembodied heads. The meaning of the *King's* Head is perhaps obvious but no less culturally implicated in bodily rhetorics we are used to attending to in other contexts: "The King towardes his people is rightly compared . . . to a head of a bodie composed of diuers members,"[22] James I was fond of saying. But what is Ben Jonson imagined to be at the head of—the corpus of drama?[23] Of Fletcher's Head, we could ask these and other questions: Where hangs the head of the inseparable Beaumont? Lies the Phillip Massinger's Head nearby?[24] Is the two-headed sign unpostable (or counterproductive)?

Let me give a final example that takes us in a somewhat different direction. The bookseller Walkley's sign of "the Eagle and Child" might seem unremarkable, until one translates its allusion to the Ganymede myth.[25] At this sign was sold (among other books) *Philaster,*[26] a play that dwells at length upon a master's erotic relation with his boy-servant. The play seems both presided over by the Ganymede myth (returning repeatedly to accounts of Philaster's ganymedic "taking up" of the page Bellario[27]) and a significant reversal (or mutualization) of the trajectory of desire in the classical tale; Philaster remarks that "the love of boys unto their lords is strange."[28] Maybe it is just happy coincidence that this homoerotic myth, widely viewed as such in early modern England,[29] should appear both within this play and on its title page as a bookseller's address. But even if this connection was not deliberate, following the printing of *Philaster* it has the potential to be read as a resonance by the browser in Walkley's shop or the reader of this text. If Ganymede was also taken to "represent intelligence, or rational thought" and "le[a]d people to love of divine truth,"[30] that only makes the resonances of Walkley's Eagle and Child more complex, potentially figuring an intersection, present elsewhere in this culture, of homoeroticism, learning, and books.[31] These signs, I am suggesting, do not escape the possibility of a reading within the extended social texture of their culture, a texture woven in part in and by the play-texts themselves. While we might tend to see the "internal" Ganymede references as deriving from Beaumont and Fletcher and Walkley's sign ("external" to the play) as Walkley's choice, all of this evidence seems to me to be potentially inside-out or outside-in; none of the signs I've discussed seem evidence that is merely *evident*—simply to be "seen out," in the etymological sense of that word.

There are thus other questions to be asked of these signs: at the sign of the Adam and Eve, or the Eagle and Child, what kinds of readers, readings, and reading practices were reflected, or produced? Who is addressed by these address signs? What kinds of texts and readerships and eventually authorships may have gathered at them?[32] What other kinds of practices and/or identifications are mobilized by Adam and Eve, or Jupiter and Ganymede, and to what extent do books as material objects serve as mediations or conduits in that process? What makes a sign lucrative as a notation of location in this culture?[33] When and how is it possible to sell at the sign of an authorial head, recognizable as such? With an engraved Shakespeare likeness so prominently available in the folio collections of 1623, 1632, 1663–64, 1685, why is there no sign of Shakespeare's Head? To steal a sign from the first Beaumont and Fletcher folio, why is there no sign, on the streets of seventeenth-century London, of a "Parnassus *biceps*"—a two-headed Mt. Parnassus?[34] Finding an author's head—much less his hand—may raise as many questions as it answers.

Notes

1. *The Excellent Comedy, called The Old Law: Or A New way to please you,* By Phil. Maßinger. Tho. Middleton. William Rowley (London: for Edward Archer, 1656), sig. A1; Wing STC M1048; Greg #766. Within the catalogue itself (present in only some of the play's surviving copies), the play is attributed to Massinger. Catalogue reprinted in W. W. Greg, *A Bibliography of the English Printed Drama*

to the Restoration, 4 vols. (London: for the Bibliographical Society, by Oxford University Press, 1939–59), vol. 3: 1,328–38.

2. "An Exact and perfect Catalogue," *Old Law,* sig. A1.

3. See Henry Plomer, *A Dictionary of the Booksellers and Printers Who Were at Work in England, Scotland, and Ireland from 1641 to 1667* (Oxford: The Bibliographic Society, 1907, rpt. 1968), 148.

4. "A true, perfect, and exact Catalogue of all the Comedies, Tragedies, Tragicomedies, Pastorals, Masques and Interludes, that were ever printed and published, till this present year 1661," in *Tom Tyler and His Wife. An Excellent Old Play* (London: 1661), sig. A1. Greg #820.

5. I've briefly discussed elsewhere the problems of evidence these lists represent, see "Playwrighting: Authorship and Collaboration," *A New History of Early English Drama,* ed. John D. Cox and David Scott Kastan (New York: Columbia University Press, 1997), 357–82. For a reading of the list that emphasizes the veracity of attributional information over the cultural reading I'll advance here, see W. W. Greg, "Authorship Attributions in the Early Play-Lists, 1656–1671," *Transactions of the Edinburgh Bibliographical Society,* ii (1946) 305–29, also Greg, *Bibliography* 3: 1,319–20.

6. *The Careless Shepherdes. A Tragi-Comedy . . . Written by T. G. Mr. Of Arts* (London: for Richard Rogers and William Ley, 1656). Wing STC G1005; Greg #761. Catalogue reprinted in Greg, *Bibliography* 3: 1,320–27. This catalogue is thought to be slightly earlier than the *Old Law* catalogue; see Greg, *Bibliography* 3: 1,319, 3: 1,328n.

7. Compare this format with that of the lists' distant descendant, the modern, author-organized *Short Title Catalogue.*

8. "A true, perfect, and exact Catalogue," in *Tom Tyler.*

9. "A True, perfect, and exact Catalogue of all the Comedies, Tragedies, Tragi-Comedies, Pastorals, Masques and Interludes, that were ever yet Printed and Pubished, till this present year 1671," in *Nicomede. A Tragi-Comedy, Translated out of the French of Monsieur Corneille, By John Dancer* (London: for Francis Kirkman, 1671). Greg prints one version of Kirkman's list, "basically [that] of the 1661 edition" (3: 1319), to which he appends the advertisement from the 1671.

10. "An Advertisement to the Reader," in *Nicomede,* 16 of the catalogue.

11. The existence and reproduction of the lists themselves speaks to this, and Kirkman also writes, "I have been these twenty years a Collector of [plays], and have conversed with, and enquired of those that have been Collecting these fifty years" ("An Advertisement to the Reader," in *Nicomede,* 16 of the catalogue). More evidence for what I am calling this "bibliophilic culture" is the series of apparent collector's marks in one of the Folger Library copies of the *Careless Shepherdes* catalogue (G1005, copy 2); a seventeenth-century reader has marked many of the titles with a horizontal dash, and at the end of the catalogue there appears a series of numbers in the margin: "505 26030": "505" corresponds to the number of title entries in the list; "230" may represent the number of titles owned or read, though the number of entries (eventually) marked is closer to 380. Similarly, in the Houghton Library copy of this catalogue, an early reader has written consecutive numbers after the titles of selected plays in the list, perhaps indicating those he/she owned.

12. It is significant that the three major folio collections of drama by men come first in Kirkman's discussion—either because those collections may have produced the popularity that the list records, or because they make accessible a certain kind of evidence of authorial productivity that Kirkman is interested in recording and using to organize.

13. *Nicomede,* 16 of the catalogue.

14. For some general comments on the use, duplicate use, and circulation of shop signs, see Peter W. M. Blayney's impressive and deeply informative study *The Bookshops in Paul's Cross Churchyard,* Occasional Papers of the Bibliographic Society, no. 5 (London: The Bibliographic Society, 1990), 10. I am deeply indebted to the research in Blayney's book, which also discusses the location and circulation of a number of particular signs in detail.

15. A search of the online *English Short Title Catalogue* indicates that many of these signs continue on imprints intermittently through the end of the seventeenth century; the dates in the text above (which should be understood as approximate) emphasize the earlier period because they are drawn from "Index 3D: Signs," in *A Short-Title Catalogue of Books Printed in England, Scotland, and Ireland and of English Books Printed Abroad 1475–1640,* ed. Katharine F. Pantzer, (London: The Bibliographical Society, 1991), 3:232–40. See also Blayney, *Bookshops.* Thus far I have been able to locate no sign prior to the Jonson's Head that indicates a personal name; the exceptions are some signs associated with saints and saints' heads—the George, St. Michael, St. Paul's Head and St. John's Head (see Blayney, *Bookshops,* 97–103, and *ESTC*), and one historical/classical figure (the Lucrece [Blayney 82, 87–88]); it is not clear that all of these are "head" signs. Interestingly, there is a Seneca's Head sign in the late seventeenth century (in signage, if not in folio, does classical authorship postdate English authorship?), recorded in John Bullord's *Bibliopolii Littleburiani pars prima:* "At Mr. Varennes, at Seneca's Head near Exeter-Change in the Strand" (1696, *ESTC*).

16. Plomer records Robert Pollard selling at the sign of the Jonson's Head from 1655–58 (*Dictionary,* 148). Blayney notes that the Plomer, ed., *Dictionaires* contain sometimes inaccurate and incomplete dates (*Bookshops,* 11–12), and a search of the online *ESTC* yields one additional 1659 imprint for Pollard (Wing D464); all other Pollard imprints at the Jonson's Head are 1655–58.

17. Kirkman is remarkably mobile; Plomer lists six locations at which he sold books, and the narrative of his bookselling and collecting life is of great interest to the history I am here sketching. See Plomer, *Dictionary,* 110–11. There is some evidence that Kirkman and Pollard worked in conjunction with each other, at least on one imprint, according to the *ESTC,* which records the following: *Lusts dominion, or, the lascivious queen. A tragedie.* Written by Christofer Marloe, Gent. London: printed [by Jane Bell] for F. K[irkman] and are to be sold by Robert Pollard, at the sign of Ben Johnsons head, on the back-side of the Old-Exchange, 1657. Jane Bell was also apparently the printer for *The Old Law* edition in which the catalogue sold by Archer and Pollard appeared; see Jeffrey Masten, "Textual Introduction," *The Old Law,* in *The Complete Works of Thomas Middleton,* general ed. Gary Taylor (Oxford: Oxford University Press, forthcoming).

18. On this, see Margreta de Grazia, *Shakespeare Verbatim: The Reproduction of Authenticity and the 1790 Apparatus* (Oxford: Clarendon, 1991), chapter 1; Joseph Loewenstein, "The Script in the Marketplace," *Representations* 12 (1985), 101–14; Jeffrey Masten, *Textual Intercourse: Collaboration, Authorship, and Sexualities in Renaissance Drama* (Cambridge: Cambridge University Press, 1997), chapters 3–4; Stephen Orgel, "What is a Text?" in *Staging the Renaissance: Reinterpretations of Elizabethan and Jacobean Drama,* eds. David Scott Kastan and Peter Stallybrass (New York: Routledge, 1991), 83–87; Peter Stallybrass and Allon White, "The Fair, the Pig, Authorship," *The Politics and Poetics of Transgression* (Ithaca: Cornell University Press, 1986), 27–79.

19. De Grazia makes an analogous point about reading authorship in the preliminaries of the 1623 Shakespeare folio; see *Shakespeare Verbatim,* 11.

20. Nigel Smith, *Literature and Revolution in England 1640–1660* (New Haven: Yale University Press, 1994), 24.
21. John Heminge and Henrie Condell, "To the Great Variety of Readers," in *Mr. William Shakespeares Comedies, Histories, & Tragedies* (London: by Isaac Iaggard, and Ed. Blount, 1623), sig. A3.
22. *Minor Prose Works of King James VI and I*, eds. James Craigie and Alexander Law (Edinburgh: Scottish Text Society, 1982), 74.
23. In the context of bodily rhetorics, it is interesting to contemplate the meaning of the sign of the "Maiden head," at which books were sold at least in 1668 and 1600 (*ESTC*). Other maiden('s) head signs are discussed by Blayney, *Bookshops*, 50, 65–66.
24. Massinger was buried in Fletcher's grave; see Masten, *Textual Intercourse*, 1–2.
25. See Ovid, *Metamorphoses*, 10.155ff.
26. Walkley published the first and the second editions of the play, see: *Philaster. Or, Loue lies a Bleeding. Written by {Francis Beaumont and Iohn Fletcher} Gent. The second Impression, corrected, and amended* (London: for Thomas Walkeley, and are to be solde at his shoppe, at the signe of the Eagle and Childe, in Brittaines Bursse, 1622), (Q2).
27. In Francis Beaumont and John Fletcher, *Philaster*, ed. Dora Jean Ashe, Regents Renaissance Drama series (Lincoln: University of Nebraska Press, 1974), see 2.1.5–7, and Bellario's speech to Philaster (after s/he is discovered to be Euphrasia):

> I saw a god,
> I thought, but it was you, enter our gates.
> My blood flew out and back again, . . .
> . . . .
> Then was I call'd away in haste
> To entertain you. Never was a man
> Heav'd from sheepcote to scepter, rais'd
> So high in thoughts as I.
>
> (5.5.165–72)

28. *Philaster*, 2.2.57.
29. The work of Leonard Barkan, *Transuming Passion: Ganymede and the Erotics of Humanism* (Stanford, Calif.: Stanford University Press, 1991) and James Saslow, *Ganymede in the Renaissance: Homosexuality in Art and Society* (New Haven: Yale University Press, 1986) on visual art strongly suggests that the Eagle and Child sign would have been legibly homoerotic; see also the commentary on the homoeroticism of the myth in Bruce Smith, *Homosexual Desire in Shakespeare's England: a Cultural Poetics* (Chicago: University of Chicago Press, 1991); Mario DiGangi, *The Homoerotics of Early Modern Drama* (Cambridge: Cambridge University Press, 1997); Gregory W. Bredbeck, *Sodomy and Interpretation* (Ithaca: Cornell University Press, 1991).
30. Richard Knowles, ed., *As You Like It*, A New Variorum Edition of Shakespeare (New York: MLA, 1977), 64.
31. Aspects of this intersection have been addressed by Elizabeth Pittenger, "Dispatch Quickly: The Mechanical Reproduction of Pages," *Shakespeare Quarterly* 42 (1991): 389–408; Bruce Smith, *Homosexual Desire in Shakespeare's England: a Cultural Poetics* (Chicago: University of Chicago Press, 1991); Alan Stewart, *Close Readers: Humanism and Sodomy in Early Modern England* (Princeton: Princeton University Press, 1997). See also Jonathan Goldberg, *Sodom-*

etries: Renaissance Texts, Modern Sexualities (Stanford, Calif.: Stanford University Press, 1992); Richard Rambuss, *Spenser's Secret Career* (Cambridge: Cambridge University Press, 1993).

32. An answer to these questions would depend at least preliminarily on a search of all the books sold at/bearing these signs. I choose these examples because they can stress an opposition between same-sex and cross-sex signs, but we could also attend to the resonances of biblical vs. mythological, the reproductive family vs. a notion of the family that includes servants, etc. For the early modern Ganymede myth as rearticulating concerns of apprentice-family relations that might well have been relevant to book- and print-shops, see Di Gangi, *The Homoerotics of Early Modern Drama,* chapter 2.

33. Eric Wilson brilliantly probes the implications of the shop sign in the context of an emergent capitalist economy; see "Abel Drugger's Sign," in *Historicism, Psychoanalysis, and Early Modern Culture,* ed. Carla Mazzio and Doug Trevor (New York: Routledge, forthcoming, 2000).

34. *Comedies and Tragedies Written by {Francis Beavmont and Iohn Fletcher} Gentlemen,* (London: for Humphrey Robinson and Humphrey Moseley, 1647) frontispiece. The quoted phrase appears in the Latin poem below the frontispiece portrait; the poem is translated in an appendix to Lois Potter's recent Arden edition of *The Two Noble Kinsmen.* Despite the book's title and general rhetoric, the frontispiece depicts Fletcher alone, a configuration that may well have influenced Kirkman's choice of sign; on the folio portrait, see Masten, *Textual Intercourse,* 121–25.

Murder in Guyana

Patricia Parker

THE MURDER IN THE *Mouse-trap of Hamlet* happened in Vienna: of this we are assured by the most prominent editions (which feature the murdered Duke "Gonzago" along with his wife "Baptista"). Harold Jenkins's Arden *Hamlet* reads: "*The Mousetrap*—marry, how tropically! This play is the image of a murder done in Vienna"; Philip Edwards's New Cambridge *Hamlet* "The Mousetrap. Marry how? Tropically. This play is the image of a murder done in Vienna"; G. R. Hibbard's Oxford *Hamlet*: "The Mousetrap, Marry, how? Tropically. This play is the image of a murder done in Vienna."[1] The Riverside, Bevington, and more recent Norton editions all similarly present a murder in Vienna.[2] Editorially speaking, the case is closed. It is only when we turn to the earliest texts of the play that we find a different location for the murder—not Vienna (as in the Second Quarto and Folio) but "*guyana*," the location in the First Quarto (Q1):

> *Hamlet*: Mouse-trap: mary how trapically: this play is
> The image of a murder done in *guyana*. *Albertus*
> Was the Dukes name, his wife *Baptista*.[3]

For anyone encountering the Q1 text for the first time, its "*guyana*" may come as a shock. However scrupulous the editorial collation, we find no trace of "*guyana*" in the textual apparatus of most modern editions, where even in the "band of terror" itself Q1's "*guyana*" has been "disappeared."[4] Edwards cites other Q1 variants on the same text page, but not "*guyana*." Of his choice of the Folio's "Tropically," he notes, "As a trope, a figure of speech. Q1's 'trapically' shows the Joycean pun." But he does not inform the reader that the line that contains Q1's "trapically" is immediately followed by "The image of a murder done in *guyana*." Hibbard similarly omits "*guyana*," though he cites other Q1 variants in his collations and glosses.⁵ Jenkins comments of his "marry, how tropically!" that "the Q1 spelling suggests pronunciation and brings out the pun," but nowhere discloses Q1's different location for the murder, not even in his Long Note, which he dedicates not to the early texts' variants "*guyana / Vienna*" but rather to Urbino, which does not appear in any of them: "Vienna might perhaps be a misreading of Urbino (U and V being interchangeable) or otherwise suggested by it"; "It appears to be true that the play *The Murder of Gonzago* (and accordingly the death of King Hamlet) is based on an actual murder, that of the Duke of Urbino in 1538." Jenkins acknowledges that some adjustments may be necessary to make the intended "Urbino" fit, even apart from more material considerations of printing: "Gonzago" was the name (though not exactly) not of the murdered Duke of Urbino but of his alleged murderer, Luigi Gonzaga; the Duke's wife's name was "Leonora" rather than "Baptista," though an "earlier Duke of Urbino had married Battista Sforza."⁶

Such arguments may be necessary for a theory that comes closer to fulfilling Pope's emendation of "tropically" to "topically": readers of the recent Norton edition still learn that "Shakespeare seems to base *The Moustrap* on an extremely muddled version of the Duke of Urbino's alleged 1538 murder by Luigi Gonzaga."⁷ Jenkins states confidently that the combination of Gonzaga's "name" with "the unusual method of killing" (poison in the ears) "leaves no doubt that we have here the prototype of the murderer in *Hamlet*." But even the proposed congruence of the name of Luigi Gonzaga, alleged poisoner of Urbino, with the poisoned "Gonzago" of Vienna in Q2 and F, does not work for the Q1 text, where the Duke murdered in "*guyana*" is named "Albertus," difficult to see as a printing (or other) error for "Gonzaga."

Leaving Urbino aside, what about "*guyana*" for Vienna? Most comments on Q1 "*guyana*" assume that it is simply a *mistake* for "Vienna," often in ways reflective of the view that Q1 represents some form of "memorial reconstruction." (It has been reported that even the famed Orange Tree production of Q1 directed by Sam Walters in 1985 was not true to its "*guyana*." Nicholas Shrimpton's review claimed that its "Mousetrap took place in familiar Vienna rather than surprising 'Guyana' "; but here—as with the theory of "memorial reconstruction" itself—so much depends on the reliability of the reporter.⁸) Even before the rise of the New Bibliography, or the Arden, New Oxford, or Cambridge editions that assume some version of reconstruction, the variorum commented on its choice of "Vienna": "COLLIER: The *Guiana* of Q1 perhaps arose from the shorthand-writer having misheard the name."⁹ A somewhat different version of *"guyana"* as error or mistake is offered by Kathleen O. Irace, editor of the 1998 Cambridge edition of *The First Quarto of Hamlet,* which (among other editorial alterations) replaces Q1's "sallied flesh" with the "sullied flesh" that appears nowhere in any early text. Irace prints not the Q1 text of these lines ("Mouse-trap: mary how trapically: this play is / The image of a murder done in *guyana*"), but yet another conflation ("Moustrap. Marry how? Trapically. This play is the image of a murder done in Guiana"),¹⁰ revealing only in the usual small print at the bottom of the page that her edition (with its modernized "guyana") actually prints the Folio's "Marry how?" Her notes at the back comment that Guiana, a "tropical region in north-eastern South America, [is] an unlikely location for *The Murder of Gonzago.* Q1's reading could be emended to 'Vienna' from Q2 and F (3.2.239), or, like certain other readings unique to Q1, this word could be retained to help reinforce Hamlet's troubled mental state." Her introduction briefly acknowledges that Guiana "would not have been entirely unfamiliar to an Elizabethan audience," since "both Raleigh and Chapman described a voyage to Guiana in works published in 1596," Raleigh's *Discoverie of the large, rich, and bewtiful Empyre of Guiana* and Chapman's "De Guiana, carmen Epicum," prefixed to Lawrence Keymis's *A Relation of the Second Voyage to Guiana.*"¹¹ But she returns even here to the assumption that Q1's *"guyana"* could "be useful to an interpretation emphasising either Hamlet's troubled mental state or pretended madness," turning an assumed textual mistake into a psychological symptom, error but of a different kind.

The presentation of Q1 in the series edited by Graham Holderness and Bryan Loughrey is more faithful to the Q1 text than Irace is. But they also offer in their own gloss on Q1's *"guyana"* and "trapically" a telling instance of how difficult it is to stay within the "material" text, or to guard its discrete textual boundaries, even when the distinguishing (or celebrating) of that text is a primary objective. Holderness and Loughrey comment as follows: "trapically: i.e. the title is derived from a trope, a figure of speech, and the action takes place in a tropical location ('*guyana*'). The other texts print 'tropically'. The word also puns on 'trap.' "¹² There is no explanation offered as to why *"guyana"* appears in Q1. But its "tropical location" is used to gloss the "tropically" found *not* in Q1 but in Q2 and F—a crossing of textual boundaries that undoes the notion of the discrete text itself, even while it may suggest ways in which different texts of *Hamlet* pirate from each other (or a larger nexus in which "tropically" might be playing not just with its rhetorical but also with its geographical sense, as in the tropical location of "*guyana*," even if neither appears materially within the same single text).

What then do we do with Q1's "*guyana*"? No modern editor, however scrupulous, can be expected to reproduce all existing variants. But there is reason now, I would argue, to record "*guyana*" in future editions. It is possible that it represents an "error" of some kind, including one in some way related to the material conditions of printing, even if, unlike Q2's "the Lady shall say her minde freely: or the black verse shall hault for't," it cannot be explained by something like the possible confusion of "c" and "n" in secretary hand. In the absence of clear evidence that it *is* an error, it is also possible that Q1's "*guyana*" is a different location, with different associations from the "Vienna" of Q2 and F. I have found myself thinking about it in relation to the "*Guiana*" of the folio *Merry Wives,* which is clearly affected by the contemporary associations influenced by Raleigh's and other reports ("She is a Region in *Guiana*: all gold, and bountie: I will be Cheaters to them both, and they shall be Exchequers to mee: they shall be my East and West Indies, and I will trade to them both"). The Guiana that Raleigh famously described as "a countrey that hath yet her maydenhead,"[13] relating discovery itself to a sexualized female "countrey," figured as the paradigm of undiscovered countries, as well as of rival triangles for imperial possession, and of the problem of the credibility of travelers' tales or reported evidence: perhaps guyana is not that far removed from *Hamlet* after all. Death itself is described as an "undiscouered country" (Q1) in all three of the early texts of the otherwise radically divergent "To be or not to be" soliloquy. And all three early texts include evocations of empire in Aeneas's tale to Dido, Julius Caesar and Brutus, Marcellus and Nero, even if the less certain "Claudius" is described as the consort of an imperial jointress and as pirate or cutpurse of empire and the rule only in Q2 and F.

I first came to Q1's "*guyana*" from pondering the ways in which all three early texts of *Hamlet* often sound more like *Othello* than we might think (including Q2 and F's lines on Gertrude's battening on "this Moore"—whose corresponding Q1 text gives this rival King and husband a "face like *Vulcan*," as in the "black as Vulcan" of *Twelfth Night*). In the midst of *Hamlet* texts that harp repeatedly on blackness, on the spotted or maculate, adulterate, stained, soiled, "sallied" or sullied, the "Baptista" of this "*guyana*" murder scene (the name in all three texts for the wife of the *Mousetrap,* which famously appears in the form that recalls the Baptist) is part of this network, suggesting the washing of the Ethiope that the King's speech in the Prayer Scene (again, of all three texts) relates to washing white as snow. The prayer scene of Q1 stresses the blackness of the King's "adulterous fault" ("say thy sinnes were blacker then is ieat, / Yet may contrition make them as white as snowe") and his desire to be washed "cleere" ("O that this wet that falles vpon my face / Would wash the crime cleere from my conscience!"), a metaphorics that continues as the scene proceeds ("let the deuell weare blacke," "sute of Sables," "damnable faces," "croking raven," "Thoughts blacke," "mixture rancke, of midnight weedes collected"). And in Q1—as in the others—polarities of black and white, like the Ghost who describes himself as an angel but may be "damned," themselves turn tropically, complicating the very attempt at clear distinction.

All of this may be immaterial, the result of considering too closely or the mixture rank of my own desire to intermingle texts that should be kept discrete. Perhaps all that matters here is to hope that this occulted murder in guyana will out.

Notes

1. Harold Jenkins, ed., *Hamlet* (London and New York: Methuen, 1982), 302; Philip Edwards, *Hamlet, Prince of Denmark* (Cambridge: Cambridge University Press, 1985), 163; G. R. Hibbard, ed., *Hamlet* (Oxford and New York: Oxford University Press, 1987), 261.

2. Q1 (1603) text is cited here from *The Three-Text Hamlet: Parallel Texts of the First and Second Quartos and First Folio,* eds. Paul Bertram and Bernice W. Kliman (New York: AMS Press, 1991), 146.

3. *The Riverside Shakespeare,* ed. G. Blakemore Evans et al. (Boston: Houghton Mifflin Company, 1974) is a notable exception, but it cites Q1's "*guyana*" only in its textual endnotes, making no comment on it on the text page itself, though, like other editions, it does comment on tropically / trapically.

4. Jenkins, *Hamlet,* 507-8.

5. *The Norton Shakespeare, Based on the Oxford Edition,* ed. Stephen Greenblatt et al. (New York and London: W.W. Norton, 1997), 1,713.

6. See Shrimpton's report in *Shakespeare Survey* 39 (1986): 191–206, esp. 194–95, analyzed in Janette Dillon, "Is There a Performance in this Text?" *Shakespeare Quarterly* 45, 1 (spring 1994), 74–86, esp. 83; Holderness and Loughrey's introduction (28–29); and Bryan Loughrey's "Q1 in recent performance: an interview," in Thomas Clayton, ed., *Q1 Now* (Lincoln: University of Nebraska Press, 1991), 123–36.

7. Horace Howard Furness, ed., *A New Variorum Edition of Shakespeare,* vol. III, *Hamlet* (Philadelphia: J.B. Lippincott Company, 1877), 255.

8. Kathleen O. Irace ed., *The First Quarto of Hamlet* (Cambridge: Cambridge University Press, 1998), 40 and 70.

9. Ibid., 16.

10. Graham Holderness and Bryan Loughrey, eds., *The Tragical Historie of Hamlet Prince of Denmarke* (New York and London: Harvester Wheatsheaf, 1992). See text on p. 75 and gloss on p. 122.

11. Raleigh's *Discoverie,* cited from Richard Hakluyt, *Principal Navigations,* 12 vols. (Glasgow, 1904; rpt. New York, 1969), 10:428. All of these issues—including the credibility of Raleigh's report in particular—are treated by Louis Montrose and Mary C. Fuller in well-known articles that first appeared in *Representations* 33 (winter 1991).

The Art of the Lacuna

Stephen Orgel

In 1517 the Roman printer Giacomo Mazzocchi published a volume of portraits of famous ancients derived from his own coin collection; the book is discussed in a forthcoming essay by Sean Keilen, who called it to my attention. (I deal here with some issues about the book that are not covered by Keilen, and with two of the book's sequels.) Each woodcut is provided with a brief biography by the distinguished historian of Roman antiquities Andrea Fulvio. The book, entitled simply *Illustrium Imagines,* appeared under a draconian license from Pope Leo X threatening anyone anywhere in the world who published a competing volume "in the same or larger type" with excommunication—the relation between typography and heresy here is notable; so is the implication that the actionable element is the size of the type.

The collection is systematic only in that it is roughly chronological and groups members of the same family together. All the figures are historical with the exception of Janus, who appropriately begins the book, and all are Roman with the exception of Alexander the Great and Cleopatra. Not all emperors are present, however, and there is no attempt to fill in the blanks, or to make the iconography comprehensive. The book gives the impression of a real coin collection, though only the obverses, showing the illustrious faces, are recorded, and while the profiles are in fact quite accurate, the woodcuts nevertheless show what we might call a certain negotiation with verisimilitude. For example, the Alexander portrait is certainly based on a coin of Alexander, much elaborated—and possibly via a marble relief of Alexander by Verocchio, now in the National Gallery in Washington—but on real Alexander coins his name is on the reverse, not the obverse, and, of course, in Greek. The armed head, moreover, is a portrait of Athena, not the emperor—though Mazzocchi would not have been aware of this: it was taken to be a portrait of Alexander until the eighteenth century.

Alexander the Great, from Andrea Fulvio, *Illustrium Imagines,* Rome, 1517

The Art of the Lacuna

Cornelia, and Pompeia, wives of Julius Caesar, from *Illustrium Imagines,* Rome, 1517

But the book contains three striking anomalies. Julius Caesar is grouped with various members of his family, including four wives: Cornelia, Pompeia, Calpurnia, and Cossutia. Now Cossutia was in fact not Caesar's wife. According to Suetonius, she was engaged to him, but the engagement was terminated in favor of a more politically advantageous marriage to Cinna's daughter Cornelia, who became Caesar's first wife: this is laconically explained in Cossutia's caption. Nevertheless, coins were issued by both Cossutia's family and Caesar's describing her anticipatorily as "Uxor Caesaris"—hence, no doubt, the confusion. But Cossutia's picture is blank. What does it mean? Perhaps that Mazzocchi knows such coins exist, but his collection does not include one. But then why include her at all? The collection as a whole is, as I say, neither systematic nor complete—and if one were going to omit a wifely coin, Cossutia's would surely be the obvious candidate: she was not Caesar's wife. An ideal of numismatic completeness, however, is apparently being implied here, and, as Keilen shrewdly remarks, the blank

COSSVTIA VXOR. CAES. **XVIII**

Fuit hęc familia equeſtri & diues neq;
prius repudiata q̃ in matrimonium du
éta.

Cossutia, fiancée of Julius Caesar, from *Illustrium Imagines*, Rome, 1517

The Art of the Lacuna

portrait serves as evidence of the authenticity of the entire enterprise—Cossutia has been neither omitted nor invented. She is the exception that proves the rule.

Two other lacunae show the same scholarly tactics in reverse. The heads of Plaudilla Augusta and Antonia Augusta are depicted, but without captions. Now both these names are problematic. The honorific Augusta stamps them as the wives of emperors, but no such empresses exist. Plaudilla should in fact be Plautilla: she is Fulvia Plautilla, the wife of Caracalla, called Plautilla Augusta on her coins—was Mazzocchi's example worn or otherwise partly illegible, and was she therefore unidentifiable? Antonia Augusta, however, is altogether anomalous. She is apparently the elder daughter of Mark Antony and Octavia: they had two daughters, both named Antonia, Antonia Maior and Antonia Iunior, and Antonia Iunior appears a few pages later. Antonia Maior was not an empress, but perhaps she was called Augusta as the niece of Augustus; however, I can find no record of any coins bearing her portrait. In any case, Andrea Fulvio certainly recognized both her name and Plaudilla's as anomalies.

"Plaudilla Augusta" and "Antonia Augusta," from *Illustrium Imagines*, Rome, 1517

Once again, both coins could simply have been omitted, but the lacunae testify to the project's scholarly integrity.

Now what happens next? In 1524, François Juste, in Lyons, published a new edition of *Illustrium Imagines*—as it happens, in smaller type, perhaps to be on the safe side of excommunication. It follows the format of Mazzocchi's volume quite precisely, with one significant exception: while Plaudilla and Antonia remain unidentified, the space for Cossutia's picture is no longer empty. It has been filled with the portrait of the emperor Claudius who, unbearded and boyish, looks feminine enough. As the Alexander/Athena coin indicates, however, gender in such cases was less significant than attributes. The substitution of Claudius for Cossutia would have been impossible with the 1517 woodcut, in which Claudius is crowned; whereas his 1524 laurel wreath is equally suitable to Cossutia. Only Claudius's name poses a problem. In both the Harvard and Newberry copies, and I assume therefore in all, it has been obliterated with printer's ink, apparently by hand, and in the printing house—the woodcut itself could not simply be

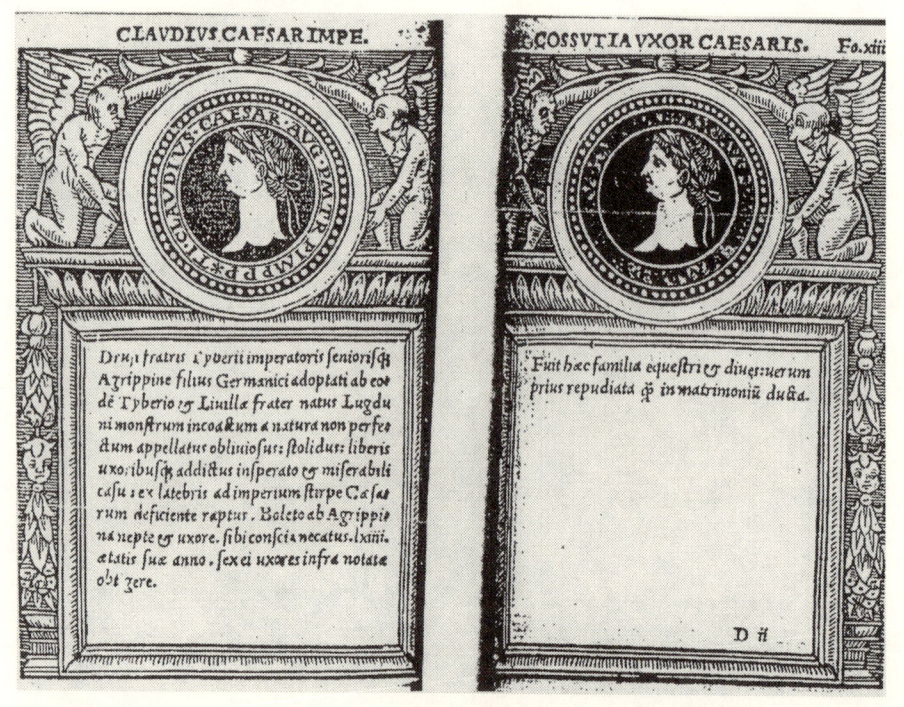

Claudius Caesar and Cossutia, from François Juste's edition of *Illustrium Imagines*, Lyons, 1524. Reproduced by permission of the Newberry Library.

altered, since it had to be used again for Claudius. *Illustrium Imagines* has here ceased to be a coin collection, a record of images drawn from the material remains of the past, and has become an iconology, fanciful when necessary; and everything, even missing things, is illustrated.

A page of Tyrants, from Johann Huttich, *Imperatorum et Caesarum Vitae*, Strassburg, 1534

And now the third step: starting in 1525 and extending into the 1550s the Strassburg printer Johann Huttich issued a series of new editions of the book, initially under the title *Imperatorum Romanorum Libellus.* These follow Mazzocchi's original edition in leaving Cossutia's picture blank, though they also tidy things up by omitting the baffling Plaudilla and Antonia. But for Huttich, Cossutia has in a sense become the norm: the Strasbourg collection is greatly expanded, largely by the addition of blank heads. This effectively turns the book back into a coin collection, with the blanks to be filled by the individual collector; the book's greatest value is its record not of what is there, but of what is lacking: it is the reader's coin collection now. But it also transforms the nature of the book as a testimony to the historical reality of material objects. The evidence Huttich's missing heads provide is the evidence of things not seen, things to be sought. The Renaissance book was less a product than a process.

The Triumph of King James
and His August Descendants

by Ana Mary Armygram

for Marta Werner

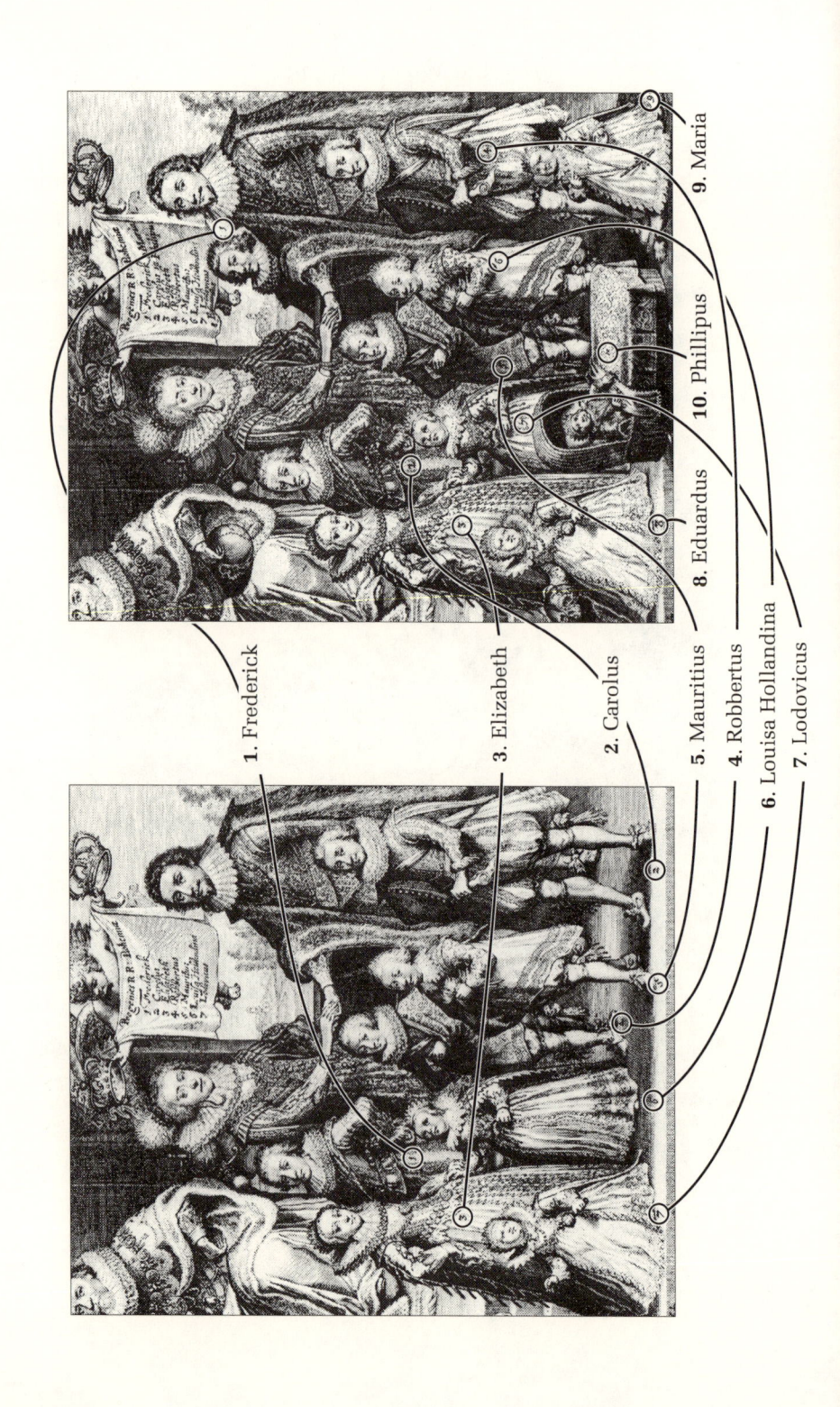

1. Frederick
2. Carolus
3. Elizabeth
4. Robbertus
5. Mauritius
6. Louisa Hollandina
7. Lodovicus
8. Eduardus
9. Maria
10. Phillipus

The Triumph of King James and His August Descendants

Willem van der Passe's engraving of the family of King James (c1622-24) is genealogical. It celebrates the Stuart line, not only in Britain (at the monarch's right hand), down through his new male heir, Prince Charles (whose older brother, Henry, between them, now rests his elbow on a skull); but also in Bohemia, through both James' daughter, Elizabeth (on his left) and, below her, closer to his grandfather than his own father (who is relegated to the edge of the composition), her eldest son, Frederick Jr.

While serving its political functions, the engraving may seem equally to be a collection of personal portraits. But don't be taken in; the revisions to the plate (c1625-30) assert the dynastic over the personal. Note what seems to be a new eldest son beside the mother. Attend closely to variant numbers on the figures, which are keyed to numbered names on the putto's banner (itself also variant), and you'll see what happened. When the maturing Frederick acquired a new representation, his old one became a hand-me-down. Look at the evidence: in the first state, "1" is on Frederick's hip; but it appears beside his new head in the revision — in which that "1" on the hip was re-engraved as "2". In other words, the same old face and body now re-present Carolus, not Frederick! The image of Carolus passed in turn to Robbertus — and so on, many images cascading down the burgeoning royal family, economically, until Mauritius became Louisa Hollandina in pants; she became Lodovicus in skirts (not such outrageous garb for a *very* young boy in that era); and he, formerly Lodovicus living, became newly-born Eduardus dead. (You *do* see the new skull? It's *not* a yo-yo.)

Meanwhile, back in Britain, Charles' hand, which formerly rested flat on an allegorical Bible, inscribed *"Religium et Constantia"*, now grasps the hand of a woman allegorical. *Very* economically, the engraver recycled the tablecloth as the lower part of her gown. Merely rubbing the plate here in a vertical swath, he lightened the lines, and so evoked a royal leg. (A delicate touch.) And, rounding the square foot of the table leg, he called forth a royal shoe. Otherwise, from her waist down, you couldn't tell her from a — well, in fact, it never was a *pure* tablecloth *qua* tablecloth. Wasn't it *always* something of a skirt in waiting? And it is the mark of the *finest* minds to discern this *solely* with reference to the first state. For the putto's crown held high above the deer park and table loaded with books never *really* did make much sense. They just comprised a peripheral place eventually to slot a royal woman in — a conduit of legitimacy. And are we *really* surprised that, though the putto's banner, *"Progenies Iaco: et: An: RR: Mag: Britan:"*, was delicately re-engraved to mark the son's change of *rank*, from *"Carolus Pr:"* to *"Carolus Re:"*, the royal consort What's-her-Face was never even *named*?

In life, her name was Henrietta Maria. If you think this is her portrait, contrast these snippets from the second state and the *third* (c1660-70), executed after van der Passe's death. In life, it was her *husband* lost his head. But in art, he keeps it — and *she* sports a new one. (In fact, she's all new from the bosom up!) You get the picture?

Note

Willem van der Passe (c1598-c1637) and the *four* states of this engraving are discussed in Arthur M. Hind, *Engraving in England in the Sixteenth and Seventeenth Centuries, a Descriptive Catalogue*, 3 vols., CUP, 1952-64, Vol. 2 ("The Reign of King James"), pp. 285-301, especially 295-97. (The complete plate has five columns of engraved text below it, each of eleven or twelve lines; they are not shown here.) Images of the first two states are © The British Museum, and the third is © The Ashmolean Museum, Oxford, to both of whom my gratitude for permission to reproduce their copies.

© A. M. Amygram

II
Clothes, Properties, Textiles

The "Signification" of William Reynolds's Clothes

KATHERINE DUNCAN-JONES, ed.

Modernized extract from a letter dated 28 January 1589 from the unemployed soldier William Reynolds to Walter Cope (BL MS Lansdowne 99, fols. 25–26).

MASTER COPE, I MOST HUMBLY recommend me unto you. . . . It hath pleased God now once again to move me to write to you, an Inferior person, that which he hath since in mercy showed to me, even the joyfullest tidings that ever was for England, which is now my third alarm to waken England, and the sweetest melody that ever England heard. . . . Although I have no library to increase profound knowledge yet I say he reads well and has good religion which preferreth the fear and love of God before the fear and love of mortal men. . . . I was touched for superstition, but who can better devise than God hath put into my mind, and I hope well for the advancing of his glory for my twelve days in black must take effect hereafter, yet will they think that which I mean to do to be my foolish and vain superstitious invention. . . . Upon Saturday last at night I desired God in my prayers that he would vouchsafe to teach me to understand his will, and suddenly I conceived the long and lamentable exile of the Jews, then I bowed myself toward the East and worshipped the Lord for that sweet conceit, and then again I conceived that after the twelve days, I should make me a suit of some pure white, and a cloak of pure sky color striped with some small lace of gold, and to line my cloak with a seawater green, and to make me a scarf of yellow, white, and green, a scabbard of red velvet, a white scarf about my right arm, and although some such motions had heretofore a little glimmered in my mind yet now when I perceived that God would make England pure and precious in his sight, which is but a small island compassed about with the sea, and that the sky, even God his word, should be clear, and therefore even Christ should shine clearly upon thee most comfortably, then I bowed myself the second time to the Lord, yet I conceived more, that my other cloaks bought before by me at a venture were brought to me by God and had their signification too, and here is my greatest grief, that as I bought the other by my friends' help, so would I buy the black and white too myself if my ability would serve, wherefore herein in respect of my country's honor I desire help for God's sake with speed (6 Psalm). Then considering better of my first cloak which was white mingled with red, and that when I bought it first I would not by no means line it, no, not the collar, for then it could not simply betoken God his wrath, then considering the second suit of tawny, I understood it best became my sad and penitent mind. Yet the darkness of my country England, by my cloak of russet lined with seawater and stockings of seawater, so that I could not step forth of England but into the sea which I compassed me about, and that the sky, God's word, was so darkened with the thick clouds of our sins that the sun, Christ, could not shine through it, also now I did perceive that many things which I have done spoke and writ before had a great signification, Yea the Lord moved me yet again to look well upon myself, and to compare myself to England: then I stood still a little while musing and pondering thereof, and suddenly I was ravished with joy above measure, then I laughed, I wept, and I rejoiced greatly, holding up my hands to heaven, saying, "O Joy of Joys, O wonder of wonders, O most true concent[1] of heavenly harmony, O Lord, Lord, how sweet and comfortable is thy majesty and mercy to weak man, even dust, Wherefore O England come, come, come."

Note

1. "Concent," the technical musical term, rather than "consent."

"His Apparel Was Done Upon Him": Rites of Personage in Foxe's *Book of Martyrs*

Laurie Shannon

KING LEAR NOTORIOUSLY MAKES the case that to be naked, unadorned, or "unaccommodated" is, literally, to not-be; like the unreal number zero, such a person is "an O without a figure."[1] Though this logic arguably covers anybody, Lear's own case in the matter of investiture is special: as king he is "invested" with an "office" or "dignity," the period's idiom for what we might call an official capacity. This essay will consider the material relations (cloth rites as well as social interactions) involved in adorning a person into—or out of—being.[2] In particular, it will assess early modern formulations of what we still term "public figures."[3] The "public person" (often the sense of the term "the great") maintains a juridical status apart from private persons. So instead of primarily viewing a public/private split as occurring "within" a single self, early modern English culture seems largely to understand it as separating categorically different forms of personage. Aemilia Lanyer, for example, construed "the great" as those who "are placed in . . . Orbes of State," apart from others who might wish to be near them; Francis Bacon devoted an essay entitled "Of Great Place" to this status or class.[4]

Public personage enjoys, of course, a special relation to clothing and costuming. In *Twelfth Night,* when Malvolio believes in his own sudden, apparent access to "greatness" ("some are born great, some achieve greatness, and some have greatness thrust upon 'em"), he determines both to adopt the fashions of going yellow-stockinged and cross-gartered *and* to spout "arguments of state" and "read politic authors" (3.1. 138, 148). Greatness, like clothes, is "put on" in Malvolio's account. Ceremonies of investiture often establish an individual with the marks of "place." But it is not simply a matter of wearing "the robes of office"—we also see a fascination with the social interactions that transfer the robes and with their status as *borrowed* attire. Shakespearean examples abound and emphasize office-holding as the temporary possession of a loaned garment. Lear himself compounds his divestiture of royal estate with "Off, off, you *lendings* / Come, unbutton here" (3.4.103); the Duke in *Measure for Measure,* deputing powers to his substitute, has "*lent* him our terror [severity], *dressed* him with our love [mercy]" (1.1.19). Against our quotidian sense of dressing oneself, in one's own clothes, what does it mean to be formally dressed in or stripped of borrowed clothes—by someone else?

Instead of reviewing an instance of political divestiture, I propose to assess an episode in John Foxe's *Book of Martyrs*: the degrading of Nicolas Ridley and the executions of Ridley and Hugh Latimer on the same day in 1555 under the Marian prosecution of Protestants. Foxe's narration of these cases provides special interest for three reasons. Ridley's divestiture[5] reflects the originally ecclesiastical jurisprudence underlying "the king's two bodies" theory of the relation between a mortal person and perpetual office, a decretal known as *Quoniam abbas*.[6] But unlike this relatively esoteric legal rule, the incident was public and theatrical; its dissemination in Foxe's martyrology further established the story in, at once, both popular and national culture.[7] Perhaps most interestingly, though, we see the ceremony of divestiture juxtaposed with other strategies and semiotics of dress. Specifically, Foxe's text stages a powerful, though ultimately incomplete, contestation of the power of clothes either to confer or cancel personage. Against a doctrine of institutional and legal office materially effected by rites of dress, Foxe sets a Protestant semiotic of (only virtual) nakedness as a competing theory of the relation of clothes to persons. But either way, personage is specified through events that are physically interactive and that depend on cloth transactions. Foxe's prose, like George Cavendish's *Life of Wolsey* or Edward Hall's *History of the Noble Houses of Lancaster and York,* records an inventorying fabric sense that immediately notifies the modern reader of the poverty of his or her vocabularies for cloth.

What we might call a Protestant semiotic of dress emerges straightforwardly, and it derives from a familiar distinction between mere material (decorated, deceptive) externalities and an interior, "naked" or plain truth. In Foxe's account of Latimer's conversion, he describes how Latimer "forsook the School doctors and other such fopperies and became an earnest student of true divinity."[8] "Fopperies" is a key switching point; it casts orthodox doctrine as a grossly overlaid, worldly fashion; a disguising of "God's Word' in a showy, misleading, and affected costume. Against "fopperies," Foxe immediately sets Latimer's "Sermon on the Cards," which he describes as having "overthr[own] all external ceremonies not tending to the necessary furtherance of God's word" (294). The logic here suggests that embodiment and materiality, as such, threaten "the Word," which presides over the passage as an immaterial standard in danger of being falsely covered.

Ridley's degrading from "the dignity of priesthood"[9] extends Latimer's logic, and Foxe's account stresses Ridley's critique of externalities and costume: "they put upon Ridley the surplice with all the trinkets appertaining to the mass. As they were putting on the same, Ridley did vehemently inveigh against the Romish bishop [the Pope] and all that foolish apparel, calling him Antichrist and the apparel foolish and abominable—yea, too fond for Vice in a play" (306). The reference to theater and the illusions of drama, of course, provides a foretaste of the antitheatricality that would develop later in the century. Here, though, the emphasis upon folly and abomination highlights a vision of a truth endangered by potential investments in materiality.

Foxe's narrative nevertheless deploys its own impeccable and spectacular sense of fabric. Both Latimer and Ridley enter perfectly attired for the roles they will perform in the mid-century theater of Protestantism. Brought before the Bishop of Lincoln to be examined "upon certain assertions," Latimer appears in what we can only consider the costume of Humilitas, a counterpart to the appareled "Vice in a play": "Latimer bowed his knee down to the ground, holding his hat in his hand, having a kerchief on his head and upon it a nightcap or two, and a great cap with two broad flaps to button under the chin, wearing a threadbare Bristow frieze gown girded with a penny leather girdle, at which hanged by a long string of leather his Testament, and his spectacles without case depending about his neck upon his breast" (302). Here we recognize Latimer's characteristic "displaying modesty." Foxe's detailing of the poverty of Latimer's attire ("threadbare," "frieze," "penny leather," "without case") invokes a powerful and loamy iconography. Shakespeare later will compress this linkage of moral fiber and homespun cloth in *Love's Labour's Lost* as "russet yeas and honest kersey noes" (5.2.414). Foxe's outfitting of Latimer here prepares a weighty theatrics of plainness for ensuing events, as we will see.

Meanwhile, Foxe recounts the rite of degradation, Ridley having been adjudged "to be degraduated from all ecclesiastical order" (306). What is most striking about the episode is the severe detachment of dressing and undressing from any trace of individual volition—almost all agency in this matter is given to those with custody of Ridley. In fact, we have already been presented with a life of Ridley in which his daily habits included a session of prayer "every morning, as soon as his apparel was done upon him" (292). Just as ecclesiastical garments are being "*put upon*" Ridley here, we see in the passive grammar that dressing was sometimes an event expressing social relations of one kind or another, even on a "normal" day. But in the appropriations of Ridley's body to strip him of his office and of both men's bodies in "secular" executions, this deindividuated practice of the relation of clothes to persons takes on spectacular effects; these are effects Foxe is concerned to critique in the name of a conscience that is "inviolable."[10]

During Ridley's degradation, the officiators first "put upon" Ridley "the trinkets of the mass" or "mass gear" and then they sequentially remove it again (306–7). As they manipulate his body, Ridley launches a fierce disputation of the very terms by which the divestiture proceeds, inveighing "vehemently . . . against . . . all that foolish apparel" (306). They hold Ridley's hands onto the chalice and wafer when he promises to drop them. When lastly they remove the surplice from his back, Foxe offers Ridley's last, deeply rhetorical question: "What power be you of, that you can take from a man that which he never had?" (306). This profound contestation of the social and institutional effectiveness of investiture in the first instance, while others are dressing and undressing Ridley, makes formidable Protestant theater—even as it casts church orthodoxies as mere (if violent) puppeteering.

The final passages conjoin both official and Protestant costumings with the extraordinary high-impact physicality of being publicly undressed, by others. The costumes of execution are tailored to the character and station of the two men. Ridley wore "a fair black gown, furred and faced with foins, such as he was wont to wear being bishop, and a tippet of velvet furred likewise about his neck, a velvet nightcap upon his head and a corner cap upon the same, going in a pair of slippers to the stake" (308). Latimer's attire, though, not only typifies his spiritual self-presentation in life—it also triggers the precise affective response in the audience that was traditionally attributed to rhetorical effectiveness: "After [Ridley] came Latimer in a poor Bristow frieze frock all worn, with his buttoned cap and kerchief on his head, all ready to the fire, a new long shroud hanging over his hose down to the feet; which at first sight stirred men's hearts to rue upon them" (308). Stirred by rhetoric, stirred by cloth: the detail implies Latimer's subsequent words to Ridley that together they will light a candle for Protestantism in England. Commanded to prepare themselves (undress), "they with all meekness obeyed" (309). Ridley removes his gown and tippet and gives them to his brother-in-law; "some other apparel that was little worth he gave away; other the bailiffs took . . . some plucked the points off his hose; happy was he that could get any rag from him" (310). The ritual dissolution of Ridley's person is enacted socially in these commanded and coerced deliveries of his attire to bystanders of every kind. Deliberating whether he should die in his truss, his brother-in-law concluded it would only increase the pain when it might instead do a poor man some good; Ridley then "unlaced himself" and went "in his shirt" to the stake.

Latimer's disrobings are only more explosive. After Ridley's obedient self-stripping, "Latimer gave nothing, but very quietly suffered his keeper to pull off his hose and other array, which was very simple" (310). In Latimer's case, such an undressing effects a transfiguration, one driven by a reversed semiotic of weakness and strength: "Being stripped into his shroud, he seemed as comely a person to them that were present as one should li[ke]ly see; whereas in his clothes he appeared a withered and crooked, silly old man, he now stood bolt upright, as comely a father as one might behold" (310). Ridley, "being" "in his shirt," Latimer "stripped" "into his shroud"—the ambivalent grammars reflect both a state of undress and the purest forms of covering. The martyrs are alive and transfigured in the naked costumes of sleep and death. Foxe's text partly contests the institutional arrangements and orthodoxies behind the power of clothes to "make (or unmake) the man." But he is also a citizen of the cloth economy, the "worn world," Peter Stallybrass has described: the details of dress cannot be overlooked, cannot even be resisted; they are materially relevant to transactions in personage.

Notes

1. William Shakespeare, *King Lear,* in *William Shakespeare: The Complete Works,* ed. Alfred Harbage (New York: Viking Press, 1969), 3.4. 101; 1.4.183–84. All subsequent Shakespeare references are to this edition.
2. For a detailed analysis of this process, especially in its relation to the the-

ater and theatricality, see Peter Stallybrass, "Worn worlds: clothes and identity on the Renaissance stage," in *Subject and Object in Renaissance Culture,* eds. Margreta de Grazia, Maureen Quilligan, and Peter Stallybrass (Cambridge: Cambridge University Press, 1996), 289–320.

3. U.S. Constitutional case law reflects this tradition of a differentiated nomenclature. See *New York Times v. Sullivan,* 376 U.S. 254 (1964) and its subsequent elucidation in *Curtis Publishing v. Butts,* 388 U.S. 130 (1967) and *Gertz v. Robert Welch, Inc.,* 418 U.S. 323 (1973). These cases establish the responsibilities of the press regarding defamation of, respectively, "public officials," "public figures," and "private persons."

4. Aemilia Lanyer, "A Description of Cooke-ham," in *The Poems of Aemilia Lanyer,* ed. Susanne Woods (Oxford: Oxford University Press, 1993), lines 105–12; Francis Bacon, "Of Great Place," in *Francis Bacon: A Compilation of the Major Works,* ed. Brian Vickers (Oxford: Oxford University Press, 1996), 359–61.

5. No record of Latimer's degradation survives.

6. This reasoning underlies the "legal fiction" of corporate perpetuity: predecessor and successor are accorded identity, as "one person," since "a delegation made to the Dignity without expressing a proper name passes on to the successor"; quoted and discussed at length in Ernst Kantorowicz, *The King's Two Bodies: A Study in Medieval Political Theology* (Princeton: Princeton University Press, 1957), 385–96.

7. For a discussion of this phenomenon, see Jesse Lander, "Foxe's *Books of Martyrs*: printing and popularizing the *Acts and Monuments*," in *Religion and Culture in Renaissance England,* eds. Claire McEachern and Debora Shuger (Cambridge: Cambridge University Press, 1997), 69–92.

8. John Foxe, *Foxe's Book of Martyrs,* ed. G. A. Williamson (Boston: Little, Brown and Company, 1965), 294. Subsequent references are to this edition and will appear in the text.

9. Ridley was degraded from the priesthood only; for somewhat hazy reasons, his prosecutors refused to recognize his episcopal orders. For an assessment, see David Loades, *The Oxford Martyrs* (Bangor, Wales: Headstart History, 1992), 215–16.

10. For a persuasive account of the production, rather than the dissolution, of Protestant selfhood in the flames of the Marian persecution, see Janel M. Mueller, "Pain, persecution, and the construction of selfhood in Foxe's *Acts and Monuments*," in McEachern and Shuger, eds., *Religion and Culture in Renaissance England,* 161–87.

Handkerchiefs and Early Modern Ideologies of Gender

WILL FISHER

I BEGIN WITH A STORY from Renaissance England about a handkerchief. It is a tale of intrigue and jealousy, involving a man anxious about a woman's purity and some impertinent trifling. The plot is simple: one man becomes enraged when he sees the woman's linen in the hands (and even touching the face) of his rival. This story is not, however, the one told by William Shakespeare. Shakespeare's version would not be written for another forty years. It is Sir Thomas Randolph's account of an incident that occurred at Hampton Court in 1565. It involves Queen Elizabeth I and two of the most influential courtiers at the time, Leicester and Norfolk.

One day in March 1565 Elizabeth watched as her favorites played tennis for her amusement. The weather was warm and Leicester had apparently become "hot" and was "sweating." During a break from the action the two men came over to the area where the Queen was sitting, and then, suddenly and without warning, Leicester snatched "the Queen's napkin out of her hand and wiped his face" with it. Seeing this gesture, Norfolk was immediately incensed: he "said that he [Leicester] was too saucy," and "swore that he would lay his racket upon his face." Following this threat, there "rose great trouble" and blows eventually ensued. Finally, Randolph notes that afterward "the Queen [was] offended sore with the Duke" for his behavior.[1]

In order to better understand this incident, there are two things that we need to bear in mind. First of all, it is worth noting that it takes place relatively early in Elizabeth's reign and that at the time Leicester was, despite Norfolk's opposition, actively vying for the Queen's hand (and perhaps even her handkerchiefs). In fact, just a year before the affair at Hampton Court, Leicester had had a portrait of himself painted in which he gently caresses a handkerchief

Figure 1. Anglo-Netherlands School, *Robert Dudley, 1st Earl of Leicester (with Dog)*, c. 1564. Reproduced by permission of a private collector.

tucked away in his purse (Fig. 1). In a recent article on the portrait, Jacob Voorthuis suggests that this napkin may well have been a token of affection from the Queen herself.[2] Furthermore, the composition of Leicester's portrait is virtually identical to that of a portrait Norfolk had painted of himself the preceding year, 1563. In Norfolk's portrait, his body is posed in the same position as Leicester's, and he too fingers a handkerchief in his purse (Fig. 2).

Secondly, the handkerchief was a relatively new cultural artifact, and therefore its social connotations and the rules governing its use were still in process of being defined. Fashion historians often point out that the handkerchief was first popularized in Europe during the Renaissance. In England, this accessory came into widespread use during the sixteenth century, reaching the peak of its popularity during the reign of Elizabeth. The *OED* indicates that the term "hand-kercher" first appeared in English in the 1530s. As its name implies, the handkerchief was conceptualized as a version of the Medieval "kerchief" specifically intended for the "hand."[3] Norbert Elias has argued that the adoption of this object and others like it (for example, the fork, separate bowls for eating, etc.) was an important part of "the civilizing process."[4] Moreover, he suggests that the use of these utensils by certain groups of people ultimately helped to establish social distinctions and map out differences of status. But if Elias provides an incisive analysis of how new types of class identity were formed through the development of a new system of manners and through new cultural artifacts like the handkerchief, he is largely silent on how these social processes might have been inflected by questions of gender. What I am interested in here is the role the handkerchief played in materializing early modern notions of femininity, and the female body. In particular, I believe that the increasing social importance of the handkerchief might be viewed in relation to the patriarchal ideology that figured women as "leaky vessels." Gail Paster has brilliantly demonstrated the pervasiveness of this trope, noting that Renaissance "medical texts, iconography, and proverbs of oral culture" all describe women as being more "watery" than men.[5] These descriptions of women's humoral "nature" have encoded within them pejorative ideas about women's character and behavior: the images of "leaky" women "reproduce a virtual symptomatology of woman, which insists on the female body's moisture, secretions, and productions as shameful tokens of uncontrol."[6]

We can see some of these issues or concerns made manifest in Randolph's account of the incident at Hampton Court. First, Nor-

Figure 2. Hans Eworth, *Thomas Howard, 4th Duke of Norfolk*, 1563. Reproduced by permission of a private collector.

folk's angry outburst about Leicester wiping his sweat on Elizabeth's handkerchief may well have been a displaced reaction to Leicester's attempts to "soil" the Queen's purity by forming a marital (or sexual) alliance with her. It is not particularly surprising to find that Norfolk was anxious about protecting Elizabeth from being "tainted" by Leicester since the purity of the Virgin Queen was a widespread cultural preoccupation. Nor, for that matter, is it particularly surprising to find that Elizabeth's handkerchief was the locus for Norfolk's anxieties. Handkerchiefs were, of course, well-known tokens of love.[7] But they were also objects that were involved in regulating the body and keeping it "pure." Moreover, we should note here that Elizabeth certainly seems to have been aware of the ideological figuration of women as "leaky vessels," and at times even manipulated it for her own purposes. The most notable example of this is the sieve portraits that she had painted of herself starting in about 1579 (see, for example, Fig. 3). The sieve in these images is a symbol of virginity, alluding to Petrarch's *Triumph of Chastity,* where the Roman Vestal Virgin Tuccia proved her purity by carrying water in a sieve without spilling a drop. The crucial point here is not simply that Elizabeth had herself represented as a "pure" virgin, but more specifically, that her virginity was symbolically linked to her ability to control leakage. In other words, Elizabeth's sexual continence was likened to the Vestal Virgin's miraculous ability to contain the flow of water from the sieve—the implication being that Elizabeth also has the "miraculous" ability to control her own leaky body. When seen from this perspective, the Queen's handkerchief emerges as yet another instrument for materializing her body as a classical body (to use Bahktin's terms), that is to say, for materializing it as an entity that is closed off and under control. Indeed, both the handkerchief in Randolph's account and the sieves in the portraits are associated with Elizabeth's purity, and in both cases that purity seems to be associated with a kind of corporeal continence.

But if the handkerchief was thus an instrument of self-fashioning for Elizabeth and also, more generally, an artifact that helped to produce the patriarchal ideology that figured women as "leaky" vessels, its role in these processes was necessarily complicated by its prosthetic nature, by its transferability. Thus, even if these accessories were, as Stephanie Dickey remarks in an article on them, "almost exclusively a female attribute" in Renaissance "history painting," "theater," and "portraiture," we cannot forget that the handkerchief was a detachable part and as such could not be tied

Figure 3. Quentin Metsys the Younger, *Elizabeth I ("The Sieve Portrait")*, c. 1583. Reproduced by permission of the Pinacoteca Nazionale, Siena, Italy.

exclusively to any one particular group or person. Indeed, the different stories about the provenance of the handkerchief in Shakespeare's *Othello* demonstrate the problematic gendering of this article. At one point, Othello tells Desdemona that the handkerchief was a given to him by his dying mother (3.4.52ff), and at another he claims that it was "an antique token / My father gave my mother" (5.2.210). These conflicting accounts highlight the handkerchief's ability to move among different hands, and more specifically, to move between differently gendered hands. Once we have recognized this, it becomes apparent that it was the ideological work of "history painting," "theater," and "portraiture" to make it seem as if handkerchiefs were simply "a female attribute."[8]

In Randolph's account, it precisely the transferability of the handkerchief that is at issue: the accessory is taken from Elizabeth by Leicester. Furthermore, in this particular case Leicester appears to be as much, if not more, of a "leaky vessel" than the Queen. When seen from this perspective, Norfolk's comment that Leicester was "too saucy" would imply not only that he had been "impertinent" with a social superior, but also that he was quite literally too "sweaty."[9] Leicester's excessive perspiration therefore becomes an indication that he is an inappropriate partner for the Queen: it is a sign of both his inherent "baseness" (his "lowly" class status) and his excessive heat (his indecorous sexuality).

Finally, we should acknowledge that the handkerchief itself is a strangely contradictory artifact. According to Dickey, although "the aristocratic connotations of the handkerchief stem . . . from two factors" (first, "its costliness as a material object, finely woven, embroidered and sometimes even adorned with pearls," and second, "its implicit function to absorb bodily fluids, foul odors, and other indignities the bearer is by implication too civilized to deal with in a more casual fashion"), in practice "these two connotations are antithetical" for "to employ a costly, elaborately decorated article like the embroidered handkerchief . . . for actually blowing the nose would be . . . unthinkable."[10] This incongruity has radical implications: it means that, on the one hand, the handkerchief is associated with purity (with clean, white linen), but on the other hand it is also associated with impurities (like "base" bodily fluids). In Elizabeth's case, these antithetical qualities are foregrounded. While it is clear that the Queen's handkerchief, as I have already suggested, helped to construct her purity, it is unclear whether the item itself is pure or impure: that is to say, whether it simply attests to the Queen's inherent purity (demonstrating that her body is like the "miraculous" sieve that does not leak), or whether it maintains the Queen's purity by absorbing impurities. Moreover, Leicester's affront will appear to be different depending on how we understand the object: in the first instance, the transgression would be that Leicester has contaminated the Queen's pristine napkin, and by extension, the Queen herself, whereas in the second, it would be that he has dared to mix his own bodily fluids with those of the Queen.

If Randolph's account of the incident at Hampton Court thus illustrates the contradictory nature of the handkerchief, I hope that it also begins to demonstrate the extent to which Renaissance notions of femininity were bound up with historically specific material objects. Indeed, historicizing the early modern body and early modern ideologies of gender would seem to necessitate being attentive to the prosthetic accessories that worked to materialize them.

Notes

1. This incident is described in several of Elizabeth's biographies, especially Elizabeth Jenkins's *Elizabeth and Leicester* (New York: Coward-McCann, Inc., 1961), 115–16. Neville Williams provides a direct quotation of this section of Randolph's letter in *All the Queen's Men: Elizabeth I and Her Courtiers* (New York: Macmillan, 1972), 91.

2. Jacob Voorthuis, "Portraits of Leicester," *The Dutch in Crisis 1583–88: People and Politics in Leicester's Time* (Leiden, 1988), 58–59. Cited in *Dynasties: Painting in Tudor and Jacobean England 1530–1630,* ed. Karen Hearn (London: Tate Publishing, 1995), 96–97.

3. See the *OED*'s entry for "handkerchief."

4. Norbert Elias, *The Civilizing Process,* trans. Edmund Jephcott (Oxford: Blackwell Books, 1994).

5. Gail Kern Paster, "Leaky Vessels: The Incontinent Women of City Comedy," in *The Body Embarrassed: Drama and the Disciplines of Shame in Early Modern England* (Ithaca: Cornell University Press, 1993), 25.

6. Ibid., 52.

7. See Diana O'Hara's discussion of handkerchiefs as love tokens in "The Language of Tokens and the Making of Marriage," *Rural History* (1992): 1–40.

8. Dickey focuses almost exclusively on Dutch painting, but Juana Greene makes a similar observation about English painting. According to Greene, the handkerchief is a common prop "in the portraiture of the Elizabethan, Jacobean, and Carolinian periods": as she puts it, there are "many paintings depict[ing] noble and gentry women holding large lace-edged handkerchiefs." Stephanie S. Dickey, "Women Holding Handkerchiefs in Seventeenth-Century Dutch Portraits," in *Beeld en zelfbeeld in de Nederlandse kunst, 1550–1750* [*Image and self-image in Netherlandish art, 1550–1750*], ed. Reindert Falkenburg, Jan de Jong, Herman Roodenburg, and Frits Scholten, *Kunsthistorisch Jaarboek 1995,* vol. 46 (Zwolle: Waanders Uitgevers, 1995), 340. Juana Greene, " 'For Love and Money, Love and Ware Weele Sell': Merchandising and Marrying in *The Faire Maide of*

the Exchange." Unpublished Manuscript. I thank Juana for sharing her work with me.
   9. The *OED* lists "sweat" as one of the available meanings of "sauce" during the Renaissance.
   10. Dickey, "Women Holding Handkerchiefs," 336.

Elizabeth's Embroidery

Maureen Quilligan

THE ELEVEN-YEAR-OLD Princess Elizabeth covered a manuscript volume that she presented as a gift to her stepmother Katherine Parr in 1544 with an embroidered sleeve or chemise, for which she, apparently, had done the needlework.[1] Embroidered in bright turquoise blue and decorated with an interlaced design picked out in still-shiny silver thread, the volume makes an elaborate gift, with Katherine's initials, "K.P.," raised up in cotton batting–stuffed relief in the center of both back and front covers. Raised-work embroidered silver flowers are at each of the four corners, probably pansies, forming a pun on the French word for thoughts, "pensees." The French pun is appropriate because the manuscript is of Elizabeth's translation of Marguerite de Navarre's *Miroir de l'Ame Pecheresse* [*The Mirror or Glass of the Sinful Soul*]. More cotton batting is used to raise cord-marks on the book's spine, as if the embroidered cover were part of the manuscript's actual binding, allowing the book to mimic authorship of a bound manuscript volume such as one might find in a library.

Paradoxically, the contrast between the smooth, nearly professional perfection of the gobelin-stitched embroidery in its elaborate interlaced design and the rather awkward italic printing of the manuscript itself, if it does not betray the hand of a more mature sewing teacher, reveals that even for royally born Elizabeth, the needle was a far more practiced instrument in her eleven-year-old hand than the pen.[2] She had not yet come under the tutelage of Roger Ascham, who, after age fourteen, had a pronounced effect on her handwriting. Perhaps the most important aspect of this object—which may help us to understand how the embroidery assists rather than detracts from her writerly authority—is that she dedicated the volume to her stepmother. Such a dedication may be no more than an attempt to please a queen of pronounced Protestant sympathies by translating the work of another, but it is uncanny

Figure 1. MS Cherry. Reproduced by permission of the Bodleian Library, University of Oxford.

that the text of this translated poem, sent from one female family member to another, covered in a personally worked textile, results in a gesture that looks oddly like the trade in woven heirloom items that Annette Weiner finds generic to female communities and that, she has brilliantly argued, requires us to revise our sense of the

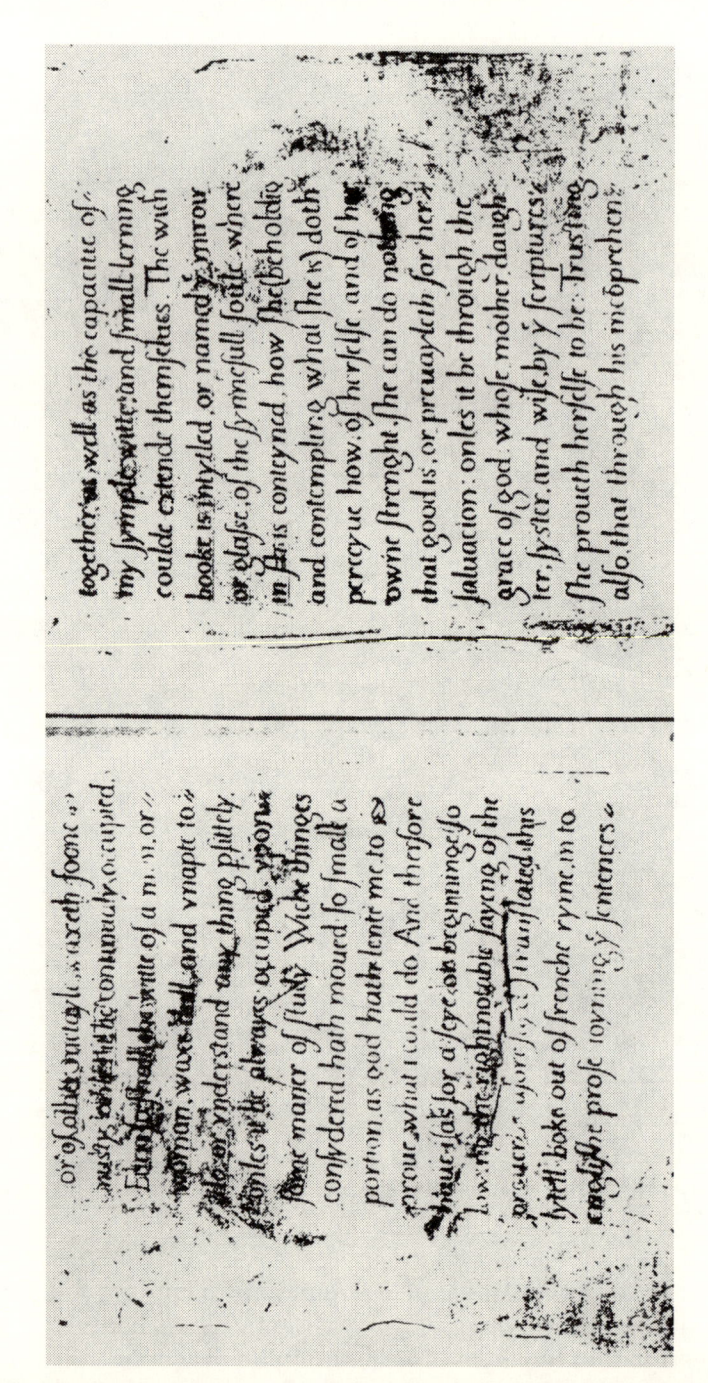

Figure 2. MS Cherry: fols. 2ᵛ-3. Reproduced by permission of the Bodleian Library, University of Oxford.

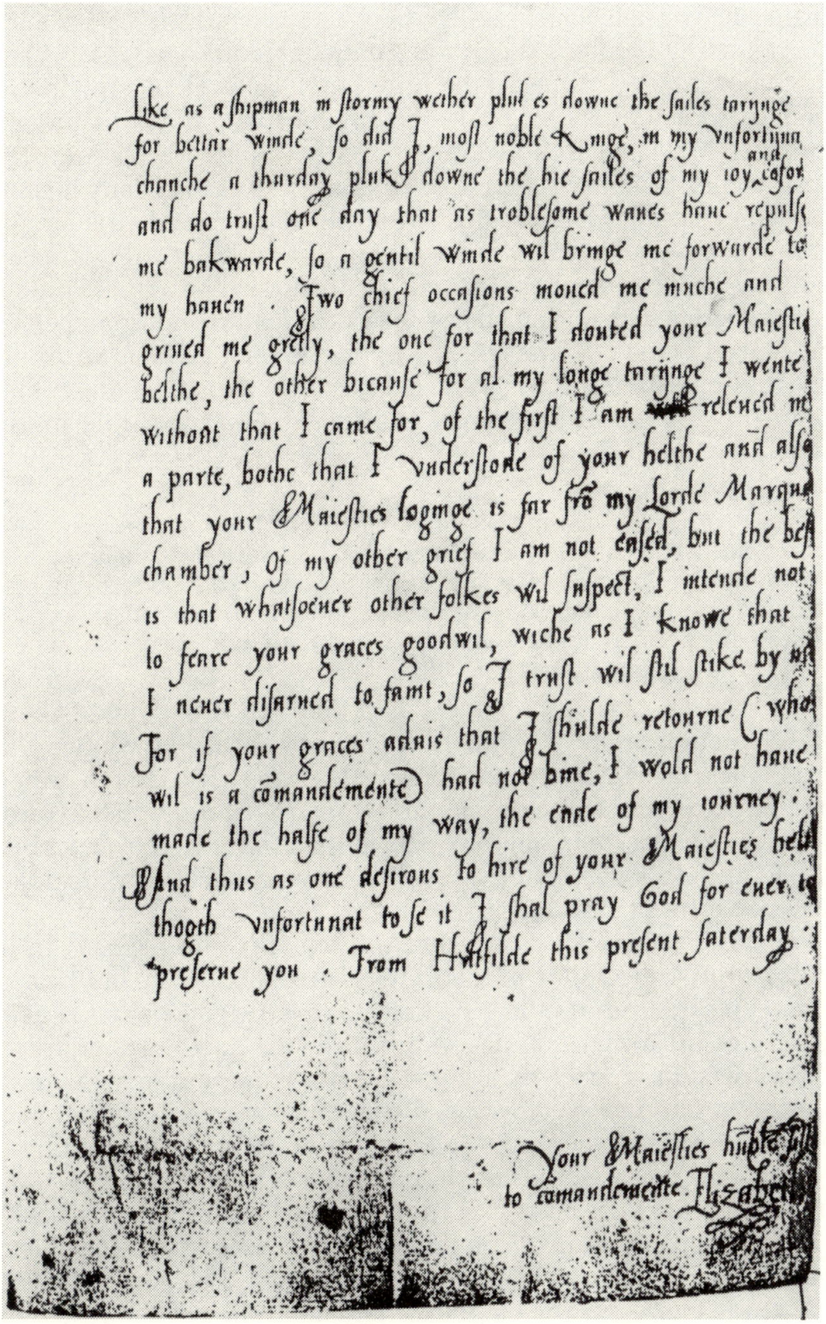

Like as a shipman in stormy wether pluckes downe the sailes tarijnge
for bettar winde, so did I, most noble kinge, in my vnfortunat
chanche a thursday plukd downe the hie sailes of my ioy, and cofor
and do trust one day that as troblesome wanes haue repulsed
me bakwarde, so a gentil winde wil bringe me forwarde to
my hauen. Two chief occasions moued me muche and
grieued me gretly, the one for that I douted your Maiesties
helthe, the other bicanse for al my longe tarijnge I wente
without that I came for, of the first I am releued in
a parte, bothe that I vnderstode of your helthe and also
that your Maiesties logmoe is far fro my Lorde Marques
chamber, Of my other grief I am not eased, but the best
is that whatsoener other folkes wil suspect, I intende not
to feare your graces goodwil, wiche as I knowe that
I neuer disarned to famt, so I trust wil stil stike by me
for if your graces aduis that I shulde retourne (whos
wil is a comandemente) had not bine, I wold not haue
made the halfe of my way, the ende of my iourney.
And thus as one desirous to hire of your Maiesties helthe
thoogh vnfortunat to se it I shal pray God for euer to
preserue you. From Hatfilde this present saterday

Your Maiesties humble
to comandemente. Elizabeth

Figure 3. From Alfred Fairbank and Berthold Wolpe, *Renaissance Handwriting*, p. 66. (See note 2.)

"traffic in women" outlined by Lévi-Strauss and Marcell Mauss.[3] Indeed, using Weiner's theory of "inalienable possessions" as central to her understanding of the function of some gift-giving in Elizabethan society, Lisa M. Klein has argued that 1544 was the year Elizabeth had been established in the succession by an act of Parliament, although she was still illegitimate.[4] As a gift to a female member of her father's family—in which Elizabeth now had a slightly more secure place—the woven nature of the object calls attention to its inalienable status.[5] Klein never discusses the actual contents of Elizabeth's translation (her concern is for the embroidery), but the central trope of incest insists upon the endogamous withholding from circulation of the female speaker. Elizabeth's one remark about the content of the translation insists upon multiple intimacies:

> The which book is entitled, or named, *The Mirror or Glass of the Sinful Soul,* wherein is contained how she (beholding and contemplating what she is) doth perceive how of herself and of her own strength she can do nothing that good is, or prevaileth for her salvation, unless it be through the grace of God, whose mother, daughter, sister, and wife by the scriptures she proveth her self to be.[6]

Such a metaphor speaks directly against the traffic in women that, according to Lévi-Strauss, the incest taboo was supposed to protect: the textual content of a woman-to-woman gift of cloth, as Weiner has further suggested, and the endogamous status of the object indicate Elizabeth's very youthful self-citing at an anthropologically very powerful position for a female.[7]

We usually understand the pen and needle to be opposed in the protofeminist discourse of the Renaissance, of course, but here, in Elizabeth's first production, the pen and needle go together in a first gesture of intrafamilial authorship. Indeed, Ann Jones and Peter Stallybrass have recently argued that far from confining women, embroidery and sewing, especially in an aristocratic setting, were means for artistic display: "Whatever repressive and isolating effects sewing as a disciplinary apparatus might have been intended to produce, women used it both to connect to one another within domestic settings and to articulate public roles for themselves in the outer world."[8]

Nothing expresses the claims for female agency possible to make for embroidery and sewing more clearly than the cloth-draped interior of Hardwick Hall. Covering as much interior surface as the famous windows by Smythson—by which the house is known through its jingle, "Hardwick Hall, more glass than wall"—the embroideries and other cloth hangings made by Elizabeth, Countess of Shrewsbury, her women, and her professional male embroiderers, are often of militant female virtues as well as more passive kinds. One set of very large appliqué hangings—made from recycled ecclesiastical cloth bought by two of Elizabeth's husbands during the dissolution of the monasteries—celebrates famous historical women along with their personified virtues: Zenobia (Maganimity and Prudence), Penelope (Patience and Perseverance), Lucretia (Chastity and Liberality), Cleopatra (Fortitude and Justice), Artmesia (Constancy and Pietas—Aeneas's heroic virtue). Other panels represent various female allegorical virtues conquering famous tyrants: Faith squashing Mahomet, Hope against Judas, Temperance conquering Sardanapalus.[9] The Hardwick Hall records reveal that in 1591–92 Bess gave Elizabeth's embroiderer a large sum of money to work pieces for a gown for the Queen; such payments are perhaps in lieu of the actual cloth that may have been given at various other times (Levey, 36).

Elizabeth's manuscript sleeve is on a much smaller scale than these gifts, of course; but it is clear that its transferral is the beginning of the object's familiar circulation which will work to increase (or decrease) the creator's reputation.[10] The eleven-year-old Elizabeth asks Katherine to keep the volume private, at least until its faults have been corrected: "But I hope that after having been in Your Grace's hands there shall be nothing in it worthy of reprehension and that in the meanwhile no other (but your highness only) shall read it or see it, lest my faults be known of many" (112). In essence asking for collaborative correction, Elizabeth fearfully expects that many will read the volume and, while not exactly assuming "publication" thereby, she reveals her concern for the performance as one by which she will be judged. One of the faults about which she worries is clearly her understanding of the French she has translated, but it is the entire object, including the embroidery, which would have been displayed by the Queen when she offered it to another reader. Elizabeth's needlework as well as her verbal mastery are both on display in the gift. At eleven she would not have known, of course, that the text would be reprinted five separate times throughout her reign; its reproduction in print means that the text ceases to be a private and inalienable object— but for all that it does not cease to work to increase the authority of Elizabeth and of the women whose writing it accompanies in the massive compilation in which it appears in 1582, Thomas Bentley's three-volume *Monument of Matrons* (later expanded to five volumes). In a very real sense, this print version of the text merely replicates in monumentally public form the authority the embroidery-covered object implicitly had within it.

Notes

1. Margaret H. Swain, "A New Year's Gift from the Princess Elizabeth," *The Connoisseur* 36 (1973): 258–66. I am indebted to Martin Kauffman, Department of Western Manuscripts, Bodleian Library, Oxford, for this reference and for aid in handling the volume.

2. Alfred Fairbank and Berthold Wolpe, in *Renaissance Handwriting: An Anthology of Italic Scripts* (London, 1960), 67, argue that Elizabeth was at the time a student of the writing tutor Jean Belmain, and that Ascham and Grindal only influenced but did not radically change her elegant hand. See figures 2 and 3.

3. Annette Weiner, *Inalienable Possessions: The Paradox of Keeping-While-Giving* (Calif., 1992); see especially chapter 2, "Reconfiguring Exchange Theory."

4. Lisa M. Klein, "Your Humble Handmaid: Elizabethan Gifts of Needlework," *Renaissance Quarterly* (1997): 459–93.

5. See Klein, p. 465.

6. Marc Shell, *Elizabeth's Glass* (Lincoln: University of Nebraska Press, 1993), 111.

7. For the now classic discussion of Levi-Strauss on which most feminist uses of the traffic in women rest (including Weiner's) see Gayle Rubin, "The Traffic in Women: Notes on the Political Economy of Sex," in *Towards an Anthropology of Women,* ed. Rayna Reiter (New York: 1975), 157–210.

8. See Ann Jones and Peter Stallybrass, "The Needle and the Pen," in *Worn Worlds: Clothes and Identity in the Renaissance* (forthcoming).

9. Santina M. Levey, *An Elizabethan Inheritance: The Hardwick Hall Textiles* (London: 1998), 69.

10. Susan Frye, "Sewing Connections: Elizabeth Tudor, Mary Stuart, Elizabeth Talbot, and Seventeenth-century Anonymous Needleworkers," in *Maids and Mistresses: Women's Alliances in Early Modern England* (Oxford: 1999), 165–82, emphasizes the differences between Elizabeth Tudor's girlhood embroidery and Elizabeth Talbot's heroic wall hangings; without an appreciation of the theoretically powerful incestuous content of the translated text, it is difficult to see the similarities between the two Elizabeths' needlework. For further discussion see "The Case of Elizabeth" in my *Incest and Agency: Female Authority in the Renaissance* (forthcoming).

Cheerful Givers: Henslowe, Alleyn, and the 1612 Loan Book to the Crown

S. P. Cerasano

THE CIRCULATION OF MATERIAL objects—in the form of gifts, bribes, and loans—has long been central to understanding power relations in early modern Europe. Historians continually remind us that these transactions were part of the everyday traffic of social and political affairs, especially within patronage networks. As Linda Levy Peck explains, the complex patron-client relationship of the period was conceived of as a "mutual exchange of benefits." However, as she also notes, service to a notable patron was both a sign of status and a burden.[1] Consequently, personal and political rewards bred financial obligations, not uncommonly for the individual in service to a greater lord. Given their subtle nature these transactions are frequently difficult to identify. However, one particular window into such obligations is preserved in British Library Additional MS. 27,877, in which are listed the names of persons who contributed to a loan to King James in 1612.

The book consists of over one hundred pages and catalogs within these roughly six hundred names. The first section of the book is organized according to the officers of various legal courts—Chancery, King's Bench, Common Pleas, the Exchequer, and Star Chamber. There follows a brief section headed "Merchant Strangers," listing many French and Dutch merchants who contributed to the loan. However, the largest portion of the book records, on a country-by-country basis, lenders' names, the sums lent, the dates of payment to the collectors, and the dates that the funds were transferred to the Exchequer of Receipt. Approximately six to ten names are listed per each "day of payment," suggesting that the collectors contacted lenders individually and, even perhaps, personally.

Although termed a "loan," the lenders understood implicitly

that, given the Crown's financial circumstances in 1612, they might never receive repayment of the loan; or that repayment might indeed take a very long time. To begin with, King James had inherited a substantial debt from Elizabeth I, as well as a public revenue system that, in Conrad Russell's phrase, was "close to the point of breakdown" when James ascended the throne. Additionally, the effects of serious long-term underfunding had begun to take their toll. By the beginning of James's reign no more than 10 percent of households in the country were required to pay the lay subsidy taxes periodically approved by parliament. Moreover, other factors strained the budget. The Jacobean court was much more expensive to operate than Elizabeth's had been. The King, Queen, and Prince Henry each ran his or her own household. Then there was the problem of conspicuous consumption that, as David Loades explains so well, was seemingly inherent in the aristocracy: "Aristocratic households were traditional centres of power, patronage and conspicuous consumption."[2] Unfortunately, King James and Queen Anne excelled at prodigality. Their time at court was marked by displays such as the Jonsonian masques, the ostentatious funeral of Prince Henry, and the lavish wedding of the Princess Elizabeth—the latter two occurring in the period around 1612. All this exacerbated the Crown's financial problems and made even more desperate the need for the loan. What had been the Crown's customary expenses of £300,000 per annum, during the reign of Elizabeth in peacetime, rose initially under James to £400,000, and to £550,000 by 1614.[3] Thus, the loan was one of Robert Cecil's last initiatives to reduce the Crown's debt before his death in May of the same year.[4]

The loan book represents a collection of names headed by aristocrats, those loyal both to the Crown and to the conservative faction led by Cecil. Not surprisingly, the list reads like a social register, including such personages as Sir William Bowyer, Sir William Killigrew, Sir George Coppin, and Sir Henry Billingsley. Sir Jerome Bowes, sometime ambassador to Russia, also contributed, as did Sir Thomas Vincent, Sir George and Sir Nicholas Carew, and Sir Thomas Heneage. More than several wealthy women also contributed, some widowed, who were members of eminent noble families, such as Susan, Lady Stanhope and Lady Elizabeth Kitson. There are other familiar names as well, including John Donne (who just over a decade later became Edward Alleyn's father-in-law), Fulke Greville, and Robert Fludd, the well-known physician, alchemist, and rosicrucian.[5]

Philip Henslowe and Edward Alleyn appear together on fol. 140[4] under the section devoted to Surrey, which spans just under two pages. They are the only persons listed in the loan book in any way connected with theatrical interests.[6] However, they are doubtless included because of their social backgrounds—each was armigerous by birth—and also they shared the position of Master of the Royal Game at the time. (They acquired the position in November 1604, through Sir William Steward, the King's good friend, who had acquired the patent from the Crown just a few months earlier.[7]) In the context of the other lenders Henslowe and Alleyn's "liberality" (as it would have been termed then) placed them well within the upper echelon of the lenders. The donations ranged from just over £6 to £50. Most gentlemen lent sums in the lowest range, while many titled nobles were content to loan £20 each. Within this group were Henslowe and Alleyn, who lent £10 and £15 respectively, placing them in league with significant landowners such as Sir Thomas Hunt, and just beneath Sir Lionel Cranfield, a businessman legendary for his wealth, who lent £20.

In the realm of their extensive holdings the money lent by Henslowe and Alleyn reduced their own value very little, though the amounts of their donations were substantial for the time. If nothing else their loans were meager in comparison with the money they earned through their ownership of the Bear Garden. Moreover, their involvement in court circles protected their own political and financial interests. Solidarity with royal factions offered immunity from certain types of reproach and legitimized their activities outside of the court circle. In retrospect, it seems that the 1612 loan fell at an advantageous moment. It was a pivotal year for Henslowe and Alleyn. Having encountered resistance from the Middlesex authorities in building the Fortune in 1600, they had relied upon the support of the Privy Council and the Queen to allow them to continue with this project. Now, twelve years later, they were making plans to convert their existing Bear Garden into a unique structure, a combination playhouse-baiting arena called the Hope, which was constructed the next year. Therefore the good will of the Crown was politically useful as an assurance that future projects would be supported. The Masters of the Game would have argued that if there was to be a Royal Game, periodically exhibited at court for the entertainment of the king and foreign visitors, it had to be practiced on a regular basis. Consequently, Henslowe and Alleyn needed a rebuilt Bear Garden to assist in this; not to mention that the business generated by the baiting in London was a hefty portion of their income. But, concurrently, Henslowe and Alleyn were well aware of the growing animosity of the city fathers toward the public stage. Given this, they might well have been wary that the London officials could argue that Southwark didn't need another playhouse. So however their plans were greeted, the royal imprimatur was politically useful.

Quite predictably, the liberality toward the Crown, as it is exemplified in the 1612 loan book, did not stop there. If the court was a place of conspicuous consumption it was also a place of conspicuous obligation, and Alleyn continued on in royal service until his death. In April 1619, Alleyn purchased a musket, coat of armor, and horse in order to outfit Sir Jeremy Turner, Muster Master of the Surrey trained bands. One month later, Alleyn and his wife traveled to Somerset House to attend the funeral of Queen Anne. On 24 March 1620 Alleyn visited Whitehall to attend the festivities celebrating King James's accession. On 8 September of the same year Alleyn's wife contributed £3 to the Queen of Bohemia's aid.[8] Such gifts and gestures were the currency that allowed them, and others, to get along in the murky waters of the Jacobean court circle.

Nor was the magnitude of their individual loans or gifts the most significant factor in reading their activities. Rather, these transactions would have been considered part of the reciprocal nature of the Crown's patronage, a sign that all was well in their mutual relationship, a symbol of the lenders' faithful adherence to their liege. Likewise it gave the lenders solidarity with other members of the aristocracy. In part, their acceptance of a royal patent placed Henslowe and Alleyn in positions of both power and obligation. In other part, the mutuality of patronage coupled virtue with the giving and ennobled their relationship with the Crown. Gift-giving was the mirror of Divine practice.[9] As was stated in 2 Corinthians 7–9 of the King James Bible, first printed in 1611: "God loveth a cheerful giver." Hence, Henslowe and Alleyn would have been pleased to have been thought of as being among those who supported the Crown in a time of need; and they would have thought themselves honored in that obligation. Thus, their appearance in the 1612 loan book speaks to yet another way in which the theatrical world came together with the world of the court. Furthermore, it illustrates that the theatrical world could be inhabited by men like Philip Henslowe, who spent their time brushing shoulders with the court not only to promote their own social aspirations, but to nurture and protect their business interests from within the corridors of conservative power.

Notes

1. Linda Levy Peck, *Court Patronage and Corruption in Early Stuart England* (London: Routledge, 1993), 15–17, 33, and elsewhere throughout the introduction and chapter 1. For ways in which the circulation of gifts influenced international politics see Gustav Ungerer, "Juan Pantoja de la Cruz and the Circulation of Gifts between the English and the Spanish Courts in 1604/5," *Shakespeare Studies* 26 (1998): 145–86.

2. David Loades, *Tudor Government* (Oxford: Blackwell, 1997), 236.

3. Christopher Durston, *James I* (London: Routledge, 1993), 24, 26–27.

4. Alan Haynes, *Robert Cecil: Earl of Salisbury, 1563–1612* (London: Peter Owen, 1989), 194–205, 212.

5. The community of names preserved in the manuscript constitutes several social groups. Many of those listed in the loan book had dealings with Henslowe and Alleyn during their careers. Given the brevity of this essay, I will have to explore these connections elsewhere.

6. The London and Middlesex pages are equally devoid of persons with theatrical interests. Also, unhappily, when all roads leading to Shakespeare's biography seem to come to dead ends, this manuscript is no exception. The Warwickshire pages are totally blank.

7. George F. Warner, *Manuscripts and Muniments of Alleyn's College of God's Gift at Dulwich* (London: Spottiswoode, 1881), 68.

Henslowe's affiliation with the court extended back to 1593 when he was appointed a Groom of the Chamber. He later became a Sewer of the Chamber and then a Gentleman Pensioner. E. K. Chambers, *The Elizabethan Stage* (Oxford: Clarendon Press), I, 44. Edward Alleyn's family had also been associated with the court, his father serving as a Gentleman Porter.

8. Warner, *Manuscripts and Muniments*, 178, 183, 186.

9. Peck, *Court Patronage,* 13ff. Barbara Rosenwein writes about these tendencies in an earlier context in *Negotiating Space: Power, Restraint, and the Privileges of Immunity in Early Medieval Europe* (Ithaca: Cornell University Press, 1999), especially chapter 7, "A Gift-giving King."

The Secret History of Richard Bellasis

LENA COWEN ORLIN

To TURN TO PROBATE DOCUMENTS for a cultural history of some early modern English *what*s—the goods and possessions of private life—is to discover the extent to which this is a history of early modern *where*s. Postmortem inventories were intended to be about the *what*s and their *how much*es, and so they remained for the poor, the unpropertied, and those in service, whose inventories generally listed only ready money and apparel. But for persons with anything more, possessions were categorized as well as appraised. One indexing system was generic: clothing was still listed as a separate category, as were plate, any jewels, bed and table linens, sometimes pewter. The second system was cartographic, with household furnishings listed under the names of the rooms in which they were found. Wills, meanwhile, identified objects in a number of ways, only one of which was descriptive. They could also specify location (William Wryghte left his son "my hutch in the loft which standeth by my bedside on that side which I lie on"); they could particularize by value (Agnes Hunte gave her daughter the "best" mattress, the "worst" bolster, and the "middle" tablecloth); and they could refer to provenance (Thomas Duckett assigned his daughter "a great brewing kettle that was my mother's" and "a little kettle bought at Waltham Fair last").[1] As a by-product of their designated functions, wills and inventories often indicate where goods were at the time of their owner's death, where they had been in their earlier history, and where their appointed future would take them.

No will full of *where*s is more interesting than that of Richard Bellasis, probated in 1600.[2] The wealthy, unmarried Bellasis, second son of a knight, named twenty-eight legatees: a brother, a sister, five cousins, eight nieces, six nephews, four servants, and three others. (He also remembered unnamed and unnumbered "yeomen servants," "servants at husbandry," and "women servants," and there were bequests for poor parishioners, poor prisoners, a free grammar school, and local roadworks.) Distributing his cash and personal goods among his kin, Bellasis wrote with so high a level of detail that from his will alone it is possible to compile a substantial inventory of his house at Morton in Durham.

He had a *hall* with a great wainscot dining table, forms (benches) and stools, and painted cloths on the walls. The *bedchamber over the hall* was Bellasis's own, with its bed, chests, coffers, desks, tables, pictures, hangings, and, just outside the door, a press or cupboard "where my apparel useth to lie." The *old parlor* contained another bed, more chests—one at the foot of the bed and one at its side—hangings, and also a chair "with a leather seat and back, which I do use to sit in." On the stair landing outside the *old high chamber over the old parlor* was a "London chest covered with black leather and banded with iron," holding damask and diaper linens; inside the chamber were two beds, two linen chests, more hangings, and a press. The *new parlor* had a little iron chest and a "long table" covered with Bellasis's "best Turkey carpet." His "best featherbed" was in the *great chamber over the new parlor,* which also had valuable tapestry hangings, wainscot cupboards, chairs, stools, and pictures. In the *little chamber next unto the great chamber* and the *little green chamber* were two more beds, more hangings, and more pictures; in the *gallery,* pictures; and in the *study,* a great press.

Although he required his nephew Charles Bellasis to live in the house as a condition of its bequeathal to him, Bellasis gave the contents of the great chamber, new parlor, and gallery to nephew Bryan Bellasis; the little chamber to sister Jane Hedworthe; the little green chamber to nephew John Pullen; half the old high chamber to niece Isabell Hedworthe; the other half to niece Margrett Hedworthe; the old parlor to nephew John Hedworthe; and the hall and the bedchamber over it to servant Margrett Lambert. Bellasis's habit of bequeathing room contents whole, rather than giving a table here and a bed there, intensifies the sense of a "world in little" dismembered by his death. Bellasis also split in thirds his remaining household stuff (among two nieces and a servant), his English books (three nephews), his armor and weapons (three nephews), and his farm animals and feed (two nephews and a servant). Plate was widely distributed, and two jewels went to his brother and a cousin.

The most extraordinary *wheres* of this will, though, concern the "ready current coin" shared out among twenty-five heirs. Bellasis documents over £64 in his study, "within a little purse of silk ribbon, within a little leather bag, which is put within a white leather shoe," which is tucked behind two books on the top shelf of the press in his study, "where the glasses stand." £100 are "laid within the bottom of the table chair" (a chair with a hinged back that could be lowered over its seat to form a table) "which standeth before [his] bedside, and hath ever some books and papers and hourglasses standing on it." £800 in three parcels—two "lapped up" in thin pieces of lead and one "within a little wooden box"—are walled in the "west side of the little dark stair that goeth down out of my bedchamber at Morton into my study there, about three quarters of a yard above the upper step." £200 are stowed "under the boards, betwixt two joists and the ceiling . . . hard under the first stepping up towards" a north window in a chamber. And £200 are in a wooden box "walled up in a hollow place within the wall" of the great chamber, "about one yard above the floor" in the southwest corner. In a study Bellasis maintained in another house, in Jarrow, £100 are stored in a "great iron chest."

Secretly, Bellasis added a "schedule" of these and other repositories to the will he had signed publicly, in the presence of seven witnesses, a month-and-a-half before (on 6 February 1596). The schedule was emended four times before his death. He first erased as "disbursed" some of his original entries: £100 in a box under the lowest shelf of the press in his study, £60 in a bag on the middle shelf, £100 in the bottom of a barrel in his wine-and-beer storehouse. Later, he recorded new deposits, among them £100 in a desk, £160 in two leather bags on the press, £100 in a chest in his bedchamber, and £129 13s. 4d. in the chest at Jarrow. Eventually, all but the last were again erased as spent. Finally, in February 1598, Bellasis wrote that he divided £400 among eight leather bags on his study press. At the time of his death, the cash reserves came to £1,194 3s. 4d., with £800 behind the wall of his study stair, £464 2s. on the press in his study, £200 under the floorboards at the chamber window, £200 behind the great chamber wall, £100 in the bedside table chair, and £229 13s. 4d. in the chest at Jarrow. The conspicuously active cash flow refutes his editor's speculation that Bellasis may have been "a penurious and suspicious miser, who loved to visit his treasured hoards." So, too, do the monies walled away and inaccessible, the funds at Jarrow that Bellasis says he "did never since peruse, or see," and a loan of £100 left unrecalled "for the easing of" one William Blitheman. In his own remarkably personal will, nephew Charles Bellasis paid tribute to the generosity of his "very good uncle."[3]

In the case of Richard Bellasis, the accidental cartographic effect of his will is exaggerated by an unorthodox life. Had he had a wife, son, or daughter to transmit his secret knowledge to, there might have been no need for the careful documentation of his hidden deposits. To prevent anyone coming after him from claiming the funds as some sort of domestic treasure trove, however, Bellasis autographed the description of each cache and also named witnesses to them. William Blitheman and William Thursbie could testify that they had locked his £100 in the chest at Jarrow. His servant Margrett Lambert could depose that she had "helped" to place the £800 in the stairway wall and the £200 walled up in the great chamber, that she was told of the £200 beneath the chamber floor and the £100 in the bedside table chair, and that she knew also of the money in the storehouse.

Margrett Lambert shared all the secrets of Morton save for those of the study; repeatedly, Bellasis characterizes her as solely "privy" to the hidden repositories.[4] When his scattered legacies to her are assembled in a coherent list, they also indicate that she was surprisingly well provided for: £100 and all the monies in his bedchamber (at least another £100), an impressive collection of plate, the London chest with its linens, one third of all the household stuff not otherwise bequeathed, two yokes of oxen, six milk cows, one third of all other farm animals and feed, and, tellingly, the most intimate of his goods. These were the contents of his bedchamber, the chair he customarily sat in, and the furnishings of his hall—the last, objects that in a more normative life would have been left to his son but that he withheld from his chosen successor to the house at Morton. Lambert was also the only woman among the seven witnesses to the will, the only woman among five executors, and the only person to appear as both witness and executor.

The secret history suggested here is among the more extraordinary by-products of an early modern testamentary instrument. Sexual intimacies between master and servant were undoubtedly common enough, but the administrative context for this revelation—the processes of property transfer—ironically reveals a profound emotional intimacy, as well. It also shows Bellasis to have been aware of his responsibilities to a distinguished family, and the demands of family and his relationship with a woman he identifies as his "servant" may well have been in conflict. Honoring both familial convention and an unconventional relationship, the will of Richard Bellasis is more forthcoming than most diaries of the sixteenth century. The wills of William Wryghte, Agnes Hunte, and

Thomas Duckett (cited at the outset of this essay) are less sensational in what they disclose, but they, too, suggest the excesses of private meaning that could attach to public probate documents.

Notes

1. All citations are from the series of *Essex Wills,* ed. F. G. Emmison. For Wryghte (1569), see vol. 2, *Essex Wills (England), 1565–1571* (Boston: New England Historic Genealogical Society, 1983), no. 850. For Hunte (1586), see vol. 5, *Essex Wills: The Archdeaconry Courts, 1583–1592* (Chelmsford: Essex Record Office, 1989), no. 1188. For Duckett (1563), see vol. 2, no. 34.

2. *Wills and Inventories from the Registry at Durham, Part II,* ed. Rev. William Greenwell, *Publications of the Surtees Society,* 38 (1860), 337–45. I modernize his transcriptions. Bequests of lands and leases are omitted from the discussion that follows.

3. Excerpted by Greenwell, *Publications of the Surtees Society,* 339–40.

4. The only goods in which Lambert did not have a share were books and armaments. On the study as a private, masculine space, see my "The Key and the Cogito," in *Private Matters and Public Culture in Post-Reformation England* (Ithaca: Cornell University Press, 1994).

Creating a Silk Industry in Seventeenth-Century England

LINDA LEVY PECK

IN 1599 THOMAS MOFFETT wrote an elaborate poem, "The silk wormes and Their Flies,"[1] describing the silkworms he had seen when he was in Tuscany in 1579 and issuing a nationalist call to his countrymen to raise silkworms and to wear silk clothing, a call that countered contemporary sumptuary laws: "rise hearts of English race. / Why should your clothes be courser than the rest? / . . . Begge countrymen no more in sackcloth base, / Being by me of such a trade possest / That shall enrich yourselves and children more / Than ere it did Naples or Spaine before."[2]

Contemporaries commented on the richness of English clothing. Looking back to 1574 the historian William Camden wrote "In these dayes had very great excess of Apparel spread it selfe, all over England . . . whilst they jetted up and downe in theyr Silkes, glittering with gold and silver eyther imbroydered or laced."[3] In the 1590s John Stow documented both the production and retailing of silk. "There were more silk shops in Cheapside during the latter years of Elizabeth than there had formerly been in all England. . . . In the yeere 1599 was devised, and perfected the Art of knitting or weaving silk stockings, wastecoates, and divers other things, by engines or steele loomes by William Lee."[4]

As the income of the landed increased in the late sixteenth and early seventeenth centuries, clamor for luxury goods increased.[5] Imports of silk doubled in the 1590s.[6] In 1559 silk fabrics had made up 3.3 percent of the imports to London. By 1622 this had grown to 5.1 percent. The increase in raw materials was more dramatic. In 1559 1.1 percent of the imports were silk; by 1622 this had risen to 7.5%. In the seventeenth century the new silk industry was almost entirely dependent on importation of raw materials. In 1622 London imported silk worth £118,000. By 1640 this had reached

£175,000, in the 1660s £263,000 and by the end of the century £344,000, amounting throughout the century to 23–29 percent of the total value of imports.[7] Silk, either raw or "thrown into thread for the weavers at Spitalfields and elsewhere to work on," was the most valuable of all the raw material imports throughout the middle and later seventeenth century.[8] It was brought in by the Levant Company from the eastern Mediterranean, later augmented by imports from Italy. Its production, however, was uncertain because it depended on weather in those areas of the Mediterranean where silk worms dined on mulberry leaves.

In response to such uncertainty and because of the increasing cost of imports, the Stuarts, like the Medici and the Valois, tried to create domestic silk industries. As a result, interest in sericulture burgeoned in the first decade of the seventeenth century.[9] The campaign to create the raw materials for the silk industry took place both in print and in orders to local magistrates to ensure that the entire population planted mulberry trees.

King James argued for import substitution and technology transfer. He eschewed his loss of custom revenues in the name of public utility and jobs. In his preface, "Instructions for the increasing of mulberie Trees and the breeding of silk-wormes, for the making of Silke," James stressed how successful the King of France had been in establishing the silk industry. Adopting Henri IV's approach, James ordered "those of ability" to distribute 10,000 mulberry plants at 3 farthings a plant or 6s. a hundred:

> all thinges of this nature tending to plantations, increase of Science, and works of industrie, are things so naturally pleasing to our owne disposition, as wee shall take it for an argument of extraordinarie affection towards our own person . . . our Brother the French King hath since his comming to that Crowne, both begun and brought to perfection the making of Silkes in his countrie, whereby he hath wonne to himself honour, and to his subjects a mervailous increase of wealth.[10]

What England lacked were mulberry trees. There were three different types of mulberry trees: black, white, and red. It was the white mulberry on which the silkworms thrived. The red mulberry had been found growing in the wild in Virginia by early explorers. Nicholas Geffe, in his translation of Oliver de Serres's work on silkworms, urged the massive and continuing import of mulberry trees and the imitation of continental nurseries. Geffe offered "within five yeeres to furnish England with ten millions of white Mulberrie plants or upwards which may be generally dispersed, for the good and benefit of the whole kingdome."[11]

The silk worm project was on conspicuous display at court, with the expansion of the Mulberry Gardens, four acres on the current site of Buckingham Palace. One of the Grooms of the Chamber got three months expenses "whilst traveling about with the king's silk worms withersoever his Majestie went."[12] In 1609 Queen Anne had her portrait painted in a gown covered with embroideries of silkworms[12] and in 1616 commissioned Inigo Jones to build a silkworm house at Oatlands. John Bonoeil, author of an important 1622 tract on sericulture for Virginia, was the keeper of the gardens, vines, and silkworms at Oatlands.[14]

While these early efforts to raise mulberry trees did not succeed in England, the sense of the importance of a domestic silk industry remained strong throughout the century. The focus then turned in two different directions: the first to raise mulberries in Virginia to replace the tobacco crop, a view promoted from James I to John Locke, the second, to sponsor the manufacture of "raw-silk into broad silk fabrics." The English silk industry benefited enormously from Huguenot silkworkers who migrated to London during the French wars of religion in the 1580s. They were augmented with another wave of skilled craftsmen after the Revocation of the Edict of Nantes.[15] Concentrated in Spitalfields, silk weaving became so successful by the end of the century that its exports successfully challenged both the French and Italians. The Crown fostered this skilled labor force and banned imports to improve its market position. By the 1730s Thomas Lombe introduced factories, based on Italian designs, to the English silk industry.

Notes

1. Thomas Moffett, *The silkewormes and their flies* (London, 1599), ed. V. H. Houliston, *Medieval and Renaissance Texts and Studies,* vol. 61, (Binghamton, N.Y., 1989). The poem was dedicated to the Countess of Pembroke. Moffett relies on Marcus Hieronymus Vida's *De Bombyce* (Italy, 1527) dedicated to Isabella d'Este. An even earlier poem on silkworms, *Bombyx*, was published in Rome in the 1490s (introduction, xii–xiii). I am grateful to Albert Braunmuller for this reference.

2. Ibid., 70. Moffett's poem drew praise from Nathaniel Baxter in 1606 in his *Sir Philip Sydney's Ourania* (London, 1606): "Her forme, her life, her foode, her worke, her end, / By Doctor Muffet is eloquently pen'd." Quoted in the introduction, xviii The date is significant since it suggests the mounting interest in the silkworm in the first decade of the seventeenth century.

3. During the Alençon courtship in 1581 Queen Elizabeth ordered that cloth of gold, velvet, and silk were to be reduced in price by 25 percent so that lords and ladies could be richly clothed. C. T. Onions, *Shakespeare's England*, 2 vols. (Oxford, 1916), 1:94.

4. Quoted in Onions, *Shakespeare's England*, 1:20, 102.

5. Christopher Clay, *Economic Expansion and Social Change: England 1500–1700*, 2 vols. (Cambridge, 1985), 2:26.

6. Ibid., 2:39, 124.

7. Ibid., 2:125.

8. Ibid., 2:161.

9. The Crown "saw it as a means of reducing the large sums spent annually on the import of manufactured silk from abroad." Clay, *Economic Expansion and Social Change*, 2:39.

10. The king's letter was "given under our signet at Westminster 16 November 6 James I."

11. Oliver de Serres, *The Perfect Use of Silk[-]Wormes and their benefit With the exact planting, and artificiall handling of Mulberrie trees whereby to nourish them, and the figures to know how to feede the Wormes, and to winde off the Silke And the fit maner to prepare the barke of the white Mulberrie to make fine linnen and other workes thereof. Done out of the French originall of D'Olivier de Serres Lord of Pradel into English, by Nicholas Geffe Esquier* (London, 1607), STC 22249. Geffe's postscript, p.3.

12. *CSPD 1611–1618*, 555; July [18?], 1618; Frank Warner, *The Silk Industry of the United Kingdom* (Drane's, London, 1921), 537–38.

13. T. B. Pugh, "A Portrait of Queen Anne of Denmark at Parham Park, Sussex, *The Seventeenth Century*, 8, 1 (autumn 1993), 167–80, 170–71. I am grateful to Helen Payne for these references.

14. After his death he was replaced by John Tradescant, who had an annuity of £100 a year. The Mulberry Gardens, located in St. James, were tended by the Tradescants, gardeners to Charles I. Quoted in Prudence Leith-Ross, *The John Tradescants: Gardeners to the Rose and Lily Queen* (London, 1984), 93–94.

15. Clay, *Economic Expansion and Social Change*, 2:39.

III
Languages of Materiality

Words as Things

Margreta de Grazia

Is a word a thing? It depends, of course, on what is meant by *thing*. If sensible properties constitute thingness, then a word is certainly a thing. It exists either as a sound to be heard or a mark to be seen. There is a long tradition, however, of denying words the status of things. In the short essay that follows, I will suggest that this tradition begins when words are required to *represent* things or matter. If words are to give a clear representation of things (empirical or notional), they must forego their own thingness.

At the beginning of the seventeenth century, Bacon draws a strong line between words and things. To emphasize the inferiority of words to things, he compares words to three forms of representation:[1] a flourish on the initial letter of a patent or limned book; the statue Pygmalion fell in love with; a painting like Zeuxis's famous still life of grapes that looked so real a blackbird tried to peck them.[2] This mistaking of the unreal for the real is what Bacon terms "Pygmalion's frenzy," a madness like idolatry that fixates on the image rather than the thing the image represents. In all three instances, the forbidden graven image is imagined as being itself immaterial. It offers up nothing of its own to read, to embrace, to eat. But, of course, all these forms of representation *do* have substance of their own, though it is not the same as that of the thing they represent. The flourish is made of ink on paper, the statue of stone, the painting of canvas and pigment. If these images were granted materiality, they would themselves become things worthy of the desire (to study, love, eat) that is the due of what they represent. Their pursuit then would be impelled not by a mad "frenzy" but by perfectly reasonable interest.

If words are to serve as transparent representations of things, their own thinglike or sensible properties must be overlooked. Or else remade in the image of what they represent. Thus Bacon hinted at an alternative system of notation that would work "without the help or intervention of words."[3] Its characters, he speculated, would resemble the things they represented, either physically as pictographs or conceptually as ideographs. In the second half of the century, Bacon's suggestion materialized in the project sponsored by the Royal Society to devise an artificial language. John Wilkins, for example, in his 800-page *An Essay Toward a Real Character, and a Philosophical Language* (1668) describes a set of characters intended to represent directly the objects or notions common to all men.[4] Each character stands for a thing or an idea, and when properly distributed and combined they are to correspond with empirical observation or philosophical ordering. In these attempts, characters are designed in the likeness of the things they represent; their own material attributes are forged to match what they stand for. Words, it might be said, have been phased into things. Indeed it is not much of a leap to Swift's satire of the Royal Society's linguistic projects. Gulliver stumbles upon an academy whose members have abolished words altogether and communicate solely by brandishing things. If a long conversation is anticipated, huge bundles are assembled; for shorter ones, a few items under the arm will do.[5]

The Royal Society was also concerned with improving the use of ordinary language. In his *History of the Royal Society* (1667), Thomas Sprat commends the Society's commitment to aligning words with things; he reproduces several of its reports, which are exemplary in their description of "so many things almost in an equal number of words."[6] John Wilkins's first consideration is to assign marks or names to all things and notions in order to attain "a just *Enumeration*." Ordinary language is riddled with two defects that upset this ideal balance: homonyms and synonyms. Either there are not enough words to match things or else too many. In the case of homonyms, one word is used for many things: *bill,* for example, is used to mean weapon, bird's beak, and written scroll. Homonyms include not only puns or clenches, but also words that have become equivocal as a result of the figurative extension of their literal meaning. Words like "break, bring, caste, cleare, come, draw, fall, hand, keep, lay, make, pass, put, run, set, stand, take," Wilkins maintains, have from thirty to a hundred "several senses."[7] Ordinary language is also rendered "obnoxious" by its possession of synonyms. Though less abundant in English than in some other languages (Arabic, for example, possesses "above a thousand several names for a *Sword,* and 500 for a *Lion,* and 200 for a *Serpent,* and fourscore for *Hony*"), it is still rife with "superfluities," as is demonstrated by his long table of redundant and therefore dispensable words. "END, aim, mark, goal, drift, intent, effect, purpose, design, scope, reach, reason, final, tend"; "SIGN, badge, token, mark, note symptome, symbol, index, indication, cue, print, scarr, track, signature, signifie, beacon, becken, boad, foretoken, presage, prodigie, portentous, ominous, auspicious."

Yet, significantly, what are regarded as defects to be removed in the seventeenth-century artificial language schemes are precisely the characteristics to be cultivated in the rhetorics of the earlier century. The principles of synonymy and homonymy are at the heart of the most influential treatise on language use in the sixteenth century, Erasmus's *De Utraque Verborem ac Rerum Copia* (1512). There one learns the basic techniques of expanding and contracting words in order to attain the copiousness and brevity that are key to eloquence. Though the treatise is best known for its listing of some 150 variations for saying "I was pleased to receive your letter," and some 200 for saying "I will remember you as long as I live," it also insists on the importance of reducing wording. In contrast to the Baconian economy of so many words for so many things, words are by design made both to fall short of things or to exceed them. Linguistic virtuosity requires exercise in wielding the material properties of words: their duration as sound when spoken and their extension as marks when written.

The flagrant incommensurability of words and things in *De Copia* indicates how far the ends of rhetoric lie from the linguistic ideal of one-on-one representation. Indeed a radical transformation of the classical pair has occurred as they are transmitted from one century into the next, from the domain of rhetoric to that of natural philosophy. Erasmus's *res et verba* pairing extends as far back as the rhetorics of Cicero and Quintillian. In the sixteenth century, the Latin binary is translated as things and words, or matter and words. But in the seventeenth century *things* or *matter* come to lose their rhetorical sense of *things to be discussed* or *subject matter*; they refer instead to *empirical things* or *physical matter*.[8] It was precisely this newer kind of *res* that was found lacking in rhetorical celebrations of *verba*. Copious words were thought to conceal a dearth of things. In this respect, the sixteenth-century humanists were considered no different from New World Indians. Lacking ontological and epistemological *things,* the "Schoolmen," according to Sprat, "wanted *matter* to contrive, and so, like the Indians, onely express'd a wonderful artifice in the ordering of the same feathers in a thousands varieties of figures."[9]

To answer our opening question: a word is a thing in the sixteenth but a nonthing in the seventeenth century. In the domain of rhetoric, whose purpose was persuasion and not representation, a word was permitted to retain its materiality, for it was the source of this power. There is no better evidence of this than Puttenham's discussion of the sensory quality of words and figures in his *The Arte of English Poesie* (1589). Words, he insists repeatedly, need to possess physicality in order to impress the mind: "the minde being no less vanquished with large loade of speech, than the limmes are with heauie burden."[10] The understanding is reached via the "sensible approaches" of the ear and eye. A term was borrowed from the Greek in order to single out this physical power: *energia,* defined as "forcibleness" by Sidney and as "a strong and virtuous operation" by Puttenham.[11] It is through rhetoric then that *energy* enters the language before becoming, along with *matter,* the subject of physical science or physics.[12] Possessing both matter and energy, words might themselves have been the object of scientific inquiry.

Notes

1. "Here therefore [is] the first distemper of learning, when men study words and not matter. . . . And how is it possible but that this should have an operation to discredit learning, even with vulgar capacities, when they see learned men's works like the first letter of a patent or limned book; which though it hath large flourishes, yet it is but a letter? It seems to me that Pygmalion's frenzy is a good emblem or portraiture of this vanity: for words are but the images of matter; and except they have life of reason and invention, to fall in love with them is all one as to fall in love with a picture." *The Advancement of Learning,* in *The Works of Francis Bacon,* ed. James Spedding, Robert Leslie Ellis, and Douglas Denon Heath (London, 1857), 3:284.

2. In his dedicatory ode to *The History of the Royal Society,* Abraham Cowley refers to Zeuxis's painting (Pliny, Bk. 35) in crediting Bacon for having led men away "From Words, which are but Pictures . . . To Things." See *History of the Royal Society by Thomas Sprat,* ed. Jackson I. Cope and Harold Whitmore Jones (1667; London: Routledge & Kegan Paul Ltd., 1959), stz. 4, B2.

3. *De Augmentis Scientiarum* in *Works,* 4:439.

4. John Wilkins, *An Essay Toward a Real Character and Philosophical Language* (1668; Menston, Eng.: The Scolar Press Limited, 1968).

5. Jonathan Swift, *Gulliver's Travels,* ed. Peter Dixon and John Chalker (London and New York: Penguin, 1985), 230–31.

6. Cope and Jones, *History of the Royal Society,* 132.

7. Wilkins, *An Essay Toward a Real Character,* 17–18.

8. On the alteration of the classical *res* in seventeenth-century discussions of words and things, see A. C. Howell, "Res et Verba," *ELH* XIII (1946), 121–42.

9. Cope and Jones, *History of the Royal Society,* 15.

10. George Puttenham, *The Arte of English Poesie,* eds. Gladys Doidge Willock and Alice Walker (Cambridge: Cambridge University Press, 1936), 198–209.

11. Ibid., 142.

12. Brian Vickers has argued that the capacity of rhetoric to move was increasingly stressed between 1540 and 1640: "Of the three goals of rhetoric, *movere, docere, and delectare,* movere became the most sought-after." See "On the Practicalities of Renaissance Rhetoric," in *Rhetoric Revalued: Papers from the International Study for the History of Rhetoric,* ed. Brian Vickers (Binghamton, N.Y.: Medieval and Renaissance Texts and Studies, 1982), 136.

The Matter of Sounds

Gary Tomlinson

> *Caliban:* Be not afeard: the isle is full of noises,
> Sounds and sweet airs that give delight and hurt not.
> Sometimes a thousand twangling instruments
> Will hum about mine ears; and sometimes voices
> That, if I then had waked after long sleep,
> Will make me sleep again; and then, in dreaming,
> The clouds methought would open and show riches
> Ready to drop upon me, that, when I waked,
> I cried to dream again.
>
> (3.2.133–41)

CALIBAN'S FAMOUS SET-PIECE in *The Tempest* does not lead where its beginning seems to point. From an enumeration of sounds, songs, and musical instruments, he veers toward a vision of the heavens bursting with palpable riches. From a state of sharp, wakeful cognizance, he drifts toward sleep and dreams.

Somewhere far behind Caliban's dream stands the archetype for all musical dreams through the Middle Ages and Renaissance: Cicero's *Somnium scipionis,* dispersed widely enough in Macrobius's *Commentaries* to become a commonplace in praises of music and its powers. If, however, Scipio's dream is a straightforward Neoplatonic *anamnesis,* leading the soul back through the musical spheres toward its heavenly origins, Shakespeare's *somnium calibanis* is something else again. It does not point upward toward musical quintessence and, finally, transcendent immateriality. Instead Caliban's noises and songs seem positively to induce the opposition at the heart of his dream: immaterial heavens versus the too-solid riches they would shower down on him. Sonic forces seem to be positioned here at a liminal meeting-point of matter and nonmatter. From this place they confront interpretations of early modern ontologies that would straightforwardly separate the two.

Caliban's positioning of sounds and songs would not have surprised a Renaissance Neoplatonist. The most influential sonic ontology of the period, Marsilio Ficino's, consistently emphasized a similar liminality.[1] In his often reprinted *De vita libri tres,* an elaboration on Plotinus dedicated to therapeutic and astrological magic, Ficino arranged mundane materials and phenomena of the human soul alongside the heavenly spheres whose influxes they might attract. Words, songs, and sounds (undifferentiated from one another: a point to which I will return) occupied the middle space, dedicated to the sun. Beneath them came more or less solid material substances—metals, plants, vapors, and so forth (associated with the moon, Mercury, and Venus)—while above them ranged immaterial psychic phenomena: conceptions of the imagination (Mars), the deliberations of reason (Jupiter), and intuitive understanding (Saturn).

Also in *De vita,* and elsewhere throughout his later writings, Ficino connected sounds and songs to the human *spiritus.* This too marked the borderline positioning of sounds, since spirit was the most liminal of human faculties. In Ficino's view, capping a history of pneumatology reaching back to ancient times, spirit joined body and soul—and hence, since the human organism was located at the midpoint of the cosmos, material and immaterial realms all told. Ficino's ambivalence in defining spirit shows that it did not admit of identification as either matter or nonmatter; it was, he wrote, "almost not a body but a soul; or again, almost not a soul but a body."

The implications of this ambivalent spirit are far-reaching. It cannot be equated with Descartes's animal spirits, the most subtle materials of the human body (though these grew out of Ficinian and other pneumatological traditions). These later spirits remain stolidly material, however thin they might be; because of this they cannot come in contact with the immaterial soul. In affirming the impossibility of such contact they inaugurate the dualism of the Cartesian legacy. Ficino's spirit, instead, escapes dualism through its ineffable liminality. It suggests the possibility that Renaissance materialities were always in touch with nonmatter—if in ways difficult to perceive from a post-Cartesian perspective. Ficino's spirit operates as a bridge between the material and immaterial realms of the cosmos rather than marking, as Descartes's spirits, one edge of the chasm separating them.

Song, in its association with spirit, sits planted in the middle of the bridge. For this reason its effects cannot be analyzed either as technological (as material interactions with the body) or as psychological (immaterial alterations of soul). Neither can they be explained as both simultaneously, in the manner of so many post-

Cartesian, dualistic axioms of correspondence between material and immaterial worlds. The early modern effects of song must instead be explained as a *singular* interaction with the body/soul unit that extends at once from material to immaterial realms, confirming the juncture of and contact between the two: call it a *metatechnology*.

In Ficino's ideological frame (and Caliban's and—can we doubt?—Prospero's as well), the power of sounds and song provides an archetypal instance of this metatechnology. But it is by no means the only instance current through the late Renaissance. Many other operations of nondemonic, white magic are metatechnological as well. These include, in some conceptions, the making of material charms and talismans and even writing itself—the potent writing, in the case of *The Tempest,* of Prospero's book. They include also a whole class of mechanical operations considered magical by della Porta, Campanella, and others: operations involving devices such as flying machines and other marvels, which we can only understand as magical if we appreciate the metatechnological forces they were once seen to activate. The idea of a metatechnology penetrates deeply into early modern praxis, touching on operations we tend instead to conceive as technologies and blurring the clear distinction of material and immaterial we tend to project onto the period.

The locus of song's spiritual, metatechnological operation is the imagination or phantasy, one of the lower faculties of the soul. Through its airy motions, song imprints an image on the imagination, a phantasm on the phantasy—an ostensibly material inscription on an immaterial medium that takes us to the heart of the magical evasion of philosophical dualism. In this operation, song is no different than words, sounds, or pictures. All of them inscribe images on the immaterial phantasy. For Ficino and the broader Renaissance tradition he informed and represents, there is no epistemological distinction between the meaningfulness of words, of songs, of images.[2]

For this reason Pierre Iselin is not quite right to state that musical messages in *The Tempest* are "either semanticized, or de-semanticized."[3] His terminology raises the possibility of a distinction between words and other signs that is not borne out in, at least, the magical epistemologies at work in the play. The semantic values of words in early modern magic—and, indeed, across a broader spectrum of the psychologies of the period—arose from the same flux of images, materially impressed on an immaterial medium, that allowed songs, noises, pictures, and other signs to be meaningful. The thunder that utters the name "Prosper" to Alonso signifies in the same manner as the hummings, buzzings, and twanglings heard by the other visitors to the island. Its greater *interpretability* does not set it apart in any deep way from those other, less scrutable signs. If anything, indeed, it marks it as superficial, and them as signs more deeply imbricated in the mysterious workings of the cosmos.

The common epistemology of all these different signs is one reason why the list of signifying sounds Caliban names in his speech cuts so wide a swath through the sonic universe. Noises, sounds, sweet airs, twangling instruments, and voices (singing? speaking?): the list cannot be domesticated within the category "music," at least not in the narrow, exclusionary currency of its modern western usage. Instead Caliban's list taps into a universal, imagistic signification on which Renaissance confidence in magical powers was built. Music in *The Tempest*—a well enough trodden topic in Shakespeare studies—still admits, then, of this rethinking: it is not separable in any modern sense from all Prospero's and Ariel's sonic resources on their island, or indeed from their other resources. It is nothing more and nothing less than the material/immaterial, metatechnological, imagistic epitome of their magical arts all told. This, along with cursing, Caliban seems to have learned well from Prospero.

Notes

1. For a detailed account of Ficino's views of song and sounds, see my *Music in Renaissance Magic: Toward a Historiography of Others* (Chicago: University of Chicago Press, 1993), chapter 4.
2. For an argument to bolster this assertion, see ibid., 115–21.
3. Pierre Iselin, " 'My Music for Nothing': Musical Negotiations in *The Tempest*," *Shakespeare Survey* 48 (1995): 135–45. Iselin's article as a whole usefully brings to bear on *The Tempest* several topics I dwelled on in *Music in Renaissance Magic*: Ficino's *De vita,* musical furor, musical soul loss, iatromusic, and the flux around 1600 of auralist and visualist discourses. I am indebted to Olivia Bloechl for bringing this essay to my attention.

The Language of Framing

Rayna Kalas

At the end of John Lyly's 1580 prose narrative, *Euphues and His England,* there is an epistolary exchange containing *Euphues' Glass for Europe,* a description of England addressed to the ladies of Italy. Protesting that he could not possibly do justice to the glory of Elizabeth, Lyly says that the *Glass* is a frame rather than a painting: "I hope, that though it be not requisite that any should paynt their Prince in England, that can-not sufficiently perfect hir, yet it shall not be thought rashness or rudeness for Euphues, to frame a table for Elizabeth, though he presume not to paynt hir."[1]

Lyly fabricates a classical authority for his frame. The putative source is Pliny, who in a passing reference, notes Alexander's public edict proscribing all depictions of him except those made by specific named artists.[2] But Lyly embellishes the anecdote with a fictive account of Parrhasius, and his frame.

> When Alexander had commanded none should paint him but *Appelles,* none should carve him but *Lysippus,* none engrave him but *Pirgotales, Parrhasius* framed a Table squared everye way twoo hundred foote, which in the borders he trimmed with fresh colours, and limmed with fine golde, leaving all the other roume with-out knotte or lyne, which table he presented to *Alexander* who no less mervailing at the bignes, than at the barenes, demaunded to what ende he gave him a frame with-out a face, being so naked, and with-out fashion being so great. *Parrhasius* answered him, "Let it be lawful for *Parhasius, O Alexander,* to shew a Table wherein he would paint *Alexander,* if it were not unlawfull, and for others to square Timber, though *Lysippus* carve it, and for all to cast brasse though *Pirgotales* engrave it." *Alexander* perceiving the good minde of *Parrhasius,* pardoned his boldnesse, and preferred his arte: yet enquyring why hee framed the Table so bygge, hee answered, that hee thought that frame to bee but little enough for his Picture, when the whole worlde was too little for his personne, saying that *Alexander* must as well be praysed, as paynted, and that all hys victories and vertues, were not for to bee drawne in the Compasse of a Sygnette, but in a fielde.

> This aunswer *Alexander* both lyked & rewarded, insomuch that it was lawful ever after for *Parrhasius* both to praise that noble king and to paint him.[3]

What Parrhasius presents to Alexander is not the ornamental quadrilateral of a modern frame, but a prepared wooden panel: he "framed a Table" of immense proportions "without knotte or lyne" decorated only at the borders and otherwise left blank. He does not presume to paint the table, only to craft it. Following a brief exchange, Alexander, "perceiving the good minde of *Parrhasius,* pardoned his boldness, and preferred his arte." Alexander, seeming to reward the painter as much for his craftiness as for his craft, grants him dispensation both to praise and to paint.

If Parrhasius gains through his cunning the right to practice the "arte" of praise, his frame is also a reminder that praise is an *arte* or *misterie* which, like any other, involves the manipulation of matter. The crafting of this gigantic frame is more like squaring timber than carving it, more like casting brass than engraving it. Drawing the anecdote to a close, Lyly applies the example of Parrhassius to yet another list of artisans whose work is "but begun for others to ende," and includes among them Euphues himself. Implicitly acknowledging the hierarchy of trades that privileges intellectual over manual arts, Lyly nonetheless compares Euphues's framing of praise to artisanal labor: "hee that whetteth the tooles is not to bee misliked, though hee can-not carve the Image."[4]

Lyly's anecdote, with its customary guise of humility, is easily read as a bid for the preferment of his own art, especially since Elizabeth was another sovereign who sought to mandate the production of her image.[5] What I wish to stress, though, is that Lyly seeks to authorize his prose through the device of a material frame. By using the frame to epitomize verbal craft, Lyly links the figurative language of praise to the mechanical arts. Lyly's invention of a blank king-sized frame as the metaphor for his prose exemplifies the material nature of language in the second half of the sixteenth century, when framing was related to questions of craft rather than aesthetics and was identified not with the visual but with the verbal.

In the sixteenth century, the word *frame* did not have as its primary sense, as it does today, the alienable quadrilateral ornament surrounding a painting. For one thing, as Lyly's text indicates, before oil painting on canvas became the norm, frames were prepared together with the background panel. So when *frame* was used in the context of painting—and until the end of the century its use was far rarer than "table" or "border"—it referred to a different kind of structure than what we call a frame today. The word was more likely to refer to the internal design or structure of a thing, the skeleton of a barn, for example, or the admixture of a potion. More frequently, *frame* was used as verb, and as such, it palpably evoked the thing in its making. Though *frame* was rarely used in the context of visual images, it was used throughout the poetic treatises of the late sixteenth century to describe the organization of language: Samuel Daniel's *A Defence of Ryme,* for example, says that "All verse is but a frame of wordes."[6] *Frame* conveys the sense that language is ordered by abstract principles, but the word names that order only as it is materially manifest in speech and writing. Like the practitioners of any *misterie,* rhetoricians were concerned to show that their *arte* was adapted to the materials with which they worked.

As Lyly's text attests, in the sixteenth century, before framing was associated with the adornment of a consummate aesthetic object, framing was about predicating the way a thing is to be wrought. The poetic tracts are concerned to define poetry as a material substance so that the framing of poetry is a craft practice just like the framing of any other material object. Thomas Lodge, writing here about classical poets, says that poems should be framed as potions: "what so they [poets] wrot, it was to this purpose, in the way of pleasure to draw men to wisedome: for, seeing the world in those daies was vnperfect, yt was necessary that they like good Phisitions should so *frame* their potions that they might be applicable to the quesie stomaks of their werish patients" [emphasis added].[7] The object, whether it be a poem or a potion, is framed with its practical end in sight; its making is determined by the matter to which it is "appliable." Framing is not an a priori scheme, but forethought that is bound to the telos, or purpose, of a thing: framing is dictated by the object toward which it is directed.

Human industry is most esteemed when it shows not the ingenuity of the craftsman per se, but aptness to an order already present in the materials at hand. Because divine order is manifest in all of created nature and because the tools of any trade are adapted to the materials worked upon, tradesmen labor according to a divine order. As Thomas Wilson explains in his 1560 *Arte of Rhetorique*: "By an order we devise, we learne, and we frame our doings to good purpose: the carpenter hath his square, his rule and his plummet, the tailor his meet yard and his measure, the mason his former and his plaine, and every one accordyng to his callyng frameth thynges thereafter."⁸ We "frame our doings to good purpose" because physical nature directs us to that purpose.

Roger Ascham addresses the crafting of language in similar terms in *The Schoolmaster*. The various discourses of poet, historian, philosopher, and orator, he writes, "differ one from another in choice of words, in framing of sentences, in handling of argumentes, and use of right forme, figure, and number, proper and fit for every matter."⁹ If, as Wilson says, "every one accordyng to his callyng frameth thynges [language] thereafter," where the arts of language are concerned, discourse and genre comprise the "order" by which the poets and orators "devise" and "frame" their "doings to good purpose." Genre may be a more abstract tool than a "plummet" or a "plaine," but the text emphasizes that the materials of language are made "fit for every matter" through "framing" and "handling." Given its root, the word *handling*, even when it does not expressly signify manual labor, evokes a kind of making that is scaled to mortal hands. William Webbe commends Virgil's framing of verse because it is quite literally handled by the poet: "first you may marke how Virgill always fitteth his matter in hande with wordes agreeable unto the same affection which he expresseth: as in his Tragicall exclamations, what patheticall speeches he frameth."¹⁰ Virgil frames speeches "agreeable unto the same affection" as tragedy by fitting the "matter in hande with wordes."

The priority that is granted to the framing or handling of language coincides with the priority of rhetoric in English vernacular logics, though that coincidence has been elided by the tendency to understand rhetoric in terms of style rather than craft.¹¹ The relation of rhetoric to logic tends to be characterized in aesthetic terms as a distinction between style and substance: between ornamental flourish and the sublime idea. I propose that that there is also evidence, in sixteenth-century theories of language, to see rhetoric as the worldly artifice or material crafting of a natural and enduring logical ideal. In his *Rule of Reason,* Thomas Wilson follows Agricola and the scholastic tradition in dividing logic into *inventio* and *judicium,* the two principles of classical dialectic, or the logic of opinion. However, Wilson inverts the conventional order, placing *judicium,* which concerns the arranging of words into propositions and syllogisms and thus is more like rhetoric, before *inventio,* which, in the tradition of Aristotle and Cicero, is about the searching out of topics. "The first parte standeth in framing of thynges aptly together, knitting woordes for the purpose accordingly & in

Latin is called Iudicium. The seconde parte consisteth in finding out matter, and searching stuffe agreable to the cause and in Latin is called Inventio." Wilson draws attention to his inversion of these principles and offers the following explanation:

> And now some wil saie that I should first speake of the finding out of an argument, before I should teache the waye how to frame an argument. Truthe it is that naturally we finde a reason or we beginne to fathom (fashion) the same. And yet notwistanding, it is more mete that the ordering of an argument should be first handeled: forasmuche as is that no more profit a man to find out his argument, except he first know how to order the same and to shape it accordingly (which he doth not yet perfectly know) then stones or Timber shal profite the Mason or Carpenter, which knoweth how to work upon the same. A reason is easier found than fashioned for every manne can geve a reason naturally and without arte but how to fashion and frame the same, according to the art, none can do at all, except that they be learned.[12]

Wilson acknowledges that argument always begins with finding a reason, but says that "an argument should be first handled" as a mason or a carpenter handles stones or timber in order to learn "how to fashion and frame the same, according to the art." In essence, Wilson foregrounds craft and rhetoric in his logic.

Ralph Lever's *Arte of Reason, rightly termed,* Witcraft, *teaching the perfect way to argue and dispute* also suggests extent to which, before dialectic was streamlined with scientific logic under the rubric of method, English vernacular logic was strongly identified with both craft and rhetoric.[13] Lever's text, thought to have been written in the 1550s though it was published in 1573, is one of the earliest English vernacular logics.[14] In his *Witcraft,* Lever replaces classical terminology with invented English words like "saywhat" and "shewsay." As he explains in the "Forespeache," "Wee have also framed unto ourselves a language, whereby we do expresse by voyce or writing, all devises that wee conceyve in our mynde: and doo by this means let men look into our heartes and see what wee thinke." The English have "framed unto" themselves a particular language that conditions the "devices" of the "mynde" and through that native tongue the thoughts of the population are best known. In English, as Lever's subtitle evinces, wit is literally crafted. English lends itself to being crafted because it shares with the other Germanic languages a peculiar capacity for forming compound words out of single and double syllable word combinations. Lever's vocabulary exemplifies both the "speciall grace" and the craftedness of the English tongue: "As for the devising of newe termes, and composing of wordes, our tonge hath a speciall grace, wherein it excelleth many other, and is comparable with the best. The cause is, for that the most parte of Englishe wordes are shorte, and stande on one sillable a piece. So that two or three of them are ofte times fitly joined into one."[15] This conception that language is "joined" is not a peculiarity of Lever's invented lexicon: Patricia Parker has demonstrated that the mechanics of joining—and the "rude mechanicals" generally—were central to vernacular discourses on logic and rhetoric in the sixteenth century.[16] When Lever explains that "Witcraft is a cunning to frame and to answere a reason," he is describing a material as much as an ideal practice.

In Lyly's anecdote, Parrhasius simultaneously presents Alexander with a crafted object and an occasion for "enquyring." Insofar as Alexander questions Parrhasius about his curious object, the crafted frame provokes a kind of logical or dialectical exchange; the frame and the dialogue together constitute proof of Parrhasius's ability to praise. In the sixteenth century, the liberal arts—reconfigured under the influence of humanism to include not only rhetoric, logic, and the other liberal arts inherited from the medieval scholasticism, but also those developed out of the interest in classical texts such as poetry and history—would have been classed above the mechanical arts, yet Parrhasius wins rights to practice those arts through the imbrication of logic and craft.[17] Lyly's device of the frame conjoins the liberal and mechanical arts in a manner that does not abide by a strict hierarchical division of trades that esteems intellectual arts over manual ones. Nor does Lyly's frame abide by the division of nature from artifice that, as Patricia Parker has pointed out, was a correlative of that hierarchy.[18] Parrhasius crafts an object that seems entirely artificial since it is all apparatus and no mimesis—"a frame with-out a face"—yet holds the promise of being most like the nature of things: in this frame, Alexander's "victories and vertues" can be drawn not "in the Compass of a Sygnette, but in a fielde." Lyly's frame, and framing in general, reveals that the particular materiality of language in the late sixteenth century was a hybrid of natural and mechanical orders.

Notes

1. John Lyly, *The Complete Works of John Lyly*, ed. R. Warwick Bond, vol. 2, *Euphues and His England* (Oxford: Oxford University Press, 1967), 204.

2. "The same monarch [Alexander], too, by public edict, declared that no one should paint his portrait but Apelles, and that no one should make a marble statue of him except Pyrgoteles, or a bronze one except Lysippus." Pliny the Elder, *Natural History,* trans. and ed. John Bostock and Henry Thomas Riley (London: George Bell, 1890), 7:38, 184.

3. Lyly, *The Complete Works,* 204.

4. Ibid., 205.

5. In 1563, a Proclamation approving strict control of her image was drafted, though it was not issued; the Privy Council did not order the censorship of Elizabeth's image until 1596. David Howarth, *Images of Rule: Art and Politics in the English Renaissance 1485–1649* (Berkeley and Los Angeles: University of California Press, 1997), 102.

6. Samuel Daniel, *A Defence of Ryme* (1603) in *Elizabethan Critical Essays,* ed. G. Gregory Smith (Oxford: Oxford University Press, 1904), 1:359.

7. Thomas Lodge, *Defence of Poetry* (1579), in *Elizabethan Critical Essays,* 1:66.

8. Thomas Wilson, *The Arte of Rhetorique* (1560), facsimile reprint of the 1585 edition, ed. G. H. Mair (Oxford: Oxford University Press, 1909), 157.

9. Roger Ascham, *The Schoolmaster* (1570), ed. Lawrence B. Ryan (Charlottesville: University Press of Virginia for the Folger Shakespeare Library, 1967), 138.

10. William Webbe, *A Discourse of English Poetrie* (1586), in *Elizabethan Critical Essays,* vol. 1, 256. Poesy is often characterized as a balance between industry and magnanimity. So although Webbe commends Virgil for framing speeches by fitting the "matter in hande with wordes," George Chapman, in his *A Defence of Homer* criticizes Virgil for not being magnanimous enough in his framing of the *Aeneid*: "where *Virgill* hath had no more plentifull and liberall a wit than to frame twelve imperfect bookes of the troubles and trauailes of *Aeneas, Homer* hath of as little subject finisht eight & fortie perfect" (*Elizabethan Critical Essays,* 1:299). Chapman's remark reveals that framing connotes making rather than completion since he uses the verb "frame" in contrast to "finisht." In any even, it should be noted that Webbe may be playing on the classical characterization of logic as a closed fist and rhetoric an open hand.

11. Though he himself was carefully to note the strength of logic and dialectic in English scholasticism, Kristeller's general statements about the supremacy of rhetoric in Renaissance humanism have been influential. For instance, he borrows from the fine arts one of the "important reasons" for defending a rhetoric-centered, humanist Renaissance. "The concept of style as it has been so successfully applied by historians of art [the author notes Panofsky] might be more widely applied in other fields of intellectual history and might thus enable us to recognize the significant changes brought about by the Renaissance, without obliging us to despise the Middle Ages or to minimize the debt of the Renaissance to the medieval tradition." Paul Oskar Kristeller, *Renaissance Thought: The Classic, Scholastic and Humanist Strains* (New York: Harper Torchbooks, 1961), 93. Brian Vickers has argued that the privileging of rhetoric depends on a division of logic from eloquence, and from rhetoric, which is not entirely applicable to the sixteenth century: "If we were to regard *elocutio* as mere ornament then its rise to dominance in the sixteenth century would be inexplicable, unforgivable almost." *In Defence of Rhetoric* (Oxford: Clarendon Press, 1988), 283. On the relationship between logic and rhetoric in the English Renaissance, see Wilbur Samuel Howell, *Logic and Rhetoric in England 1500–1700* (Princeton: Princeton University Press, 1956).

12. Thomas Wilson, *Rule of Reason conteinyng the arte of logique* (London, 1551), B1r–B2r.

13. This streamlining of logic under the general term, method, has been identified with Ramus and his follows since Walter J. Ong's *Ramus, Method and the Decay of Dialogue* (Cambridge, Mass.: Harvard University Press, 1958).

14. On the date of composition of Lever's *Witcraft*, see Howell, *Logic and Rhetoric*, 57–63.

15. Ralph Lever, *The Arte of Reason* (1573), facsimile reprint in *English Linguistics 1500–1800*, ed. R. C. Alston (Menston, Eng.: Scolar Press, Ltd., 1972), no. 323.

16. Patricia Parker, *Shakespeare from the Margins: Language, Culture, Context* (Chicago: University of Chicago Press, 1996), 83–115.

17. According to Ong, by the end of later middle ages, most of the arts faculty in European universities were logicians rather than theologians. And by the end of the sixteenth century, logic—which had once capped the trivium of grammar, rhetoric, and the logic insofar as it was taught last among the three and was considered a preparative for the more advanced study of the quadrivium—had effectively been shifted to the quadrivium. Not only had logic become the basis for the more advanced study of the quadrivium, the quadrivium itself, Ong argues, was more a quadrivium in word than in deed. University education was not limited to geometry, astronomy, music, and arithmetic, but included "arts" such as history and poetry. "The seven liberal arts nowhere appeared as the real and complete framework of instruction." Rather, Ong writes, "It will be noted here how far the trivium-quadrivium framework has disintegrated, for dialectic or logic has migrated from the trivium to be associated with 'physics' and the rest of 'philosophy' which constituted the reality existing where the quadrivium was dutifully assigned to be." Ong, *Ramus, Method and the Decay of Dialogue*, 138–39.

18. Parker notes that while the "mechanical" or "artifactual" are often positioned against the "spontaneous or natural," the former are often identified with matter: "In the vertical hierarchy of the mind as separated, or "singuled," from matter and the material . . . the mechanical also designated not only the practical as opposed to the contemplative but more generally an association with the material." Parker, *Shakespeare from the Margins*, 85.

Shakespeare Writing Matter Again: Objects and Their Detachments

Jonathan Goldberg

*W*RITING MATTER: *From the Hands of the English Renaissance*[1] was initially conceived as a Shakespeare book. The plan had been to develop the argument presented in chapter 4, "Shakespearian characters: the generation of Silvia," of my previous book, *Voice Terminal Echo*,[2] which had considered various instances of the coincidence of character in its scriptive and dramatic meanings from *Two Gentlemen of Verona* and *Titus Andronicus* to *Twelfth Night*, *Hamlet*, and *Cymbeline*, among other texts. The point of such an exercise, of course, was to depsychologize character and to contest the transcendentalizing aims implicit in arguments for unique individuality. Character books, pedagogical, and secretarial manuals were cited, the trajectory of the letter and the letter writer pursued in *Writing Matter*. The Shakespearian aim of the project only was realized in an essay, "Hamlet's Hand",[3] which represents an initial attempt to read the manuals in which handwriting was taught alongside the play. More important than such connections was the work done in that essay and several others that argue the significant relationship between the textual situation of Shakespeare's plays and their representations of texts—the letters circulated, forged, read; the questions of who reads, who writes, and why always matters for understanding circuits of power and desire.[4]

I take this occasion to recall those earlier projects to encourage work that might further specify the connections between textual conditions, textual properties, and textuality in its broadest sense (in Shakespeare among others). Such work must be wary about supposing that seeing that there is nothing but text necessarily evades transcendentalizing if it allows the admission (as both Derrida and Marjorie Garber would) of ghosts if not quite spirits into the machine. But it needs also to be wary about attaching substance to letters and thereby transcendentalizing materiality as inalienable possession or the thing itself. Richard Halpern's account of handwriting in *The Poetics of Primitive Accumulation*[5] provides terms by setting textual production along the materialist path of a regulated volatility, a path to be connected to the commodity as an object of dispossession, volatized in exchange, fantasized and fetishized as possessions that rather possess their possessors. These are objects loosed from fixed property relations, signs that will not serve as the indexicals Sidney imagined that characters bear onstage.

Plays by Shakespeare may have more letters in them than any other significant prop, props displaying (im)propriety. The circulation of letters is barely contained by the kind of empiricist gesture that counting might suggest. In the second act of *King Lear,* to take one example, Regan claims to have received a letter from Goneril a scene before the letter carrier arrives, while the delivery of the letter as later recounted by Kent describes a scene that cannot have taken place; in the letter as Regan reads it, Goneril tells her that she is about to arrive, something that she could not possibly have written in act one when she dispatched the letter, since her decision depends on events subsequent to the posting of the letter. These dizzying refusals remind us of the post in posting. They make plotting and retrospection coincident. If letters can arrive before they were sent, or vice versa, then before and after are—literally—preposterous. Letters, moreover, can find their proper recipients even when they are disguised and known to no one (how do Kent and Cordelia correspond?); they can convey true sentiments even when they are forged (Edmund does know his brother's character). Letters are the material form of uncanny knowledge, the vehicles of desperate idealizing hopes. Unfounded, they found modernity. Oswald, the fluid character most allied to the desacralizing regimes of modernity (as Halpern argues), unmoored from old property order and from gendered propriety as well (his service lubricates all sorts of promiscuity), is a postman—a secretary and letter carrier. When Edgar intercepts and kills him, he speaks for the first time *in propria persona.*

The circulation of letters in this play must be related to its textual condition; the fact that there are two *King Lear*s means only that there once were more than that, and that no text of the play ever will be anything more than just that—one text among a number whose sum we can never total. Fifty at a clap, Lear exclaims, a piece of knowledge he gets from nowhere in 1.4—or from some (lost) text of the play; or from the kind of knowledge the play intimates travels by the post. Nothing comes of noting.

In its foundational illusoriness, the play of the letter is to be related to the so-called scene at Dover where we look into an abyss that we cannot see. Recently, both times an essay of mine on that moment was reprinted, its two final sections were omitted; the punch line of the essay was thereby refused—that the double texts of *King Lear* won't even ground the deconstructive reading that the essay offers. Further, that the play traffics in a scene of failed vision replicated elsewhere, notably in *Cymbeline* when Imogen's vision cracks seeing Posthumus sailing away. The effect of the Dover Cliff scene in *Lear* is intimately tied to the father-son pair and the pathos of blinded visionary patriarchy (for more on this, see forthcoming work by Christopher Pye); the founding spot where vision is annihilated may always be misogynistically understood as the dark and vicious place of begetting (Imogen points Posthumus until he is nothing more than the tip of her needle, a gnat to be pricked, nothing more than a speck in the air). That the viewer in classic accounts of perspective is presumptively male—and that Imogen is not (or, rather, that the character is not while the gender of the player—boy—refuses the modern taxonomy of diacritical gender difference, male and female)—suggests that the oedipal drama of *King Lear* is as historically contingent as is the movement of the post.[6] Literally.

Notes

1. Jonathan Goldberg, *Writing Matter: From the Hands of the English Renaissance* (Stanford: Stanford University Press, 1990).
2. Jonathan Goldberg, *Voice Terminal Echo* (New York and London: Methuen, 1986).
3. Jonathan Goldberg, "Hamlet's Hand," *Shakespeare Quarterly* 39, 3 (1988): 307–27.
4. See, e.g., "Textual Properties," *Shakespeare Quarterly* 37.2 (1986): 213–17; "Rebel Letters: Postal Effects from *Richard II* to *Henry IV*," *Renaissance Drama*, n.s. 19 (1988): 3–28; " 'What? in a names that which we call a Rose': The Desired Texts of *Romeo and Juliet*," *Crisis in Editing*, ed. Randall McLeod (New York: AMS Press, 1994); "*Romeo and Juliet*'s Open Rs," *Queering the Renaissance*, ed. Jonathan Goldberg (Durham, N.C.: Duke University Press, 1994).
5. Richard Halpern, *The Poetics of Primitive Accumulation* (Ithaca: Cornell University Press, 1991).
6. "Perspectives: Dover Cliff and the Conditions of Representation," in *Shake-

speare and Deconstruction, ed. David Bergeron and G. Douglas Atkins (New York: Peter Lang, 1988), excerpted in two Macmillan New Casebooks, *King Lear,* ed. Kiernan Ryan (1993); *Shakespeare's Tragedies,* ed. Susan Zimmerman (1998). The final remarks here glance at the project of my most recent book, *Desiring Women Writing* (Stanford: Stanford University Press, 1997).

When We Were Capital, or Lessons in Language: Finding Caliban's Roots

Ian Smith

> Do you know why people like me are shy about being capitalists? Well, it's because we, for as long as we have known you, *were* capital.
>
> —Jamaica Kincaid, *A Small Place*

In his *Cosmography in Four Books, Containing the Chorography and History of the Whole World* (1674), Peter Heylyn makes the following pronouncement on blacks in Africa, particularly those inhabiting the region known as "Terra Nigritarum" or the "Land of Negroes": "The Inhabitants, till the coming of the Portugals thither, were for the most part so rude and barbarous, that they seem to want that use of Reason which is peculiar unto Man."[1] African barbarism connotes the nonhuman, a state of nature bordering on the bestial, and implies complete ignorance of "all Arts and Sciences" that are here set apart as the peculiar province of European literacy and civilization.[2] Critiques of Africans' speech recur, speech serving as the performance by which one's membership in the intellectual production of a community is validated. From John Lok's travels beyond Guinea to eastern Africa in 1555, we come upon the curious Troglodytica who "have no speech, but rather a grinning and chattering."[3] Thomas Herbert presses the animal metaphor that is implicit in Heylyn's appraisal to the limit when he makes the literal connection between the apish speech of Ethiopians and their supposed practices of bestiality: "Their language is apishly sounded (with whom tis thought they mix unnaturally)."[4] As a living antithesis to a spectrum of European values, Africans seemed to embody a concept of barbarism whose capacious contours included fundamental differences that could be gauged in language. The "barbarous," debased speech of Africans has, notably, an inverse relationship to the category of rhetoric and eloquence that constituted a central discipline in the English humanist educational program in the sixteenth century and stood as an important feature of an evolving English identity.[5]

Surprised to learn that Caliban, the "monster of the isle" in Shakespeare's *The Tempest* (1611), can speak, Stephano asks, "Where the devil should he learn our language?" (2.2.66–68). In addition to extending the network of intertexts among Heylyn, Herbert and Lok, the drunken butler's question invokes the trope of barbarism whose venerable classical roots had pervaded English and European intellectual, humanist traditions.[6] However, *The Tempest*'s figuration of the "barbarous" Caliban includes the accusation of subhuman potential while bringing together the otherwise separate fields of rhetoric and geography in significant ways. Recent criticism has tended to write Caliban in an American colonial context, but as the son of Sycorax, though he was born on the island that Prospero now rules, Caliban is African or, even more precisely, a Barbarian.[7] In his own narrative account of competing ownership of the island and its surviving inhabitants—specifically Caliban and Ariel—Prospero retells the story of Sycorax's banishment from her native Algiers in North Africa, one of the four kingdoms, as they were sometimes called (the others being Morocco, Tunis, and Tripoli), that Europeans had known collectively as "Barbary" ever since business contacts were first forged by medieval Christian merchants. Both Prospero and Miranda's treatment of Caliban recalls Heylyn's supposedly providential history of the intervention of Europeans in African affairs; that is, until their "coming . . . thither" Caliban was and continues to be no more than a barbarous brute who must "want that use of Reason which is peculiar unto Man." Consistent with the early modern European deployment of this polyvalent identity, Shakespeare has the Italians specify language as the area in which their superiority entitles them to raise the barbarous Caliban to the level of competent slave. Hence Miranda's outburst at a resistant Caliban upon his first appearance in the play: "Abhorred slave, /. . ./ I pitied thee, / Took pains to make thee speak, taught thee each hour / One thing or other" (1.2.353–57).[8] But Caliban knows that in reality he had little "profit on't" (1.2.365) and that language training was designed to indoctrinate and inculcate as well as provide a ready medium for the issuing of orders concerning the various domestic duties that as slave laborer he must carry out on pain of torture.[9] Prospero's books, which Caliban recognizes as the ultimate source of the magus's power, are situated along the continuum of language, literacy skills, and study that becomes identified with Europeans. In assuring themselves of Caliban's innate barbarism and of his cultural heritage as a Barbarian, Prospero and Miranda set out to provide language training as a crucial disciplinary measure in what is, after all, a colonial culture in epitome and, thereby, confirm the important racial nexus of geography and language in the early modern period that is fully implied in the negative descriptor "barbarous" as it relates to Africa.

The Tempest evokes the important distinction between "barbarian" and Barbarian—the Greco-Roman influenced rhetorical traditions and the geographic awareness of North Africa and its perceived role of Mediterranean cultural antagonist in sixteenth- and early seventeenth-century European history.[10] Writing in 1589, Puttenham reminds us, however, that in common English usage "barbarism" and its cognates had effectively erased the Arabic roots of the terms' applications to Africa and its people, generally, in favor of superimposing an unbroken but *false* etymological link with the Greek *bárbaros* and its subsequent Roman inscription.[11] With greater philological acumen, then, Heylyn observes that the name that became synonymous with Africa itself, "Barbary," denotes linguistic defect, being derived "from Barbar, signifying in their Language an uncertain murmur."[12] Still, Puttenham's remarks underscore the degree to which Englishmen in the late sixteenth century were prone to hear the cultural echoes of Greece and Rome when they used the terms "barbarism" and "barbarian" in relation to Africa. Thus the label "barbarian" functions as a rhetorico-geographic pun whose phonological materiality masks a linguistic "colonialism" at work in English and European usage as a preferred Greco-Roman system becomes the model for citing the contemporary African.

Shakespeare, with a pointed reanimation of the specificity of North Africa in the etymological geography that links Rome, Africa, and Renaissance England, invites us to fill out the historical intertext of Algiers which in his own time had become synonymous with an array of commercial activity and slavery.[13] For his own part, Trinculo, the jester, coming upon the cowering and partially hidden Caliban, sees there economic opportunity writ large and dreams of transporting him to England where "this monster makes a man" (2.2.30–31). Indeed, the "monsters" of Africa had already contributed to the making of Englishmen as early as Hawkins's slave raids in the 1560s.[14] With increasing degrees of success over the following century, Englishmen carried off Africans to other shores where their labor in the fields of English overseas enterprises materialized historically the paradigmatic versions of labor, financial interest and slavery that, respectively, Prospero demands, Trinculo in grim comic imitation fantasizes, and Algiers connotes. Shakespeare throws into sharp relief the colonial implications of Prospero's island regime and the pervasive exploitative vision of Africa that has trickled down through the social ranks even to the level of the jester Trinculo. Caliban's violent curse at Prospero and Miranda already signals an awareness of the barbarous, material fate that lay behind seemingly innocuous lessons in language.

Notes

1. Peter Heylyn, *Cosmography in Four Books, Containing the Chorography and History of the Whole World.* (London: Philip Chetwind, 1674), 4.1: 44.
2. Ibid.
3. Richard Hakluyt, *The Principal Navigations, Voyages & Discoveries of the English Nation,* 12 vols. (Glasgow: James MacLehose, 1904), 6:169.
4. Thomas Herbert, *Some Years Travels Into Divers Parts of Asia and Afrique. Describing especially the two famous Empires, the Persian, and the Great Mogull: weaved with the History of these later Times.* (London: Richard Bishop, 1638), 18.
5. On the importance of rhetoric in the school curriculum as well as literary achievements in English and their relation to national identity, see Richard Helgerson, *Forms of Nationhood: The Elizabethan Writing of England* (Chicago: University of Chicago Press, 1992) and T. W. Baldwin, *William Shakespere's Small Latine and Lesse Greeke,* 2 vols. (Urbana: University of Illinois Press, 1944).
6. For a discussion of the relation of classical barbarism to English Renaissance constructions of Africans, see my "Barbarian Errors: Performing Race in Early Modern England," *Shakespeare Quarterly* 49 (1998): 168–86.
7. The "colonial" readings of *The Tempest* have often assumed and American context and assign Caliban a native "Indian" identity. I have argued here for an African Caliban, and by implication, a so-called Mediterranean or Old World reading of the play that must complement the American echoes; Jerry Brotton also calls attention to the Mediterranean reading in " 'This Tunis, sir, was Carthage': Contesting colonialism in *The Tempest,*" in *Post-Colonial Shakespeares,* ed. Ania Loomba and Martin Orkin (London: Routledge, 1998). The "colonial" approach has itself generated heated debate. For a convenient summary of the important sources and relevant arguments, see Russ McDonald, "Reading *The Tempest,*" *Shakespeare Survey,* 43 (1990): 15–28; we should also add R. Knapp, *An Empire Nowhere: England, America and Literature from "Utopia" to "The Tempest"* (Berkeley: University of California Press, 1992). For a more recent objection to the "colonial" approach, see Leo Salingar, "The New World in *The Tempest,*" in *Travel and Drama in Shakespeare's Time,* ed. Jean-Pierre Maquerlot and Michèle Willems (Cambridge: Cambridge University Press, 1996).
8. William Shakespeare, *The Tempest,* ed. Frank Kermode (London: Methuen, 1954). All citations are taken from this edition.
9. Prospero commands:

> Fetch us in fuel; and be quick, thou'rt best,
> To answer other business. Shrug'st thou, malice?

> If thou neglect'st, or dost unwillingly
> What I command, I'll rack thee with old cramps,
> Fill all thy bones with aches, make thee roar
> That beasts shall tremble at thy din.
>
> (1.2.368–73)

10. Among the several references on North Africa, I will cite only Fernand Braudel's *The Mediterranean and the Mediterranean World in the Age of Philip II*, vol II, trans. Siân Reynolds (Berkeley: University of California Press, 1995).

11. See George Puttenham, *The Arte of English Poesie*, ed. Edward Arber (London: Alexander Murray, 1869), 257–58. The *Oxford English Dictionary*, second ed. (1989) notes also that "Barbary" is etymologically related to the Arabic "*barbara* 'to talk noisily and confusedly' (which is not derived from Greek [*bárbaros*])."

12. Heylyn also notes that according to one hypothesis, "bar" in "Barbary" could also mean "a *Desart*, which doubled, made up first *Barbar*, and after *Barbary*" (4.1:21).

13. See John B. Wolf, *The Barbary Coast: Algiers Under the Turks 1500 to 1830* (New York: Norton, 1979); Andrew C. Hess, "The Battle of Lepanto and its Place in Mediterranean History," *Past and Present* 57 (1972): 53–73.

14. See Hakluyt, *The Principal Navigations,* 10: 8, 65–66.

Trinket, Idol, Fetish: Some Notes on Iconoclasm and the Language of Materiality in Reformation England

JAMES J. KEARNEY

> Ha, ha, what a fool Honesty is? And Trust, his sworn brother, a very simple gentleman! I have sold all my trumpery; not a counterfeit stone, not a ribbon, glass, pomander, brooch, table book, ballad, knife, tape, glove, shoe tie, bracelet, horn ring, to keep my pack from fasting. They throng who should buy first, as if my trinkets had been hallowed, and brought a benediction to the buyer.
>
> —William Shakespeare *The Winter's Tale* 4.4.598–605

IN *THE WINTER'S TALE,* AUTOLYCUS, Shakespeare's roguish peddler, gloats over his ability to pass off his shabby merchandise, his trinkets and trumpery, to an undiscriminating public. In doing so, he associates the fervor of his naïve consumers with those who throng after all things hallowed, those who believe in the power of the sacred object to bring a benediction to the godly buyer. That is, he associates his credulous patrons with Catholics. This association is suggested not only by his explicit reference to hallowed objects and bought benedictions, but is implicitly present in the words "trinket" and "trumpery." As David Kaula argues, "the terminology Autolycus applies to his wares belongs to the verbal arsenal of anti-Catholic polemical writing in Reformation England. Again and again such words as "trumpery" and "trinkets" appear in the Protestant diatribes against what were considered the mercenary and idolatrous practices of selling indulgences, crucifixes, rosaries, medals, candles and other devotional objects."[1] The word "trinket" is of particular interest because its etymology is obscure; the word seems to enter the English language in the 1530s when, according to the *Oxford English Dictionary,* three different meanings of the term were theoretically operative: "a tool, implement, or tackle of an occupation"; "a small ornament or fancy article"; and "decorations of worship" or "religious rites, ceremonies, beliefs, etc. which the speaker thinks vain or trivial."[2] In practice, the *OED*'s third definition relating to "vain or trivial decorations of worship" tends to color other uses of the word. Indeed, many of the early uses of the term denigrate women and Catholics as people who not only misunderstand the value of objects but who might also have powerful and unnatural relations to them.

The significance of the fact that "trinket" seems to have entered the language, or, at least, become more fashionable, during the decade of the Henrician Reformation is strikingly apparent when we turn to the *OED*'s first entry under the "vain or trivial decorations of worship" rubric. In a 1538 letter to Richard Rich, Dr. John London recounts some of his iconoclastic efforts in the Henrician dissolution of the monasteries: "I have pullyd down the image of your lady at Caversham, with all trynkettes abowt the same, as schrowdes, candels, images of wexe, crowches, and brochys, and have thorowly defacyd that chapell."[3] Hugh Hilarie provides a similar list of papist objects in his 1554 anti-Catholic poem, *The Resurrection of the Masse: The Masse Speaketh,* when he denounces "Aultare clothes, corporasses and cruettes / Copes, vestementes, albes, boke, bell and chalice / Candelstickes, paxe, and suche other trynckettes."[4] The word "trinket" recasts both London's peculiar inventory and Hilarie's motley collection as catalogues of Catholic folly. Unlike more traditional forms of iconoclastic discourse such as the Elizabethan Church's authorized "Homilie against perill of idolatrie," which granted enormous power to the treacherous material object, the reformed language of "trinkets" worked to demystify the material dimensions of religion by rendering it trivial.[5]

No English reformed work attempts to denigrate the "idolatrous" materialism of the papists more than John Foxe's *Acts and Monuments.* At the beginning of the ninth book, "containing the Actes and thinges done in the Reigne of King Edward the sixt," Foxe includes a woodcut that portrays "The Papistes packing away their Paltry."[6] Depicting the removal of statues, crosses, mitres, elaborate folios, and, of course, Catholics from England, this woodcut represents a graphic version of the iconoclastic lists of London and Hilarie. The woodcut portrays the Catholics loading themselves and their "paltry" onto a ship of fools and trifling baubles ("The Ship of the Romish church") headed for foreign shores, with the decree—"Ship ouer your trinkets & be packing you papists." The text which the woodcut purports to illustrate, however, does not discuss Catholic trinkets and papist paltry. Rather, it celebrates the ascension of Edward VI, declaring him the second coming of the biblical boy-king and revered iconoclast, Josias. The implication is that just as Josias clashed with Old Testament idolaters so his antitype Edward would contend with the superstitious and idolatrous papists. Here, the papist trinkets of the woodcut seem both to help link Edward to an Old Testament iconoclasm and to suggest that there is some qualitative difference between the dark majesty of Old Testament idolatry and the triviality of papist baubles.

The term trinket could also be extended outward from lists and images of pernicious material objects to include any manifestation of religious materialism. In one of his *Six Sermons* Henry Smith associates the term "trinket" with all the "inventions" of Catholic doctrine and ritual: "then they inuented Purgatory, Masses, Prayers for the dead, and then all their trinkets."[7] Similarly, Foxe associates trinkets with the idolatrous innovations of the Catholic Mass itself. In a section of *Acts and Monuments* mocking the elaborate ceremony of the Mass, the running header is "The popes trinkets with the Canon of the Masse described" (1275–77). Having reproduced and ridiculed the Catholic Salisbury Use, and recounted a reformed history of "how and by whom this popish or rather apish Masse became so clamperde and patched togither" (1274), Foxe turns his attention to "such trinkettes as were to the foresaide Masse appertaining or circumstant, first, the linnen albes and Corporasses" (1276). Foxe then mockingly provides an index of frivolous objects and absurd innovations. As Foxe's example makes clear, terms like "trinket" helped the reformers cast their indictment of religious materialism as satire. If the established discourse of iconoclasm described the perils of the idolatrous object, the language of "trinkets" dismissed the material dimension of religion as farce. If iconoclasm struggled with the fundamental problems of representation and materiality that have shadowed Christianity throughout its history, the "common sense" language of trinkets suggested that the ridiculous innovations of Catholics were both easily perceived and easily "sent packing." Indeed, one could argue that by helping Reformers rethink Christian iconoclasm as a demystifying discourse, "trinket" and related terms anticipate, or lay the groundwork for, the modern discourse of fetishism.

"Fetish," of course, is modernity's preferred term to describe a perceived improper relation to objects. In a recent series of important essays, William Pietz has produced a genealogy of the fetish,[8] tracing the modern understanding of the word to the seventeenth-century voyage narratives of Protestant merchants trading on the African coast. I am attempting here to supplement Pietz's genealogy of the fetish by taking seriously his observation that in the early seventeenth century the understanding of the fetish was set within the "theoretical frame . . . of Protestant Christianity's iconoclastic repudiation of any material, earthly agency."[9] What is traditionally understood as iconoclasm broadly defined—the violent attack on the material dimension of religion—and the discourse decrying fetishism are distinguished by the relative power each discourse imputes to the material object. Traditional iconoclasm grants the idolatrous object an extraordinary power. As Ann Kibbey argues in a study of "Iconoclastic Materialism," "what historians and critics have misconstrued as a categorical opposition to images was actually a devoted, if negative, act of reverence, and a very self-conscious one at that. Although iconoclasm appears to have been a rejection of all images, in their own way the iconoclasts believed very deeply in the power of icons."[10] In the Elizabethan separatist Henry Barrow one can find evidence of the kind of "negative reverence" that Kibbey argues is constitutive of iconoclasm. Barrow was an iconoclast for whom, as Keith Thomas argues, "the arrangement of the very stones of church buildings was so inherently superstitious that there was nothing for it but to level the whole lot to the ground and begin again." Barrow writes that "the idolatrous shape so cleaveth to every stone, as it by no means can be severed from them whiles there is a stone left standing upon a stone."[11] Understanding the objects of "superstitious" worship as spiritual materializations of the demonic, iconoclasts like Barrow treat the material dimension of religion with a perverse respect.

If a vehement iconoclasm is always a kind of idolatry insofar as it grants the offending object immense power, the discourse of anti-fetishism is always an exercise in demystification. The modern conception of the fetish always implies distance, always implies an anthropological gaze that suggests that the barbarous other is guilty of some fundamental error in his/her relationship to objects. Protestant polemic of the sixteenth century tacked back and forth (sometimes in the same treatise, sometimes in the same sentence) between a negative iconoclastic reverence for the bewitching and beguiling object and a series of belittling gestures that reduced the material dimension of Catholic worship to the superstitious and unenlightened veneration of trash, trumpery, and trinkets. And it is precisely in these demystifying gestures that one can find a prehistory of the fetish. Prior to the emergence of the notion of the fetish on the coast of Africa in the early seventeenth century, reformation thinkers, entrenched in controversies surrounding icons and idols, vestments and sacraments, had been engaged in a century-long meditation on materiality and the veneration of objects. By reexamining the lexicon of this meditation we can begin to explore the historical relation between the traditional Christian understanding of iconoclasm and the emergence of the modern discourse of fetishism.

Notes

1. David Kaula, "Autolycus' Trumpery," *Studies in English Literature, 1500–1900,* 16 (1976): 289. In addition to Shakespeare, Spenser and Milton, Kaula finds these words used in the following texts: Jan vander Noot's *A theatre . . . of voluptuous worldlings,* trans. T. Roest (1569); William Tedder's *The recantations as they were seuerallie pronounced by Wylliam Tedder and Anthony Tyrell* (1588); John Mayo's *The popes parliament* (1591); Francis Bunny's *A comparison betweene the auncient fayth of the Romans, and the new Romish religion* (1595); George Gifford's *Sermons vpon the whole booke of the Revelation* (1596); John Racster's *William Alabasters seven motives* (1598); John Rhodes's *An answere to a Romish rime* (1602); George Downame's *A treatise concerning Antichrist* (1603); Samuell Harsnett's *A declaration of egregious popish impostures* (1603); Jean Chassanion's *The merchandise of popish priests* (1604).

2. *Oxford English Dictionary,* second edition (1992).

3. Reproduced in Thomas Wright's *Three Chapters of Letters Relating to the Suppression of Monasteries; Edited from the Originals in the British Museum by Thomas Wright* (London: Nichols, 1843), 224.

4. Hugh Hilarie, *The Resurreccion of the Masse* (Strasburgh, 1554), B8r.

5. For the "Homilie against perill of idolatrie" see *Certaine Sermons or Homilies Appointed to be Read in Churches in the Time of Queen Elizabeth,* facsimile of 1623 ed., eds. Mary Ellen Rickey and Thomas B. Stroup (Gainesville, Fla.: Scholars Facsimiles and Reprints, 1968).

6. John Foxe. *Actes and Monuments of matters most speciall and memorable* (London: Peter Short, 1596), 1178.

7. Henry Smith, "The Sweete Song of Old Father Simeon, in Two Sermons," *Sixe Sermons Preached by Maister Henry Smith* (London, 1593), 26.

8. "The Problem of the Fetish": "The Problem of the Fetish, I," *Res* 9 (1985): 5–17; "The Problem of the Fetish, II," *Res* 13 (1987): 23–45; "The Problem of the Fetish, IIIa," *Res* 16 (1988): 105–23.

9. "The Problem of the Fetish, II," *Res* 13 (1987), 40.

10. Ann Kibbey, *The Interpretation of material shapes in Puritanism: A Study of rhetoric, prejudice, and violence.* (Cambridge, Eng.: Cambridge University Press, 1986), 42.

11. Quoted in Keith Thomas's *Religion and the Decline of Magic* (New York: Scribner, 1971), 58, 59.

REVIEW ARTICLE

Playing Companies and the Drama of the 1580s: A New Direction for Elizabethan Theatre History?

PAUL WHITFIELD WHITE

THE 1580S HAS BEEN A PERPLEXING DECADE for theater historians. For one thing, scholars writing surveys or histories of a theater in which the dominant figure, William Shakespeare, does not appear until the following decade, are not quite sure how much of the 1580s to include in their chronological range of materials, if any. Some include all of it (for example, *The Cambridge Companion to English Renaissance Drama [1580–1642]*), some part of it (for example, The Oxford History of English Literature's *The English Drama 1586–1642*), and some none of it (for example, *The Professions of Dramatist and Player in Shakespeare's Time 1590–1642*). The most recent volume of this type, *A New History of Early English Drama,* covers the 1580s but attempts to avoid the pitfalls of periodic designations altogether by using the term "early" to describe its chronological range.[1]

For scholars interested in plays of high literary merit, a major problem is that the decade lacks sustainable focus from beginning to end. In so far as it is treated as a period at all, the 1580s tends to be carved up into unequal halves to highlight development or change. Critics are fond of referring to the post-1587 period as the "breakthrough years," marking "the expansion" and "flowering" of Elizabethan drama, a time when the first playhouse on the Bankside (the Rose) opens and when the drama emerges from the inexplicable dumbshows, jog-trot verse, mongrel-tragicomedy and primitive stage effects described in such works as *The Schoole of Abuse* (1579) and *The Apology of Poetry* (1581).[2] Without denying that the drama of Kyd, Marlowe, and the other University Wits represents a major artistic advancement, this scenario underestimates the extent to which the theater was already a complex, technically sophisticated—not to mention highly popular—institution in London at the *beginning* of the decade. We need to keep in mind that as early as 1567 England's first known playhouse, the Red Lion, opened in Stepney with an enormous stage, forty feet wide by thirty feet deep, equipped with a trap door and a "turret of Tymber" supporting a floor eighteen feet above the stage which was probably used for ascents and celestial figures.[3] Since the Red Lion discovery effectively dislodges "1576" as the year in which the urban playhouses were established, we are now looking at a London theater industry well into its second decade of operation by 1580. Indeed, by that year at least ten professional acting companies were performing plays, many regularly on weekdays, at nine or ten different commercial playing venues in the London area.[4] When the city politicians and preachers raised a storm of opposition to their existence in the early eighties, the players were sufficiently self-confident and self-asserting to respond with perhaps the first "anti-puritan" play of the period, "The Play of Plays." Unfortunately, this play (described by Gosson) has vanished into oblivion along with most others of the 1580s.[5] For the period 1580 to 1589, *The Annals of English Drama* lists 86 titles, for which 53 texts survive, most of the latter dated in the final years of the decade.[6] Yet these numbers represent a fraction of what once existed. William Ingram offers a plausible argument for upwards of 200 plays written per year in the late 1570s, and I see no reason for a significant decrease during the 1580s.[7]

The implications of this loss for researchers of the 1580s is far-reaching. It certainly raises questions about when, and at what pace, linguistic, artistic, and technological advances occurred during the decade. To be sure, playhouse audiences may not have seen, or heard, anything like *Tamburlaine* when it debuted on the London stage in the summer of 1587. On the other hand, Peele's *Arraignment of Paris* was already experimenting with flexible blank verse for court drama as early as 1581, and who is to say that Peele or one of the other Wits did not write blank-verse plays designed for the professional stage between then and 1587 which anticipated Marlowe's poetic dialogue?[8] Indeed, Kyd's *The Spanish Tragedy* may be such a play, although a few critics have been willing to posit an early-to-mid-1580s date, despite the fact that the play's action covers the pre-Armada years in Spain and makes no mention of the event itself.[9] Considering the sophistication of Lyly's plays of the early 1580s (often overlooked as relevant to the professional stage because Lyly is misleadingly labeled a "court playwright"), and the fact that Queen's Men, with their twelve full-time actors, were performing "large-cast" plays as early as mid-1583, we should perhaps reconsider the theory that the "great drama" of Elizabethan England suddenly burst upon the scene in the late 1580s.

In what follows I wish to consider several recent books and articles which raise just such questions and problems about the 1580s I have touched on here. They challenge us to reconsider our assumptions and perceptions about professional acting companies, theatrical conditions at the court and in the universities, the relationship between major playwrights like John Lyly and their patrons (both noble and public), and the career of the popular playwright in the 1580s and after. These topics are important in themselves within the 1580s timeframe, but they also have significant implications for our understanding of Shakespeare and the theater of the following decades.

Some of the best new scholarship produced on the 1580s has to do with the playing troupes, defying a long tradition in theater history that attempting to approach the Elizabethan theater from the perspective of the players constitutes an exercise in futility. "To treat intelligibly any of the several dramatic companies at the end of the [sixteenth] century," wrote W. W. Greg in 1908, "demands a knowledge of the constitution of other companies and of the sequence of other events such as at present can hardly be said to exist."[10] Greg was writing two years before John Tucker Murray's two-volume *English Dramatic Companies 1558–1642* and fifteen before E. K. Chambers four-volume *Elizabethan Stage,* both of which vastly increased the body of material known about the troupes. Nevertheless, his general pessimism, combined with literature scholars' focus on individual authors and plays, held sway, with very few exceptions, until the present decade, and even today G. K. Hunter, who highlights the above-quoted passage by Greg in the opening pages of his *English Drama 1586–1642* (1997) echoes Greg's conviction when he asks rhetorically, "Can we . . . say anything that will make linkage between company and repertory more than a historical pipedream?"[11]

Two important new books on playing companies respond affirmatively to this question, but before considering them we should draw attention to the Records of Early English Drama project to which recent scholarship on the troupes owes much of its source material.[12] The REED volumes, of course, supply records for all aspects of drama from the Medieval period through to 1660, but their findings with respect to touring acting companies and their patrons represent the most important archival work on the troupes since the days of Chambers and Murray. Quite strikingly the published volumes to date indicate that the touring of professional companies peaked in the 1580s (with the 1590s not far behind), with 435 performance incidents (including dismissals) by fifty-seven playing troupes, most of which were sponsored by the higher nobility.[13] The implications of this are potentially explosive when we consider the now-prevalent view that increasingly as Elizabeth's reign went along, dramatic activity withered away in the provinces. Might we now consider the possibility that in many communities in the provinces there were more, rather than fewer, opportunities to see plays at the mid-point of Elizabeth's reign?[14] Another interesting finding of the REED research is that in a decade when many of us thought that Protestant religious authority was firmly estranged from the popular stage, we find among the patrons of these acting companies names typically associated with advanced Protestants—Warwick, Huntington, Essex, and of course Leicester. This linkage between moderate puritanism and the stage is one of the claims of Sally-Beth Maclean and Scott McMillan, as we shall see shortly.

The first major book in the past decade to address troupe playing in the 1580s, and for the early modern period as a whole, is Andrew Gurr's *The Shakespearean Playing Companies.* Drawing on the author's vast knowledge of Elizabethan theater history over the past thirty-five years, this book traces the operations of some thirty-five professional adult and boys' troupes performing in the London area under Elizabeth and the early Stuarts. The study divides into two chronologically ordered sections, the first discussing aspects of the companies as an industry, such as patronage, travelling, day-to-day operations and significant general developments and changes over an eighty-year period; the second section treating the histories of the individual companies. The two-part design results in some overlap and repetition, but of the kind we have grown to accept from reading Chambers *Elizabethan Stage.* Gurr's best insights concerning company/repertory linkage apply to the later years when the rivalry between London-based companies, fixed in their own playhouses, forged differences in the repertories. Yet as he observes, through the 1580s there is no evidence of any one company working exclusively in London and affiliated with a single playhouse, not Leicester's (often linked to the Theatre in Shoreditch by virtue of its being built by James Burbage, a Leicester player) not even the Lord Admiral's (often thought to be based at the Rose from 1587 onwards). It was not until 1594 that their patrons arranged for the Admiral's Men and the Lord Chamberlain's Men to settle at the Rose and the Theatre respectively. His claim that troupes resolutely stuck to their traditional practice as nomadic entertainers well into the 1590s is born out by REED records and by the work of Sally-Beth Maclean and Scott McMillin on the Queen's Men noted below. While Gurr believes that no one company or individual took a controlling or interventionist role in the changes experienced by companies during the era, he does regard the establishment of the Queen's Men in 1583 as pivotal in securing legitimate status for professional playing in London during the decade, in popularizing the all-important large-cast play, and in providing a model for setting up the "duopoly" of the Lord Chamberlain's Men and the Lord Admiral's Men a decade later in 1594.[15] He is especially illuminating about the activities of theater patrons on the Privy Council, favoring Charles Howard as the prime-mover on behalf of the theater community from the early 1580s through the remainder of Elizabeth's reign. (As we shall see, Gurr's view of Howard's early prominence does not square with Maclean and McMillin's account of events of 1583.) There is much new information in this book about the professional troupes operating in the 1580s, eighteen of which are identified—most notably Sussex's, Leicester's, Warwick's, Worcester's, Derby's, Oxford's, the Lord Admiral's, and the Queen's, although the book limits its analysis only to companies who operated in London and appeared at court.

If Gurr's study is comprehensive in the sense that it analyzes and surveys the companies across the early modern era, *The Queen's Men and Their Plays,* by Sally-Beth Maclean and Scott McMillan, explores in depth all aspects of a single, major playing troupe's operation and history—personnel, repertory, touring itinerary, and patronage, along with its broader social and political contexts. This approach is not unprecedented,[16] yet in devoting an entire book-length study to a major troupe in the heyday of Elizabethan professional theater, *The Queen's Men* is a first, and its findings and conclusions not only provide a model for future projects of this kind, but have important implications for a range of related fields in the discipline, from textual criticism to Shakespearean biography. Because the history of the Queen's Men is so central to our understanding of the English theater of the 1580s, it will be worth considering that history in some detail.

The Queen's Men begins by focussing in on 1583, the year the court, in an extraordinary move, hand-picked the twelve best actors in the nation to form a new company under the Queen's patronage. Past critics have accounted for the company's formation in two ways: first of all, as a grand gesture by the court to demonstrate to the anti-theatrical City fathers the monarchy's endorsement and protection of professional playing, and secondly, as a means by which to end the embarrassing rivalry among the leading noblemen's troupes—Sussex's, Leicester's, Derby's, and Oxford's—for holiday performances at court.[17] MacLean and McMillin, however, downplay the court's supposed adversarial role against the city, observing that in draining the best acting talent from the nation's most celebrated companies to form the Queen's Men, the Privy Council was hardly offering protection to the playing community; rather they were in effect "reducing the number of companies and the number of theaters active in London, a point on which the council may have been the silent and unacknowledged allies of the city."[18] The authors see the amalgamation of Paul's Boys with the Chapel Children to form one royal juvenile company as part of this court policy of reduction implemented in 1583, although, as Gurr suggests, this merger may have taken place at least one year earlier.[19]

Where the authors most boldly depart from previous scholarship, however, is in their claim that Sir Francis Walsingham was the prime mover behind the Queen's Men's formation. Since the days of Chambers, critics have been baffled by the role of the Queen's puritan-leaning secretary in authorizing the Revel's Office to create the company and in subsequently defending it against the City government. Surely Walsingham was merely filling in for the ailing Lord Chamberlain Sussex in 1583, Gurr suggests, when the real initiative for the royal troupe came from those truly appreciative of the stage, namely Charles Howard and his relative, Edmund Tilney, the Master of the Revels.[20] Yet why did not Sussex's deputy, Lord Hunsdon, or the Vice-Chamberlain, Sir Christopher Hatton, both also Privy Councillors, act on his behalf? Why instead was it Sussex's political opponent who appointed the company? Maclean and McMillin, I believe, are right on target in arguing that Walsingham followed earlier secretaries of state (Thomas Cromwell in the 1530s, Lord Burghley under Edward VI and during the opening years of the Queen's reign) in recognizing the political usefulness of a popular acting troupe to advance the monarchy, propagating a centrist-oriented Protestantism that exposed the dangers of international Catholicism and the indigent religious radicalism which, in the 1580s, emerged as presbyterian puritanism. Walsingham was allied throughout the 1580s with the Earl of Leicester's moderate puritan policies, and the authors' note that Leicester's own documented support of drama to advance his political interests, as well as his close links with the new troupe (three of his own troupe's players joined it, the Lord sponsoring the troupe on several occasions) suggest that he played a mentoring role to the company, advising Walsingham on decisions concerning them. More speculative is the book's claim that the Queen's Men contributed to Walsingham's espionage operations while travelling the realm. This is difficult to prove but it is entirely plausible considering the extensive research linking artists of every kind—including travelling entertainers—to intelligence work in England during this period and earlier.[21]

With their interlude-style dramaturgy and repeated emphasis on "truth" and "plainness," especially in their history plays (which they popularized, if not invented, in the 1580s), the Queen's Men's repertory confirms for Maclean and McMillin that the company was formed "to spread Protestant and royalist propaganda through a divided realm and to close a breach within radical Protestantism."[22] This propaganda is most evident, at least in its anti-Catholic aspect, in *The Troublesome Reign of King John,* where the laying on of hands and swearing of allegiance to the Pope at the altar of St. Edmundsbury was a piece of iconoclastic theater popular since the days of John Bale and continuing through the 1630s when *The Cardinal's Conspiracy* attacked the ceremonialism of the Laudian church in a similar fashion. Yet, in complicating our understanding of religion/theater relations in the 1580s, the authors observe the central role the Queen's Men in challenging presbyterian puritans (as well as Catholics) near the end of the decade when they were embroiled in the Martin Marprelate controversy, staging plays in defense of the Elizabethan bishops and established church. As far as I can see, however, the Queen's Men were, for the most part, engaged in religious propaganda with a small "p." In such plays as *The Famous Victories* and even *Friar Bacon* comic buffoonery and pronounced visual effects dilute any serious religious message intended. We need to keep in mind that whenever didacticism enters the commercial domain of the public playhouse its teeth are inevitably blunted by the tacit agreement that paying spectators come to be pleasured, not preached to. *The Queen's Men and Their Plays,* nevertheless, contributes to the reconfiguring of religion/theater relations during the 1580s and after. Until fairly recently, the professional theater was seen as a purely secular institution—forged out of humanist and capitalist interests, if not forced to be secular by censorship against religious matters in plays. Shortly, we'll note that Catholicism also had its place on the stage.[23]

Some of the most original research in *The Queen's Men and Their Plays* concerns the touring itineraries of the company. The Queen's Men were the most widely traveled, the most profitable, and the best known acting company in sixteenth-century England, sometimes splitting into two troupes (this they did from their inception, not later on as is usually thought). They followed routes well established over half a century earlier; the main circuits were in East Anglia, the Southeast, the Southwest, the Midlands, the West Midlands, the North East, and the North West. Contrary to received opinion, they did not tour because of any failure to gain a foothold in London; the road was their political mandate and the provinces their targeted audience and main source of revenue. Records indicate that they sometimes had a spring tour, usually a summer one, and often spent the fall in London, though not apparently lodged in a resident playhouse but "touring" the city's many venues, mostly the inns within the city walls. They were, needless to say, attendant at court where they held a monopoly among professional troupes during the 1580s. They visited London less later in their career, and indeed may have lost their acceptance there, where they usually performed only during the fall and Christmas seasons anyway, due to the Marprelate controversy of 1588–90. Ironically, the Marprelate writers appropriated the jesting, satirical rhetoric of Tarlton and the Queen's Men in attacking the established church. Whether they were staging unlicensed plays or were initially backed by the Revels Office only to have that support withdrawn when the attacks and counter-attacks got out of hand, remains unclear.

The company's reduced market in London, however, was also related to the popularity of Marlowe whose poetic artistry and magnificent characters the Queen's Men could not match in their own plays. That the company attempted to fight to get its audience back is evident from the printed edition of *The Troublesome Reign* (published in 1591), where Marlowe is slighted in the address to the reader's attack on Tamburlaine, that "infidel," and in the play itself where the hero closely echoes Faustus in his expressions of spiritual despair; however where Faustus succumbs, John overcomes despair to attain Christian faith and be the forerunner to Queen Elizabethan and England's Protestant monarchy: "The anti-Marlowe motive is neatly dovetailed into the celebration of Elizabeth's lineage, these being the Queen's Men to the last."²⁴ Whatever happened to their London market in the late 1580s, the company went back on the road to resume their busy touring schedule, performing in cities, towns, and private households throughout the realm. Their playing venues varied but included guildhalls, great halls in private homes, church houses, and some churches as well. The guildhalls, such as the famous surviving one at Leicester, were remarkably small in comparison to the venues of a thousand spectators or more that the Queen's Men were accustomed to in London, and the book might be pressing it a bit in saying that at the Leicester guildhall "the Queen's Men would have performed before audiences conservatively estimated at three hundred."²⁵ I would guess audiences of at least three-hundred for a Tarlton-led Queen's company, but not within the cramped quarters of the guildhall. We might seek them, rather, next door within the spacious nave of St. Martin's Church where playing troupes had entertained (probably much larger) audiences earlier in the century. Missing from the book too is an analysis of performance settings within the four royal palaces where the company played before Queen Elizabeth and the court. This gap is filled, however, by John Astington's study discussed below.

The question of Shakespeare's relationship with the Queen's Men has been repeatedly debated. *The Queen's Men and Their Plays* convincingly shows that the extant published texts of the troupe's monarchical history plays are not "bad quartos" resulting from later memorial reconstructions of Shakespeare's comparable histories. On the contrary, Shakespeare is indebted to the Queen's Men's repertoire for the plots of his second Henriad, *King John,* and *King Lear*. It is therefore not implausible that Shakespeare may have joined the Queen's Men in some capacity in the mid-to-late eighties. This hypothesis competes with E. A. J. Honigmann's explanation of "the lost years," that Shakespeare's schoolmaster years "in the country" led him to a Catholic household in Lancashire, and from there on to the rival professional company of Lancashire's leading magnate, Fernando Stanley, Lord Strange.²⁶ Several players in this troupe, it has been noted, eventually restructured to form, along with Shakespeare, the Lord Chamberlain's Men in 1594. Yet Park Honan's cautious new biography of Shakespeare suggests that these hypotheses are not entirely incompatible. Following his return from Lancashire to Stratford where be married in his early twenties, Shakespeare might have "attached himself to the Queen's Men," and "he could have gone with the actor John Heminges from there straight into Strange's Men."[27] Assuming this were the case, it would be ironic to find that while Marlowe was changing the face of Elizabethan drama, Shakespeare was sticking it out with the Queen's Men in the late 1580s waiting for the chance to make his own contribution to the stylistic demise of the Queen's Men's plays through his participation in the blank-verse revolution.[28]

Much of what Gurr, Maclean, and McMillin say about the conditions leading to the increased sophistication of professional drama in the 1580s is reaffirmed in John Astington's *English Court Theatre 1560–1642,* the first full-length study of the theater at court under Elizabeth and the early Stuarts.[29] As Astington documents, the partnership between the Revels Office and the professional players underwent a kind of reversal around the mid-point of Elizabeth's reign. Up until 1580 or so, the Revels Office set the standard for scenic spectacle through its lavishly produced plays and masques, and it supplied the theater community with costumes for lease. However, with the Office's sharp curtailment of expenditures following Lord Treasurer William Cecil's restructuring of court finances, the Revels became increasingly dependent upon the professional companies who now replaced court-produced masques and lavish "shows" with their own staged productions. By the time Henslowe was turning a major profit at the Rose in the 1590s, the London playhouses may have been better equipped than the Revels Office itself. A theme emerging from Astington's book is that the Revels Office significantly stimulated the development and continued success of professional drama in the 1580s, not only by the enlightened regulation of its new Master, Edmund Tilney (granted authority to license plays and players nationwide by a 1581 patent) but by its policy of reliance on professional players for holiday entertainment at the royal court.

Yet there is much more in the book to discover besides Revels/players relations. Working very much in the vein of such theater historians as John Orrell, Alan Nelson, and William Ingram, Astington spells out in considerable detail the highly varied architectural and performance conditions at the mainly temporary court theaters constructed at the four royal palaces of Hampton Court, Richmond, Greenwich, and St. James. Repeatedly contradicted in the evidence is Richard Southern's universal model of Tudor hall performance with the actors set up before the lower screen and extending their action across the broad expanse of the hall floor. Astington states that we also need to be suspicious of the old view that the Revels' budget cuts resulted in a much simpler use of performance space at court in the late eighties,[30] since the platform stages built by the Office of the Works's carpenters and joiners and decorated by its painters for some events were elaborately equipped with mechanical traps (for ascents and descents) and three-dimensional (and often curtained) stage houses. Many of the stages were remarkably small in scale, like the 14-foot square stage built in the Great Chamber at Richmond where several troupes performed in 1588–89. Astington's chapter on "Artists and artisans" gives some much deserved attention to the virtually never-mentioned craftsmen working behind the scenes to produce, in some instances, spectacular effects: the stage-machinist John Rose who build the mechanical trap inside a gigantic rock for the *Knight of the Burning Rock* in 1579 and an apparatus for moving clouds around the same time; the Lizard family of painters—William, John, Nicholas Jr., and Lewis who decorated various stage houses, properties, and ceilings, through to the mid-1580s; the wire-drawer Edmund Burchall who rigged up chandeliers and other hanging lights with wire cables for performances by the Queen's Men and Paul's Boys in 1587. The book draws on recent historical scholarship in its discussion of court audiences, noting that with a woman monarch on the throne, her female companions, maids of honor, and wives and daughters of leading nobles were both visible and prominent at court performances,[31] which helps to explain the many direct addresses to female spectators in a play like Lyly's *Gallathea* (ca. 1584). *English Court Theatre* is not for those looking for political or cultural readings of drama staged before Elizabeth and her early Stuart successors; rather, in concentrating "on the physical and aesthetic conditions under which actors worked when they performed at the Tudor and Stuart courts"[32] and in providing twenty-one plans and illustrations of the theaters and an index of court performances between 1558 and 1642, Astington's study establishes itself as the standard authority and most comprehensive reference source on English court theater during the early modern period.

Whereas Astington and others have explored the relationship of court theaters to the commercial playhouses of the London area, less attention has been given to the connections of both types to staging at the universities. Alan Nelson's *Early Cambridge Theatres* advances our knowledge considerably on these fronts. As with theaters at court, one is struck by the considerable scale and complexity of the staging apparatus in the typical college hall, transforming it from a rather sparsely decorated space into a full-fledged theater, marked on all sides by timber structures for galleries, platforms, staircases, and multiple leveled stage houses. Rarely, if ever, at Cambridge, was the lower hall screen used as a backdrop or second-level balconies used for acting. While Astington argues that temporary court stages were build anew for each occasion, with the lumber reused for other purposes afterwards, Nelson shows that at Cambridge even the most complex stages were prefabricated and demountable, placed in storage after their use each year. His book gives us a vivid sense of the *process* involved in putting on a play performance. Actors and musicians (the non-students among them drawn from the town waits, others brought in from London) rehearsed as much as a month in advance in a nearby acting chamber (usually somewhere within the master's quarters); carpenters, painters, and other hired artisans began preparations a week in advance, with students paid to dine in the town while the hall was detained. Prior to and during the performances, costumed guards called stagekeepers wore visors and carried torches to control crowds and potential rivalries between colleges.

In redating the sophisticated staging in Queen's College Hall from 1638 (Leslie Hotson's long accepted claim) back to 1546, Nelson suggests that Cambridge may have been instrumental in developments leading up to the early Elizabethan playhouses. Challenging John Orrell's claim that classical models of architecture influenced Burbage's design of the Theatre, Nelson offers a powerful counter-argument that medieval English principles of stage construction took precedence over imported models in London, as in Cambridge. He also raises questions about the use of trapdoors and upper galleries for stage action (neither are much evident in Cambridge) and supports recent claims about audience seating and configuration in the amphitheaters (e.g. seating directly behind and above the stage). But, as Nelson suggests, the Cambridge discoveries may be more useful in reconstructing Blackfriars and other "private" indoor theaters in London, with which college halls such as Queen's had the most in common.[33]

In an earlier article Nelson notes that the twenty-five plays on record for performance at Cambridge during the 1580s were, for Shakespeare and his contemporaries, "more noticed, more remembered, more admired, and more imitated" than those of any previous decade, and despite their coming after the heyday of the 1550s and 1560s.[34] With Latin the dominant language of the college stage, the most influential play was *Pendantius* (1581), a debunking of

Gabriel Harvey which established a trend in stage satire lasting into the 1630s. The most important Cambridge playwright of the decade was Thomas Legge, among Francis Mere's "best for tragedy," who wrote the historical trilogy *Richard Tertius* (1579), followed by *Solymitana Clades,* or *The Fall of Jerusalem,* another trilogy and "the longest play ever written in England," recovered after 400 years in 1973.[35] Chambers suspected that the latter piece might have been the same play as *The Destruction of Jerusalem,* which was performed at great expense and with much fanfare at Coventry in 1584 in place of the recently defunct mystery cycle (see note 14 above).[36] This would have made the young scholar of St. John's College, Oxford, whom the city paid the handsome amount of £13.6s.8d, into a plagiarist, but the identification now seems highly unlikely. Oxford's theatrical culture was no less fully developed than Cambridge's in the 1580s, with the famous William Gager presiding at Christ Church, but Oxford's heyday lay ahead in the first two decades of the next century. Unfortunately, apart from a few articles by John Elliott, Jr., we do not have either updated records or commentary on Oxford for the early modern period (Elliott's REED volume on Oxford is forthcoming),[37] and indeed a full-length survey of drama and theater at the universities together has not been undertaken since Frederick Boas's now somewhat out-dated *University Drama in the Tudor Age* published in 1914.

Elizabethan Oxford's most distinguished and influential playwrighting graduate was John Lyly, the one major English playwright for whom we have extant plays extending across the decade of the eighties. Lyly's relation to the royal court and to the public theater has been significantly revised in the past few years. A casualty of recent criticism is the perception of him as an obsequious (if belatedly disgruntled) panegyrist of Queen Elizabeth who steered clear of controversial issues. Thus, in an article on *Endymion* and *Midas,* David Bevington sees Lyly calling for a tolerant policy towards loyal English Catholics such as his own patron, the Earl of Oxford, during the years when England witnessed the execution of Mary Queen of Scots and the failed invasion of the Spanish Armada.[38] In the first book-length study of Lyly since the 1960s, Michael Pincombe argues that while Lyly complimented the Queen through his panegyical figure of "Eliza," he "became increasingly sceptical and hostile of courtliness as he went on."[39] If an early play like *Campaspe* expresses the anxiety of the court poet who fears the political misinterpretation of his art, late plays such as *Gallathea* are more overtly critical of the Elizabethan cult of the virgin queen. Pincombe shows that Lyly's Ovidian-inspired eroticism sometimes ran counter to his panegyric of Queen Elizabeth. He partially accounts for this ambivalence by the fact that Lyly's plays were at least as much produced for the paying gentry spectators at Blackfriars and Paul's playhouses as for an audience before the Queen.

Taking Pincombe's lead in this respect, Kent Cartwright reconsiders Lyly's place within the commercial London theater and the popular dramatic canon of the late 1570s and 1580s. Challenging the persisting view that Lyly's drama is exclusively court-centered, static, and intellectual, Cartwright demonstrates that the plays are full of the theatrical vitality and visceral delight of the popular chivalric romances and moral interludes contemporaneous with them and condemned by the antitheatricalists.[40] Moreover, Lyly may have been England's first "serial" dramatist, repeating in play after play the same mixture of mythological and romantic characters, Ovidian transformations, and witty prose dialogue, which his audiences at the commercial indoor theaters and at court came to expect. Lyly's debt to the public theater raises the question of whether he may have penned some of these other popular plays, and may have done so before he shows up in court records in 1583/84. According to Pincombe, Lyly's career as playwright occurred quite by accident in 1583 when his patron, the Earl of Oxford, secured for him the lease of Blackfriars to manage, and write plays for, the new children's company created from the merger of the earl's own boys with those of the St. Paul's and Chapel Royal companies.[41] Thus Pincombe places Lyly as a mere spectator of plays prior to this and the writing of his accomplished comedy *Campaspe* presented at court on 1 January 1584. Yet the Paul's/Chapel troupe may have merged as early as 1582 with Lyly at the helm. Gurr suggests that Thomas Giles, successor to Sebastian Westcote as Almoner to St. Paul's on the latter's death in 1582, "appears to have linked Paul's Boys with the Chapel Boys, and to have taken on John Lyly as his deputy."[42] Be that as it may, the earl of Oxford patronized both an adult company led by the famous Dutton brothers who were active at the Theatre in Shoreditch and a children's playing troupe—one man and nine boys—who traveled in the provinces during the early 1580s (the latter were paid two shillings each for performing at Bristol in 1581).[43] It is therefore plausible that Lyly wrote for one, possibly both, of these companies, as might be suggested by Gabriel Harvey's remark that Lyly had "played the Vicemaster of Poules, and the Foolemaster of the Theater for naughts . . . sometime the diddle-sticke of Oxford, now the very bable of London."[44] Writing in 1593, Harvey might have been alluding to Lyly's involvement with the Marprelate controversy in the late 1580s when, it now seems clear, Lyly was writing comedies, possibly for performance at the Theatre as well as at Paul's, in support of the ecclesiastical establishment. But I would not discount Chambers' conjecture that Lyly's fellow Euphuist Stephen Gosson may have been praising Lyly when in 1579 he spoke of "the two prose books played at the Belsavage, where you shall find never a word without wit, never a line without pith, never a letter placed in vain."[45] I think it unwise, therefore, to single out Lyly as the one University Wit who managed to avoid writing for the popular stage. Like the rest of them, he was constantly in debt, and writing for the common players was a way of avoiding poverty.

The University Wits—Lyly, Robert Greene, Thomas Lodge, Thomas Nashe, and Christopher Marlowe—are generally recognized to have been at the center of the drama's transformation during the late 1580s. This is not the occasion to discuss the criticism of their plays individually, yet the most compelling recent discussion of their collective importance is found in the long-overdue Oxford History of English Literature volume, *English Drama 1586–1642: The Age of Shakespeare* (1996), by G. K. Hunter. Hunter argues that the Wits (he gives the non-university Kyd and Shakespeare "associate memberships")—were socially positioned to arrive at the right historical moment in the Elizabethan theater's development to enrich the drama in quality and significance.[46] This humanistically educated and short-lived generation of writers were somewhat estranged from a political and religious establishment which had no suitable place for their prodigious talents and liberal views. Most of them, therefore, found themselves writing for the rapidly burgeoning professional stage with its demand for playscripts, despite their disdain for such work. For Hunter, however, the Wits' importance for the future of Elizabethan drama is not to be found initially in their plays but in their prose fiction where the personalized mode of the genre's narration, combined with the Wits' marginalized lifestyles and viewpoints, enabled them to give individuated voice to prodigals, outcasts, and subversives opposed to the current social order.[47] It was not until Marlowe's *Tamburlaine* came along in 1587, however, that his fellow Wits were provided with a model of adapting such "outsiders" from prose fiction to the popular stage, which until then was hemmed in creatively by demands for social consensus and conventional morality, most clearly exemplified in early Elizabethan "estates moralities." As Kyd's *Spanish Tragedy* demonstrates, however, the innovations of the Wits did not bring an end to the older dramaturgy; instead, those innovations were absorbed into the mainstream dramatic tradition.

Hunter aligns the Wits with a Burckhardtian model of individualism ushered in by the Renaissance, a model dismissed by the 1980s postmodern critique of Francis Barker and Catherine Belsey who countered with their own theory that the modern, autonomous, inward-looking self did not develop until the latter seventeenth century, although signs of it first appear in English drama with *Hamlet* ("I have that within which passes show").[48] However, Hunter's notion that the Wits forged individualism out of the "unbridgeable gap between self-valuation and the values of the world" coheres with other recent literary studies on the history of the subject by David Aers (exploring the late Medieval period), Alan Sinfield, and Katherine Maus.[49] Where Hunter stresses Humanism as the main ideological source of the Wits' self-identity, these critics stress the importance of religion, and particularly Protestantism, in the development of interiority and in opening the way for sceptical, heterodox subject positions found in such plays as *Tamburlaine, The Jew of Malta, Doctor Faustus,* and *The Spanish Tragedy.* Where I think further exploration can be done in this vein is with the Wits' prose writing downplayed or ignored by Hunter: Greene's *The Repentance of Robert Greene* and Nashe's *Christ's Tears Over Jerusalem,* both of which show their authors' Calvinistic credentials, often overshadowed by their Humanism. As Deborah Shuger observes, while *Christ's Tears* is a politico-religious diatribe against the decadence and spiritual indifference of late Elizabethan London, this Protestant "passion narrative" introduces the reader to an interior spiritual landscape of sin, fear, violence and eroticism. The extent to which the warrior culture of Marlowe's *Tamburlaine* is yoked together with Christian retribution is found in Nashe's depiction of a Christ spurned by his bride, the Church. "Emulating Tamburlaine, Christ first offers 'the Jewes the White-flagge of forgivenesse and remission, and the Red-flag of shedding his Blood for them, [and] when these two might not take effect . . . the Black-flagge of confusion and desolation.'"[50] Nashe and Greene both project in their religious prose writings deeply personalized expressions of suffering and spiritual alienation that are useful in further illuminating the plights of Faustus and Hieronimo.

That the Wits perceived themselves as serious writers who resorted to playmaking only out of financial necessity is well established, yet few critics have explored their connection with the specifically literary culture of the 1580s and 1590s. One recent book that does, however, is Patrick Cheney's *Marlowe's Counterfeit Profession: Ovid, Spenser, and Counter-Nationhood*.[51] We tend to think of Marlowe first and foremost as a playwright, but Cheney convincingly shows that Marlowe self-consciously conceived of himself as a poet whose identity was shaped by and subsequently modified the Elizabethan literary system. At the center of Cheney's book is the rivalry Marlowe had with Edmund Spenser, whose verse is echoed (always ironically, often in parodic form) repeatedly in Marlowe's surviving plays and poems. Cheney argues that Marlowe self-consciously pursued an Ovidian career path, countering the Virgilian course of his rival, and that in satirizing the pretensions of "the Brytayne Orpheus" to be England's great poet, Marlowe substituted himself as the age's new poet, a "counter-nationalist" who championed pleasure over didacticism as the main end of poetry. What comes clearly into focus in both Hunter's and Cheney's studies is that playwrighting for the public theaters throughout the eighties continued to be considered professional hackwork, undeserving of the individual recognition accorded to poets, and it was, of course, as poets that the Wits aspired to be recognized. Only in the nineties did dramatists' names begin to appear on playbills, and it would be another decade or so—with the increasing popularity of *published* plays—that they would be accepted as serious writers, yet even then they remained associated with "common players." It is only because of a contemporary's passing remark that we know Kyd's authorship of *The Spanish Tragedy*, the most talked-about play of its time, and it would be well into the seventeenth century before Marlowe's name would be published on the title page of his *Tamburlaine* plays.

The names of acting companies and their patrons, *not* playwrights, are what counted for playgoers, and if we are to learn more about the 1580s and its importance for English theatrical culture both in London and in the provinces, we need to research their histories in more depth. Current studies are limited by the existing records, but REED and other archival researchers are adding new materials every year. By bringing to our attention new evidence, by working imaginatively with already existing materials, and by questioning old, weakly supported assumptions, future scholarship will bring the theatrical landscape of the 1580s more clearly into focus and by doing so, show that some parts of the terrain are very different than we currently suppose.

Notes

1. A. R. Braunmuller and Michael Hattaway, eds., *The Cambridge Companion to English Renaissance Drama* (Cambridge: Cambridge University Press, 1990); G. K. Hunter, *English Drama 1586–1642, The Age of Shakespeare,* The Oxford History of English Literature (Oxford: Clarendon, 1996); Gerald Bentley, *The Professions of Dramatist and Player in Shakespeare's Time 1590–1642* (Princeton: Princeton University Press, 1986); John Cox and David Kastan, eds., *A New History of Early English Drama* (New York: Columbia University Press, 1997).

2. See Philip Edwards, "William Shakespeare," 112–59 in *The Oxford Illustrated History of English Literature*; Eric Sams, *The Real Shakespeare* (New Haven: Yale, 1995), 64; Muriel Bradbrooke, *The Rise of the Common Player* (Cambridge: Cambridge University Press, 1962), viii–ix. For a fine, book-length study of the 1580s, see *Elizabethan Theatre XI* (Port Credit: Meany, 1990), and particularly the essay by John Astington, "The London Stage in the 1580s," 19–32.

3. Janet S. Loengard, "An Elizabethan Lawsuit: John Brayne, his Carpenter, and the Building of the Red Lion Theatre," *Shakespeare Quarterly* 34 (1983): 298–310; see also Astington, "The London Stage," 4–5.

4. These included the four city inns—the Bull, the Bell, the Cross Keys, and the Bell Savage; three, possibly four, suburban amphitheatres—the Theatre, the Curtain, Newington Butts (it is unclear how long the Red Lion remained open after 1567); and the two indoor children's playhouses—one at Paul's and the other at Blackfriars. For more on the acting companies, see the discussion of REED below.

5. Stephen Gosson, *Playes Confuted in Fiue Actions* (London, 1582), 202; cited in *The Elizabethan Stage,* 4 vols (Oxford: Clarendon, 1923), 4:217–18.

6. Alfred Harbage, S. Schoenbaum and Sylvia S. Wagonheim, eds., *Annals of English Drama 975–1700*, 3d edn. (London: Methuen, 1989).

7. William Ingram, *The Business of Playing: The Beginnings of Adult Theater in Elizabethan London* (Ithaca: Cornell University Press, 1992). Sally-Beth Maclean and Scott McMillin, however, suggest that after 1583 the theatre decreased in size but became more stable and profitable. See the discussion of *The Queen's Men* below.

8. On Peele's blank verse, see G. R. Hibbard, "From 'iygging vaines of riming mother wits' to 'the spacious volubilitie of a drumming decasillabon,'" *Elizabethan Theatre XI*, 55–74.

9. But see Arthur Freeman, *Thomas Kyd: Facts and Problems* (Oxford: Clarendon, 1967).

10. W. W. Greg, ed., *Henslowe's Diary,* 2 vols. (London, 1904–8), preface to part 2; cited in G. K. Hunter, *English Drama 1586–1642, The Age of Shakespeare*, vi.

11. Hunter, *English Drama 1586–1642*, 362.

12. The six (out of fourteen total) volumes published this decade by REED are as follows (all volumes published in Toronto at University of Toronto Press): *Herefordshire/Worcestershire,* ed. David N. Klausner (1990); *Lancashire,* ed. David George (1991); *Shropshire,* ed. Alan Somerset (1994); *Somerset, including Bath,* ed. James Stokes and Robert J. Alexander (1996); *Bristol,* ed. Mark C. Pilkinton (1997); *Dorset/Cornwall,* ed. Rosalind Conklin Hays and C. E. McGee/Sally L. Joyce and Evelyn S. Newlyn (1999). For other work on the troupes not addressed below, see Peter H. Greenfield, "Touring," *A New History of Early English Drama,* 251–68; and various essays in *Elizabethan Theatre X*.

13. I want to thank Alan Somerset for supplying me with data and statistics on the troupes and their patrons from REED's computer files. The files are based on all published volumes of REED. Somerset and Sally-Beth MacLean have under-

taken a joint project to make the REED patron data available electronically. Some of those files are currently available at www.utoronto.ca/patrons.

14. Consider the city of Coventry in 1584 when unprecedented civic funds were spent on the one-time performance of *The Destruction of Jerusalem*, a great outdoor spectacle in the manner of the town's old mystery play cycle (retired in 1579). According to REED records, Coventry citizens also enjoyed thirteen visits by touring acting companies that year (actually down from eighteen visits the previous year).

15. Gurr, *Shakespearean Playing Companies* (Oxford: Clarendon, 1996), 65.

16. Suzanne Westfall devotes a chapter to the Henrician Duke of Suffolk's Men in her *Patrons and Performance: Early Tudor Household Revels* (Oxford: Clarendon, 1990), and I have done the same for John Bale's company under Thomas Cromwell in *Theatre and Reformation: Protestantism, Patronage, and Playing in Tudor England* (Cambridge: Cambridge University Press, 1993), chapter 1.

17. See *The Elizabethan Stage*, 1:291; J. Leeds Barroll, "Drama and the Court," *The Revels History of Drama in English Volume III*, ed. Clifford Leech, et al. (London: Methuen, 1975), 4–27.

18. Sally-Beth Maclean and Scott McMillin, *The Queen's Men and Their Plays* (Cambridge: Cambridge University Press, 1998), 10.

19. Gurr, *Shakespearean Playing Companies*, 222.

20. Gurr, *Shakespearean Playing Companies*, 197.

21. See Charles Nicholl, *The Reckoning* (London: Jonathan Cape, 1992); John Archer, *Sovereignty and Intelligence: Spying and Court Culture in the English Renaissance* (Stanford: Stanford University Press, 1993); Curtis C. Breight, *Surveillance, Militarism, and Drama in the Elizabethan Era* (London: MacMillan, 1986).

22. Maclean and McMillin, *The Queen's Men*, 166.

23. See the discussion of Lyly below. For a new study on Protestant culture and the Renaissance stage, which includes works by Marlowe and Kyd from the fifteen-eighties, see Huston Diehl, *Staging Reform: Reforming the Stage* (Ithaca: Cornell University Press, 1998). This is an important book, but it overstates its case about the extent to which plays like *Doctor Faustus* and *The Spanish Tragedy* demystify the dazzling and potentially idolatrous images of the popular stage. I review it elsewhere, in *Review of English Studies*, forthcoming.

24. Maclean and McMillin, *The Queen's Men*, 158.

25. Maclean and McMillin, *The Queen's Men*, 68.

26. E. A. J. Honigmann, *Shakespeare: The "Lost Years"* (Totawa, NJ: Barnes and Nobles, 1985). The theory about Shakespeare and the Queen's Men is developed by Eric Sams, *The Real Shakespeare: Retrieving the Early Years, 1564–1594* (New Haven: Yale, 1995); see especially chapter 14.

27. Park Honan, *Shakespeare: A Life* (Oxford: Clarendon, 1999), 109. Honan calls Honigmann's evidence for the sojourn among the Hoghtons and Heskeths "inconclusive" in his discussion of biographical traditions, yet earlier in the book he owes a good deal of a chapter (5) to this evidence which he treats in sympathetic terms.

28. Maclean and McMillin, *The Queen's Men*, 165.

29. John Astington, *English Court Theatre 1558–1642* (Cambridge: Cambridge University Press, 1999).

30. On page 89, Astington says this view is expounded by E. K. Chambers in his chapter on "Staging at Court" in volume II of *The Elizabethan Stage* (Oxford: Clarendon, 1923), but I find no such thesis expressed in the chapter, which appears in volume 3, not in volume 2.

31. Astington, *English Court Theatre*, 164.

32. Astington, *English Court Theatre*, ii.
33. Alan Nelson, *Early Cambridge Theatres* (Cambridge: Cambridge University Press, 1994), chapter 8.
34. "The London Stage in the 1580s," *Elizabethan Theatre XI*, 19–32; 22.
35. Nelson, *Early Cambridge Theatres*, 22.
36. See Chambers, *Elizabethan Stage* 3:408–9.
37. John R. Elliott, Jr., "Early Staging at Oxford," *A New History of Early English Drama*, 68–76; and Elliott, "Queen Elizabeth at Oxford: New Light on the Royal Plays in 1566," *English Literary Renaissance* 18 (1988): 218–29.
38. David Bevington, "Lyly's *Endymion* and *Midas*: The Catholic Question in England," *Comparative Drama* (Special Issue: "Drama and the English Reformation"), 32 (1998), 26–46.
39. Michael Pincombe, *The Plays of John Lyly* (Manchester: Manchester University Press, 1996), viii–ix.
40. Kent Cartwright, "The Confusions of *Gallathea*: John Lyly as Popular Dramatist," *Comparative Drama*, 32 (1998): 207–39. The discussion is given a broader context in Cartwright's *Theatre and Humanism: English Drama in the Sixteenth Century* (Cambridge: Cambridge University Press, 1999), 167–93.
41. Pincombe, *Plays of John Lyly*, 16.
42. Gurr, *Shakespearean Playing Companies*, 222.
43. Gurr, *Shakespearean Playing Companies*, 222.
44. A. B. Grosart, ed., *The Works of Gabriel Harvey*, 3 vols. (London, 1884); cited in Gurr, *Shakespearean Playing Companies*, 222.
45. Chambers, *The Elizabethan Stage*, 3:412.
46. Hunter, *English Drama 1586–1642*, chapter 3, "The Emergence of the University Wits."
47. Hunter, *English Drama 1586–1642*, 31.
48. Hunter, *English Drama 1586–1642*, 31; Francis Barker, *The Tremulous Private Body*. New York: Methuen, 1984; Catherine Belsey, *The Subject of Tragedy: Identity and Difference in Renaissance Drama*. New York: Methuen, 1985.
49. Hunter, *English Drama 1586–1642*, 33. See David Aers, "A Whisper in the Ear of Early Modernists; Or, Reflections on Literary Critics Writing the 'History of the Subject," *Culture and History 1350–1600*, ed. David Aers (Detroit: Wayne State UP, 1992); Katherine Maus, *Inwardness and Theater in the English Renaissance* (Chicago: University of Chicago Press, 1995); Alan Sinfield, *Faultlines: Cultural Materialism and the Politics of Dissident Reading* (Berkeley: University of California Press, 1992).
50. Debora Kuller Shuger, *The Renaissance Bible: Scholarship, Sacrifice, and Subjectivity* (Berkeley: University of California Press, 1994), 119.
51. Patrick Cheney's *Marlowe's Counterfeit Profession: Ovid, Spenser, and Counter-Nationhood* (Toronto: University of Toronto Press, 1997).

REVIEWS

English Court Theatre 1558–1642
By John H. Astington
Cambridge: Cambridge University Press, 1999

Reviewer: Herbert Berry

"English court theater" embraced two very different kinds of drama. One was effectually an adjunct of the regular professional theater that served mainly the general public. It consisted of plays and performers brought into the court from the professional playhouses of London for the amusement of courtiers. The other consisted of largely amateur entertainments that originated in the court—a form of them called "masks" current in Elizabethan times and the more familiar "masques" of later times. They were written partly to resemble plays but were really elaborate manifestations of high art and fashion performed for, and usually by, the nation's elitest elite.

In his book, Professor Astington has set out to treat both from 1558 to 1642, not just performances but everything to do with performances, down to details of carpentry and painting and the wages of the people who worked on them. He is especially aware of the ways in which the English court theater related to art and style, domestic and European. And he appends a useful list of "all known performances of plays and masks/masques at royal palaces and houses" during the period (221–67).

Much of this matter has been gone over by well-known predecessors, but he manages to deal with it not only more extensively and in greater detail than others have done but often with fresh conclusions derived from new information. He persuasively dispels, for example, the tendency to think that before the architect Inigo Jones arrived at court early in the seventeenth century the staging and decoration of court entertainments were unsophisticated, "crude and rough" (142, 145).

The book is organized into six chapters. They concern the administration of departments at court involved in mounting performances; the houses and palaces, "royal places," where performances took place; specific rooms used for performances within houses and palaces; "artists and artisans" who worked on performances; audiences who attended performances; and "royal occasions" (a sampling of specific performances). The scheme seems reasonable, but it requires Astington in each chapter to deal with both kinds of drama from one end of the period to the other, and he freely strays beyond a strict understanding of the subject of the chapter. The result is much repetition and summarizing, hence thinly argued assertions. Moreover, because he means to arrive at conclusions about every aspect of the subject, he supplies many gaps in evidence with guesses, some of which resemble facts. A striking virtue of the book, however, is that he is everywhere cautious, sensible, and knowledgeable.

The list of performances at court is less useful than it could be because, unlike its predecessors (in volumes by E. K. Chambers, M. S. Steele, G. E. Bentley, and others), it does not offer sources of the information it contains. Also, the reader must find whether a performance is of a professional play or an amateur entertainment by deciding whether the performers mentioned seem a professional or an amateur group. The list does not quite include "all known performances," either. It omits one that Nathaniel Tomkyns, the clerk and registrar of Queen Henrietta Maria's council, mentioned in a letter of 29 July 1634. "The Queen," he wrote "is preparing to entertain ye King with a Galanteria (as they call it) at Holdenbye wch being within her ioynture, she holds as her own howse." Holdenby House was a "royal place" in Northamptonshire. It had been bought by James I, and on Henrietta Maria's marriage with Charles I it became part of her jointure. In July 1634, the court was on progress. Professional London players, the Prince's men, had been paid £100 to go along and should, therefore, have taken part in the "galanteria."[1] The King would be in Holdenby House thirteen years later when Cornet Joyce famously arrested him.

The book includes illustrations of places where performances took place, but only ancient ones that can be deceptive. Astington points out from written evidence, for example, that the ground plan of the Great Chamber at Whitehall was 30 by 60 feet, but the illustration is an ancient drawing that shows it as nearly square, (50–51). Modern plans illustrating written evidence would have been welcome, not only of the relevant rooms but of palaces and especially of Whitehall with an indication of where the modern street lies. Curiously, John Norden's map of Middlesex and part of Surrey (1614) is reproduced on page 2 to show the location of royal places in and near London, but it actually shows, vaguely, only Oatlands, Hampton Court, and Greenwich.

One questionable idea offered as fact is that the Crown chose to house the Revels office "in the centre of theatrical activity" in London (13–14, 25) rather than at Whitehall. The office was, however, in London from the start, long before there were any real playhouses. It was in Warwick Lane near Newgate until 1547, then in Blackfriars until 1559–60, when it moved, still well before the coming of playhouses, to a building belonging to the dissolved Priory of St. John of Jerusalem. It was there when playhouses did appear and remained there until 1607–8, "close," Astington writes, "to . . . the Theatre, the Curtain, and eventually the Fortune." The Priory building was, however, a bracing walk from all those playhouses and even from nearer ones. Moreover, when eventually a playhouse (the Red Bull) did open nearby, several hundred yards north on St. John Street, the Crown moved the office to Whitefriars. Had the Crown wanted the office to be in the center of theatrical activity up to the late 1590s at least, it should have considered premises in Gracechurch Street or Bishopsgate. The location in Whitefriars was, Astington adds, "at the centre of the circle formed by the seventeenth-century playhouses," and it was actually next door to the Whitefriars playhouse. But that playhouse was the westernmost of the current playhouses, and no playhouse was built farther west until 1617. The office next appeared in St. Peter's Hill, south of St. Paul's, in 1612, which was relatively near only one functioning playhouse, the second Blackfriars, and later still it appeared in the parish of St. Mary le Bow, Cheapside, near no playhouse.

Another dubious fact is used to locate where musicians played in theatrical structures erected at court. Because, as Astington believes, musicians in London "playhouses were accommodated on a second storey of the tiring house," they were accommodated similarly at court (144, 200, 201, 206–10), and, moreover, actors could perform there, too. While musicians obviously played somewhere in London playhouses, however, no direct evidence has them playing in the second story of a tiring house or, for that matter, in any other specific part of a playhouse. Direct evidence does have paying spectators in the second stories of several tiring houses, especially that at the Boar's Head.

One may also hesitate about a number of statements having to do with dramatic activity during the reign of Elizabeth (104). Despite, Astington writes, the "unprecedented surge in quality and quantity" of such activity in London during the last twenty years of the reign, "the breadth and variety of dramatic activity in England as a whole was actually reduced during Elizabeth's reign." And, presumably during the last twenty years of the reign, "many small groups of players [in the provinces] succumbed to fewer, larger, tightly organised groups under the patronage" of courtiers. So far as quantity goes, however, none of these statements is true of at least one west country town, Bridgwater in Somerset. In the twenty years before the reign, from 1537–38 to 1557–58, ten named companies of players and one unnamed company appeared in the town nineteen times. In the first half of the reign, from 1559 to 1579–80, twelve named companies appeared there twenty-three times. In the last half, from 1580–81 to 1603, thirteen named companies and six unnamed companies appeared there thirty-one times.

"The budgets for the most expensive Stuart masques," Astington writes, "were counted in the thousands of pounds" (158). But the budget for at least one was counted in the tens of thousands. In February 1634, the four Inns of Court spent "above" £20,000 to mount James Shirley's *The Triumph of Peace* at Whitehall and then at Merchant Taylors' Hall, and the court must have spent further sums for incidentals. When Astington comes to discuss that masque, he misses the patently genuine statement of its cost but depends twice on a letter that is apparently one of J. P. Collier's forgeries (177, 187). In it, a real lawyer, Justinian Pagett, supposedly describes taking part in the masque. Collier published the letter but did not say where he had found it, and nobody else has reported seeing it. Astington assumes that artificial lighting was used only at the private playhouses "like the Blackfriars" (219), but the public ones used it, too, when night comes early during the winter (as the Boar's Head documents also show). He states that both private playhouses in Blackfriars were in medieval halls and another at St. Paul's "is likely to have been" (75), but only the second one in Blackfriars clearly was. The first one there probably was not, since it was in an old buttery, and the one at St. Paul's probably was not, either, since it should have been in the Almonry of the Cathedral, which in the time of the playhouse was no medieval hall.[2] In listing the master of the Revel's emoluments (16–17), he omits the fees that at least some playhouses paid to stay open and those that many entertainers paid for the casual use of a playhouse.

Readers, finally, who seek to verify much of Astington's most important new material, which comes from thirty-three rolls of royal accounts (PRO, E. 351), will complain that he could have made their task easier. For he cites only rolls, many of which contain dozens of sides of writing. His "Skaffolde Tymbre," "poles," and "mastis of ffire" from an account belonging to the reign of Henry VIII (82), for example, occur somewhere on the fifty-eight large sides of writing of E. 351/3245.

But any book that aspires to be definitive in a large and complex subject, as Professor Astington's does, must give readers pause now and then. There is vastly more in this book that is shrewdly informative, new, and very useful.

Notes

I have read only the uncorrected page proofs of this book, which the publisher has supplied in advance of publication to enable an early review. Things to which I refer, therefore, may have disappeared or been altered between proof and book.

1. The entertainment has been noticed in print since 1872, but the name of the place has been mistranscribed as "Hulembey," which identifies neither a royal nor any other place. See H. Berry, *Shakespeare's Playhouses* (New York, 1987), 141; *CSP Dom., 1629–31,* 37.

2. For the one at St. Paul's, Astington relies on a statement in which E. K. Chambers read more into his sources than they reveal. See H. Berry, "Where was the Playhouse in which the Boy Choristers of St. Paul's Cathedral Performed Plays" (forthcoming in *MaRDiE*), note 12 and elsewhere.

In Praise of Scribes: Manuscripts and Their Makers in Seventeenth-Century England
By Peter Beal
Oxford: Clarendon Press, 1998

Reviewer: *Laetitia Yeandle*

This is a splendid book, an exemplary piece of writing on an overlooked topic. How many of us, poring over the manuscripts upon which we depend for so much of what we know of the history and literature of the past, have given much thought, perhaps any thought, to the people to whom we are indebted for copying these manuscripts, wondering who they were or why they copied them or in what circumstances they did so? On the whole they are nameless, reminding us of the law-writer Nemo in *Bleak House,* their names unrecorded in their manuscripts, so unlike contemporary publishers and printers who advertised themselves conspicuously on their title pages. What Peter Beal has done in this book is focus attention on the professional scribe of the early modern period in England, a person whom he describes as "someone who simply writes or copies something by hand, for whatever purpose," and on his confrères the clerk, the scrivener, and the secretary. Peter Beal has scrutinized countless manuscripts of the period and tells us what he has found out about the scribes and how they worked together and were organized, no longer working in a monastic scriptorium removed from society at large. Many of Beal's insights have come from carefully considering the actual texts as physical objects. He constantly impresses upon us how important manuscript publication continued to be despite the existence of the printing press. Even the printed form with blanks to be filled in by hand caught on only gradually. Printing and manuscript cultures existed side by side long after the introduction of printing.

The book is divided into five chapters, each self-contained, each lavishly illustrated and amply footnoted. In each scribes play a central role. The first chapter, "In praise of scribes," spells out the scribe's place in society and what is known of the conditions under which he worked. Beal reminds us that, besides providing copies of many kinds of manuscripts, he was also responsible for drawing up documents at all levels of administration, from royal warrants with the royal sign manual to everyday business documents. On him depended the accuracy of the wording and phrasing, an all-important factor, especially in legal documents. Since the work of the scribe led to his sometimes serving as stationer, notary, usurer, or banker, he easily became the butt of satires, and Peter Beal regales us with many quotations that he has found in all kinds of writings.

The second chapter is entitled " 'It shall not therefore kill itself; that is, not bury itself': Donne's *Biathanatos* and its text." Given its subject and the attitude of the times, Donne was hesitant about making his work widely available. Peter Beal considers Donne's stated wish that it should neither be printed nor burned, and how, by presenting a copy to at least two friends whom he could trust, he hoped both to preserve his work and at the same time limit its readership.

The third chapter, and the one that particularly appealed to me, is a tour de force. It is entitled "The Feathery Scribe." Except for the scribe's name, which still eludes him, Beal has been able to discover an amazing amount of information about this individual. Thanks to this professional scribe's distinctive and flamboyant hand, and Beal's wide-ranging knowledge of manuscripts, Beal has been able to assemble a list of 115 manuscripts with works copied by this person—state papers, parliamentary journals, political tracts, legal and antiquarian treatises, religious discourses, biographical accounts, poetry, and so on. The solid information he was able to gather about these manuscripts—the number that are duplicates, the number where Feathery was but one of several scribes, the relation of these manuscripts to others, their early owners if not their first owners—made him realize that here he had an example of a scribe busy working in a scriptorium in London for a certain clientele in the 1620s and 1630s, a scribe who at some point seems to have had his own scriptorium. Part of his evidence has come from the predominance of certain watermarks in the paper where Feathery was not the only scribe and where the same hands keep recurring, suggesting teamwork. He has found that Feathery's hand is sometimes associated with that of a known antiquary and collector, Ralph Starkey (d. 1628), who both copied documents himself and commissioned copies of texts that interested him, to the extent that he ran into trouble with the Crown for having access to and owning state papers that were not for general consumption. In fact, Beal raises the question whether Feathery was contributing to the atmosphere of discontent of the 1620s and 1630s. By supplying copies to antiquaries like Sir Robert Cotton as well as to those who were beginning to question some of the actions and statements of the Crown, and who were becoming increasingly interested in the precedents of recent history, Feathery was responding to a need, but not, Beal thinks, overtly promoting dissent. Feathery and scribes like him were bit players in the national debate that led to the English Civil War. With the relative freedom of the press that came about in the first years of this conflict, scribes like Feathery were in less demand and in fact evidence of his activities stops on the threshold of the 1640s. Sadly, there are no known records relating to the purchase or sale of Feathery's copies with his name attached that would substantiate Beal's findings and give us the scribe's true identity. Peter Beal has found only one note in Feathery's hand, alas unsigned, showing he received 5 s. for copying two works.

The fourth chapter, " 'Hoping they shall only come to your merciful eyes': Sidney's *Letter to Queen Elizabeth* and its transmission" is about a letter that reached many eyes both when it was written in 1579 and later. Sir Philip Sidney wanted to try to dissuade the Queen from her proposed marriage to the Duke of Alençon. Although the original does not exist, the text was sufficiently topical at various times in the next hundred years to have been spasmodically copied—and edited—whenever the political climate reminded people of the possible dangers of a foreign marriage. The variants among the copies make the construction of a stemma a nightmare. At least nine copies are wholly or partly in Feathery's hand; they are not taken from the same exemplar.

The fifth chapter, on " 'The virtuous Mrs Philips' and 'that whore Castlemaine': Orinda and Her Apotheosis, 1664–1668," is a cautionary tale of how the opposite to what an author states she wants to happen can happen. To a woman of Katherine Philips's social standing, manuscript circulation was more genteel than print publication, but she discovered that allowing copies to be made left her without authorial control. Considering how anxious she was to be respected for her "virtue" and "honour," it was ironic that, not four years after her death in 1664, Charles II's mistress, Lady Castlemaine, should play one of the two leading female roles in the first production of Mrs. Philips's translation of Corneille's play *Horace* at Court.

At the end of the book are six appendixes that give even more depth to these several studies: quotations about seventeenth-century clerks and scriveners from contemporary works; a checklist of one hundred and fifteen manuscripts with one or more works copied by the Feathery Scribe scattered all over the British Isles and the United States in twenty-eight repositories; a catalogue of eighty-nine manuscript works found in the study of Ralph Starkey after his death in 1628, some of the titles of which correspond very closely to known manuscripts in Feathery's hand; a list of thirty-seven known manuscript texts of Sir Philip Sidney's letter to Queen Elizabeth; Katherine Philips's letter to Lady Fletcher; and John Taylor's verse satire on Katherine Philips. As well as the usual lists of plates, figures, and abbreviations at the beginning, there is also an index of manuscripts cited that runs to seven pages, as well as a full bibliography and a general index.

Because of the author's perceptive treatment of his story and the

103 excellent plates, *In Praise of Scribes* presents a fresh picture of the manuscript world of the seventeenth century to be read alongside *Sir Philip Sidney and the Circulation of Manuscripts 1558–1640* by H.R. Woudhuysen and *Scribal Publication in Seventeenth-Century England* by Harold Love. If one wants to read it for pleasure one can; if one wants to pause to consider the evidence, one can. In fact the book and its footnotes are a mine of information on many aspects of manuscript culture generally, providing summaries of what is known, for example, on the cost of copying manuscripts, the time taken to copy them, and so on. One can see how Beal's approach could be a model for more studies of this kind. If only we had a way to classify different handwritings less distinctive than Feathery's and did not have to rely on the visual memory of a Peter Beal, who can scan hundreds of manuscripts and remember the details for future reference. So many scribes are waiting to be identified if only with descriptive terms like the "Master of ——" used to distinguish one anonymous early painter from another.

In Praise of Scribes grew out of the Lyell lectures delivered in May 1996. The lectures were established by the will of the bibliophile, James P. R. Lyell (1871–1949), the Readers being asked to apply themselves to the "science of books and manuscripts." Peter Beal has joined a lengthening list of illustrious Readers who have delivered these lectures beginning with Neil Ker in 1952. The series gave him the opportunity to explore in depth new ways of looking at old manuscripts.

The Politics of the Stuart Court Masque
Edited by David Bevington and Peter Holbrook
Cambridge: Cambridge University Press, 1998

Reviewer: R. Malcolm Smuts

More than thirty years ago, Stephen Orgel rejuvenated the study of Stuart court masques by treating these spectacles as serious political documents. The volume under review, which grew out of a 1993 seminar in Newcastle, Australia, demonstrates that the interpretive tradition he founded has now spread to three continents without any loss of vitality. The publisher's blurb asserts that these essays break new ground by replacing a "monolithic view of culture and power in the production of masques" with an emphasis on the ways in which "rival [court] factions . . . represent their clash of viewpoints through dancing and spectacle." The editors' introduction and the following essay by Martin Butler both develop this claim, politely criticizing Orgel's work and subsequent New Historicist scholarship for exaggerating the degree of control exercised by the King, overlooking "the conflicting arenas of interest within court culture," and giving undue weight to "the idealisms of Tudor-Stuart political theology" at the expense of "the actual processes through which things happened" (9). Earlier studies are also taken to task for equating the masque's political message with its "poetic form" (22) in ways that overlooked the importance of nonverbal elements in performances, as well as the problem of assessing audience responses. As a corrective to these shortcomings, the editors and Butler advocate an approach that is more alert to the diversity of viewpoints within the court and the particular circumstances surrounding individual masques and more prepared to allow for politically ambiguous readings.

This is a trenchant and persuasive argument, but one that will prove easier to outline in theory than to implement through specific studies. For the kinds of investigations being advocated require both a detailed knowledge of the social and political history of the court and a capacity to supplement textual analysis through investigations into aspects of masque performances that are often poorly documented. Unfortunately recent work by historians does not provide as much assistance as one might hope. Revisionists have exploded Whig stereotypes of Stuart absolutism, while stressing the ideological diversity and factionalism of the court. But they have not yet produced a sufficiently detailed and convincing picture of factional rivalries and policy debates at the political center to provide a solid basis for literary scholarship, especially during the early and middle years of James I, when most of the masques on which scholars have concentrated were performed. Although historians including Linda Peck, Pauline Croft, and Neil Cuddy have certainly given us a much fuller picture of the Jacobean court than the one available to Orgel thirty years ago, a great deal more work needs to be done in this area.

Not surprisingly, some essays in this collection succeed better than others in overcoming these obstacles and breaking genuinely new ground. On the one hand, Barbara Lewalski's contribution simply reiterates the generalizations of an older generation of scholarship about the "culture wars" of the 1630s and their relationship to the alleged moral laxness of Stuart court culture, supporting its case with predictable quotations from William Prynne and Lucy Hutchinson. Lewalski does cite the important work of Erica Veevers on French Counter-Reformation influences in masques written for Henrietta Maria but she ignores nearly all other recent historical investigations of the Caroline court. She also neglects important new work on political libels and scandal-mongering being carried out by Croft, Alistair Bellany, and Thomas Cogswell, which might have deepened her central argument.[1]

Stephen Orgel's rather discursive essay makes several interesting observations but its central preoccupation with the cultural construction of race and gender seems to have little connection to the collection's main themes. Its inclusion in this volume merely emphasizes how far the pioneer in the field has moved away from the main concerns of younger scholars who are trying to revise his insights. David Bevington's chapter comparing the masque incorporated in Shakespeare's *The Tempest* to Campion's nearly contemporary *Lord's Masque* is more carefully integrated and closely argued. Yet it ultimately reveals the difficulties of assessing audience reactions solely on the basis of textual analysis. Bevington gives a persuasive account of the kinds of responses that Campion and Shakespeare probably wanted to evoke but produces no direct evidence of how actual spectators reacted to either production. Hugh Craig's discussion of the changing nature of the Jonsonian antimasque also employs a traditional method of textual analysis, without attempting to explore surrounding historical circumstances. It does show, however, that the masque's formal structure was capable of conveying a more complex view of power than Orgel and other previous critics have allowed.

Several other essays use innovative methods to shed real light on court masques, though without discussing court faction in any detail. Tom Bishop's essay on the relationship between tradition and innovation in these entertainments is conceptually stimulating, though not always convincing in its conclusions. It opens up a line of investigation into ways in which court culture was sometimes used to reinvent historical rituals that may well yield important results in the future. Nancy Wright provides a convincing account of how the Merchant Tailor's Company used entertainments presented to James I and Prince Henry to enhance its own corporate dignity through association with royalty, while also parrying Crown demands for financial concessions. Barbara Ravelhofer does a superb job of interpreting a sparse body of evidence to reconstruct changing dance styles employed in masques around 1620. She then goes on to provide a suggestive discussion of why some contemporaries perceived new dance steps as affronts against masculinity. David Lindley's companion piece on music is less satisfactory, partly because the author usually responds to lacunae in his evidence by assuming that musical scores cannot have done a very effective job of conveying political meanings. Whether correct or not this view does little to advance understanding of how masques did communicate through means other than words. Lindley does, however, make a sustained attempt to deal with a crucially important, though poorly documented and inadequately studied dimension of masque performances. All the essays in this group seek to move beyond a strictly textual approach, either by studying nonverbal elements in masque performances or by indicating how masque tropes can be related to broader political, social, and cultural features of the period. The fact that they do not shed much light on the volume's ostensible theme in no way diminishes their intrinsic interest.

This leaves four essays—by Paul Hammer, Martin Butler, Peter Holbrook, and Leeds Barroll—that do deal directly and substantively with the relationship of court entertainments to political faction. The most successful of these is Hammer's analysis of the speeches framing an appearance by the Earl of Essex at an Accession Day joust of 1595. Through a careful analysis of the extant manuscript sources, Hammer shows that this entertainment was almost certainly crafted by Essex and a team of intellectuals in his household, rather than by Francis Bacon alone, as Richard McCoy and other earlier scholars had supposed. Hammer goes on to argue that the main intention was to impress the joust's public audience, rather than the Queen herself. This was one of several attempts by the Earl in this period to cultivate a flattering public image, in the hope that by doing so he would ultimately be able to pressure Elizabeth into granting him more influence than she wished. It was a risky and provocative strategy that ultimately backfired disastrously.

Barroll's essay illuminates the relationship of court entertainments to social and political competition in a different way, by carefully examining the identity of the women invited to perform in Queen Anne's masques and the ways in which they were paired together on stage. If the resulting conclusions have less impact on our understanding of political competition among court heavyweights than those reached by Hammer, they unquestionably advance understanding of Anne's use of the masques both to reward individual courtiers and to signal her favor for groups like Essex's former associates. Barroll here provides a model of how careful attention to performative elements of masques, combined with a knowledge of social alignments at court, can yield new insights.

The contributions of Holbrook and Butler develop broadly similar arguments that exemplify both the strengths and limitations of the attempt to make factional competition the key to the masques. Each attempts to show how specific masques sought to mediate disagreements over foreign policy within the court's ruling group, which divided a peace-loving King from his more warlike sons, Henry and Charles. The recognition that such disagreements existed represents an important advance over interpretations that treat the Stuarts as a uniformly pro-Spanish dynasty. But a view of court politics as a running battle between a pacific hispanophile king and his anti-Spanish heirs is still probably not complex enough to provide an entirely satisfactory framework for analysis of masques spanning the period 1610 to 1624. Contemporaries did often associate Henry and Charles with a more aggressive line toward the Habsburgs, and in certain periods, like the early 1620s, this perception was demonstrably correct. But the conventional view of James as a consistent pacifist pursuing policies of "appeasement" underestimates the complexity and flexibility of his views on European affairs, especially before the outbreak of the Thirty Years' War. The evolution of Jacobean foreign policy, particularly between the Treaty of London in 1604 and the Battle of White Mountain in 1620, remains among the least studied aspects of the period. Until much more work has been done in this area, generalizations about peace and war factions within the court need to be treated with caution.

Moreover, foreign policy considerations intersected with both domestic political concerns, like the chronic shortage of cash in Stuart coffers, and "ideological" issues including England's obligations to European Protestants and James's horror of religiously inspired rebellions. To some degree the King's views can be illuminated through his own writings. Although Orgel and new historicist scholars quoted selectively from James's Scottish treatises, *Basilikon Doron* and *The Trew Law of Free Monarchies,* in developing a picture of Stuart ideology, works produced by the King in England, such as the pamphlets written during the Oath of Allegiance controversy, have been almost entirely ignored by students of the masque. Court sermons, which have now been illuminated through the research of Peter McCullough and Lori Anne Ferrel, represent another important but neglected body of sources potentially capable of illuminating relationships between factions, political events, and cultural attitudes among the ruling group at Whitehall.[2] For all his simplifications, Orgel was undoubtedly correct in thinking that masques often represented politics in ways deeply shaped by theological assumptions. This insight needs to be refined and developed rather than discarded as masques are reinterpreted in light of a deeper understanding of their historical contexts. Butler and Holbrook have arguably construed the foreign policy issues underlying Jacobean masques too narrowly, by failing to investigate ways in which fundamentally religious concepts of royal authority may have shaped and constrained debates over England's relations with Europe.

In short, literary scholars need to be wary of assuming that they can unlock the political meanings of court masques merely by replacing a whig concept of Stuart absolutism with a revisionist emphasis on court faction. Historians have not reached consensus concerning the role of faction at Whitehall during most of this period. There is general agreement that in certain periods, notably the 1590s and the years of Buckingham's ascendancy, faction became a serious problem. But the situation during the remainder of the reigns of Elizabeth I, James I, and Charles I is far less clear. Although there was always competition over power and patronage, as well as *some* disagreement over policy issues, it has not been established that clear factional alignments resulted. Historians also currently disagree sharply over whether factional disputes sometimes involved fundamental issues of principle. The demise of the old view of mounting court-country conflict has had the effect of revitalizing, rather than settling, debates over the character of Stuart political thought and culture and the degree of consensus or conflict over ideological values.[3]

As a number of essays in *The Politics of the Stuart Court Masque* show, innovative studies of masques can sometimes contribute to a deeper understanding of court politics, in ways that affect historical interpretations. To some extent, however, studies of masques will always remain dependent on broader research into surrounding historical contexts. Reliance on inadequate social and political history will inevitably yield flawed understandings, no matter how meticulous the textual analysis. Pointing this out is not intended as a criticism of scholars like Bevington, Holbrook, and Butler, who have done more than their share of holding up one end of an interdisciplinary dialogue. It is intended as a warning that students of the masque should not assume that historians know as much about the internal history of the Elizabethan and early Stuart court as they sometimes like to pretend. What is ultimately needed is a good deal more genuinely interdisciplinary collaboration and research, including attention to cultural documents *other than* masques and poems by authors like Ben Jonson. Sermons, pamphlets, newsletters, and anonymous squibs and libels all have something to teach us about the environment in which court entertainments were created and performed, though these sources are only beginning to receive the attention they deserve. Ironically, the best way of placing masques in a better historical perspective may sometimes be to turn our attention elsewhere. For until we learn more about other forms of cultural expression employed in the early seventeenth century, readings of masques will always proceed in something of a vacuum.

This volume of essays amply demonstrates how far historicist interpretations of the masque have progressed since the 1960s. By doing so, however it also shows how much work remains to be done in this field. In exposing the limitations of Orgel's work and new historicist scholarship the contributors have underlined a number of vexing problems that cannot be solved through the conventional sources and methods of literary scholarship. This challenge has provided a considerable stimulus to interdisciplinary work and methodological innovation, resulting in some striking achievements. Yet progress in understanding the nonverbal dimensions of masque performances, the reactions of contemporary audiences, and the political contexts in which these entertainments were originally embedded remains limited. With few exceptions, political interpretations of court masque remain heavily dependent on textual analysis, supplemented by contextual insights deriving mainly from historical studies that remain patchy and uneven in their coverage of the relevant issues. Until more high quality work is produced on the social, political, and cultural history of the court, historicist studies of masques will continue to face serious obstacles. Although there is no easy solution to this problem, it is important to face up to it squarely.

Notes

1. Alistair Bellany, " 'Railinge Rymes and Vaunting Verse': Libellous Politics in Early Stuart England, 1603–1628," in *Culture and Politics in Early Stuart England,* ed. Kevin Sharpe and Peter Lake (London: 1994); Pauline Croft, "Libels, Popular Literacy and Public Opinion in Early Stuart England," *Bulletin of the Institute for Historical Research* 68 (1995): 43–69; Thomas Cogswell, "Underground Verse and the Transformation of Early Stuart Political Culture," in *Political Culture and Cultural Politics in Early Modern England: Essays Presented to David Underdown,* ed. Susan Amussen and Mark Kishlansky (Manchester, Eng.: Manchester University Press, 1995).

2. Peter McCullough, *Sermons at Court: Politics and Religion in Elizabethan and Jacobean Preaching* (Cambridge, Cambridge University Press, 1998) and Lori Anne Ferrel, *Government by Polemic: James I, the King's Preachers and the Rhetorics of Conformity, 1603–1625* (Stanford, Stanford University Press, 1998).

3. The two poles are best represented by the works of Glenn Burgess (consensus) and Johan Somerville (ideological disagreement), although there is a spectrum of intermediate opinion.

Press Censorship in Elizabethan England
By Cyndia Susan Clegg
Cambridge: Cambridge University Press, 1997

Reviewer: Cecile M. Jagodzinski

In *Press Censorship in Elizabethan England,* Cyndia Clegg (Pepperdine University) seeks to rehistoricize the debate about the nature of censorship, the role of the author, and the supposedly hegemonic stance of the Elizabethan religious/political state. She attempts to modify Annabel Patterson's suggestion that the inconsistent application of censorship laws allowed for ambiguity and accommodation on the part of both author and censoring bodies; rather, Clegg claims that press censorship was haphazard, infrequent, and invoked only in cases that threatened to harm the Queen's person, national security, or "the order of law" (197). These cases, rather than being "representative of early modern censorship practices," were reactive responses to "particular and local events and personalities" (xiv). Clegg asks the reader to dispel his or her late-twentieth-century notions about freedom of information, freedom of the press, and authorial autonomy, and instead to sympathize with a sixteenth-century social structure that was attempting to maintain its authority (and its image) in the face of the new mechanism of print. This implicit endorsement of the censors is carried throughout the book.

The study is divided into two major sections: part one deals with "the practice of censorship," and takes a historical approach, with its review of the early English printing and publishing industry, Marian and Elizabethan licensing laws, and actual licensing and authorizing practices. Clegg discounts the Stationers' Company as an agent for censorship, regarding it as a trade union to which the Crown had delegated authority over printing. Elizabeth's reaffirmation of Queen Mary's charter of the Company (even though it included the duty of suppressing the "detestable heresies ... of Holy Mother Church"), the role of the High Commission in silencing religious dissent (and therefore controlling relevant printed matter), and the low percentage of books actually registered with the Stationers through the 1590s all argue for the soundness of Clegg's position regarding the Company. However, Clegg uses other historical data to begin her apologia for the limited amount of censorship that she says does occur in the period. For instance, in establishing her argument for the reactive nature of press control, she notes that no statutes between 1558 and 1603 dealt specifically with control of the press (though there were laws against treason, sedition, and libel that encompassed printed matter), and that the purpose of the 1559 Injunctions legislating religious conformity was chiefly ecclesiastical in intent and not an attempt to ban all dissent. Clegg seems to be suggesting that censorship as a mere by-product of the enforcement of laws and statutes is perhaps excusable, and cannot really be construed as censorship at all.

The second part of the book is comprised of six case studies of censored texts, a kind of "acts and monuments" of martyred books, suggests Clegg. In these examinations of particular incidents of censorship, we learn exactly how accidental was the prosecution of offenders, and how subject authors and publishers were to the vagaries of political trends and rumors. Clegg's review of the case of George Gascoigne's *A Hundredth Sundrie Flowres* (1573) and *The Posies* (1575), for example, points to Gascoigne's subtle revisions to the 1575 text, in which he directs readers to a moral reading of the text in order to deflect attention from the real danger to himself—being accused of possible slanders. Clegg shows that John

Stubbs was punished, not simply for opposing Elizabeth's marriage to the Duke of Alençon (there was general turmoil over the prospect), but for publishing his opposition at the same time that Elizabeth regarded the negotiations with France as a profitable political exercise. Stubbs, in fact, may have been a political insider, for his arguments against the marriage are marked, suggests Clegg, by recourse to the sort of discourse common to those in the highest levels of government; after his punishment and imprisonment, Stubbs went on to comfortable positions as steward of Yarmouth, secretary to Lord Willoughby de Eresby, and member of Parliament. Clegg's chapter on Holinshed's *Chronicles,* with its excellent close readings of the cancels and cancellanda in the "Historie of England" and "Historie of Scotland" sections of the book, illustrates the role of censorship in the self-fashioning of the early modern English government. The revisions remove all hint of official entrapments, anti-Catholic diatribe, and Privy Council factionalism; in their place are narratives of English law and justice at work.

Clegg's exoneration of the censors is perhaps most evident in her chapters on Catholic propaganda and on the Marprelate tracts. She faults earlier historians of Counter-Reformation Catholic publishing (perhaps rightly so) for failing to distinguish between the censorship of Catholic devotional works and seditious works advocating the overthrow of Elizabeth. She discounts the prohibition and seizure of *all* Catholic printed books as of small consequence in the face of their danger to the Elizabethan state. Similarly, in her discussion of the Marprelate texts, Clegg remarks on the small number of Puritan texts that were actually censored. These, however, were exceptional, argues Clegg, for their libeling of Elizabeth's bishops as "pettie popes" (187), for violating "the conventions of the dispute about reform" (193), and, oddly, for their "challenge of civility and reason" (197). In the last chapter, dealing with the heretofore puzzling 1599 bishops' ban of nine books (mostly satires and epigrams), Clegg is very successful in noting that censorship occurred most frequently when printers and authors presented their work to the public at inopportune moments. All nine of the censored works were thought to be connected in some way with the Earl of Essex, Robert Devereux's expedition to Ireland; their suppression was the bishops' manner of protecting Essex and, by extension, the government of England.

While one may quarrel with Clegg's apparent justifications for Elizabethan censorship of printed material (as a defense against treason, libel, and sedition), this book gives students of censorship and print history some valuable new readings of significant chapters in the rise of sixteenth-century nation-state, England.

Discontinuities: New Essays on Renaissance Literature and Criticism
Edited by Viviana Comensoli and Paul Stevens
Toronto: University of Toronto Press, 1998.

Reviewer: Jean E. Howard

What has happened to Renaissance studies since the many innovations of the 1980s? That is the central question posed by this collection of essays, many of which comment on some aspect of the state of the field as the decade of the 1990s draws to a close. In their lively introduction, Paul Stevens and Viviana Comensoli take the position that early modern studies has remained a site of innovation and energy throughout this period and has not, as some have argued, fallen into the critical doldrums. They believe, however, that no single kind of work dominates the field despite the fact that most critics now agree that literature, in the editors' words, "does political work" (x). Beyond that, they find early modern studies marked by lively contestation among a number of research agendas and theoretical paradigms. The title of the collection, *Discontinuities,* is, in fact, meant to signal the ongoing rifts, contradictions, and productive debates informing the field today.

I suspect not everyone will agree that the critical momentum, the sheer outpouring of energy and excitement that marked Renaissance studies in the 1980s, has continued unabated into the present. Nonetheless, a number of Renaissance scholars find plenty of life in the machine even now; and most would agree that while forms of historicism play a major role in the field, there is no critical consensus about what constitutes the proper business of criticism or the proper way to go about it. Of special importance, therefore, is where the editors and the contributors to *Discontinuities* locate the key faultlines and the central debates within the field now. What urgent questions are being engaged? Which critical projects pose explicit or implicit challenges to one another?

The collection as a whole is not entirely satisfactory in clarifying these matters though it contains some excellent individual essays and though the editors use the introduction to point out a number of conflicting assumptions among the writers whose work they have gathered. Perhaps the most successful juxtaposition in the volume occurs in part 2: "What to Do With Shakespeare?" where Elizabeth Hanson compares *Eastward Ho* to *The Merchant of Venice* to make the point that we have to stop studying only Shakespeare if we want an adequate historical understanding of the Elizabethan and Jacobean period, and Karen Newman reads *Timon of Athens* to argue that the cultural cachet of Shakespeare continues to make him necessarily central to teaching and research efforts. Real questions are posed through the juxtaposition of these essays. What do we want and expect from the big canonical authors in the field: Milton, Shakespeare, and Spenser? Do we simply capitalize on their name recognition value to address issues of contemporary interest now? Can one produce an "historical" understanding of the period from any single author? If not, what would constitute a sufficient range of texts? And how does one market other authors—with one's students as much as with textbook and publishing houses? These are questions that have to be addressed every time a book of criticism dealing with Renaissance matters is written or a syllabus constructed.

Three other sections organize the collection: part 1: "Recovering Women's Writing: Historicism vs. Textualism," part 3: "Rethinking Subjectivity: The Turn to Lacan," part 4: "Political Engagement and Professional Discontinuities." The polemics in some of these essays are fairly tired. My eyes glaze when I hear, again, that poststructuralism discredited the idea of agency just when women became subjects of history, or when an essay begins, again, by detailing the seven mortal sins of Stephen Greenblatt. Moreover, certain key developments in contemporary studies make no appearance in this volume. There are no essays dealing with the new textual studies that have destabilized as effectively as poststructuralism received notions of author and text; no essays consider the appropriate geographical coordinates within which to study the textual productions of an early modern nation state. New work on cartography, colonialism, race, and material culture makes no appearance. There is feminism in the volume, but few signs, except for Karen Newman's contribution, of the queer Renaissance.

This sounds grouchy on my part. Of course no collection can be comprehensive. But for a volume that self-consciously wishes to document the continuing vitality of, and discontinuities within, early modern studies, this one looks back to the work done in the 1980s a bit too often, in the process missing some of what has made the 1990s most interesting.

That said, there are a number of useful and provocative essays in the collection. Linda Woodbridge underscores the complexity of bringing social history and literature into conjunction; Tracey Sedinger, critiquing new historicism, makes good use of Slavoj Zizek's work to challenge what she sees as the naive suturing of the subject to the social in new historicist work; Susan Zimmerman nicely synthesizes the ideas of Bataille, Mary Douglas, and Lacan to explore how effects of horror are produced in early modern tragedy by the foregrounding of interstitial and marginal states where cultural taboos can be transgressed. The volume ends with two vigorously iconoclastic essays. Barry Taylor powerfully critiques the received narrative that British cultural materialism embodies "real politics" while American new historicism is politically timid, overly professional, and burdened by theory. Provocatively, he sees this as an interested narrative that obscures the theoretical debates within the left in Britain and unproductively holds in place misleading binaries between history and poststructuralism, politics and textuality. Sharon O'Dair ends the volume with a useful discussion of how Weberian and Marxist understandings of class differ and then a no-holds-barred attack on academic leftists who attack capitalism, scorn the consumerism of others, and yet themselves scramble for the rewards of the academic status system. (You get all this *and* a reading of *Timon of Athens*.) One does not have to agree with all O'Dair says to feel that in this essay there are several debates worth continuing, even if the result might not be consensus, but a continuing process of productive contestation. Such debate, I think, is what the editors of *Discontinuities* aspired both to document and to promote, and their collection goes some way toward realizing those aspirations.

Death, Desire and Loss in Western Culture
By Jonathan Dollimore
London and New York: Routledge, 1998

Reviewer: Mario DiGangi

Readers of *Shakespeare Studies* will be familiar with British cultural materialist Jonathan Dollimore from his incisive analyses of Renaissance drama in *Radical Tragedy* and *Sexual Dissidence*, as well as from *Political Shakespeare*, the influential anthology he edited with Alan Sinfield. In method and scope, Dollimore's new study most closely resembles *Sexual Dissidence*, an account of the development of "perversion" from a theological into a sexual concept across a span of centuries. *Death, Desire and Loss*, a study of "the strange dynamic which, in Western culture, binds death into desire," is similarly ambitious (xii): it encompasses the writings of ancient philosophers and theologians (Plato, Epicurus, Seneca, Augustine); Renaissance essayists, poets, and playwrights (Montaigne, Ralegh, Donne, Spenser, Shakespeare); and a host of nineteenth- and twentieth-century philosophers, theorists, and novelists (including Marx, Nietzsche, Freud, Bataille, Foucault, Conrad, Mann, and Lawrence). *Death, Desire and Loss* also revisits some central concerns of Dollimore's previous scholarship: the significance of both materialist and psychoanalytic accounts of society and subjectivity; the cultural dynamics of identification, desire, and displacement; the modern preoccupation with homosexuality as a "focus of fundamental social, psychic, and aesthetic conflicts" (281); the various ways in which "the early modern may be said to anticipate the modern" (116). Although readings of Shakespeare occupy relatively little space in *Death, Desire and Loss* (only one fourteen-page chapter focuses exclusively on his works), Dollimore's astute observations on the sonnets, *Romeo and Juliet*, and *Measure for Measure* aptly illustrate his thesis that early modern thinkers regarded mutability as the primary force bringing desire into intimate proximity with death.

While acknowledging the influence of ancient pagan as well as Christian philosophers on Renaissance thought, Dollimore suggests that the early modern period witnessed an "intensified preoccupation" with the notion of mutability as "an instability which simultaneously disintegrates and drives both the world and the self" (68). As far as English writers are concerned, Dollimore sees variations on this idea in Thomas Browne's intuition of adversity as latent within felicity; in Donne's meditations on life as a process of dissolution; and in Ralegh's recognition of the paradox that death, while rendering all human endeavors vain, nonetheless spurs us to further action. Dollimore suggests that for all these writers, "death is not merely an ending but an internal undoing"; consequently, the "absolutely other is found to inhere within the self-same as nothing less than the dynamic of its dissolution" (76). This apprehension of death produces significant psychological and social consequences. In *Measure for Measure,* for instance, Duke Vincentio deploys such a philosophy of death as a means of social control. Instructing Claudio to be "absolute for death," the Duke places mutability at the very core of identity and of desire. If this is so, then life is a kind of death: subjected to such knowledge, the transgressively desiring Claudio readily (if only temporarily) submits to the Duke's authority.

The typically early modern notion that "death is not merely the eventual termination of life, but an impossible mutability within life itself" (115) centrally informs the erotic dynamics of Shakespeare's sonnets. Not surprisingly, Dollimore develops this argument via some of the more familiar poems about the destructive power of mutability and desire, such as sonnets 65 ("Since brass, nor stone, nor earth, nor boundless sea"), 129 ("Th' expense of spirit in waste of shame"), and 147 ("My love is as a fever, longing still"). His analysis of these poems is not entirely new, especially the argument that the poet, by recording the young man's beauty, compensates for loss: he "empowers himself by writing unforgettably of the powerlessness of everything under the sway of time" (106). Nonetheless, Dollimore puts a compelling spin on this familiar reading when he suggests that the poet, while submissive to death, also identifies with and is possibly even enamored of its awesome power (105).

Dollimore then turns to *Romeo and Juliet,* in which the paradoxical eroticism of the sonnets—the "internalization of mutability as desire" (108)—is fully displayed. Rather than rehearse commonplace observations about the tragic intertwining of sex and death, Dollimore explores the "perverse" implications of the jarring claim that this play constitutes "an adult fantasy *about* adolescent desire" (109). Because for adults "adolescent sexuality is something idealized from the position of loss," the adults' perception of Romeo and Juliet's desires in the play is deeply, and disturbingly, ambivalent (111). Dollimore demonstrates this thesis most provocatively in the case of Juliet's father. Confronted with the death of Tybalt (and hence with his own mortality), Capulet seems to project onto his daughter his own desire for the youthful Paris, with whom he also identifies. Haunted by "the failure and loss which is mutability" (111), however, adults not only idealize young love, but also associate it with death, which represents at once the condition of mutability and its longed-for end. Romeo participates in this inherently ambivalent erotic economy, for his replacement of Rosalind with Juliet reveals the experience of desire as an internal, ever-present, death: an "impossible mutability within life itself" (115).

Death, Desire and Loss in Western Culture is not, of course, a book about Shakespeare. Because Dollimore aims to trace the connection of death and desire across an enormous span of Western culture (his reading of *Romeo and Juliet* accommodates Plato as well as Freud), there is no attempt to provide a comprehensive account of Shakespeare's various treatments of this subject. What Dollimore does offer, through partial readings of a few culturally central texts, is an insightful assessment of Shakespeare's place within a long history of Western speculation about the paradoxical embrace of desire and death.

Aemilia Lanyer: Gender, Genre, and the Canon
Edited by Marshall Grossman
Lexington: University Press of Kentucky, 1998

Reviewer: Karen Robertson

In 1611 Aemilia Lanyer introduced her poem *Salve Deus Rex Judeorum* with a sequence of dedicatory verses that sought patronage from a hierarchy composed of Queen Anne and nine court ladies. That early patronage bid seems to have failed, but at last she has found her sponsors—albeit nearly four hundred years later. Marshall Grossman, editor of this collection of eleven essays, displays an admirable commitment to Lanyer's work. With his selection, for this first critical volume, of well-known scholars including David Bevington, Leeds Barroll, Barbara Lewalski, and Susanne Woods, editor of the Oxford University Press edition of the poem, Lanyer has returned to the highest circles. Any newcomer to the poem can now turn to these essays for analysis of the politics of patronage, the rhetorical strategies of the poem itself, and its religious poetics. Never again will a reader have the pleasure and terror of reading an unannotated text, and insight will be cushioned and guided by the essays in this volume. How well served is Lanyer by this book?

This volume of essays, including both a bibliography and an index, is a worthy testimony to Marshall Grossman's "evangelical" passion for the merits of her work. Encouraged to read Lanyer by his colleague Jane Donawerth, who literally put a packet of materials on women writers into his mailbox, Grossman has commited himself to the labor of the production of a careful and serious volume of essays. The excitement of that political and literary effort is signaled in Grossman's preface.

For Grossman, in both his introduction and in his essay "The Gendering of Genre," the inclusion of women writers in the canon exposes the gendered nature of the seemingly neutral canonical (male) voice. By setting Lanyer beside Donne and Jonson he explores that process. While I agree with the argument and see the process as opening intriguing pedagogic possibilities, I must register a faint dissatisfaction. Perhaps the gender of the authoritative voice is a discovery that must be recapitulated by each generation, though Simone de Beauvoir made the point in *The Second Sex*. Perhaps the strategy of the argument itself, by promising insights into familiar texts, tends to subordinate the new to the familiar. Some of the critics in this volume are not yet entirely confident about the intrinsic value of Lanyer's work, although they welcome it for the light it casts on canonical work.

Lanyer's entrance into modern literary studies has two sources—one through the biographical research of A. L. Rowse and his dramatic "discovery" of Shakespeare's "dark lady," and the other through the pressure and energies of feminist scholarship that, in the search for women's voices, has uncovered, edited, and taught the work of a number of women writers of the early modern period. The dedicated labor of second-wave feminist scholars whose editions provide crucial anchors for the analysis of the discourses of gender can be traced in the useful annotated bibliography provided by Karen L. Nelson, although not all the essays address that range of material. This volume, by placing a discussion of Rowse's claims as the first essay replicates the gender hierarchies of literary history and gives Rowse's damaging claim undue prominence. Since this volume comprises nearly half of the twenty-five articles on Lanyer listed in the MLA bibliography for 1999, that replication of canonicity may have an effect on developments of subsequent scholarship. That would be a pity, since the essays in this volume do provide solid and sober introduction to the problems and issues of Lanyer's entrance into the canon and collects a valuable set of essays on the problems and questions of Lanyer's feminist poetics.

The first essay is David Bevington's witty demolition of the principles guiding A. L. Rowse's discovery of Shakespeare's "dark lady." Bevington uses the subject of Rowse's biographical claims as an opportunity to take up the battle between the historians and the literary critics. Bevington exposes Rowse's tendentious techniques of literary detection and his tendency to flatten poetic invention. For Rowse, all poetry is simply disguised autobiography. After a teasing series of concessions, Bevington shows that Rowse's confident identification of Lanyer as the dark lady is based on speculations about the provenance and ordering of the sonnets while in manuscript between 1590 and 1609, and a casual confidence about the stability of the meanings of words, in particular the polysemy of the word "begetter" in Thomas Thorpe's dedication of the first edition of the sonnets to Mr. W. H. Bevington uses Rowse's Lanyer as an illustration with which to chastize the certainties of some historical readings of literary texts and to demonstrate the tools and interpretive subtleties of literary scholarship. While Rowse readily provides egregious examples, Lanyer herself seems less important to the issue. Like any lady fought over, she becomes a prize in the battle of critics, for the heroics of editorial detection. Who best deciphers Simon Forman's hand, Rowse or Stanley Wells? Was Lanyer "brown" or "brave" in youth? It is fair to say that this essay engages with Lanyer's first appearance in modern literary history; unfortunately the terms in which she is framed reinscribe canonicity, for the marginalized female poet enters a very great while after Shakespeare and Southampton.

The second biographical essay that opens the volume, "Looking for Patrons" by Leeds Barroll, offers a more direct examination of the biographical circumstances of the production of a volume of poetry by a woman and of Lanyer's agency in her seeking of patronage. Barroll takes up three topics: the claims for a relationship between the Countess of Kent and the young Aemilia Bassano; the court connections of Alfonso Lanyer, whom Aemilia married in 1592; and the possible error that Lanyer committed in her hierarchizing of court ladies in the dedicatory poems. Barroll uses his considerable historical knowledge of the Tudor and Jacobean court to examine Lanyer's competitive bid for patronage in the dedicatory poems, and in particular the claim registered in Simon Forman's diary and echoed in the dedicatory verse that Susan Bertie, Dowager Duchess of Kent was "mistress of my youth." Barroll's method is interrogative as he traces the paths of the dowager Countess of Kent and the daughter of Baptist Bassano, a court musician. Using the fuller documentary records available for the marriage and whereabouts of an aristocratic woman, Barroll seeks those moments when Susan Bertie and Aemilia Bassano may have crossed paths sufficiently to have established a relationship. He finds two moments. Susan Bertie's husband was restored as Earl of Kent in 1572 and Susan became countess for a year before his death the following year, when Aemilia Bassano was between three and four years old. "It is hard (albeit not impossible) to suggest a set of circumstances in which the very small daughter of a court lutenist might obtain a mentoring relationship with a countess" (32). Or Susan Bertie, as dowager countess, might have taken on the role of mentor, particularly after the death of Aemilia's father when the child was seven in 1576, but the domestic arrangements of the young dowager countess are uncertain. It is assumed that she returned home to her parents' house in Grimsthorpe or resided at court, thus offering little opportunity for sponsorship of a young girl. Barroll's scrupulous tracing of the divergent paths of a very young girl and the newly widowed countess serves as a corrective to too hasty assumptions about the meaning of the biographical claims of the dedicatory verses. Barroll then explores the significance of Alfonso Lanyer's court connections and his patronage efforts on the part of his wife. Barroll concludes his biographical study with an analysis of the mistake in judgment Lanyer committed in her hierarchizing of the various court ladies in her dedicatory poems, by comparing Lanyer's patronage bid with the more canny dedications of Samuel Daniel and Ben Jonson. He observes that the prominence that Lanyer gives to the Countess of Cumberland, both in the dedicatory poems, and in the fabric of the poem itself, honors an aristocratic woman whose power at court was limited. He observes further that placing the Countess of Bedford after the Dowager Countess of Pembroke was "a strategic error" (40).

Barroll's careful reading of the dense networks of connection and patronage of the court revises sentimental notions of court politics and notions of feminine circles of support. "What I am suggesting is that we attempt, with great and respectful care, to situate Lanyer's admirably bold bid for patronage within the hard exigencies of her social milieu, attempting neither to idealize nor to diminish her status and accomplishments" (42).

There follow five essays that analyze the feminist poetics of the text, most notably that of Janel Mueller, "The Feminist Poetics of *Salve Deus Rex Judaeorum*." Barbara K. Lewalski's essay "Seizing Discourses and Reinventing Genres" provides a magisterial introduction to the ensuing essays on the poetics of the *Salve Deus*. She summarizes the various genres appropriated by Lanyer for her display of poetic talent: ode, sonnet, dream vision, verse epistle, prose epistle, religious lament or complaint, defense, elegy. This useful summary directs attention to the radical innovation of the text—the daring narrative of Pilate's wife defending Eve and pleading for the release of Christ, a moment expanded from a hint in the Gospels—and compares Lanyer's handling of the materials of the country house poem in the elegaic "Description of Cooke-ham" with Ben Jonson's "To Penshurst."

Three of the essays analyze Lanyer's mobilization of a radical theology for poetic authorization, expanding Lewalski's brief claim that Lanyer's poem "lays some groundwork for the female preachers and prophets of the Civil War period" (53). Susanne Woods explores Lanyer's use of religious vocation to authorize her boldness in self-presentation as a poet. Kari Boyd McBride argues that the radical theology of the dedicatory poems place Lanyer "in the lineage of religious visionaries such as John Bunyan, Margaret Fell, Anne Hutchinson, and John Milton" (79), a claim substantiated in Janel Mueller's "The Feminist Poetics of *Salve Deus Rex Judaeorum*."

Susanne Woods, Lanyer's exemplary editor, broadens her work on the poem to expand our understanding of Lanyer's strategic use of religion to establish her authority as a poet. Woods teases out the significance of the word *grace,* which she observes occurs over ninety times in the poem, and compares Lanyer's dedications with those of Daniel, Ralegh, and Jonson, to demonstrate her conversion of "traditional notions of grace into an empowerment of her own agency and the female point of view" (87).

Woods's observation of "the ongoing and subtle tension through the poem between the petition and the gift, between the poet distinct and humble and the poet identified with her lofty dedicatee" (87) as a common feature of patronage poems provides a delicate adjustment to the persuasive but somewhat exhaustive analysis of Kari Boyd McBride of the complexities of client-patron relationships. While McBride valuably emphasizes the way the poet displaces inherited class privilege through her use of religious authority, the word "venom" to describe the poet's address to Anne Clifford seems overstated (74). Anne Clifford, as daughter, is rightly encouraged to emulate her mother, and acknowledgment of the daughter's inferiority to the mother seems only just. Were the desired patron to detect "venom" in the voice of the poet (74), then the poet's search for patronage might well fail.

Janel Mueller's insightful essay places an analysis of Lanyer's poem within the trajectory of feminist and postmodernist historicism, as part of the process of developing "an eventual set of useful generalizations about the conditions that empowered female authorship in preindustrial and pre-Enlightenment Europe" (102). Conceding that Lanyer holds essentialist notions of feminine and masculine and teleological purposes that are not our own, she sees Lanyer as "every bit our contemporary in her resolve to locate and articulate transformative possibilities in gender relations that will bear their own urgent imperatives for enactment. . . . In her handling, universalism and essentialism directly empower a feminism that proves rich, outrageous, and originary by any present-day standard" (101). This essay most clearly evokes the process of discovery that the poem offers to students in the classroom as the screen of past belief, which at first seems orthodox and rigid, gives way to a recognition of the bold radicalism of the text. Confident about the agency of the female poet, Mueller situates the poem thickly within literary and feminist history. Citing among others Joan Kelly, Constance Jordan, Gayle Green, Coppélia Kahn, Joan Scott, and Judith Newton, Mueller demonstrates an easy familiarity with interdisciplinary feminist criticism. This essay places Lanyer's poem within the trajectory of women's writing in Europe, comparing the possibilities for authorship with those available to Christine de Pisan, and argues that Lanyer's defense of women in the poem is an intervention in and challenge to a contemporary discursive construction of women—their appearance as evil tragic protagonists on the early Jacobean stage. Provocative and energetic, this essay establishes possibilities for further reading by setting the poem against the Jacobean Cleopatra plays, among texts from the controversy over women, and beside a male poet's version of Christ's passion,

Giles Fletcher's *Christs Victorie and Triumph in Heaven, and Earth, Over and after Death*. Mueller's argument that Lanyer "uses her portrayals of Christ and actual good women to trace the impact of feminine or feminized virtue on the masculine side of a range of standing dichotomies that mark conceptions of social and political relations" (117) demonstrates a poet as vigorous and aware in her challenge to misogyny as Christine de Pisan two hundred years earlier. Mueller's analysis culminates in her examination of the "unique outspokenness" of Eve's Apology, a reading that captures the drama and shock of the poem.

Naomi Miller's essay, "(M)other Tongues: Maternity and Subjectivity," an analysis of the maternal and matriarchal bonds that link women, usefully complements Mueller's essay and amplifies McBride's insight into the conflicts between women documented in the poem, by reminding us that however ambivalent the relationship to those women, "Lanyer's decision to claim the authority of her writing voice specifically in relation to a community of women, however ambivalently constructed, is in itself a daring move which insists upon the enabling potential of female homosocial bonds" (156). The essay places that analysis within the context of women's wills and careful disposition of property to daughters rather than sons as a context from which to examine the specifically female estate, governed by "a maternal authority conceived in intellectual and spiritual rather than merely physical terms" (162).

Michael Morgan Holmes extends the analysis of the female homosocial communities of the poem, drawing on queer theory to argue intriguingly that the dedications of the work to prominent women "suggest[s] that, if we accept that same-gender desire plays a vital role in the *Salve Deus*, female homoeroticism could play a role nearer to the center of official ideology than is commonly thought" (p. 169). That provocative suggestion does not address the issue of Lanyer's failure to achieve sponsorship. Holmes suggests that the spiritual devotion evoked in the poem is closer to Catholic imagery, a claim that puts him in conflict with those authors in the collection who see Lanyer in line with radical protestant voices. Despite these caveats, the insight that homoeroticism "enabled Lanyer to negotiate the complex relations between social hierarchies and gender identities" (183) offers a valuable resolution to the conflicts Lanyer attempts to negotiate.

Two final essays conclude the volume. Achsah Guibbory in "The Gospel According to Aemilia: Women and the Sacred" reads the inventions of the *Salve* within the context of biblical hermeneutics to situate the remarkable expansion provided by Lanyer in the defense of Eve offered by Pilate's wife. Boyd Berry closes the collection with an analysis of Lanyer's rhetorics of digression in the poem.

Barbara Bowen, in a talk at the Shakespeare Association last year, enjoined us to read these women writers more thickly. This volume begins that task and sets out fruitful directions. Further comparison of the religious poetics of Counter-Reformation and Protestant women, the history of defenses of Eve, the homoerotics of female communities, and Lanyer's response to the representations of Cleopatra, to name a few. A subject absent from this volume is a deeper consideration of the social status of converted Jews in England and what Baptist Bassano's origins may have meant to his daughter. Bowen's own work has explored the racial implications of the poem, as a community of white women is imagined through the exclusion of the dark outsider, a reminder that a poet we celebrate may participate in discursive practices that have damaging consequences. This absorbing collection of essays establishes a ground from which we may develop further, denser readings of this bold and imaginative early modern writer.

The Story of All Things: Writing the Self in English Renaissance Narrative Poetry
By Marshall Grossman
Durham and London: Duke University Tress, 1998

Reviewer: Judith H. Anderson

As the title of Marshall Grossman's *Story of All Things* might suggest, his argument, which at times becomes a hermeneutic meditation, resists easy summation. In the main, he is concerned with the content of the form and with the changes of literary form—substantive form—over time and in relation to other kinds of material, social, and ideological changes. But even more basically, he is concerned with the "rhetoric of the self," the figures poets choose to represent subjectivity and to register their response to history (xi–xii). While Grossman uses Augustine as a point of reference throughout, briefly discusses Dante and Petrarch, includes a chapter on Spenser, and recurrently invokes the example of Shakespeare, his focus for about half the book is on the seventeenth century: Donne, Marvell, and Milton. His argument is larger than these particular focii indicate, however, including, for example, notable discussion of Joel Fineman's work, to which he acknowledges a considerable debt, and provocative criticism both of New Historical anecdotes and of Stephen Greenblatt's view that psychoanalysis, as we know it, is not a historical mode of interpretation for Renaissance writings.

Invoking the work of Hayden White, Grossman categorizes the rhetorical figures by which poets represent the subjectivity of their characters: on the one hand, as metaphor and synecdoche, the figures of similarity, continuity, and wholeness, and on the other hand, as metonymy and irony, the figures of difference and discontinuity. The former two are "the brakes of the tropological machine"; the latter two "are its engines" (50). The former align with the iconic or specular, the idealistic, and the lyric; the latter with the verbal or audible, the dynamic, and the narrative. Lyric expresses presence; narrative expresses memory, retrospection, historic process. With as many (and more) equivalences as these, it is not surprising that much of what Grossman argues is metaphorical to its core, but unlike many another, lesser story of all things, it is thoughtfully and self-consciously so. His awareness of the implications of his methodology is acute and unflinching and lends considerable authority to it.

The relationship of the figure of a woman to the poetic agent's desire and to the symbolic ordering of the cosmos is focal for Grossman's treatment of Spenser, Donne, Marvell, and Milton, as for his earlier points of reference, Dante and Petrarch and, in a broader sense (sexual sublimation), even Augustine. Freud conspicuously underwrites this focus, especially when Grossman turns to the seventeenth century. In Grossman's view, literary history chronicles the interpretive action of symbolic systems on the nonsignifying world, and "the great hermeneutic systems of modernity are properly the theory" for a Renaissance system distinguished by temporality and closure—that is, by narrative. Much of his effort is to show that Freudian (Lacanian, Žižekian) subjectivity is not imposed on the period but is in "conversation" with it (xxi). Since Grossman remarks the Renaissance pun in *conversation* (verbal and sexual intercourse) and refers to Renaissance narrative itself as being "conscious," perhaps the relation he intends might be described as a productive cohabitation. Thus, to demonstrate that the subject in *Paradise Lost* originates in a desire for the mother is "not only to recapitulate Freud, but also to install this formation of the subject or ego within a specific temporality" (240); or, from another direction, "Freud does not explain Spenser so much as repeat him" (141).

Grossman posits a "structure of deferral . . . integral" both to *The Faerie Queene* and to the psychoanalytical and historical contexts through which he views it (107). The poem is a "*story* of the formation of the ego in and through desire's quest for the always deferred trace of its effaced . . . origin" (121). Of the three Spenserian scenes he examines—the stripping of Duessa, the hermaphroditic figure of reunion in the 1590 ending, and Calidore's interruption of Colin's vision of the Graces on Mount Acidale—the last speaks most directly to the "thematic consciousness" of the narrative's structural deferral (111). Right after five repetitions of the word "midst" within thirty-six lines, on Acidale the poet "appears . . . to have thrust into the middest to discover what most concerns him. And what does he discover? Not the Fairy Queen, not the universal virtue of Magnanimity, not the epideictic model of the perfect gentleman, not, in fact, any gentleman at all, only himself: 'Poore *Colin Clout*' " (133). Grossman seems really to mean "himself," Edmund Spenser, since this passage is preceded by pages in which the origin of *The Faerie Queene* is located in Spenser's erotic fantasy, as it well might be. But Colin Clout is a role, and Colin's lass is encircled and enabled by the Graces; indeed, the whole vision is infused by the Muse. As these figures are weighted in *The Faerie Queene*, they have a great deal to do with history and memory (cultural, racial, literate). Grossman's discovery is neither original nor invalid, but it does seem in need of further complication.

Grossman's discussions of Donne, Marvell and Milton are especially valuable. In Donne's *Anniversaries*, he sees a univocity of style and content: "This [univocal] ground, which is in a given historical moment more or less conscious of the ways in which rhetoric reconfigures *being*, constitutes the metaphysics of Donne's metaphysical style, the use of style as a primary mode of philosophical elaboration" (165). Grossman persuasively proposes that we take Donne at his word when he tells us *The First Anniversarie* is a postmortem on the world, and *The Second* is a progress to a better one. What this means in his perceptive reading of the *Anni-*

versaries is that Donne chronicles the production of the self as difference, "as that which is *not* (and cannot be) represented adequately" (166). Donne uses the death of Elizabeth Drury "to represent the failure of (Petrarchan) love . . . as a historically mediated event" (174). In a generic sense, then, "shee" in the *Anniversaries* is Laura, or, a self-signifying universe, ontologically homogenous and dominated by metaphor. Writing from a time between sublimations, so to speak, Donne "encounters the repressed, the excess that cannot be accommodated to the symbolic system" (179).

In Grossman's reading of the seventeenth century, "the ideological tensions arising from the reorganization . . . of social life . . . [are] experienced as an inward division of the self," and poets of the period reflect and reflect on this division in poems "suspended between iconic and verbal representation and lyric and narrative genres" (218). In the writing of Marvell and Milton, "allegory [finally] gives way to narrative" and metaphor surrenders to metonymy and irony (197). Because my views on allegory are on record elsewhere, I'll just observe that Grossman's distinctions between allegory (continued metaphor) and narrative leave me skeptical and proceed to "Appleton House," where he finds an innocent, pastoral mimesis coexisting with a deceptive, illusionistic one. Lyric likewise coexists with narrative, and allegory (metaphorized oneness) co-exists with irony in this poem. On a historical plane, such co-existence aligns with that of "an eternal cycle of Fairfacian fair doings" and the poet's ironic self-presentation here and now. According to Grossman, the allegorical character expresses an inborn essence (Fairfacian fair doings) in a variety of situations, while the ironic character of this poet discovers and rewrites his own meaning (202–203). In radical contrast to the Augustinian ego, Marvell's is no longer stable.

Grossman's Freudian/Lacanian allegory of *Paradise Lost* shares considerable ground with Linda Gregerson's (as he acknowledges) but is nonetheless an illuminating tour de force. Here he asserts the "formal articulation of the constitutive role of feminine desire in the dialectical construction of the patriarchal subject" (6). He asserts as well that the F/father's position is ironical "because the feminine interiority that it suppressed, contained, and appropriated is also the ground on which it stands. Patriarchal appropriation . . . of the children succeeds only insofar as it fails" (233). Feminine interiority, the womb, is requisite to the position of F/father. The feminine psyche and the body appear to be on a continuum, an argument with immense implications—metaphorical implications, I might add. In Grossman's reading, Milton reverses the Augustinian translation of flesh to W/word; in the physical relation of Adam and Eve, Adam, whose phallic pen signifies desire, writes "the future unity of desiring and desired in and as the future of the world" (239).

The Story of All Things is not an easy book to read, although Grossman is at pains to clarify his positions, to restate and resummarize them, sometimes too often. His many metaphorical equivalences (and the language that goes with each one) and shifts in register are difficult to keep track of, as some quotations in this review might suggest. But his *Story* is a highly intelligent book, full of insight, and it deserves a serious hearing.

Discovering the Subject in Renaissance England
By Elizabeth Hanson
Cambridge: Cambridge University Press, 1998

Reviewer: *Mihoko Suzuki*

Basing its argument on Michel Foucault's theory of epistemic shifts in *The Order of Things,* and revising the new historicist narrative of the emergence of the subject in early modern England, Elizabeth Hanson's *Discovering the Subject in Renaissance England* explores the intensification of the concept of interiority in late sixteenth- and early seventeenth-century England. Hanson finds the exemplary instance of this distinctive construction of the subject in the torture of suspected Catholics during the period that saw the consolidation of power by the Elizabethan state: on the one hand, techniques of investigation presume an interiority that the torturer seeks to discover and reveal, and on the other, techniques of resistance presume an interiority that the tortured seeks to conceal. Rather than aligning the emergence of the subject with a specific class or ideological position as new historicist accounts have tended to do, Hanson stresses the *strategic* use of secret interiority by both Elizabethan bureaucrats and Catholic recusants, in which these tropes of subjectivity are used by one side and appropriated by its opponents. This paradigmatic chapter, "Torture and Truth," arrestingly and convincingly articulates the dependence of the Elizabethan state on its recusant "others" in defining itself—"through knowing and that which it can never know" (20).

The ensuing chapters of *Discovering the Subject* take up *Measure for Measure* and *Othello*; the cony-catching pamphlets of Thomas Harman and Jonson's *Bartholomew Fair*; and Francis Bacon's scientific works and *New Atlantis*. While I find the overall argument original and plausible, some of the juxtapositions and specific readings seemed forced and not entirely persuasive: for example, the deployment and repeated reference throughout the book to accounts of Dell's Case, where the testimony of a child whose tongue has been cut out is pressed into service as "an uncanny allegory" (41) of the intractability of a truth "beyond the reach of the investigators" (43); or the collapsing of various instances of "alienation"—"of the poor from the land and neighbors from one another, as well as that of the writer from his work and the reader from everything (s)he reads about" (121)—in discussing Jonson's authorial strategies. The chapter on "Bacon and the discovering subject" paradoxically fits the argument of the book too well, so that the resulting reading does not depart significantly from existing scholarship that has examined Bacon's use of the discourse of discovery and investigation for both scientific and political ends.

Readers of *Shakespeare Studies* will find that "Brothers of the State," the chapter on Shakespeare, does succeed in arriving at persuasive and innovative readings of *Measure for Measure* and *Othello*. Focusing on the rise of the proto-bureaucratic state and the intimate relationship between a ruler or commander and their deputies and subordinate officers in the chain of command, Hanson productively juxtaposes *Measure for Measure* and *Othello* to elucidate the anxiety in both plays over the representation of deputies as harboring secret purposes. This chapter significantly takes into account the question of gender, arguing for the equivalence of the social categories of subordinate officer and wife—both unknowable from the perspective of the ruler and husband. The two plays similarly bring together plots concerning marriage and the state, for women are the "medium through which the vexed relationship between the subject and the early modern state can be articulated" (56). Using Eve Sedgwick's theory of homosocial relations "between men," Hanson thus sees the construction of masculinity in these plays as a contradictory one: both a hierarchical arrangement of men and a collective domination of, desire for, and differentiation from women. The conclusion of this chapter neatly returns to the trope of torture to argue that the striking exchange of marriage for torture that marks the ending of both plays represent marriages as equivalent to state violence.

Hanson's analysis of *Measure for Measure* and *Othello* demonstrates well how new theoretical paradigms can produce useful juxtapositions and innovative readings. Here, and at its best, *Discovering the Subject* brings into play different aspects of Foucault's wide-ranging work (on epistemic shifts, on power and knowledge, on sexuality, as well as on discipline and punishment) to provide fresh insights on the emergence in Elizabethan and Jacobean England of the early modern male subject—in relation to the state and to other subjects.

Foreign Bodies and the Body Politic: Discourses of Social Pathology in Early Modern England
By Jonathan Gil Harris
Cambridge: Cambridge University Press, 1998

Reviewer: Bruce R. Smith

Near the end of *Foreign Bodies and the Body Politic* Jonathan Gil Harris cites a recent article from *The New Yorker* that compares the dissemination of misinformation over the Internet to the spread of AIDS in bath houses: "as we gear up to live in a hyper-democratic media world crawling with contagious falsehoods," the writer of the article warns, "society will need a robust information immune system" (quoted on p. 144). Far from being a faded relic of the Elizabethan World Picture, the ancient comparison of the body natural and the body politic—the topos goes back to Plato and Aristotle—lives on in the twenty-first century. Harris's purpose in *Foreign Bodies and the Body Politic* is to study that topos at a crucial stage in its evolution, when ideas about pathology were shifting: in the course of the sixteenth and early seventeenth centuries, he argues, disease was increasingly imagined, not as an imbalance of humors within the body, but, in the terms we still entertain today, as an invasion of pathogens from without. These two models of pathology in the body natural imply different ways of conceptualizing the body politic. The political ramifications of those changes provide Harris his focus as he reads three representative political tracts and a series of stage plays, paying close attention to three particular pathogens: Catholics, Jews, and witches.

Harris's study takes its place in a series of recent books about early modern constructions of the human body, including Thomas Laqueur's *Making Sex* (1990), Gail Kern Paster's *The Body Embarrassed* (1993), Jonathan Sawday's *The Body Emblazoned* (1995), and David Hillman and Carla Mazzio's anthology *The Body in Parts* (1997). The contribution that Harris makes to this (dare one call it?) developing body of knowledge is his insistence that an alternative existed to the humoral body described by Galen and his early modern disciples and taken as paradigmatic by Laqueur and his successors. It was firsthand experience of the plague and of syphilis, Harris suggests, that prompted early modern authorities increasingly to question Galen's model and to reinterpret disease as an invasion from without rather than as an imbalance within. As an authority to counterbalance Galen, Harris cites the Swiss physician Philippus Theophrastus Bambastus von Hohenheim, better known by his Latin name, Paracelsus. By emphasizing Paracelsus's idea of disease as a seed implanted in the body from outside, Harris makes a determined effort to rescue Paracelsus from his reputation today as an unscientific throwback to the mystical thinking of the Middle Ages. In the alternative model posed by Harris health in the body natural becomes, not an equipoise of humors, but impermeability to invaders. The focus shifts from the body's central organs to its surfaces and orifices. In terms of the body politic that entails a shift from internal harmony to external defenses.

If Harris is right about the currency of such thinking, Stephen Greenblatt is not altogether accurate when he remarks, in a widely cited essay, that the Algonquian Indians' explanation of disease as "invisible bullets" would have been beyond the ken of the English invaders who brought influenza, measles, and smallpox with them to the New World.[1] It also means, Harris argues, that subversion does not always come from the inside and hence, pace Greenblatt, cannot always be contained. As precedent for his approach Harris enlists both Bakhtin and Derrida. Bakhtin's idea of the classical closed body becomes a medical and political ideal in counterdistinction to the grotesque open body implied by Galenic medicine.[2] For his part, Derrida in his essay "Plato's Pharmacy" provides Harris an important critical tool in the *pharmakos* or sacrificial victim. Variously translatable as "magician," "poisoner," and "scapegoat," the *pharmakos* provided a physical body that could be destroyed as a means of assuring the survival and unity of the social body.[3] Harris puts this idea to particularly good use in his discussion of Jews and witches, two categories of persons in early modern England who were not simply Other but both Us and Not Us.

Harris's strategy in *Foreign Bodies and the Body Politic* is first to set up the two models of the diseased body, those associated with Galen and Paracelsus, and then to use the models as reference points for deconstructive readings of the three political tracts and the series of stage plays. Harris makes reference to several dozen texts, by Dekker, James I, Marston, Middleton, Nashe, Shakespeare, Spenser, Webster, and others, but he concentrates primarily on three tracts, Thomas Starkey's *Dialogue Between Reginald Pole and Thomas Lupset* (ca. 1535), William Averell's *Marvelous Combat of Contrarieties* (1588), and Edward Forest's *A Comparative Discourse of the Bodies Natural and Politic* (1606) before turning to extended discussion of three stage plays, Dekker's *The Whore of Babylon,* Marlowe's *The Jew of Malta,* and Dekker, Ford, and Rowley's *The Witch of Edmonton*. Starkey's *Dialogue* serves to illustrate the conventional metaphor of the body politic as an organic whole in which the members are equally necessary to one another, as promulgated by St. Paul in 1 Corinthians 12 and argued by Menenius in Shakespeare's *Coriolanus* 1.1. Averell's *Combat* pathologizes Catholics as foreign invaders of the body at the same time that it reinterprets Menenius's fable of the belly so that some body parts (those equivalent to the monarch and the nobility) are made more important than others. Forest's *Comparative Discourse,* a response to the Gunpowder Plot, affirms the xenophobia and hierarchization of Averell's *Combat* and goes on to add a central idea from Paracelsian medicine: that poison, by quenching other poison, can actually do a body good. (This philosophy of like countering like stands in sharp contrast to Galenic medicine, in which an overheated condition requires coldness, excessive moisture requires dryness, etc.) Hierarchy and homeopathy work together, since, in Averell's paradigm, it is the sovereign who administers the corrective poison.

Dekker's *The Whore of Babylon,* read in tandem with anti-Catholic episodes from *The Faerie Queene,* reveals the dangers that lurk in the politics of poison, in particular the danger of pathologizing the authority of the poison-giver. A probing reading of Barabas in *The Jew of Malta* as *pharmakos* gains much of its power from comparison with Shylock in *The Merchant of Venice* and Romelio in Webster's play *The Devil's Law Case.* In one of the book's most original moves Harris associates all of these invading pathogens with one bodily orifice in particular, the anus. He stresses the frightening capacity of Barabas and Romelio to be everything and nothing, to be Jew, to be Christian, to be neither: "In a fashion that comes remarkably close to anticipating the paradigms of modern microbiology, therefore, Marlowe and Webster both depict the Jew as a parasitic, pathogenic foreign body whose singular danger lies in his virus-like ability to mimic the many codes and forms of his host body's component parts for his own selfish benefit" (99). Elizabeth Sawyer in *The Witch of Edmonton* emerges as a *pharmakos* of another sort. The orifices associated with anxiety about witches are not just the anus (Henry Goodcole's pamphlet *The Wonderful Discovery of Elizabeth Sawyer, a Witch* mentions a teat on Sawyer's backside that the Devil must have sucked) but her mouth. Fear of witches, Harris argues, was in large part fear of the power of speech to make happen the malevolent things the witch spoke. In his printed pamphlet Goodcole takes great pains to affirm the authority and power of written language as against Mother Sawyer's tongue—a circumstance that calls into question Derrida's insistence that Western thinking has always given primacy to speech.

In such observations Harris is at his provocative best. In general, his arguments are most compelling when the text in question doesn't yield too readily to the deconstructive pressure he brings to bear on it. As Harris himself concedes, Dekker and his fellow collaborators on *The Witch of Edmonton* have already deconstructed Goodcole's tract, leaving Harris little to do but point out the ways in which authority is shown as being compromised in the act of fighting poison with poison. With Goodcole's pamphlet, on the other hand, Harris finds just the resistance he needs to exercise his deconstructive skill. Many readers of Laqueur, Paster, Sawday, and the Hillman-Mazzio anthology may feel that Harris's opposition of the two models of pathology is too schematic. Harris comes close to acknowledging as much: "the 'new' models of disease that informed early modern English medical and political discourses alike did not appear *ex nihilo,* but were for the most part produced within, if not entirely bounded by the epistemological horizons of, well-established Galenic and religious systems of representation" (29–30). A sense of invasion of the body through the eyes and ears is present in Plato's suspicions of sense experience. To that epistemological suspicion Christian doctrine added a fear of sin entering via the same orifices. Galenic medicine held that noisome fumes were especially dangerous to the body because material particles of the offending substance entered the body through the nose. And what about gender? Harris has a great deal to say about female tongues, but Paster's contrast between the open female body and the closed male body hardly figures here at all. As Harris insists, however, the important question is why a more modern idea of disease should challenge Galenic orthodoxy at just the moment it did. Harris's book goes a long way toward demonstrating that the reason has as much to do with politics as with rise of science.

Notes

1. Stephen Greenblatt, "Invisible Bullets: Renaissance Authority and its Subversion," *Glyph 8: Johns Hopkins Textual Studies* (Baltimore: Johns Hopkins University Press, 1981), 40–61, reprinted with alterations in *Shakespeare's "Rough Magic": Renaissance Essays in Honor of C. L. Barber,* ed. Peter Erickson and Coppélia Kahn (Newark: University of Delaware Press, 1985), 276–302, and in *Political Shakespeare: New Essays in Cultural Materialism,* ed. Jonathan Dollimore and Alan Sinfield (Manchester: Manchester University Press, 1985), 18–47.

2. Mikhail Bakhtin, *Rabelais and his World,* trans. Hélène Iswolsky (Bloomington: Indiana University Press, 1984).

3. Jacques Derrida, "Plato's Pharmacy," in *Disseminations,* trans. Barbara Johnson (Chicago: University of Chicago Press, 1981).

The Politics of Courtly Dancing in Early Modern England
By Skiles Howard
Amherst: University of Massachusetts Press, 1998

Reviewer: Peter Holbrook

Here is a highly competent book displaying all the current virtues—and vices—of our discipline. Skiles Howard has explored the political and ideological significances of dancing in the Tudor and Stuart courts. She reveals the central role of this recreation (really, as her book shows, often much more than a recreation) in the period's courtiership. Like many books in the discipline now, Howard's is conspicuously up-to-date on the secondary literature and keen to show that it is not lolling about in the Bower of Bliss of unthinking positivism (it is strongly 'theorized'). It also has the shape of not a few books in the profession currently: a general introduction, rigorously (as we say) laying out theoretical and historicopolitical issues, followed by a series of "readings" (Shakespeare, Middleton, Elizabeth Cary, Henrician and Jacobean masques, etc.). Each "reading" illustrates the political thesis.

Conventional it may be, but the book tells us things we should know. Howard demonstrates that dancing was "a site of contestation" between courtly and noncourtly interests (that story has been well told before, of course, notably by Alan Brissenden in the compact and readable opening chapter of his *Shakespeare and the Dance*). The sources record that at fifty-six Elizabeth had "six or seven galliards in a morning" as "her ordinary exercise" (quoted in Brissenden, 5); flair at dancing was possibly a competitive advantage for the aspiring courtier at James's court. Certainly for a writer like Sir Thomas Elyot, dancing, promising "not only pleasure, but also profit and commodity," formed an important part of the training of a courtier. Elyot sees it as a kind of moral art of the body, amenable to detailed moral allegorization (the Platonists, he says, as well as the sun-worshippers "in India," hold dancing to imitate the "motions harmonical" and "sundry diversities of number and time" of the "celestial bodies;" dancing communicates to one's own body "the wonderful and incomprehensible order" of the heavens). For a Puritan such as John Northbrooke, however, dancing was "an exercise . . . not descended from heaven, but by the devils of hell raised," the "enemy to chastity," and "the vilest vice of all" (quoted in Howard, 55). Moses saw the people dancing around the golden calf.

This material is fascinating, and it is good to have a book that takes the diverse social functions of Renaissance dancing seriously. It is a central thesis of Howard's that dance in this period was highly socially coded: "increasingly controlled by clearly defined norms" (16), courtly dance was yet one more way the elite marked itself off from the populace. Dance was a key element in the self-presentation of the courtier and affirmed the rank and sex hierarchies of early modern England.

Howard's basic argument—that Renaissance dance, as much as literature, needs to be thought of as playing a role within the social and political stresses in the period—is persuasive. But throughout the book I find an implicit thesis—culture is fundamentally political—to lead to the kind of exaggeration that makes untruths of insights. Is it reasonable to describe dancing as "an instrument ... of ... power" (3)? The most substantial English defense of courtly dancing in the period, Elyot's, speaks of it rather as a moral and physical training. Yes, training is intended ultimately to produce the character type fit to take a leading role in the "public weal," but dancing is not conceived merely or even primarily as an "instrument" of something else—or as political. That Machiavellian language is not Elyot's. Dancing is one of the accomplishments of a class worthy of rule, and Elyot does speak of dancing as emblematizing the differences between men and women (the actions of the man show him to be "fierce, hardy, strong in opinion" etc., the woman "mild, timorous, tractable" and so on). But here again dancing is not seen, Machiavelli-like, to be a *tool* of some other, more primary, purpose, but rather to articulate divine order. The "concord" of each of these masculine and female "qualities," "in this wise knit together ... in the personages of the man and woman dancing," gives birth to a superior, androgyne virtue (thus, "wilful opinion and tractability ... maketh constancy," "fierceness joined with mildness maketh severity," and so on). Elyot thinks prudence one of the virtues inculcated by dance, and this is a virtue useful for politicians (he cites Augustus and Henry VII), but he does not conceptualize dancing as fundamentally political; the vocabulary is ethical, religious, philosophic, etc. Now, since it was certainly possible in this age for an author to speak politically, and since Elyot, who had thought more than most about the value of dancing (and was himself no stranger to statecraft), chose not to conceive of dancing in political terms, what authorizes the critic today when he or she translates ethical, religious, and other discourses about dance into a political one? My quarrel is not with the act of translation per se (that may or not be justified) but with what I take to be a near automatic assumption in current criticism—*The Politics of Courtly Dancing* is an example of this trend—that the necessity so to translate is obvious and, in fact, in need of no defense.

Redescribing dance as something else (as, say, politics by other means) can seem historically justifiable, I admit. Take Elyot's allegorization of the "honour, ... a reverent inclination or curtsey, with a long deliberation or pause" at the beginning of the dance: "By that may be signified that at the beginning of all our acts, we should do due honour to God, which is the root of prudence. . . . And that in the beginning of all things we should advisedly, with some tract of time, behold and foresee the success of our enterprise." Such rococo moralization is surely no less strained than Howard's suggestion that "the upward training of the dancing body mirrored a concern with upward mobility, its enclosure paralleled enclosures of property, the segmentation of the dancing place was a miniature likeness of the mapping of the realm, and the expansion of the dancer's control at the center of the hall a micrometonym of the centralized state" (23). Well, I think there is a difference. Elyot's allegory is elaborate, but it participates in a dominant mindset of the culture (Christianity, as well as a prudential view of life based on classical ethics). It is rhetorical and overrefined, but, granted its affiliations with these central discourses in the period, in another sense perfectly natural. The interpretation offered by Howard is ahistorical (oddly enough, given the author's careful attention to historical context). There is nothing in the sources to make us feel easy about conceiving of dancers moving across a floor as a "mapping of the realm," nor is there anything plausible about the claim that their movements "studiously mapped the hall in a precursor of global exploration" (113). On this principle, absolutely anything can be likened to anything else: "by far the favourite dance in the early seventeenth century was the *coranto,* one that covered more ground with increasing speed, reflecting the recognition of space as open, accessible, and ripe for the taking" (114). In fact, nothing in this book obliges us to believe that "the *coranto* enacted an aggressive consumption of space, an appetite for expansion" (114); no *evidence* exists to link this dance to "the great voyages" (113) of the period; all that has been done is to liken this fast, skipping, or running dance to the rapid outward movement of Europe in the sixteenth and seventeenth centuries (one fast thing is like another fast thing—which is to say, we are simply playing about with metaphors).

As I have said, the implicit argument of this book is that *at bottom culture is political.* Sometimes the thesis appears to drive the evidence, rather than the other way round. For example, Howard argues that dancing reinforced status differences between men and women. Dances constrained women more than men: in the *galliard* the man was the dancer, whereas the woman "waited patiently to be chosen" (101). But it's not clear from the information Howard supplies that women really were sidelined in the way this suggests.

That they were less athletic in their movements than men need not imply that their dancing did not have impact. Howard says that the woman's padded gown, which "displayed the wealth and rank of her husband" (101), "estranged [her] from her body," her natural shape being concealed by it. But does the grim, Foucaultian language of this analysis realistically capture the experience of dance of the many independent-minded aristocratic women of this period? Howard quotes Italian dance manuals that urged dancing as a pastime especially good for girls, who "are not free to . . . go about the town as we [men] may without reprehension" (quoted in Howard, 102)—but then tells us that "the movements of the dances . . . served not as liberation but as additional restraint" (102). One can't help feeling that something has gone wrong here. The source suggests that dancing was liberating for women in the patriarchal societies of Renaissance Europe ("A star danc'd, and under that was I born," says Shakespeare's Beatrice), but the "reading" discovers just a refinement of oppression. That *may* be right (though surely the assumption has to be that dancing is something both sexes, in all times and places, have found liberating—were women compelled to dance in Tudor England?), but "theorizing" and "readings" won't, I am afraid, help us here. What we need are detailed (empirical, positivistic . . .) studies that indicate how early modern people may have experienced dancing. (I can't believe Howard is right, for example, when she says that courtly women "totter[ed]" about in dances because they "often" wore "high chopines" [102]: her footnote quotes the dancing master Fabritio Caroso instructing women how to "move entirely with grace, seemliness, and beauty"—even in chopines [quoted in Howard, 187, n.24]. Well, were courtly women awkward in their high shoes, as that "totter" suggests, or weren't they? Maybe they just had to read Caroso!)

I don't want to give a false impression. This is a well-documented, informative, frequently suggestive study. It is a thorough treatment of an important topic and any reader will learn a lot from it. But, as with many other books in our field today, it seems marred by overstatement and exaggeration, possibly (I am guessing here) because it subscribes to a model of research that has become standard (almost, for institutional reasons, compulsory) in the academy. Once, perhaps, in a different academic economy, a less programmatic kind of scholarship was possible (one more empirical and open to the evidence, less bent on driving home some grand thesis, more appreciative of nuance). "How can we . . . theorize . . . the ephemeral movements of the past?" asks Howard early on (and answers that "conceptual frameworks . . . must be enlisted" [4]). That's one way to go about it, but I can imagine better questions to ask, ones that would seek to specify what we can and can't know, draw appropriate distinctions, raise further problems for research—even be content with the discovery of facts about the past for their own sake.

That rather dilettantish model of scholarship would not fit well with the modern, productivist university (precisely, perhaps, why it should be resurrected as an ideal). I can't resist concluding with some general remarks about the kind of research this book exemplifies, and why it strikes me as the product of a very specific milieu. (Not bad in itself of course: we all have to come from somewhere. But *some* features of this milieu seem to get in the way of understanding Renaissance culture.) Four things can be said here. First, this milieu's outlook on life is wholly political (and relatively indifferent to, for example, the ethical, religious, aesthetic, etc.). Although we know that early modern culture was in many ways a theocratic and biblical culture, and that the language of art criticism, such as it was, moralized, this milieu is almost blind to those facts: everything (and therefore, one might suggest, nothing) is political. The view of contemporaries that dancing may have bodied forth a heavenly harmony is only an ideological ruse or example of priestcraft: we can't take this notion seriously! Second, it is highly individualistic and competitive. The idea that social stability and order (let alone hierarchy) can be valuable things, are literally unthinkable (is this true of most people even today?). If dance *does* project an idea of order and social unity, so much the worse for it! Third, this academic milieu is founded on the virtues of self-discipline and, in fact, asceticism (or, at least, delayed gratification). As a result it is wary of pleasure. (Has *any* critic in recent times viewed literature as primarily entertainment or pastime—even as a source of higher pleasure?) Culture, literature *matters*—is "productive," "constitutive," etc. of the world. Even dance must be shown to do real (that is, political) work. We can call such criticism "worldly." The profession's self-esteem now depends upon its object of study connecting up with the "real" world of power and politics. Finding the world in or just behind the text confirms the critic's sense of worth. Literature *cannot* be otherworldly, frivolous, as so many ages, including the Renaissance, have often allowed it to be. Fourth (this really follows on from my point about worldliness), it is profoundly disenchanted. Culture, as Adorno diagnosed this position, is a lie. There is no "outside" to power, politics, economics. As a consequence, aesthetic judgment is pointless—there is no such thing as the aesthetic. My feeling that Cary's *The Tragedy of Mariam* is one of the most boring plays I know is irrelevant. We don't study it for aesthetic reasons—which aren't reasons anyhow. Disenchanted criticism ("everything is political") is supposed to be progressive. Sadly, nothing could be further from the truth. Part of the reactionary and oppressive political reality of our age is a general consensus that power is all there is (power has no horizon). The cynical notion that power is absolute fits with the brutal and sinister "Just Do It" world of contemporary capitalism—just do it, because there are no contexts of judgment or value *except* this world's. The "realism" of such criticism is precisely its least oppositional quality: in dissolving everything into the political, it shows there is no alternative to power. How much more radical it would be to see culture not as merely instrumental but as occasionally articulating another scale of human values.

I am sorry to end on a grumpy note about what is in many ways a searching and even exhaustive book, but, really, is it not time to move on from this kind of demystificatory criticism (which, ironically, is not nearly as politically radical as it thinks it is)? Here is my end-of-century hope: somewhere, someone is writing a book that will help us do that by creating a yet-undreamt of paradigm for the scholarship of the future.

Shakespeare's Monarchies: Ruler and Subject in the Romances
By Constance Jordan
Ithaca: Cornell University Press, 1997

Reviewer: Katherine Eggert

In *Shakespeare's Monarchies,* Constance Jordan stakes out important new territory in Shakespearean genre studies. Other critics, dwelling upon the romances' reliance on the supernatural or their conversation of death and loss into life and reunion, have described these plays as outgrowths of Shakespeare's decades-long experiments with comedy and tragedy. Jordan, in contrast, views *Pericles, Cymbeline, The Winter's Tale,* and *The Tempest* as latter-day developments of the Shakespearean history play: "projecting their subjects through the lens of an incipient nationalism, they screen issues of a private or emotional character to concentrate on matters of public moment" (10). (Jordan does not treat *Henry VIII,* the one play that is practically inarguably both romance *and* history play.) The true topic of the romances, in Jordan's account, is the inherent instability of absolutist rule, its tendency either to degenerate into tyranny or to promote anarchy.

Jordan's reading of these four plays thus tends toward the allegorical. In her argument, the romances all center upon the family unit and upon the physical body of the monarch—his status not as god but as mortal—not because these are intrinsically interesting topics for drama in general or Shakespeare in particular, but because they serve as the best possible vehicles for a debate over the nature of government. This debate Jordan sees as primarily Jacobean in its terms, although her book's introduction traces its sixteenth-century (primarily Elizabethan) origins. Its central text is James I's *Trew Law of Free Monarchies* (1598), in which the future English king figures monarchy as so absolute that an oppressed or tyrannized people has no recourse except patience and prayer. Opposing English theorists—who, Jordan argues, were largely constitutionalist rather than republican in temperament—argue instead for some kind of contract between ruler and ruled, one that was subject to positive law (that is, common law) and that required the consent of the governed, exercised primarily through Parliament. Sir John Fortescue's *De laudibus legum angliae* (1468–70), translated by Richard Mulcaster in 1567, proves to be the most influential text in Jordan's careful tracing of the anti-absolutist tradition; as head of a "mixed" monarchy, England's ruler could exercise royal prerogative only in those arenas where no positive law obtained.

Jordan's Shakespeare is a confirmed Fortescuean in the sense that the romances detail the horrifying varieties of error to which an absolutist monarch is necessarily subject. Whether he acts as tyrant or abnegates his authority, the king's sins come to pass because he has no sense of obligation to his subjects, sees no world outside his own will and desires. Antiochus's incest, Pericles's abandonment of his daughter and kingdom, Leontes's irrational jealousy, Cymbeline's virtual abdication, and Prospero's retirement to his library all bear the mark of the Jacobean absolute monarch. Other characters serve as counterexamples and even correctives to this model of bad rule: Marina and Paulina, for example, who act (in a metaphor that commonly attached to right kingship) as good physicians, healing the ills of the state. With such corrective actions resides the importance of the plays' metaphors of the family and of the human body. Fundamental to the misguided ruler's changing his ways is his admission of his own mortality: the father must give way to his children, the human to the divine, just as the king must not insist upon his own eternity and divinity.

Jordan equally emphasizes, however, how these abstract ideas and relationships discussed by theories of rule are founded in the very material considerations of English common law, which is fundamentally a law of property rights. Just as most of the disputes in the Renaissance courts over which laws a subject might in good conscience resist turn out to be disputes over taxation, so do matters of right and conscience in these plays turn out to be about property. A monarch's overbearing will is illegitimate, in the end, because it constrains his subjects' pursuit of their livelihoods; as Jordan reminds us, the most important legal decisions of the early seventeenth century limiting royal prerogative had to do with limiting the monarch's power to grant commercial monopolies. Hence Antiochus's incest is criminal because it asserts his kingdom as entirely his own property; there is no way to secure its orderly succession to his daughter and her husband. Marina's art of inculcating virtue, which Jordan reads as an avatar of good governance, is all the more bracingly effective because it "has no persuasive or moving force outside [the] real or material settings" of the brothels in which she sells the power of her virtuous voice (64). Similarly, Jordan sees in the mystical prophecy of the westering eagle at the end of *Cymbeline* Francis Bacon's economic arguments to Parliament in favor of empire building (1606–8): empire increases the nation not through conquest, but through commerce.

The question of property provides those moments in Jordan's study that emphasize how monarchical right in these plays continues to be a contested issue, rather than one that is entirely resolved by the restoration of a reformed monarchy at the plays' ends. Ordinarily, Jordan is not much given to skeptical, ironic, or even mildly outraged readings of these plays' outcomes; she tends to identify these plays' conclusions as fashioning an enlightened (in Fortescuean terms) governmental form, no matter how many underlings (women, servants, children) have been oppressed along the way. But Jordan's reading of Caliban, for example, brings a different point of view to the fore. On the one hand Caliban, for Jordan, simply represents the bestial aspects of human nature that the temperate monarch must bring under control, both in his nation and in himself. But on the other hand, Caliban is unjustly enslaved, a laborer who is not allowed to enjoy the fruits of his work. Perhaps the most fascinating of Jordan's many enlightening historical discussions is her illumination of early disputes over whether the New World natives owned their own property and, if so, how the European colonizers might legitimately lay claim to it. In sum: Prospero has no right in common law to seize Caliban's island, and Jordan proposes that the Jacobean property owner who worried about the monarch's encroachments on his or her own rights might identify more with the savage and deformed slave than with his "enlightened" master.

Such an argument illustrates what Jordan believes to be the place of the Shakespearean stage in the debate over the nature of good governance. The romances make concrete what is abstract in theoretical discussions about government; theater gives the people a place to entertain alternative ideas of what rule consists of, and how it might operate. This is not to say that the theater urges the citizens of London on toward the barricades. Instead, Shakespeare's plays, in Jordan's view of them, have rather the same effect on their audience that Jordan's discussions have on her reader: they encourage careful, considered reflection upon and reconsideration of what are hardly settled questions. *Shakespeare's Monarchies* is in many ways the ideal kind of critical text to assign in the advanced undergraduate or graduate classroom (and I expect it will see more-than-usual classroom use). Beautifully argued and written in a way that is elegantly simple but not oversimplified, its focus is purposely narrow. Jordan is not interested in large-scale refutations of alternative readings of the romances—psychoanalytic views of the plays, in particular, do not enter into her argument. Nor does she pause much to engage the now long-standing quarrels over New Historicism and its discontents. Hers is an intellectual history of finely tuned proportions; the reader who is expecting the kind of magisterial sweep of Jordan's *Renaissance Feminism* (1990) will not find it here. What the reader of *Shakespeare's Monarchies* will find are readings of four plays, each carefully shaded in the context of crucial debates over the rights of the individual versus the rights of the government—debates that have come down from Shakespeare's intellectual world to our own.

Theatre, Finance and Society in Early Modern England
Theodore B. Leinwand
Cambridge: Cambridge University Press, 1999

Reviewer: Douglas S. Bruster

Theatre, Finance and Society is a study of emotional responses to economic situations in early modern England. One of its innovations is its comparison of literary characters with sixteenth- and seventeenth-century English persons. In chapters titled "Credit Crunch," "Debt Restructuring," "Mortgage Payments," and "Venture Capital," Leinwand expands on the new historicist technique of reading "sideways"—aligning, that is, literary texts with social documents and historical events—by reading literary characters alongside biographical sequences for their representation of "affect." The book could have been titled *Emotional Lives of Financially Over-Extended Elizabethans and Jacobeans,* if with this designation we include, along with Walter Ralegh, Lionel Cranfield, and Peter Frobisher, such dramatic characters as Antonio from *The Merchant of Venice, Michaelmas Term*'s Richard Easy, and Giles Overreach in *A New Way to Pay Old Debts.*

Yet a central problem with such grouping is that Leinwand does not sufficiently address what it means to treat literary characters as case studies in social psychology. He makes no use of the many thoughtful treatments of character in the past decade: Christy Desmet's *Reading Shakespeare's Characters* (1992), for example, could have helped Leinwand better explore the textures of characters created for the stages of this era. Literary history is neglected when it comes to the plays examined here. We learn, on one occasion, that a play "has its own narrative and generic obligations" (119)—as though structure and genre were annoying debts to be paid, rather than important resources for authors. More attention to the role of such resources in the construction of character would have made this a more compelling book.

Broadening his scope to include literary history, however, would have forced Leinwand to qualify his position on the role of economics in shaping a character's affect. This is perhaps his argument's greatest weakness, its "underdetermination" of cause. That is, Leinwand places so much emphasis on the economic basis of characters' affect that other social and psychological forces are virtually ignored. Is Antonio in *The Merchant of Venice* "sad" because of his financial dealings? To make such a claim without extensive consideration of such issues as friendship, sexuality, or even Renaissance theories of melancholy, is to gain a strong argument at the risk of losing readers' confidence when they return to the wonderfully plural dramatic texts of this era.

Leinwand often uses the word "precise" in relation to his observations, contrasting his approach with market studies supposed to be less so. Along these lines, the last sentence of this book holds that "the amplitude of aphorism is more arresting but less revealing than the fine grain of particularism" (143). Which is fine, save for the fact that the only thing likely to be precise in cultural history written by literary critics (myself included) is the bibliographical information in their footnotes. For its insights Leinwand's study often relies, in fact, on *im*precision—from its use of Lawrence Stone's generalizations about history to its repeated recourse to analogies and shared themes: "Complaint, the note of self-pity, the badge of victimization, and the ensuing hatred, these are all evident in Sonnet 134, in the Cranfield and Ingram records, and in *A New Way to Pay Old Debts*" (109); "I do see a structural homology between [John Watts's] and Antonio's, the merchant of Venice's, career paths" (128); "Like Lovewit, Burbage was something of an absentee landlord" (137); "That Daniel was himself wheeling and dealing not much less than Face or Subtle is suggested by . . ." (138). There is nothing wrong with such observations. But they are far from "precise," and it is not clear that Leinwand could have sustained the structure of this book had they been so.

This brings me to my final reservation about this study. Leinwand gives us his central discovery in saying that "the early modern English experience of the operations of credit was both elastic and profound" (13). Because it does not overturn a widely held critical position, the significance of this insight depends largely on the uniqueness of its application. That is, if the experience of "the operations of credit" were the only one that was elastic and profound, or one of the few experiences that were, the claim would be worth demonstrating. But into the statement "the early modern English experience of ——— was both elastic and profound," we could surely substitute thousands of words. To learn that significant things produce varied responses in people, and in dramatic characters, is not surprising. Nor is it clear to me that the "experience of the operations of credit" could ever be otherwise than "elastic and profound," from the beginnings of credit to the present. Thus although the concentrated comparisons of this book are engaging, I am not sure what we are supposed to learn from them.

I take no pleasure in pointing out what I consider to be this book's shortcomings. Leinwand is a careful and industrious reader who shows a close acquaintance with a variety of historical events and primary texts. His analyses are often nuanced, and his prose is quite elegant. However, I feel that this book does not succeed, as I wish it had, in sustaining a conversation with the field.

Post-Colonial Shakespeares
Edited by Ania Loomba and Martin Orkin
London and New York: Routledge, 1998

Reviewer: Peter Erickson

This collection has the distinction of being the first book devoted to Shakespeare that includes the term "postcolonial" in its title, thus announcing the intersection of Shakespeare studies with postcolonial studies. Through the vivid image of a tweezer, the introduction conveys both the power and the difficulty of the coordination that this combination involves: "If they are to come together, like two ends of a tweezer, to unpick Shakespeare from a colonial past and place him more meaningfully in a post-colonial world, then Shakespeareans need to engage critically and at some depth with post-colonial criticism and the controversies that energize it."

Equally crucial to this project is the historical reach of postcolonialism since extending its application back as far as the early modern period is especially challenging. In his contribution to *The Post-Colonial Question* (1996), Stuart Hall asks: "When was 'the post-colonial'?" His answer stresses the term's double timeframe. Postcolonial refers, first, to a specific moment in the mid-twentieth century when former colonies started to gain independence and global power relations began gradually to shift. But the term has a second, more comprehensive meaning when the origin of colonial enterprise is traced back to European international ventures from the fifteenth century on. In Hall's account, this latter starting point leads to a reformulation of the entire framework of historical periodization, and it amounts to a new view of the early modern past that makes possible the direct connection to Shakespeare. The two-part organizational structure of *Post-Colonial Shakespeares* echoes Hall's wider conceptual scope.

The second part of the collection addresses contemporary appropriations of Shakespeare, a field established by Marianne Novy's three-volume project spanning the 1990s on women's revisions of Shakespeare. The two strongest contributions in this section are those by Ania Loomba and Michael Neill. Their treatment of Salman Rushdie (*The Moor's Last Sigh*), Nadine Gordimer (*My Son's Story*), and Derek Walcott (the poem "A Far Cry from Africa" and the play *A Branch of the Blue Nile*)—all writers steeped in European literary traditions—is illuminating but relatively familiar. What makes these two essays distinctive is the attention to less well-known, less geographically traveled material.

Loomba continues and expands her earlier essay "*Hamlet* in Mizoram" in Novy's second volume, *Cross-Cultural Performances* (1993), by examining a Kathakali performance of *Othello*. Loomba finds not only that Shakespeare "becomes a junior partner" but also that the Kathakali version is not at all anticolonial. Neill describes in fascinating detail the case of a consciously cross-cultural Maori-Shakespearean amalgam, *Manawa Taua/Savage Hearts,* in which collaboration turned into intractable conflict: "In the end these divisions seem to have been resolved only by an extraordinary agreement to suppress the play at the end of its highly successful run, so that it would neither be published or made available for further performance. At the heart of the dispute lay a deep disagreement about the kinds of stories it was appropriate to tell about our history—a disagreement in which Shakespeare's ur-narrative of miscegenation [*Othello*] was profoundly implicated." Loomba's and Neill's examples serve to complicate beneficent notions of contemporary hybridity.

The heart of the collection, however, is the first part. The two opening essays by Jerry Brotton and Jonathan Burton both acknowledge Ania Loomba's "Shakespeare and Cultural Difference" in *Alternative Shakespeares, Volume 2* (1996), in which she argues that a disproportionate emphasis has been given to Europe's contact with America, with the result that "English contact with the East—India, the Spice Islands, Turkey, Persia, China and Japan—has not become part of the working vocabulary of Renaissance scholarship." Loomba's citation of her unpublished manuscript *Of Queens and Spices: Renaissance Drama and the East Indies* (1996) and the appearance of Nabil Matar's *Turks, Moors, and Englishmen in the Age of Discovery* (1999) suggest that a critical mass is starting to form that will provide a more balanced and global spectrum.

In the present volume, Brotton and Burton seek to restore a Mediterranean-based "Old World" perspective. Brotton reinterprets *The Tempest* as "a politically and geographically bifurcated play in the negotiation between its Mediterranean and Atlantic contexts," while Burton contrasts Othello's cooption with the subversive "textual mimicry" of Leo Africanus's *Geographical Historie*. Beyond this initial pair, the consistently rewarding first section is extraordinarily wide-ranging. Kim Hall's groundbreaking study brilliantly opens up the topic of racial whiteness. Margo Hendricks approaches *The Rape of Lucrece* with a view to showing how "those works that are not readily identifiable as works bearing colonialist ideologies" nonetheless contain racial implications. Avraham Oz and Terence Hawkes direct attention, respectively, to Jerusalem and Wales.

The volume's final essay by Jonathan Dollimore does not engage the core issues designated by the term "postcolonial" and his contribution functions more as a retrospective postscript to *Political Shakespeare*, which he coedited in 1985. He therefore inadvertently highlights the adjectival gap separating *Political Shakespeare* and the subsequent *Post-Colonial Shakespeares*; the specificity of the latter's key word indicates the changed critical terrain to which the new volume as a whole testifies.

The special value of *Post-Colonial Shakespeares* is twofold. First, in its forthright, unapologetic evocation of the term "race," the volume reinforces current attention to this issue in early modern studies. Second, at the same time, it also insists on greater international range in the investigation of race and, within this expanded range, places emphasis on comparative analysis that will replace a one-dimensional model of Otherness with a more differentiated sense of distinctive geographical locations.

Time-Fetishes: The Secret History of Eternal Recurrence
By Ned Lukacher
Durham, N.C. and London: Duke University Press, 1998

Reviewer: Marguerite R. Waller

A volume in the Post-contemporary Interventions series, edited by Stanley Fish and Fredric Jameson, Ned Lukacher's *Time-Fetishes: The Secret History of Eternal Return* does indeed constitute an "intervention" rather than a survey or systematic investigation of its topic. It includes brief discussions of a wide range of texts, including Heraclitus, Parmenides, Plato, Ovid, Plotinus, St. Augustine, Titian, Shakespeare, Schopenhauer, Kant, Hegel, Schelling, Freud, the Marquis de Sade, Nietzsche, Heidegger, and Derrida. The conjuring power of these names underscores the centrality that Lukacher gives to the issue he focuses on: a particular way of conceptualizing the relation between time and eternity in Western thought. Though for the most part the empirical stakes of the issue are not discussed, we are reminded in the final chapter that the question was and is a profoundly spiritual one. Throughout most of the volume, the argument is highly abstract and may be more portentous for philosophers than for other scholars in the humanities.

Lukacher's learning is engagingly cross-generational and interdisciplinary. In the context of tensions among old-school literary historians and their poststructural critics, the book's seamless integration of the scholarship of some of the great figures of twentieth-century literary and art historical studies—Ernst Kantorowicz, William Empson, S. K. Heninger, Erwin Panofsky, Roy Strong—with the poststructural projects of Jacques Derrida and others is a welcome innovation. Similarly, the discussions of Titian's painting *Bacchus and Ariadne* and of some of its ancient sources take wonderfully for granted the philosophical sophistication and legibility of visual, as well as, verbal texts. Whatever doubts one may have about some methodological aspects of this "secret history," it eschews the taxonomies and genealogies that have represented verbal and visual texts from pre-Enlightenment Europe in unnecessary and unwarranted isolation from each other. One of the most engaging results of this interdisciplinary venture is Lukacher's discussion of what he calls Shakespeare's "anamorphic" images, verbal analogues of the anamorphic visual styles being revived in Elizabeth's court. He argues, for instance, that with the hendiadic phrase "is, and is not," applied to the image of the reunion of the twins Olivia and Sebastian at the end of *Twelfth Night,* Shakespeare creates an anamorphic image of an androgynous whole. Where this image stands and how it operates depends, that is, on where the spectator stands, and where the spectator stands becomes problematized by how the image operates, and so on ad infinitum.

Lukacher's general argument is that there is a history of images, or "fetishes," which attempt to crystallize, without reducing, the impossible-to-think relations between time and eternity (these categories themselves constructed differently by different thinkers and eras). The mises-en-abyme of such a project are daunting, though, and haunt the text in a variety of ways. The notion of "eternal return," notably, is described in some instances as if it were something that happens cosmologically and historically and in other instances, more satisfyingly, as a way of naming the paradox that if "difference" is originary, then there is a way in which it is always the "same," thus confounding the significances and operations of both difference and identity. As Lukacher formulates it at one point: "At the level of the general system there is an irreducible sameness to the incessant production of difference, which means that chance and necessity are only subjective perspectives on the eternal recurrence of the same differences" (114).

Lukacher's treatment of this theoretical aporia, though, at moments risks domesticating it. Instead of allowing its ramifications to problematize the book's critical discourse, for example, the authorial voice repeatedly implies positions of scholarly knowledge and historiographical mastery. To begin with, a "secret" history would seem to require a subject who can determine what is and what is not hidden. Similarly, a "history" suggests a historian, someone in a position to distinguish, however problematically, patterns of various kinds (which depend upon difference and sameness) within the traces we attribute to the "past" (itself a problematic category). Indeed, Lukacher's tone is that of the authoritative pedagogue. It is not unusual to find the book's authorial voice offering "strong" readings and drawing universalizing conclusions: "Augustine's rejection of eternal return in book 12 of *The City of God* may . . . have closed the door for centuries to the possibility of rethinking the essential identity of Dionysos and Christ" (35); "Whether we can ever do without a mythology, regardless of how reasonable or thoughtful or ironic it might be, is finally what is at stake in Heidegger's reading of Nietzsche's doctrine" (138). Such definitive formulations do an injustice to the potential of the topic to make us much more contingent readers and thinkers.

If it is not deconstructive in method, neither does *Time-Fetishes* give us a map of constructions of time comparable to Henri Lefebvre's *The Production of Space.* There is no attempt to situate constructions of time and eternity in relation to ideology, modes of production, or history understood sociologically and politically. Nor, although Lukacher cites Gilles Deleuze's book on Nietzsche, does he make any reference to Deleuze's extended meditation on time and the cinema in *Cinema 2—L'image-temps.* The project seems to have been inspired most directly by Jacques Derrida's (non) concept of "différance," which combines the notions of differing and deferring. Ironically, though, since he situates other writers so definitively, Lukacher never situates or contextualizes is own text. He discusses neither how he became interested in eternal return, nor why other students and scholars should be interested in this crux. It is, as I have indicated, exciting to glimpse the possibilities of bringing the wealth of learning accumulated by historians of ideas together with the rigor of poststructural theory. Such an alliance will be a tricky one, however, and in this volume it does not quite come off.

Writing, Gender, and State in Early Modern England: Identity Formation and the Female Subject
By Megan Matchinske
Cambridge: Cambridge University Press, 1998

Reviewer: Kathleen Lynch

This is a hardworking first book that grapples with some key issues in the rich critical field of subject and gender formations, topics equally resonant in the personal and the political spheres (if indeed those are separable anymore). One would expect no less from a series sponsored by a major scholarly press, "designed to offer historically oriented studies of Renaissance literature and theater which make use of the insights afforded by theoretical perspectives." Within the sketchy scope of a century—from Reformation to civil war—Matchinske offers closely situated readings of the textual constructions of four women's identities.

She begins with an anecdote told by Margaret Cavendish in her memoirs, published in 1656. There Cavendish avers she virtually withdrew from social contact as a young woman waiting on the Queen at court in Oxford. Cavendish tells her reader she "rather chose to be accounted a fool" than to give the least cause for perceptions of her conduct to give rise to an ill repute from which her family would suffer as much as herself. Matchinske highlights Cavendish's choice here—one admittedly circumscribed by a clearly defined and narrow set of options, but choice nonetheless, a simultaneously proactive and reactive engagement that Matchinske sees as the key to the construction of feminine identity.

To make her point, Matchinske might also have looked to the very end of Cavendish's memoirs. There, Cavendish defends her choice to write about herself. "I write it for my own sake, not theirs; neither did I intend this piece for to delight, but to divulge, not to please the fancy, but to tell the truth, lest after-Ages should mistake, in not knowing I was daughter to one Master Lucas of St. Johns neer Colchester in Essex, second wife to the Lord Marquiss of Newcastle, for my Lord having had two wives, I might easily have been mistaken, especially if I should dye, and my Lord Marry again" ("A True Relation," 390–91).

Cavendish's determination to record and thereby examine the particularities of a singular existence is one with which Matchinske is in sympathy, as her chosen methodology is a close reading of the juxtapositions of gender and state formations in several chronologically narrated but "textually and historically discrete moments" (5). These include *The Examinations of Anne Askew,* the "Life of Margaret Clitherow," Ester Sowernam's *Ester hath hang'd Haman,* and the millennial prophesies of Lady Eleanor Davies.

They are interesting choices. For the reception of three of these voices is complicated by the layerings of their articulation—Askew's through the editorial interventions and historiographical agenda of John Bale; Clitherow's by the third-person reportage of her confessor John Mush; and Sowernam's by the pseudonymity of the pamphlet's publication. The reception of Davies's is mediated, too, by the historically shifting grounds of our understanding of pathology. The four are further interesting for the variety of genres and means of publication drawn upon. Having highlighted this range of issues in her choices, Matchinske addresses them in a somewhat cursory fashion, bowing to what she terms the insistence of theory for simplicity and redirection. But her real subject in any case is cultural resistance, and the consequences are stark in the examples here—Anne Askew burned at the stake in Smithfield; Margaret Clitherow pressed to death in York; Eleanor Davies severing her communal ties and resorting to the lonely, bitter cloak of prophesy.

Chapter 1, Resistance, Reformation, and the Remaining Narratives, is a study of the erasures on which history is built and a recovery of the gendered basis of Anne Askew's resistance to the secular articulation of spiritual authority. Matchinske examines the way the received tradition of Anne Askew's saintly martyrdom masks the secular motivations of the key players in the events, Askew included. Askew was convicted and executed in 1546, in the last year of Henry VIII's reign. Her transgression was against the first of the Six Articles enacted in 1539, the one confirming the real substance of Christ's body and blood in communion, the one that brought to a doctrinal head the ongoing contestations between conservative and reformist parties in Henry's court and church.

Askew's *Examinations* were published posthumously in 1546 and 1547 in Wesel (not Marpurg, as the title pages have it) by John Bale. Matchinske contrasts Bale's tireless promotion of an international reform movement (and his own role in it) with Askew's careful and shifting articulation of "singular truths [and] individual certainties" (43). As a woman, Askew is always responsive to the restrictions and demands of her situation—always answering specific questions, never asserting universal truths. Her evasive and shifting grounds of defense—obedient woman at one moment, inspired reader of scriptures at the next—never wholly serve either the reformist or the traditional positions of debate. But by resorting to whatever options present themselves, she challenges the very terms of the debate and insists on an interpretive—and individual—flexibility.

Matchinske would have us remember that Askew was not a victim of a widespread persecution of reformists. Instead, hers was an isolated example of a court-specific threat to Henry's unstable government at the end of his reign. She is at risk precisely because of her proximity to power, particularly to the reformist Katherine Parr and her circle of attendants. Matchinske frames her interrogation of the teleological reformation narratives in which Askew has been given a secure role in terms of personal incentive and desire, "precisely those spaces where records do not exist" (27). By presenting Askew's resistance as polyvalent and never simply contained, Matchinske persuades us that the positions she was able to occupy were multiple and multiply comprehensible—and far richer than those so "powerfully narrated by writerly men who count" (24).

Chapter 2, Framing Recusant Identity in Counter-Reformation England, takes up the case of Margaret Clitherow, a butcher's wife in York who was pressed to death in 1586 for her noncompliance with then newly articulated and closely monitored requirements for church attendance. Clitherow refused to answer or plead in her own defense. She died leaving no record or personal account of her convictions or strategies. Instead, she has been memorialized in "The Life of Margaret Clitherow," a manuscript account by one of her confessors, Father John Mush. With this documentary trail—a further remove from the woman's own words—Matchinske sets herself the challenge of writing Clitherow's voice into being, creating it anew. In doing so, she generates a cultural model that considers large-scale ideological shifts to historicize difference—both from the present moment and from Anne Askew's some forty years earlier. In Matchinske's telling, the 1580s were a more stable time than the end of Henry's reign, at least in the upper echelons of government, and the focus of persecution and normalizing restraints moved away from court to the middle ranks and more rural areas. Ecclesiastical commissions proliferated, and Clitherow was caught in one of the regulatory nets.

As in her reading of Askew's work, Matchinske attends carefully to the distinctions between Mush's agenda and narrative perspective and Clitherow's. Clitherow's challenge is to negotiate between being a good Catholic saint and a good Catholic wife (and here her religion is mapped onto the Protestant discourse of domestic relations). As a gesture of her wifely duty, Clitherow reportedly sent her hat to her husband—her head—as a last act before her death. It is this kind of performativity that Matchinske foregrounds in her investigation of Clitherow. Unlike Askew, whose negotiations are rhetorical (in keeping with her Protestant devotion to the word), Clitherow's are distinctively Catholic and performative. Before her grisly death, Clitherow was offered recourse to another subject-position, another means of legitimation: her purported pregnancy offered a reprieve from the sentence of death. But Clitherow was unwilling to substantiate it, and so refused the sanctuary of domestic obligation. Seemingly most freed by her greatest privations, Clitherow is a striking example of a more widespread Catholic phenomenon: in harboring fugitive priests and providing a moral counterpoint for outwardly conforming husbands, women subverted the usual categories of gender power relations.

If Askew and Clitherow each tested the limits of identities available to them, Ester Sowernam exploited the economic bases of those identities to trade off a narrowing of choices and a loss of female sexuality and pleasure for the legally sanctioned moral high ground. Chapter 3, Legislating Morality in the Marriage Market, examines Sowernam's choices in relation to explorations of similar matters in two contemporary play-texts, Shakespeare's *Measure for Measure* and the anonymous *Swetnam the Woman-Hater*. Matchinske takes as her point of departure for the chapter Sowernam's teasing assertion on the title page that she is "neither Maide, Wife nor Widdowe, yet really all, and therefore experienced to defend all." This has been read variously as a code for male authorship of the pseudonymous text or the legitimating grounds for a right to speak. It is also a cultural coding for "punk" or whore. Matchinske reads Sowernam's equilibrious assertion and denial of the categories of identity traditionally offered women as an acknowledgment of the conflicted and frequently unenforced state of the marriage contract in early modern England. She offers the treatment of *Measure for Measure*'s Marianne as an example of male ambivalence toward women who have been abandoned by lovers after having contracted an unwitnessed and unceremonial marriage in good faith. Sowernam positions her defense of such women in the intersections of legal and moral codes. She argues a case before two female judges, Reason and Experience, to emphasize the legal nature of marriage as an institution. Women's chastity, Sowernam argues, is a marketable moral commodity, which (though status-specific) will promote masculine reputation and honesty. The price for these negotiations to cement women's roles as social consciences—doing the work of the state from within the domestic sphere—is high. As Matchinske points out, it requires "complicity in a marriage ideology that denies women agency outside the moral sphere and continues to insist on their status as property" (102).

Chapter 4, Gender Formation in English Apocalyptic Writing, considers the prophetic writings of Lady Eleanor Davies in the 1640s. Davies was born the fifth daughter of George Touchet, Baron Audeley and Earl of Castlehaven, one of the oldest peerages in England and Ireland. At one point she advised Queen Henrietta Maria of her fortunes in childbearing, and she accurately prophesied the deaths of Lord Buckingham, Archbishop Laud, and King Charles I, as well as that of her first husband (upon which vision she promptly donned her mourning garments). Davies enjoyed some notoriety in her day, but also, as Matchinske describes, was disadvantaged by her simultaneous attempts to assume the cloak of divine prophet and turn the powers thereby gained to address her own personal, gendered concerns. Matchinske is a particularly good reader of the rhetoric of apocalyptic writing and of Davies's peculiar turns with it. Matchinske sees it as an important force in the redefinition of the English state in the civil war years. By positing insurmountable oppositions, apocalyptic rhetoric, or holy hatred as she calls it, invokes a dynamic of subject formation and social change. Further, the puritanical emphasis on looking inward for spiritual direction helps to model a more easily governable subject. Moral certainty provides the authority—not to mention an empowering impunity—for nontraditional authors such as Sowernam, Trapnell, and the other female prophets of the civil war period.

Davies seized on that platform, the only basis for authority left her following a formal denial of access to the royal family in 1633 and the revocation of her rights of jointure after her first husband's death. Prophetic power compensates for her lost aristocratic privileges. Matchinske emphasizes the ways in which Davies deviates from the more usual prophetic agenda. Though Davies engages in a history that is national in scope, as did most millennial prophets, she neither demands nor advocates militant action. Instead she deflects the expectations of her readers back into support of her own position. With all her energy invested in constructing and maintaining a platform of authority, Davies is at a kind of double jeopardy for her "subject/object doubling" (144). Above all, and in a way hearkening back to Anne Askew's choice, Davies celebrates the right to interpretation. "There is nothing so secret that shall not be discovered," she writes in the introduction to the 1645 pamphlet. "I am the first and the last, the beginning and the ending." Matchinske describes one telling narrative peculiarity that may explain Davies's lukewarm reception. Davies witholds the action of her sentences to the very end. It is a Latinate construction, but also a feminized passivity, a desire to articulate a right that is so self-referential that it was then and is often still dismissed as madness.

Rather than a conclusion, Matchinske offers Connections, Qualifications, and Agendas at the end of her book. She reiterates the outlines of a history of the formation of a gendered conscience, one that derives more and more from "an ability to establish and heed one's own moral codes" (157). She confirms her notion that identity is established through differentiation and alterity, that the severing of close ties between church and state allowed for a proliferation of regulatory discourses and practices that dispersed the source of authority while fostering a raised level of self invigilation. Finally, she defends her discussion as a beginning, "a fragmentary beginning at best" (161), and calls for multiple speakers and perspectives to be brought to bear on the same set of issues. In some ways, she summons these perspectives from the footnotes of her book where she has been tracking their intersections with her thesis. Matchinske's readers will recognize that a community of critical thinkers is already at work on these questions. Matchinske's microhistories find their place among a number of initiatives that construct feminist histories of the early modern period. As she recognizes, her book is as much a product of that nexus of studies and anthologies—the simultaneous recovery and repositioning of terms of debate—as it is a singular achievement.

Sermons at Court: Politics and Religion in Elizabethan and Jacobean Preaching
By Peter E. McCullough
Cambridge: Cambridge University Press, 1998

Reviewer: John H. Astington

If Shakespeare and his fellow actors entertained the English monarchs and their courts with a number of performances over the three days of Shrovetide, in the succeeding six weeks of Lent earnest courtiers could have been present at far many more performances of quite a different kind: the sermons delivered in palace chapels and in the quasipublic Preaching Place at Whitehall by the clergymen appointed to serve as royal chaplains. The literary and oratorical skills on display must have varied, as on theatrical occasions, but in the Jacobean years the distinguished preachers Lancelot Andrewes and John Donne frequently appeared before the King and Queen.

Peter McCullough's informative and suggestive book reminds us that if we are looking for literary influences on court culture the pulpit rather than the stage is a far more likely source. "The sermon," he insists, "not Shakespearean drama, and not even the Jonsonian masque—was the pre-eminent literary genre at the Jacobean court." Moreover, the prominence of the sermon was, under James, directly attributable to the monarch's own taste and interest: "No other literary enterprise could captivate, inspire, or even anger the king like a sermon" (125).

What one might call the performative dynamics of sermons at court were comparable to those of theatrical entertainment. The preacher in the pulpit faced the west end of the chapel, where the monarch sat with his or her immediate entourage in a private gallery, the royal closet. McCullough suggests an analogy with the divided focus of a masque (on the performance and its principal observer); this seems to me overstretched. At masques the king sat in full view at the very edge of the dancing floor and with audience all around him, whereas in the chapel closet he was largely concealed, even behind a window that required opening for the monarch to thank, or, occasionally, to rebuke the preacher at the end of his sermon. Other suggestions of the first chapter, on the architecture of preaching places, seem more compelling: the relatively confined and restricted indoor spaces of the chapels as against the large courtyard arena of the Preaching Place might be compared with the two principal kinds of contemporary playhouse. Sermons in the Preaching Place might be delivered to five thousand people, and many ordinary citizens came there not only to hear the sermon but to see the King or Queen in the window of the Council Chamber. Such "commoning" seems nearer to the occasion of a masque or play.

Although the book grew out of a dissertation on the Elizabethan court—and it has indeed matured into a fully nuanced study—its center now seems to be the long third chapter on the court of King James. James, unlike Elizabeth, was genuinely interested in the intellectual framework of religion and sought out "wit" in his preachers, as well as encouraging a variety of shades of theological and ecclesiastical outlook. The sheer number of sermons preached at the various branches of the royal court after 1603 multiplied considerably. At James's funeral service the preacher pointed out that the king had heard more sermons in twenty-two years than all the monarchs of England in the two hundred years before him, a fact not solely attributable to the change in the English church. McCullough's portrait of court culture sharpens our sense of the complexity and the serious enterprise of the Jacobean reign, and his work may be particularly recommended to those who still content themselves with the King James of Whig parody, the slobbering pedantic huntsman with a penchant for young men.

A book of this length and focus has little time for the analysis of particular sermons, although it consistently suggests further avenues of enquiry. Sermons preached at the king's accession in 1603, for example, took up the balance between mercy and judgment, a theme Shakespeare was exploring a year later. Sermons at the court of Prince Henry at St. James's on the martial responsibilities of the committed Christian evidently overlap with Jonson's "device" for the Prince's persona in the *Barriers* of 1610.

The book is a substantial contribution to modern understanding of the court in Shakespeare's lifetime. In the modern way, it is peppered with the usual selection of misprints and minor errors. French expressions have suffered disproportionately, but it is, unfortunately, the last line of the acknowledgments that should leave the author with the most egg on his face. The book comes with a potentially useful calendar of sermons on disk, but if, like me, you use Mac machinery, you will need a large, recent computer to translate it into readable form, since the (single) file is enormous. For the scholar in the study, words printed on paper still have the virtues of universal access and instant legibility.

Imagining Rabelais in Renaissance England
By Anne Lake Prescott
New Haven: Yale University Press, 1998

Reviewer: Philippa Berry

Anne Lake Prescott's witty and erudite book is the first full-length study in English of the impact of Rabelais upon English culture since Huntington Brown's *Rabelais in English Literature* (1933). This may seem surprising, given the significant influence upon English Renaissance studies of Mikhail Bakhtin's *Rabelais and His World,* whose politicized reading of Rabelaisian themes—notably his carnivalesque explorations of the grotesque body (and especially the lower bodily stratum)—gained a new and enthusiastic readership on its translation into English in 1984. Yet while *Rabelais and His World* stimulated much exciting and innovative work on the politics of festivity, food, and the body, the numerous citations of Bakhtin in critical studies of the English Renaissance published since the mid-1980s are rarely accompanied by detailed investigation of the Rabelaisian texts themselves—or by consideration of the extent and character of Rabelais's early reception in England. As the author of *French Poets and the English Renaissance,* Lake Prescott is especially alert to the myopia often displayed toward French cultural influence by critics of the Renaissance across the Channel, and in this book she makes another important contribution to expanding our critical awareness of the richness and complexity of England's cultural debt to France in the late sixteenth and early seventeenth centuries.

Lake Prescott aims to chart the extent of Rabelais's fame and influence in the century between his publication in France and the first translation of his difficult French into English by Sir Thomas Urquhart in 1653, by looking in particular at three "cultural sites" where his work and name were useful: language, the body, and fantasy. What she concludes is that while many reactions to the "French Lucian" expressed ambivalence or at least confusion toward "Rabelais the atheist scoffer," or "Rabelais the dirty-minded drunk," his work nonetheless escaped the almost universal opprobrium reserved for Aretino and Machiavelli, eliciting instead a surprising range of reactions that testify to the variety and complexity of the "cultural work" that these texts performed. Admittedly, Rabelais's *Oeuvres* rarely turn up in catalogues of private books from this period (although both Ben Jonson and Gabriel Harvey owned annotated copies), yet by 1593 John Eliot could mention Rabelais in his *Ortho-epia Gallica* and expect the name to signify something. Inevitably, Rabelais "was more likely to find explicit notice among the swaggering young, the self-consciously masculine, the cosmopolitan elite, and people with a touch of what was to be called a 'libertin' mentality," and clergymen were more likely to denounce than welcome him, but Lake Prescott demonstrates that he was also cited amicably by numerous more conservative thinkers, such as John Selden, Thomas Browne, Francis Bacon, and even James I himself.

Any study of Rabelais's early reception in England is complicated by the significant amount of "para-Rabelaisian" texts that contemporaries thought to be part of his oeuvre, and Lake Prescott traces many Elizabethan and Jacobean references to "Gargantua" that were not to Rabelais's own giant-hero, but to those of chapbooks and jestbooks such as that "du grant & enorme geant Gargantua": Rabelais's own narratives had initially drawn upon these popular chronicles and subsequently stimulated new productions in the genre. It was mainly but not exclusively this chapbook literature, Lake Prescott suggests, that stimulated the enthusiasm for giants in Elizabethan romance, producing memorable yet uniquely disturbing figures such as Orgoglio in Book I of *The Fairie Queene* (whom she reads as a *gigas erectus*—an incarnation of Redcrosse's tumescent desire). But just as Spenser's use of giants as rebels against reason and spirit contrasts strikingly with the comic and therapeutic roles accorded to Rabelais's own heroes, so Lake Prescott argues that the related themes of scatology, logorrhea, satire, and fantasy popularized by Rabelais's own work elicited a peculiar combination of fascination and revulsion among many of the writers who borrowed from or imitated him. Not surprisingly, Jonson is cited as a prominent instance of this type of response; like a number of recent critics, Lake Prescott interprets his quasi-Rabelaisian combination of festivity with scatology as "anally clenched." Predictably, too, she stresses the dark violence that informs the stylistic debt to Rabelais of Thomas Nashe, whom Gabriel Harvey flytingly termed a "huge Gargantua of prose." But she goes even further, to argue that "the English seem largely to have ignored the carnival Rabelais" (although she notes that many writers, including Shakespeare, were interested in Epistemon's account of the carnivalesque goings-on in Hell from *Pantagruel*). This seems something of an overstatement—an exaggerated reaction, perhaps, against Baktinianism?—especially since a chapter of the book explores the debt of many Stuart masques to Rabelaisian motifs.

The relative marginality of Shakespeare to this study is due to the infrequency with which direct allusions to or echoes of Rabelais appear in his corpus; yet the omission is telling, reminding her reader that Lake Prescott's concern in this book is with the sourcing of specific textual references rather than with the exploration of more generalized stylistic and thematic debts. She notes the allusion to "Gargantua's mouth" in *As You Like It*; the debt of Holofernes in *Love's Labour's Lost* to Gargantua's slow scholastic tutor, Holoferne, and that of Mercutio and Falstaff to the wily trickster and companion of Pantagruel, Panurge; as well as use of the Hell episode from *Pantagruel* in *King Lear*; but she does not examine the relationship of these allusions to the general temper of the plays in which they appear. Given this methodological caution, it is not surprising that Lake Prescott only discovers something approaching a "true Pantagruelism" in the lexicography of Randle Cotgrave, whose pervasive citation of Rabelais (as "¶ Rab") in his *Dictionarie of the French and English Tongues* enables her to state (yet even here with some hesitancy) that his language, "flowing from a lexicographical horn of plenty . . . can loosely be called Rabelaisian." Observing that, in Cotgrave's dictionary definitions, "the body itself seems more open than closed," Lake Prescott's implication is that this is a Francophiliac exception to what she sees as the more typically constipated—albeit fascinated—response to Rabelais of his English readers. Yet surely Cotgrave is not the only English Renaissance imitator of Rabelais's style who communicates a logophiliac delight in bodiliness that is festive as well as satiric? It could have been helpful, in other words, if the author had occasionally set aside the specifics of Rabelaisian citation and allusion, to consider the possibly para-Rabelaisian, but certainly gigantic pleasures of wordplay and wit provided by writers such as Shakespeare and Donne—even if we cannot always trace their textual enormities to "¶ Rab."

However, Lake Prescott's scholarly restraint offers a valuable corrective to previous critical invocations of a diffuse Rabelaisian influence on English Renaissance literature, in studies that tended to depend much more on readings of Bakhtin than of Rabelais himself. What she provides us with is a great deal of evidence, culled from a wide range of texts and authors, and analyzed with an elegant acuity, which proves that Rabelais was very widely read in French and regularly cited, often in considerable detail. *Imagining Rabelais in Renaissance England* has consequently reopened a debate that appeared to have become ossified. One hopes it will prompt further investigation of the "cultural work" performed by Rabelais, together with a critical reassessment of that more generalized debt to his writings which surely informs the works of Shakespeare, along with those of Jonson, Donne, and many others.

The Acoustic World of Early Modern England: Attending to the O-Factor
By Bruce R. Smith
Chicago: University of Chicago Press, 1999

Reviewer: Joan Pong Linton

In this groundbreaking book, Bruce Smith invites us to enter an early modern world of sounds and to inhabit, through our own embodied imaginations, the aural sensibilities of what was still largely an oral society. Smith's work is deeply resonant with ongoing scholarship that attends to the body's perceptions and agency and to the practical technologies that orient individual subjects as embodied knowers and doers in the world. In describing his project as a "historical phenomenology of listening," Smith proposes to rethink early modern subjectivity in embodied terms, aware as he is of the historical discontinuity between early modern English culture and our own. This endeavor requires redefining the relationship between readers and scholars as inquiring subjects and the historical subjects who all too often become the objects of inquiry. The result is a work that will change the way we think about early modern English society and about scholarly inquiry.

From the beginning, Smith renders with economy the complexity of aural experience through an exploration of the sound O as a physical act, a sensory experience, an act of communication, and a political performance. His approach combines early modern anatomy and rhetoric with recent theory, especially in the areas of orality and literacy, communication systems, and phenomenology. For Smith, "the phenomenology of listening offers a way of accounting for subjectivity within th[e] materialist matrix" he constructs (28). In larger scope, the book is concerned with "the *politics* of media," with the questions of who has access to representation and whose interests are served within print- and voiced-based systems. Given the continued relevance of such a concern, Smith asks readers to imagine along with him how "an ecology of voice, media, and community—an ecology based on listening—may provide some hope for the future" (29).

In locating the subject within this ecology, chapter 2 establishes the body's rootedness in space and time through analysis of the rituals and practices of early modern English society. A notable example is the rogation ritual of "beating the bounds," in which a community marks its aural boundaries at the beginning of the agricultural year. Smith here draws on folklorist Dell Hymes's "speech community" and anthropologists Barry Truax's "soundscape" and Steven Feld's "acoustemology," concepts that provide the basis for reconstruction of three early modern English soundscapes—the city, the country, and the court (chapter 3). In doing so, Smith culls from a vast array of primary materials, including medical and anatomical texts, diaries, travelogues, maps, building plans, antiquarian histories, dialogues between court and country, songs, ballads, plays, masques, descriptions of royal entries, and pageants, etc. What emerges is a thick description that accretively enriches readers' appreciation of the diverse and varying aural ecologies that make up early modern England.

Smith's phenomenology of listening is not limited to external soundscapes but extends to practices that intimately involve the sounding and listening body. In chapter 4, the discussion of orthography—a practice not usually associated with listening—draws attention to the sound registered by the writing hand, thus bringing out the oral dimension of the written word both on the page and in the body. As Smith points out, early modern writers and readers identified a person's handwriting with his or her spoken voice. Such historical specificity, by undoing the dichotomy between oral and written, invites us to rethink the disciplinary bias within literary studies that has historically privileged written or printed texts over oral performance and aural reception. And there are theoretical implications as well with respect to both the structuralist privileging of speech over writing and the obverse in poststructuralist (especially Derridean) formulation. For Smith, "one difficulty with both the structuralist and the poststructuralist models of orthography is the way they reify both 'writing' and 'speech.'" As he explains, "there is not one writing technology in early modern England but several," and these writing technologies are linked, through the body, to speech and memory: "writing 'members' speech into graphemes; the viewer of the signs *remembers*" (119, 121). Thus writing technologies orient individual subjects through their sounding, remembering bodies as ethical agents in the practice of everyday life.

In view of the ethical and political dimensions of writing, Smith observes that "it ought to be possible to construct a 'cultural poetics' of handwriting no less than a cultural poetics of gender, sexuality, and nationhood" (116). The problem, the author implies, is that, unlike a cultural poetics of gender, sexuality, and nationhood, which is in large part articulated discursively through language, a cultural poetics of handwriting is in large part articulated into practice through the sounding, remembering body. Difficulties notwithstanding, chapter 4 develops just such a cultural poetics. In broader terms, chapter 5, "Some Propositions Concerning O," can be said to "beat the theoretical bounds" for a cultural poetics of O, marking the boundaries, to name only two, where the pleasures of the body meets the pleasures of the text, and where O inhabits the Lacanian imaginary before transformation into the symbolic register. Subsequent chapters explore dimensions of this cultural poetics through analysis of specific practices involving the sounding, remembering body. Finally, because "O demands political reading, in pursuit of political listening," a cultural poetics of O is no less political (albeit less overtly so) than a discursively articulated cultural politics (26).

Indeed, an argument underlying much of this book is that a cultural poetics of O not only complements more overtly political cultural poetics but in doing so calls to mind the politics in the body. A good example is the morris dance, "a combination of combat and communion" that "enacts the dynamics of male identity-formation in early modern England." As Smith explains, "affiliation is affirmed through antagonism; bodies move in opposition yet in synchrony. That ritual act takes place beyond language, at a point where music, ambient sound, and the primal [o] ring out together" (145–46). Significantly, such gestic movements "possess *depth*: in space, in time, above all in the interiors of sounding bodies that *do* them. As such, gests are not finally readable" (166). This unreadability reminds us that, insofar as a cultural poetics is grounded in practices of the body, its political significance can never be fully articulated, so that individual subjects may not be fully aware of the cultural forces that shape them. At the same time, the depth of the sounding body may indicate an agency that eludes regulation and determination by discursive regimes of power. A cultural poetics of O can thus be said to preserve the potential of embodied subjects to make a different history, a potential that warrants hope for the future.

In "sounding" a cultural poetics of the body that resists reading, Smith's goal is ultimately "to counter the tyranny of Cartesian philosophy, with its privileging of visual experience, its ambition to speak with a single authoritative voice" (26). His cultural poetics would realize its political effect to the extent that readers begin to "listen, otherwise" for a different kind of knowledge and agency in early modern texts. This imperative or mild threat would change the direction of history, and it is perhaps the author's unillusioned hope that I find refreshing. As the multivalent title of the final chapter, the imperative to "listen, otherwise" would seem at least in part ironic. It was precisely what the English did not do in their nationalist and colonialist endeavors, a failure or refusal that, the author argues, licensed English nationals to define their linguistic boundaries against the Irish and the Welsh, and English colonists to assert the superiority of their literacy to Native American orality. For us readers, then, attempting to listen, in a different way, to the politics of "merging soundscapes" would mean becoming responsive to a past whose future is even now in the making, and for which we are responsible.

The same imperative is elsewhere operative, especially in the chapters on ballads and the theater, inviting readers to "listen, otherwise" to oral practices of which only printed texts remain. Yet, as the author claims in "Ballads Within, Around, Among" (chapter 7), "traces that the singing, remembering human body has left on printed ballads are not hard to find" (177). By analyzing specific ballads and their possible performance venues Smith explores a pragmatics of oral performance in which singers and listeners are active participants and that imagines for both "the possibility of becoming many subjects by internalizing the sounds and rhythms of those subjects' voices" (201). In turning to the theater, chapter 8 reconstructs the acoustic properties of the Globe theater (and the Blackfriars, for comparison), presenting readers with the amazing complexity of structural, material, instrumental, and vocal sound effects within the wooden O. Chapter 9 presents the oral delivery on stage as the intersection of three forms of persuasion in public life—oratory, conversation, liturgy—through which actors may assert control over their acoustic field. The author argues that "the result is, or can be, a totalizing experience of sound" within which "the playgoer willingly makes herself subject to the spoken word's gestalt of force" (271). However decentered, as is the case with many of Shakespeare's plays, the characters control of the acoustic field allows them "to establish a subject position the auditors have no choice but to share" (281).

A question remains as to whether the oral performance on stage is reducible to the three forms of persuasion and, conversely, whether the conventions of drama are fully accountable to the real-life protocols of oratory, conversation, and liturgy. Would the interplay, for instance, of poetry and prose in dramatic delivery alter in some way the "gestalt of force" inhabiting the acoustic field of the theater? If dance movements possess depth and a ballad can sustain multiple subjectivities in performance, might we not imagine for dramatic performance a range of negotiable positions between the actors' forceful persuasion and the audience's willing participation in the theatrical fiction? How might we otherwise reconcile the agency of the audience who "were far from passive listeners" with "the privileged position of theater in the formation of early modern subjects" (269, 284)?

These remarks are not meant to diminish the impressive achievements of Smith's book, however, which above all demonstrates the generosity of scholarship that "beats the bounds" for a historical phenomenology of listening. While individual chapters rethink critical practice in dealing with a variety of practical technologies, each of which can inspire many new projects, the book itself is an enactment of a philosophy of listening. In dispensing with footnotes or endnotes, the author makes possible the fullest inclusion of other voices in his text. Among them is the voice of a tribal storyteller whose unrecorded oral performance claims a community of listeners and readers in a cross-cultural dialogue with history. In retaining a trace of her voice Smith teaches us how listening to the past is a way of making the future.

Close Readers: Humanism and Sodomy in Early Modern England
By Alan Stewart
Princeton: Princeton University Press, 1997

Reviewer: *Jeffrey Masten*

In the second chapter of his substantial archive of a book, *Close Readers,* Alan Stewart describes the work of John Leland, the scholar who traveled at Henry VIII's charge to monastic libraries "to compile an inventory of the books and their locations and from them to gather information for the writing of a reformed English history" (76). Quoting Leland's later editor, Stewart notes that Leland's "technique was of 'inspecting the *Books* . . . taking *exact Catalogues,* and transcribing from them whatsoever passages he judg'd might serve to give any manner of *Light* to the *History* and *Antiquities* of this *Kingdom*' " (76, original emphasis). This is a relatively minor moment in Stewart's book, but it might serve both as a rough approximation of the compendium this book represents and as a notation of the problems it raises, at least for a book that seeks to analyze the relation of humanism and sodomy in early modern England. On the one hand, this book, like Leland's influential work, performs a crucial service in locating materials that will be of use to scholars studying these topics, and in framing and analyzing some of the relevant issues attending these materials. (For students of Shakespeare, this book will speak resonantly to everything from *Love's Labour's Lost* and *Much Ado* to *Henry VIII.*) At the same time, *Close Readers* is ultimately frustrating because it often seems more itinerary, transcript, and catalogue than sustained argument. This service/shortcoming is clear on close reading but often obvious at a glance: on many of this book's pages, the quoted material in extensive and lengthy indented extracts, plus supporting footnotes, helpfully/regrettably equals or exceeds the analytic prose that stitches together these materials.

In focusing on humanism and its emergence in England, *Close Readers* stresses that humanism is not simply an educational system, method, or ideology, but a revision in the system of personal relations; as such, it is "transactional" and relational. Building on Anthony Grafton, Lisa Jardine, and William Sherman's emphasis on motivated humanistic reading, and on Jardine's notion of "knowledge transactions," Stewart's book reimmerses humanism in the social, arguing that it "concerns more than the solitary scholar, immersed in philology: it is premised on notions of social relations and transactions" (xxvii). In the service of this thesis (linked, as we will see, with "sodomy"), the book summons an archive of impressive range, bringing together materials on John Bale, the English Reformation, and anticlerical accusations of sodomy coincident with the appropriation of the monasteries; humanist educational manuals that return with regularity to the subject of beating and the schoolmaster's relation to his boy-scholars; classical and early modern texts on male friendship; and printed and manuscript documents around the "closet," study, and "cabinet" as domestic and social space. The book travels beyond the early modern England of its title to study Angelo Poliziano and quattrocento Florence (though the book could work much harder at justifying this swerve in its itinerary). Throughout, the primary materials of study are supplemented with extensive archival research, often delving into unfamiliar and/or untranslated sources in manuscript and print. The learning evinced in these pages is immense, as Stewart often provides his own translations, or improved versions of others'.

And yet, this very extensiveness is one of this book's primary limitations. *Close Readers* often transcribes too much material at too great a length; though this would not in itself constitute an unworkable problem in an encyclopedia or data base, it is a method that can overwhelm the work of a book the intended genre of which is analysis. *Close Readers* often neglects to sort, edit, and curtail at sometimes basic levels (and Princeton University Press is partly responsible here): sometimes passages are quoted several times within a few pages (164–65) or passages are translated in both text and notes (106–107). In its laudable effort to contextualize richly, the book often follows argument-halting or -obscuring digressions—pausing, for reasons that are not made clear or essential, for example, to comment and then elaborate on the "scant" "details of the early life of John Harington" (father of the more famous translator), within a reading of Roger Ascham studying Cicero in bed with a student (140). While the survey of Ascham's life and career is highly relevant to an argument on the potential homoeroticism of pedagogic beating, the level of detail deployed even here can create opposing desires in a reader: a desire for more sorting by relevance, but as well a desire for the questions and dissonances inevitably raised by this style of recounting to be answered, analyzed, or more attentively addressed. (It's useful to compare Elizabeth Pittenger's more efficient and acute analysis of Nicholas Udall,[1] whom Stewart also treats in this chapter.)

What is required in *Close Readers,* in a sense, is a stronger sense of the humanist idea (emphasized by Grafton and Jardine) of reading toward action, productive reading. This would address not only the problem of an argument sometimes occluded by extensive fact-finding and quotation, but also what may be the most significant flaw in the book, the hazy link between the book's two central terms: "humanism" and "sodomy." If, as the book argues, the "relationality or transactionality [of humanism] leads us inexorably to sodomy" (xxvii), the inexorability of this connection is not convincingly shown in this book. Let me be clear: I write this not out of some desire to protect humanism and its legacy from a putatively tainting homoeroticism; I would see myself as an ideally receptive reader for a nuanced argument that brings together linguistic/philological/textual study and sodomy in this period, and I'm as eager as the next person to see a theory of the social that leads us inexorably toward sodomy. But too often in *Close Readers,* the reading isn't close enough to explain or illuminate this connection; if this copula is inexorable, it spends much of this book as a parallel (both sodomy and humanism are relational, both are controversial, both frequently involve relations between men) rather than as an intersection.

The moments of clarity that do emerge when the book engages in pointed local analyses are useful, resonant, and enlightening—as when Stewart notes the intersection of friendship (*symphilia*) and literary study in Ascham's use of the Greek word *symphilogeo* ("join in literary studies") (156), or, in an important footnote, sets out the multiple valency of the repeated phrase and chapter title "the proof of friends" (144, n56). (In the chapter on the Henrician appropriation of the monasteries, the book neglects the possibility of a similarly nuanced reading of "sodometrouse"—a reading that might, following Jonathan Goldberg, have analyzed the complex reference of a term that describes both the sexual practices and the ostensible religious untruth of the "sodometrouse Abbeyes," thus bringing the intersection sodomy/humanism more clearly into focus.) Some brilliant observations on the complexly secretarial/familial provenance of a manuscript document called "Instructions for a Principall Secretarie" appear in the book's final pages (185–87), and the analysis of the relationship of the characters Idolatry and Sodomy in John Bale's play *Thre Lawes* will, I hope, attract new readers and teachers to this text. The book also usefully widens its metacritical frame at important moments—for example, to read the coded erotic charge(s) behind John Addington Symonds's formative study of the Italian Renaissance.

Readers interested specifically in early modern homoerotocism will find a number of points to interest them in this book. The book's range of homoerotic focus is actually broader than the subtitle's category of "sodomy" might suggest (even in the expanded post-Foucauldian sense); it includes discussions of friendship, the bonds and affections of patronage, pedagogic pederasty, and secretaryship, as well as sodomy per se (which here includes extramarital and/or nonreproductive cross-sex relations, particularly in the discussion of clerics and the monastaries). If the book's argument about the potential homoeroticism of schoolmasters' beating of their scholars is either understood as obvious or is not sufficiently clarified (how, more precisely, is the "erotic economy" of beating sodomitical?), the chapter does include a nuanced revision of Walter Ong's argument that Latin language study functioned as an early modern puberty rite; the book argues (in a moment of laudable close reading [101–102]) that beatings coincident with grammar study were both a manning and "a radical form of 'unmanning' "—a "breaching" (dressing in men's clothes) and a "breeching" (beating). Given that much of the clearest evidence *Close Readers* cites for reading beating within sodomotical discourse appears in the late seventeenth century, a stronger sense of the emergence of homoerotic anxiety around earlier schoolmasters might be formulated through more focused analysis of specific terms of the debate. "Lewd," for example, recurs with striking (as it were) frequency in Stewart's quotations and brings together a welter of discourses and anxieties in which *Close Readers* is interested. Which of the following concurrently available meanings, for example, apply to Ascham's "lewde" beating schoolmaster (112): lay (not clerical); common, vulgar, base; unlearned; wicked; lascivious? If, as the *OED* points out, "lascivious" is the only meaning that eventually survives, analyzing this kind of through-line in the evidence, at the expense of some of the other detail in the chapter, might give us a stronger reformed history both of the schoolmaster (including the homoerotic anxieties, dangers, pleasures, repulsions, and attractions surrounding him) *and* of the emergent (class-based, learning-inflected, morally valenced) history of "lewdness." Such a strategy would only further the important aim of this chapter to disentangle an understanding of early modern pedagogic relations from the histories of particular, famous individuals pathologized in later criticism and historiography.

It is a sense of a (complexly reinvested) "lewdness" or homoerotocism that seems to disappear in the book's final chapter on the early modern closet and secretaryship (first published in *Representations*); here, the sexuality/eroticism of the scenes, spaces, texts, and social structures/relationships discussed seems only to be asserted at key transitional points. Indeed, the near absence of "sex" (however constituted) in this chapter seems to prepare the way for a nevertheless surprising sentence in the book's final paragraph. Here *Close Readers* seems to deny the possibility of a kind of analysis that will attend to the politics of both sixteenth-century humanist relations and sexuality/eroticism, asserting that "by identifying the literary output of sixteenth-century humanist England as possibly homoerotic, we effectively drain the relationships that produced that literature of their political import" (187). This assertion is belied by much of the current work around sexuality and homoeroticism in Renaissance English literature and culture (sticking narrowly to secretaryship and the closet, there is the work—hardly politically *or* homoerotically divested—of Goldberg and Richard Rambuss), and indeed by intelligent local analyses in the book itself. *Close Readers* provides an ample and learned itinerary for reading the potent political charge of male-male "transactions" in and around humanism in England. This "political import," as the book seems aware, will not be identical with a late-twentieth-century politics of sexuality (generally, or in relation to learning); still, a closer reading of the important features of the difference—the alterities and continuities of the sodomy/humanism copula—may now have an instructive political benefit all its own.

Note

1. Elizabeth Pittenger, " 'To Serve the Queere': Nicholas Udall, Master of Revels," in *Queering the Renaissance,* ed. Jonathan Goldberg (Durham, N.C.: Duke University Press, 1994), 162–89.

Jonson, Shakespeare, and Early Modern Virgil
By Margaret Tudeau-Clayton
Cambridge: Cambridge University Press, 1998

Reviewer: Rebecca Bushnell

As early as Ben Jonson's sniping at his rival's "small Latin and less Greek," Shakespeare's relationship to "insolent Greece or haughty Rome" has carried ideological weight. In this same poem where he thus singled out his fellow's ignorance, Jonson did glorify Shakespeare as the "triumph" of Britain. Indeed, Shakespeare's indifference to neoclassicism has been as much celebrated as deplored. Many scholars have delighted in narrating the victory of a vigorous native English tradition over a cold, academic, and moribund neoclassical movement. Most notably in this century, in revising the image of Shakespeare as the learned humanist poet, Robert Weimann gave us Shakespeare the man of the theater, whose vitality stemmed from the popular dramatic tradition.[1] Completing his own scheme, Jonson remains the "haughty" archclassicist, always outdone by the quintessentially British Shakespeare.

In her account of *Jonson, Shakespeare, and Early Modern Virgil*, Margaret Tudeau-Clayton contributes fascinating new material to this oft-told story. Her broader theme is the circulation of "Virgil" in early modern England, that is, the cultural uses of Virgil's texts and the images of Virgil as the perfect writer, the magician, and the natural philosopher. According to Tudeau-Clayton, in early modern English culture Virgil became what Shakespeare is now for us: "an ideal, absolute paradigm of the national poet; a repository of universal human wisdom; a stable, monolithic and sacred object of reverential attention at the centre of a homogeneous community of educated readers/spectators" (2). Even though Shakespeare may now occupy Virgil's chair, through her reading of *The Tempest* she fashions a Shakespeare who challenges this Virgil and destabilizes a Renaissance "Virgilian" cosmos that is hierarchical, atemporal, and harmonious. Her Jonson, in turn, stakes out his usual position as learned, elitist, and absolutist, or the man who would be Virgil, if he only could.

In thus investigating the recurrences of Virgil's image and text,

Tudeau-Clayton's work participates in a significant revival of scholarship on the classical tradition. This work moves beyond merely identifying textual allusions or generic imitations to investigate what was culturally and politically at stake in invoking classical authority. In Tudeau-Clayton's view, "Vigil" was a multifaceted master comprising three related personae: the "school-boy's" Virgil, the model of linguistic decorum; Virgil the magician, as he was mythicized in his afterlife; and Virgil the natural philosopher, skilled in mathematics, astrology, and cosmology. All of these "Virgils" were mobilized in fashioning a "grammar of nature" (80), an ordered world of linguistic and material decorum, replicated in society, politics, and religion.

The book's first part analyzes these figures of Virgil and their place in early modern England, while anticipating the later discussion of Jonson and Virgil. The second part performs close readings of Jonson's plays, poems, and masques, while focusing on *The Poetaster,* because it puts Virgil on the stage. The book ends with an analysis of *The Tempest,* which interprets that play as a deconstruction of Virgilian authority.

Crucial to Tudeau-Clayton's argument about Shakespeare is her attribution to him of what she calls the "Protestant turn." This "turn" was a "historicizing" way of thinking, "interrogating and dis-placing [sic] the received Virgilian mediations as groundless fictions of the past, and at the same time, dis-mantling [sic] the structure of authority and the hierarchy of privilege—in short, the politics—implied in their production and circulation as knowledge" (10). In her analysis, Jonson's work uses both the schoolboy's Virgil of linguistic perfection and the learned Virgil's image of a privileged knowledge to articulate a "Catholic" structure of "hermeneutic" authority" (11). In contrast, while *The Tempest*'s Prospero may evoke everything associated with the early modern Virgil—the schoolmaster, magician, father, and natural philosopher—the play's undermining of his authority epitomizes the "Protestant turn." In Tudeau-Clayton's words, "the play . . . stages the 'discovery' of a radical and irreducible alterity—a 'dis' or 'confused noise'—within nature, history and the human subject, a discovery which, with the dis-enchantment [sic] of nature to which it is linked, marks the onset of the modern era" (11). That is, a Virgilian and Neoplatonic universe is destabilized by all the power contained in the underworld of "Dis," which also lies in the lexical function of the prefix "dis."

As these citations from Tudeau-Clayton's argument suggest, her readings of Renaissance culture and texts take a decided poststructuralist turn (perhaps the latest descendent of the Protestant turn). She paints a picture of Renaissance culture founded on binaries of elite and low, Catholic and Protestant, Old World and New. One can also detect the influence of Bahktin's formulation of the cultural contest between the monologic and the dialogic, the classic and the grotesque. The study is obviously peppered with the stylistic mannerisms of poststructuralist criticism (culminating in the unfortunate neologism of "dis-story") (214). At the same time her argument is solidly sustained by skillful close readings that extend to meter and rhythm. Tudeau-Clayton also demonstrates that she has read broadly in the British and American scholarship in this area and that she thoroughly understands the traditions of classical scholarship, including the Virgilian commentaries and the work's complex textual history.

Because of the breadth of Tudeau-Clayton's scholarship on the Renaissance Virgil and because of the depth of her reading of Jonson's and Shakespeare's plays, *Jonson, Shakespeare, and Early Modern Virgil* unfolds an insightful analysis of the cultural politics of "Virgil." However, reader should come armed with some healthy skepticism about the book's view of Renaissance culture and the relationship between Jonson and Shakespeare, insofar as it is so clearly divided between high and low, authoritarian and radical, "catholic" and "protestant." The cultural politics of this period rarely clustered so easily on such neatly aligned sides, and there are many other stories to be told.

Notes

1. Robert Weimann, *Shakespeare und die Tradition des Volkstheaters: Sociologie, Dramaturgie, Gestaltung* (Berlin: Henschelverlag: 1967); trans. as *Shakespeare and the Popular Tradition in the Theater: Studies in the Social Dimension of Dramatic Form and Function,* ed. Robert Schwartz (Baltimore: Johns Hopkins University Press, 1978). Weimann himself saw twentieth-century Shakespearean scholarship dominated by the image of the humanist dramatist Shakespeare, as against the Romantic Shakespeare as the "poet of Nature" (xxi).

2. For one account of the politics of an absolutist classicism as opposed to the "gothic" English tradition, see Richard Helgerson's *Forms of Nationhood: The Elizabethan Writing of England* (Chicago: University of Chicago Press, 1992). For an alternative construction of the politics of of Jonson's classicism, see Don E. Wayne, *Penshurst: The Semiotics of Place and the Poetics of History* (London: Methuen, 1984).

Index

Aaron, Petero, 142
Aers, David, 280
Alleyn, Edward, 48, 126, 215–19
Anderson, Judith, 317–21
Andrewes, Lancelot, 351
Archer, Ian, 89
Archer, Thomas, 78
Arden, Katherine, 57
Aristotle, 243
Armygram, Ana, 126, 184–88
Ascham, Roger, 208, 243, 363–65
Askew, Anne, 346–50
Astington, John, 273–84, 287–91, 351–52
Averell, William, 325

Bacon, Francis, 31–32, 193, 231–35, 298, 335, 354
Bakhtin, Mikhail, 203, 324, 353, 368
Bale, John, 271
Barker, Francis, 108–9, 280
Barra, Jan, 76–77
Barroll, Leeds, 298–99, 311, 312–14
Barrow, Henry, 260
Bataille, Georges, 307
Beal, Peter, 291–95
Beaumont, Francis, 161–69
Beethoven, Ludwig, 123
Beier, A. L., 89–91
Bellany, Alistair, 297
Bellasis, Charles, 221, 222
Bellasis, Richard, 126, 220–24
Belsey, Catherine, 280
Bentley, G. E., 288
Berry, Boyd, 317
Berry, Herbert, 287–91
Berry, Philippa, 353–56
Bertie, Susan, 313
Bevington, David, 169–74, 277, 295–302, 311, 312
Billingsley, Sir Henry, 216
Bishop, Tom, 297

Blayney, Peter, 162
Blitheman, William, 222–23
Boas, William, 277
Boler, James, 154–59
Bonoeil, John, 227
Booth, Stephen, 25–31
Bowen, Barbara, 317
Bowers, Fredson, 26
Bowes, Sir Jerome, 216
Bowyer, Sir William, 216
Boys, Daniel, 154
Brenner, Robert, 95, 96
Brissenden, Alan, 328
Brotton, Jerry, 340–41
Brown, Paul, 111–12
Browne, Thomas, 309, 354
Bruster, Douglas S., 337–39
Bullen, A. H., 76
Bunyan, John, 314
Burchell, Edmund, 275
Burton, Jonathan, 340–41
Bushnell, Rebecca, 366–68
Butler, Martin, 296, 299

Caesar, Julius, 177–82
Camden, William, 225
Carew, George, 216
Carew, Nicholas, 216
Carew, Thomas, 91–92
Cartwright, Kent, 278
Cary, Elizabeth, 328, 333
Cavendish, George, 194
Cavendish, Margaret, 161, 345
Cecil, Robert, 216
Cecil, William, 274
Cefalu, Paul A., 85–119
Cerasano, S. P., 126, 215–19
Chamberlen, Peter, 88
Chambers, E. K., 267–68, 277, 288
Cheney, Patrick, 281
Christian, Robert, 57
Cicero, 236, 243

Cinna, 177
Clarke, Judith Petterson, 76
Clegg, Cyndia, 302–5
Clitherow, Margaret, 345–50
Cloud, Random, 25
Cogswell, Thomas, 297
Comensoli, Viviana, 305–7
Condell, Henry, 151
Cope, Walter, 191–92
Coppin, Sir George, 216
Cotgrave, Randle, 355–56
Cotton, Sir Robert, 293
Craig, Hugh, 297
Crane, Ralph, 23
Cranfield, Lionel 337–39
Craven, Wesley, 99–100
Crewe, Jonathan, 23–41
Croft, Pauline, 296–97
Cromwell, Oliver, 46–47, 50
Cromwell, Thomas, 270
Cuddy, Neil, 296

Daniel, Samuel, 242, 313
Davies, Eleanor, 345–50
Day, John, 56, 150
Defoe, Daniel, 54, 79
de Gratzia, Margreta, 127, 231–35
Dekker, Rudolf M., 56
Dekker, Thomas, 42–84, 325–27
Deleuze, Gilles, 93, 344
Dell, Richard, 54
Derrida, Jacques, 133–34, 248, 324, 342, 358
Descartes, R., 237–39
Desmet, Christy, 337
Devereaux, Robert, 50, 304
de Vos, Max, 141
Dickie, Stephanie, 203
DiGangi, Mario, 308–10
Digby, Mary, 57
Dobbs, Maurice, 95
Dollimore, Jonathan, 308–10, 341
Donawerth, Jane, 311
Donne, John, 216, 292, 309, 311, 319–21, 351
Douglas, Mary 307
Duckett, Thomas, 220, 224
Duffy, Eamon, 136
Duncan-Jones, Katherine, 126, 191–92
Dyce, Alexander, 76

Eccles, Mark, 62
Edmonds, Frances, 48

Edwardes, Thomas, 57
Edwards, Philip, 169–74
Eggert, Katherine, 333–36
Elias, Norbert, 201
Elliott, John, 277
Elyot, Sir Thomas, 328–33
Empson, William, 342
Erasmus, D., 233
Erickson, Erik, 110
Erickson, Peter, 339–41
Evans-Pritchard, E. E., 126

"Feathery Scribe," 293–94
Feld, Steven, 357
Fell, Margaret, 314
Ferrel, Lori Anne, 300
Ferrer, Nicholas, 150
Ficino, Marsilio, 237–39
Fidge, George, 49
Field, Nathan, 56, 76
Fineman, Joel, 318
Fish, Simon, 157
Fish, Stanley, 342
Fisher, Will, 126, 199–207
Fleming, Juliet, 125, 133–38
Fletcher, John, 161–69
Fludd, Robert, 216
Forest, Edward, 325–27
Forman, Simon, 312
Fortescue, Sir John, 334, 335
Foucault, Michel, 90, 321–23
Foxe, John, 126, 149–53, 157, 193–98, 258–61
Freud, Sigmund, 133–38
Frith, John, 154, 157
Frith, Mary, 42–84
Frobisher, Peter, 337
Fulvio, Andrea, 175, 179

Gager, William, 277
Garber, Marjorie, 56, 248
Gardiner, Stephen, 157
Gascoigne, George, 303
Geffe, Nicholas, 226
Gilbertson, William, 44, 46
Goldberg, Jonathan, 127, 135, 248–51
Goldmann, Lucien, 113
Gosson, Stephen, 279
Grafton, Anthony, 362, 363
Green, Gayle, 315
Greenblatt, Stephen, 306, 318, 324
Greene, Jack, 98

Greene, Robert, 56, 279
Greg, W. W., 26, 267
Gregerson, Linda, 320
Greimas, A. J., 109
Greville, Fulke, 216
Grossman, Marshall, 310–21
Guattari, Félix, 93
Guibbory, Achsah, 316–17
Gurr, Andrew, 268–84

Hakluyt, Richard, 96–97
Hall, Edward, 194
Hall, Joseph, 152
Hall, Kim, 341
Hall, Stuart, 339–41
Halpern, Richard, 88, 249
Hammer, Paul, 298–99
Hammon, John, 151
Hannam, Richard, 44, 46, 50
Hanson, Elizabeth, 306, 321–23
Harding, Thomas, 149
Harington, Sir John, 36, 363
Harmon, Thomas, 322
Harris, Jonathan Gil, 323–27
Harrison,William, 88, 150
Hartlib, Samuel, 88
Harvey, Gabriel, 277–79, 354, 355
Hawkes, Terence, 341
Hedworthe, Jane, 221
Heminge, John, 151
Heminges, John, 274
Hendricks, Margo, 341
Heneage, Sir Thomas, 216
Heninger, S. K., 342–44
Henslowe, Philip, 126, 215–19, 274–84
Hentzner, Paul, 61
Herbert, Philip, 151
Herbert, Thomas, 252
Herbert, William, 151
Heyleyn, Peter, 252–56
Heywood, Thomas, 160–69
Hibbard, G. R. , 169–74
Hilarie, Hugh, 258
Hillman, David, 324
Hind, James, 44, 46, 50, 52
Hirst, Derek, 91
Hobbes, Thomas, 91
Holbrooke, Peter, 295–302, 327–33
Holderness, Graham, 171
Holmes, Michael Morgan, 316
Honan, Park, 273
Honigmann, E. A. J., 273

Horton, George, 44, 46, 48
Hoskins, W. G., 89
Hotson, Leslie, 276
Howard, Jean E., 305–7
Howard, Skiles, 327–33
Howard, Zachary, 51
Hulme, Peter, 108–10
Hunte, Agnes, 220, 223
Hunter, G. K., 267, 279–80
Hutchinson, Anne, 314
Hutchinson, Lucy, 297
Huttich, Johann, 182
Hymes, Dell, 357

Ingles, Richard, 55
Ingram, William, 274
Irace, Kathleen O., 171
Iselin, Pierre, 238

Jagodzinski, Cecile M., 302–5
Jameson, Fredrick, 109, 342
Jardine, Lisa, 362, 363
Jehlen, Myra, 112
Jenkins, Harold, 169–74
Jewell, John, 149
Johnson, Samuel, 23
Jones, Inigo, 227
Jones, Richard, 31
Jonson, Ben, 27, 33–36, 61, 160–68
  301, 311, 313, 322, 354, 366–68
Jordan, Constance, 315, 333–36
Joyce, Cornet, 288

Kahn, Coppélia, 315
Kalas, Rayna, 127, 240–47
Kantorowicz, Ernst, 342
Kastan, David Scott, 149–53
Kaula, David, 257
Kearney, James, 128, 257–61
Keilen, Sean, 175, 177
Kelly, Joan, 315
Ker, Neil, 295
Kermode, Frank, 108
Keymis, Lawrence, 171
Kibbey, Ann, 260
Killigrew, Henry, 54
Killigrew, Sir William, 216
King, John, 57
King, John (1997), 149
Kirkman, Francis, 160–61
Kitson, Lady Elizabeth, 216

Klein, Lisa M., 212
Kyd, Thomas, 265–84

Lacan, Jacques, 307
Lambert, Margrett, 127, 223
Lamming, George, 107
Lanyer, Aemilia, 193, 310–17
Laqueur, Thomas, 324
Latimer, Hugh, 194–98
Leicester, Earl of, 199–207
Leinwand, Theodore B., 337–39
Leland, John, 361
Lely, Peter, 79
Lever, Ralph, 244–45
Lévi-Strauss, C., 209, 212
Lewalski, Barbara, 297, 311, 314
Lindley, David, 298
Linton, Joan Pong, 356–61
Loades, David, 216
Locke, John, 227
Lodge, Thomas, 242, 279–84
Lok, John, 252
Lombe, Thomas, 227
London, John, 258
Loomba, Ania, 339–41
Loughrey, Bryan, 171
Lukacher, Ned, 342–44
Lyell, James P. R., 295
Lyly, John, 240–47, 265–84
Lynch, Kathleen, 154–59, 345–51

Maclean, Sally-Beth, 268–84
MacPherson, C. B., 91
Macrobius, 236
McBride, Kari, 314–15
McCoy, Richard, 298
McCullough, Peter, 300, 351–52
McKerrow, R. B. 26, 30
McMillin, Scott, 268–84
Malthus, Thomas, 93
Mantoux, Paul, 93
Marcus, Leah, 24
Markham, Gervase, 52
Markham, Lewknor, 45, 48, 52
Marlowe, Christopher, 265–84
Marprelate, Martin, 271
Marston, John, 325–27
Marvell, Andrew, 318
Marx, Karl, 90, 95
Mason, Thomas, 149
Massinger, Philip, 160
Masten, Jeffrey, 160–68, 361–65

Matar, Nabil, 341
Matchinske, Megan, 345–50
Maus, Katherine, 280
Mauss, Marcel, 128, 209
Mazzio, Carla, 324
Mazzocchi, Giacomo, 175–82
Mede, Joseph, 157
Middleton, Thomas, 42–84, 160–69, 325–27
Milbourne, Robert, 154–59
Miller, Naomi, 316
Milton, John, 24, 34, 306, 314, 317–21
Moffett, Thomas, 225
More, Thomas, 88, 157
Morgan, Lucy, 57
Mueller, Janel, 314–16
Mulcaster, Richard, 26–28, 33–36, 334
Murray, John Tucker, 267–68

Nashe, Thomas, 30–32, 279–84, 325–27, 355
Navarre, Marguerite de, 208
Neill, Michael, 340
Nelson, Alan, 274–84
Newborough, Mary, 57
Newman, Karen, 306
Newton, Judith, 315
Norfolk, Earl of, 199–207
Northbrooke, John, 328
Norton, Thomas, 135
Novy, Marianne, 340

O'Dair, Sharon, 307
Okes, Nicholas, 78
Orgel, Stephen, 24, 125, 175–82, 295–96, 299–302
Orkin, Martin, 339–41
Orlin, Lena, 125, 220–24
Orrell, John, 274
Owens, Jessie Ann, 139–44
Oz, Abraham, 341

Page, James R., 145
Pallister, D. M., 90
Panofsky, Erwin, 342–44
Paracelsus, 324–27
Parker, Patricia, 169–74
Parkes, M.B., 30–33
Parr, Katherine, 126, 208, 213, 347
Partridge, A. C., 34
Paster, Gail, 201, 324, 327
Patterson, Annabel, 302

Index

Peck, Linda Levy, 127, 215, 225–28, 296
Peele, George, 265–84
Philips, Katherine, 294
Picasso, Pablo, 123
Pietz, William, 128, 259
Pincombe, Michael, 277–78
Pittenger, Elizabeth, 363
Platter, Thomas, 61
Pliny, 240
Poliziano, Angelo, 362
Pollard, Robert, 160
Polyani, Karl, 92, 94
Pooke, Richard, 53–54
Powhatan, 102
Prescott, Anne Lake, 353–56
Propp, Vladimir, 109
Prynne, William, 150, 297
Pullen, John, 221
Puttenham, George, 26–28, 33, 35, 36, 254
Pye, Christopher, 250
Pym, John, 50

Quilligan, Maureen, 126, 208–14

Rabelais, F., 353–56
Raleigh, Walter, 88, 169–74, 309, 337
Randolph, Thomas, 199–207
Rappaport, Steve, 89–90
Rastel, John, 157
Ravelhofer, Barbara, 298
Reynolds, William, 126, 127, 191–92
Rich, Richard, 258
Richardson, W., 76
Ridley, Nicolas, 194–98
Robertson, Karen, 310–17
Robinson, Abraham, 48
Robinson, Henry, 94
Robinson, James, 48
Rose, John, 275
Rosenthal, Bernard M., 146
Rowley, William, 160–69
Rowse, A. L., 311–12
Russell, Conrad, 216

Sadeler, Jan, 141–44
St. John, Oliver, 50
Sandys, George, 100
Sawday, Jonathan, 324
Scott, Joan, 315
Sedgwick, Eve, 322

Sedinger, Tracey, 307
Seiffert, Max, 141
Seldon, John, 354
Serres, Oliver de, 226
Shakespeare, Edmund, 52
Shakespeare, William, 23–41, 161–69, 273, 306, 317–21, 366–68. Plays: *As You Like It*, 355; *Coriolanus*, 93; *Cymbeline*, 248, 250, 333–36; *Hamlet*, 169–74, 248, 340; *Henry VIII*, 333, 361; *King John*, 124; *King Lear*, 105, 111, 193–98, 249–50, 355; *Love's Labour's Lost*, 195, 355, 361; *Measure for Measure*, 28, 194, 308–9, 322–23, 346; *The Merchant of Venice*, 306, 326, 337–39; *A Midsummer Night's Dream*, 28, 36; *Much Ado About Nothing*, 331, 361; *Othello*, 172, 205, 322–23, 340; *Pericles*, 333–36; *Romeo and Juliet*, 308–10; *Twelfth Night*, 172, 193–98, 248, 343; *The Tempest*, 85–119, 236–39, 252–56, 297, 333–36, 367; *Timon of Athens*, 90, 111, 306, 307; *Titus Andronicus*, 248; *Two Gentlemen of Verona*, 248; *The Winter's Tale*, 111, 257–61, 333–36
Shannon, Laurie, 126, 193–98
Sherman, William, 145–48, 362
Shirley, James, 290
Shrimpton, Nicholas, 170
Shuger, Debora, 280
Sidney, Sir Philip, 36, 294, 295
Simpson, Percy, 26, 29, 34
Sinfield, Alan, 308
Smith, Adam, 93
Smith, Alexander, 44–45, 51
Smith, Bruce R., 323–27, 356-
Smith, Ian, 128, 252–56
Smith, John, 85–119
Smuts, Malcolm, 295–302
Sowernam, Esther, 346
Spataro, Giovanni, 139, 142
Spearing, Elizabeth, 44, 46,
Spenser, Edmund, 281, 306, 325–27, 354
Stallybrass, Peter, 123–29
Stanhope, Lady Susan, 216
Stanley, Fernando, 273
Starkey, Ralph, 293–94
Starkey, Thomas, 325–27
Steele, M. S., 288

Stevens, Paul, 305–7
Steward, Sir William, 217
Stewart, Alan, 361–65
Stoddard, Roger, 145
Stowe, John, 61, 225
Strachey, William, 97, 108
Strong, Roy, 342
Stuart, James, 61, 98, 100, 215–19, 226, 299, 300, 325–27, 334, 352
Stubbs, John, 304
Stuteville, Sir Martin, 157
Suetonius, 177
Suzuki, Mihoko, 321–23
Swift, Jonathan, 232

Tanselle, G. Thomas, 147
Tarlton, Richard, 59–60
Tawney, R. H., 89
Taylor, Barry, 307
Taylor, John, 151–53, 294
Thomas, Keith, 260
Thorpe, W. A., 78
Thursbie, William, 223
Tilney, Edmund, 274
Tomkyns, Nathaniel, 288
Tomlinson, Gary, 127, 236–39
Tracy, Richard, 157
Truax, Barry, 357
Tudeau-Clayton, Margaret, 366–68
Tudor, Elizabeth, 199–207, 208–14, 215–19, 294, 300–305, 352
Turner, Jeremy, 218
Turner, William, 151

Udall, Nicholas, 363
Underdown, David, 91
Ungerer, Gustav, 42–84
Urquhart, Sir Thomas, 354

van de Pol, Lotte C., 56
Veevers, Erica, 297
Verdonck, Cecil, 141
Vere, Anne, 51
Vere, Elizabeth, 51
Vincent, Sir Thomas, 216
Virgil, 243, 366–68

Waller, Marguerite, 342–44
Walsingham, Francis, 270–71
Walters, Sam, 170
Ward, Samuel, 157
Webbe, William, 243
Webster, John, 325–27
Weiner, Annette, 209, 212
Wells, Stanley, 312
White, Hayden, 318
White, Paul Whitfield, 265–84
Wilkins, John, 232–35
Wilson, Thomas, 242–45
Wood, Eileen Meiksins, 95
Woods, Susanne, 311, 314–15
Woodshore, Joan, 62
Wright, Nancy, 297
Wryghte, William, 220, 223

Yeandle, Laetitia, 291–95

Zimmerman, Susan, 302
Zizek, Slavoj, 307, 319